THE
Comfort Carpenter
AND
Elizabeth Phelps Pinkham
FAMILY

FROM
DOVER, NEW HAMPSHIRE TO STANSTEAD, QUEBEC
WITH
LEIGHTON, HUCKINS, HUNTINGTON,
CARPENTER, BREWSTER, BACHELDOR
AND AMOS PHELPS FAMILY TIES

BASED UPON TEXT BY
Robert Earlby Pinkham
AND
UPDATED BY
Anne Louise Manrique

HERITAGE BOOKS
2022

HERITAGE BOOKS
AN IMPRINT OF HERITAGE BOOKS, INC.

Books, CDs, and more—Worldwide

For our listing of thousands of titles see our website
at
www.HeritageBooks.com

Published 2022 by
HERITAGE BOOKS, INC.
Publishing Division
5810 Ruatan Street
Berwyn Heights, Md. 20740

International Standard Book Number
Paperbound: 978-0-7884-2108-2

This family history connects to family research from specific books:

~Vital Records of Dover, NH 1685-1850 by Dover Historical Society. Heritage Books. 1990.

> *Related because of Richard Pinkham (GEN1)*

~The Ancestry of J. G. Williams and Ursula Miller by Jim Schneider and Holly Rubin. Lulu. 2013.

> *Related because of Abijah Pinkham (GEN4)*

~Our Family History by Ethelmae Eylar Carter. Burgess Publishing Co. 1958.

> *Related because of Phelps-Chartier ties to Samuel Pinkham Junior line (GEN6) (GEN7).*

American Revolution (and probable Mayflower) ties for this Pinkham branch.

The Comfort Carpenter and Elizabeth Phelps Pinkham Family
with ties to Samuel Pinkham - Amos Phelps branches

Table of Contents

Reference material:

<u>The Comfort Carpenter and Elizabeth Phelps Pinkham Family
From Dover, New Hampshire To Stanstead, Quebec
With Leighton, Huckins, Huntington, Carpenter, Brewster, Bachelder
And Amos Phelps Family Ties.</u>

Abridged from original text written by Robert Earlby Pinkham (10),
Long Point on Balsam Lake, R. R. #3, Kirkfield, Ontario, Canada, 25 March 1976.
Completed by Anne Louise Manrique (12), Los Angeles, CA, 8/2015; Revised 3/2022.

What started out as an ancestry project to add to my grandfather's family research turned into discovering our line descended from 1634 New Hampshire Quaker settlers who generations later became American Revolutionary War Patriots, facts which earned me Daughter of American Revolution status, the first in my line to prove such genealogy. While still in the process of confirming Mayflower status given few 1800 Eastern Township records to support parentage claims, this Pinkham branch verifiably founded American and Canadan towns. By 1900 some descendants of this branch had moved to the Central Valley of California where I, a fifth-generation Californian on my paternal side, was born in 1965, the child of an Ontario-Canada-born Pinkham.

Based upon text by my grandfather, Robert Earlby Pinkham, information he created by visiting Family Search centers in Utah on travels from Ontario, Canada to my California home during the 1970s, my work proves our Pinkham United States and Canadian line began three-hundred-and-eighty-eight years ago in Dover, New Hampshire…

The Pincombe family arrived at North Molton, Devon following the Battle of Bosworth Field in 1483. Prior to North Molton, the family resided at Pencombe Manor in Herefordshire. Ninety percent of Pincombe surnames have originated from Devon, England. Variant names include: Pincombe, Pencombe, Pyncombe, Pyncomb, Pincomb, Pinkham. In ancient text, "Pyne" defined "pine" and "Combe" meant a hollow or ridge where sturdy trees grew. In other words, the name Pyncombe described a pine valley. The story of my Pinkham branch goes as follows…

On 10 February 1583, Philippe Pyncombe (b. 1565, England; d. 27 August 1632, Bidenford, Devon, England) married Wilmote Beare (b. 1565, Frithelstock, Devon, England) in Bidenford, Devon, England. They had a son named Richard Pyncombe.

Richard Pyncome (b. 29 March 1585, Alvington, Devonshire, England; d. 1665, England) married Mary Russell (b. 1590, England). They had a son named Richard Pyncombe (b. 7 November 1613, Alvington, Devonshire, England; d. June 1681, Dover, Strafford, New Hampshire). Richard Pyncombe changed the spelling of his name when he arrived in Dover and became "Generation 1" of the North American NH Pinkham line.

Richard Pyncombe (RICHARD PINKHAM) sailed to Dover, New Hampshire before 1640 most likely with Captain Wiggans, a man sent to "supervise the colonists" *(Richard Pinkham of Old Dover, New Hampshire and his Descendants East and West by Charles Nelson Sinnett)* who was also was Governor of the Colony for seven years. Historians place Richard on the Good Ship *Jame M_*, a vessel that sailed from the Isle of Wight, England in 1633. One of the reasons Richard Pyncombe was chosen for the voyage was because of his devout religious faith, beliefs that would benefit him while making the difficult Atlantic crossing. Richard Pinkham's Quaker ideals included the mission to: always follow where the Spirit of God and Duty leads you. (Sinnett) Richard Pinkham (1) (b. 7 November 1613, Devon, England; d. 1681, Dover, NH) married Julia Olive Gyler (b. 1614, Devon, England; d. 1688, Dover, New Hampshire) during 1643 in Dover, New Hampshire. Devout Quakers, Richard and Julia Pinkham had three sons: John Pinkham, RICHARD PINKHAM and Thomas Pinkham (Generation 2).

RICHARD PINKHAM (Generation 1) was not only one of the first settlers of Dover, New Hampshire, but he also signed the charter of New Hampshire, a document believed to be the foundation text for the Declaration of Independence. Richard Pinkham was one of forty-two individuals (Richard Pinkhame) to sign the "Dover Combination" on 20 October 1640. The Pinkham garrison, built by Richard's son, John, in 1671, was three-quarters of a mile north of the First Meeting house on High Street. The religious beliefs of this individual may be the reason why our Pinkham line is not specifically recorded in Friends meetings given many individuals were "disowned." Historically it is noted Richard Pinkham (1) signed "the Combination" in 1640, was a proprietor in 1642, was "appointed to beat the drum on the Lord's day and take care of the meeting house in 1648, "brought a suit in court" in 1649 and made "deed of gift of his property" in 22 June 1671 to "his son John in consideration of John's agreement to maintain him the rest of his life." A Sinnett recorded description of Richard Pinkham ("a man of learning with blue eyes") includes standing next to the Friends Church beating a drum, thus confirming the role the Quaker religion played in his life.

1640 Pinkham traits as described from Charles Nelson Sinnett's book on Richard Pinkham descendants include a general description of Pinkham members: They - "welcome the call of duty," are "slow of choice"; they "do not marry early", they are "slow to choose life's work," one should "never bother a Pinkham when he is thinking," and "Pinkham descendants were in their way to great spaces of light." They were also "men of learning," "not boastful" and devout members of the Friends Church. One of the first historical mention of Friends was in 1662 when three sisters were "whipt" out of town by Magistrate Waldron. Quakers eventually comprised one-third of the early Dover, New Hampshire population.

Richard and Julia Pinkham had three sons: (Generation 2) John, Thomas and RICHARD PINKHAM (2). The firstborn son, John Pinkham, is most noted historically. John (b. 1644; d. 24 August 1724) married Rose (Martha) (b. 1655; d. 1699) Otis (whose father was Richard Otis and mother was Rose Staughton) in 1674 in Dover, New Hampshire. They had nine children: Richard (m1 unknown; m2 Mary Welch), Thomas (married Mary Allin), Amos (favorite grandson of Richard I as he was an "active Quaker"), Solomon (also noted as being an "active Quaker"), Otis (his children are all listed in Friends Church listings), James (noted as not being a good Quaker), Sarah, Elizabeth (married Samuel Nuit) and Rose (married James Tuttle) Pinkham.

A more detailed history of John Pinkham (Generation 2) and Rose (Otis) nine children (Generation 3) is as follows.

~Richard Pinkham (3) married first wife (speculated forename, Elizabeth) then second wife, Mary Welch (widow of Benjamin Welch) of Kittery, Maine (age 78), when he was eighty-five years old. John Pinkham (2) gave Richard (3J2) 50 acres of land. On 12 May 1709, he sold land to his brother, Amos. On 28 November 1718, he sold land to his brother Otis. On 27 August 1718, he sold land to Israel Hodgen. He "probably" had two daughters.

~Thomas Pinkham (3) married Mary Allin on 2 December 1700. They had four children (Generation 4); three left New Hampshire for Maine: Ebenezer

Pinkham (Harpwell, ME), Benjamin Pinkham (Boothbay, ME), Martha Pinkham (Boothbay, ME) and Joseph Pinkham (Madbury, NH).

~Elizabeth Pinkham (3) married Samuel Nute on 18 March 1718.

~Otis Pinkham (3) born 1700 Inherited the old Pinkham tract. He married Abigail Tibbets of Dover, NH in January of 1701 (daughter of Ephraim Tibbets). Otis and Abigail's children (Generation 4): Samuel Pinkham (b. 9 September 1722; Married Susannah Canning) and Anne Pinkham (b. 30 April 1724).

~Rose Pinkham (3) born abt. March 1725/6; Married James Tuttle on 7 April 1783.

~James Pinkham (3) was born in 1687 and died in 1760. He was a farmer and lumberman who sold land to his brother Otis. He married Elizabeth Smith (b. 1784; d 1828) whose father was Joseph Smith of Oyster River, MA. James and Elizabeth's children (Generation 4) were James, Thomas and Israel Pinkham.

~Solomon Pinkham (3) moved to Madbury, New Hampshire. He was a blacksmith and given a land grant in 23 June 1701 when his father, John, sold him land. He married Mary Field on 11 December 1706. Their child (Generation 4), Stephen Pinkham became a Quaker preacher.

~Amos Pinkham (3) was a favorite grandchild of Richard Pinkham (1) because he became a Quaker preacher. Amos Pinkham not only inherited land from his grandfather, Richard, and uncle, Richard, but was also given money from his father to distribute to his sisters when their father, John, died. Amos was eventually "disowned" when he married outside the Friends Church a widower, Mrs. Elizabeth Chesley (whose husband Captain Samuel Chesley was killed by Indians).

Richard and Julia's middle son, Thomas Pinkham (Generation 2) was "taxed at Dover Neck 1667 and 1668 then disappears." It is possible Thomas died after 1668 or, perhaps, if he was "not a good Quaker," "disowned."

The youngest son of Richard and Julia was RICHARD PINKHAM (b. 1672; d. 1757) (Generation 2) who married Elizabeth Leighton (b. 1675; d. September 1756) (father Thomas Leighton) in 1699 when he was 27 years old. Richard Pinkham (Generation 2) was listed as being a carpenter, owning a front lot on High Street in Dover Neck and marrying the daughter of the second Thomas Leighton, Elizabeth Leighton. Richard Pinkham (2) land rights are noted by certain events: 18 April 1699 he received land from Thomas Leighton, eldest son, grandson to the first Thomas Leighton (who was deceased), brother of Elizabeth Leighton, his wife; 2 May 1699 (the year he married Elizabeth Leighton) he conveyed the "High Street premises" to a Thomas Tibbets. From this point on two or three children were born and then on 12 May 1709 Richard Pinkham conveyed to his nephew Amos Pinkham (3) land that belonged to the first Thomas Leighton. On 12 February 1736, he conveyed land to his youngest son, Tristram (3), then sixteen. On 11 February 1748-9 he conveyed land again to Tristram (3) then twenty-eight years old. "On 2 December 1730-31 he conveyed lot #70 in the first division of Rochester, New Hampshire to son Richard (3). Richard (Generation 2) did not give land to son John (3) or (Thomas) (3) indicating the importance of the Quaker religion to Richard Pinkham (Generation 2) and that, perhaps, these two sons were not devout enough.

Richard and Elizabeth Pinkham (Generation 2) had either three or four sons (and maybe a daughter), some of whom are not recorded. Their first-born child is the link to our family although the Friends Church listing does not confirm this statement. THOMAS PINKHAM (b. 1705; d. 1757) (Generation 3) is considered the child named for the father of Elizabeth Leighton (Thomas Leighton). It is also possible he was named for Richard's perhaps disowned brother, Thomas (2), who "disappeared," a moniker Quakers would not approve. Another unrecorded birth is of an Elizabeth Pinkham (b. 1708; d.1752). Thomas Pinkham's birth of 1705 is prior to the recorded births of his brothers, John (b.1707 or b. 1696), Richard (b. 1709) and Tristram (b. 1720 or 1721) in Dover, New Hampshire. As per text taken from a genealogical source (The Ancestry of J. G. Williams and Ursula Miller by Jim Schneider and Holly Rubin), Thomas Pinkham is placed within this family (Richard Pinkham and Elizabeth Leighton) "by onomastics, religion and process of elimination."

Richard Pinkham (Generation 2) named (first) son, Thomas (Generation 3) after wife's father, Thomas Leighton, his second son, John (Generation 3) after his brother John, his third son after his father, Richard (Generation 3) and fourth son, Tristram (Generation 3). Unfortunately, search for the specifics of Thomas Pinkham's birth in 1705 are not available, but given that the firstborn was usually named for either the husband's father or the wife's father, Thomas fits into this framework. Also, because both Thomas and John, sons of Richard Pinkham (2), did not inherit land from their father, it is assumed they were either disowned or not considered good Quakers. The birth of an Elizabeth Pinkham (born abt. 1708; d. 1752) is also a mystery but she likely was named for her mother, Elizabeth Leighton Pinkham.

ELIZABETH LEIGHTON, Wife to Richard (2) Pinkham:

Richard (2) Pinkham's wife, Elizabeth Leighton, was born in Dover during 1645 and died 28 December 1674. Elizabeth's paternal grandparents were Thomas Leighton (b. 1604, Glasgow, Scotland; d. 1672, Dover, NH) and Joanna Silsby (b. 1617, Scotland; d. 1783, Dover, NH. Parents were William Silsby and Joanna Fowles.). The child of Thomas Leighton and Joanna Silsby was Thomas Leighton Jr. (b. 1642, Dover, NH; d. 1710, Dover, NH) Thomas Leighton Jr. married Elizabeth Nutter, daughter Hatevil Nutter and Ann(e) Ayers.

Elizabeth Leighton's maternal grandfather, Hatevil Nutter, was a Puritan zealot (son of Edward Nutter and Jane Fulford, b. 1598 -1603, Harlington, Bedford, England) whose uncle, Anthony Nutter was the Puritan minister of Leichestershire and Woodkirk, Yorkshire ("The American Genealogist," Vol. 72, 1997, pp. 263-84), England. Historical notations describe elder Hatevil Nutter as a cruel man who incited the historically noted whipping of Quaker women. He came to Dover after the first wave of settlers sometime before 1637 when he bought much land from Captain Thomas Wiggan. He also became partial owner of the sawmill and owned the shipyard. Puritan Hatevil did everything he could to make the life of Quakers miserable. He levied taxes against only Quakers (40 shillings) and even cut off ears if payment could not be made. Eventually, over a third of Dover citizens chose to become Quakers and his granddaughter, Elizabeth Leighton, who married into a founding Quaker Dover, New Hampshire family begun by Richard Pinkham (1). Hatevil Nutter and Ann(e) Ayers children were Abigail (Roberts), Elizabeth (Leighton), Lt. Anthony, Mary, John and Mary (Wingate) Nutter.

Elizabeth Nutter married Thomas Leighton Jr. (b. 1642, Dover, NH; d. 31 October 1677, Dover, NH). The children of Thomas and Elizabeth (Nutter) Leighton Jr. were Elizabeth (m. RICHARD2 PINKHAM), John, Elizabeth (m. Small), Mary (m. Roberts) and Sara Leighton. The children of Richard and Elizabeth (Leighton) Pinkham (Generation 3) were THOMAS, John, Elizabeth, Richard and Tristram Pinkham. THOMAS PINKHAM (3) married Sarah Bunker, Richard Pinkham married Mary Coffin in Nantucket, Masachusetts and Tristram Pinkham married Martha Hayes.

Two of Richard and Elizabeth Pinkham descendants create family lines in Canada. Thomas Pinkham's line, which is followed in detail next, was established in Quebec by 1800 with Generation 5 and 6 members, later than the other branch that settled in Nova Scotia during 1777. Richard Pinkham (3), son of Richard (2) took the "good sloop *Rochester*" in 1680 to Nantucket, Massachusetts where he resided until he died. He married Mary Coffin (b. 18 April 1665, Dover, NH) (daughter of James Coffin who purchased Nantucket and Mary Severance of Dover, NH.) in Nantucket, Massachusetts. Richard (3), brother of Thomas (3), was described as "a man of noble and sturdy character; he was no doubt a member of the Friends Church in that many of his descendants were faithful helpers of that church." Richard and Mary Pinkham (3) had two sons (4) Jonathan and Shubal Pinkham on Nantucket. Shubal married Abigail Bunker of Nantucket and had a son named Richard (Generation 5) (b. 16 October 1718). Richard Pinkham (5) married Miriam Gardiner (descendant of Joseph Austen of Dover, NH). Richard (5) and Miriam Pinkham had a son named Richard (6) (b. 27 October 1752, Nantucket, MA; d. 17 August 1830, Barrington, Nova Scotia, Canada). This Richard Pinkham (Generation 6) was a blacksmith on a Nantucket whaling vessel when the ship was "overhauled by a British man-o-war and he was impressed into the King's service" (Sinnett). The British ship sailed to Nova Scotia where Richard Pinkham and three others jumped overboard. The deserters headed toward the Nova Scotia town of Barrington, knowing there was a settlement there. Richard Pinkham (6) established a blacksmith shop and married Lydia Coffin (b. Nantucket, MA) in January of 1777. Information about this Canadian Pinkham family is listed in Canadian Cape Sable Historical Society Shelburne County records under the title: Pinkham Family.

John Pinkham born in 1707 (or 19 August 1696) in Dover, NH married Abigail Starbird (b. 29 September 1696, daughter of Thomas and Abigail Dam Starbird; d. 1747).

Elizabeth Pinkham (born abt. 1708; d. after 1752) married Samuel Cromwell, son of Joshua and Lydia Cromwell, in Dover, NH on 4 December 1747.

The youngest of Richard (2) and Elizabeth Pinkham's sons was Tristram Pinkham (3). Tristram was born during 1712 in Dover, NH. Tristram Pinkham married Martha Hayes (b. 16 August 1721, daughter of Samuel Hayes and Leah Dam of Dover, NH; died abt. 1762, Dover, NH) and died 1789 in Steuben, Maine. He and his descendants (4) (Tristram Jr. - b. 1748, Dover, NH; d. 13 December 1825, Steuben, ME; married Ann Leighton in Barrington, NH. The children of Tristram Jr. and Ann Pinkham were -5- Martha, Margaret and Sarah Pinkham) founded Pinkham Bay and Pinkham Mill, Maine.

Dover, New Hampshire was founded in 1632 and shortly thereafter Richard Pinkham arrived from Devon, England. Events such as, the Massachusetts Bay Colony claiming Dover in 1641, the first sawmill being erected in 1648, the first schoolmaster being hired in 1662, Indian Wars raging from 1675 until 1725 and "Quaker women being whipped out of town" in 1662 life prove life the new world was difficult and harsh. Fortunately, for Quaker Richard Pinkham (1), an official Friends Meetinghouse was established (1680) one year before he passed away (Sinnett). Historically, Dover is considered one of the oldest continuous settlements in New Hampshire and the seventh oldest in the United States.

To review, PHILLIPE PYNCOME married Wilmote Beare in 1583 in Devon, England. They had a son, RICHARD PYNCOMBE, who was born in 1585 and married Mary Russell born 1590 in Alvington, Devon, England. They had a son, RICHARD PINKHAM, born 7 November 1613 in Devon, England who married Julia Olive Gyler (born 1614 in Devon, England) during 1643 in Dover, New Hampshire. They had a son RICHARD PINKHAM (b. 1640 in Dover, NH) who married Elizabeth Leighton (b. 1675) in 1696 in Dover, NH. Richard Pinkham (2) had children: THOMAS, John, Richard, (Elizabeth) and Tristram Pinkham who became third generation members of the United States Pinkham family.

THOMAS PINKHAM (b. 1705, Dover, NH; d. 1744, Dover, NH) (Generation 3) married Sarah Bunker (b. 20 October 1699; d. 1755, Dover, NH) (Father: John Bunker; Mother: Dorcus Field Bunker) in 1731. Records list Thomas as being involved with the military and the 1740 Cuba Expedition, as well as, being a fisherman. For whatever reason, his birth as child of Richard and Elizabeth Pinkham (3), grandchild of Richard and Julia Pinkham (1) was not recorded by the Friends Church. He married at age twenty-six and never knew his grandfather, Richard Pinkham (1).

SARAH BUNKER, Wife to Thomas Pinkham (3):

The history of Sarah Bunker's ancestry concludes with a queen of Scotland in the ancestral line. Sarah Bunker was born on 20 October 1699 in Dover, NH where she died in 1755. She was the mother to ABIJAH, Joseph, Sarah and Mary PINKHAM (Generation 4). Sarah Bunker's father was John Bunker (b. 1667, Dover, NH; d. 8 July 1707, Dover, NH) and his parents were James and Sarah Bunker). SARAH BUNKER's mother was DORCUS FIELD (b. 1688; d.1718) and her only sibling was Elizabeth (Bunker) Jacobs (b. 25 Feb. 1706) who married Daniel Jacobs, and had daughter Patience (Jacobs) Willey (b. 1744, Madbury, NH). John Bunker's siblings were James Bunker Jr., Joseph and Sarah Bunker. John Bunker's father, James, was born in 1628 in England and died in Dover, NH in January of 1698. Sarah's uncle, John's brother, James Bunker Jr., was the Constable of Dover (d. 1722, Dover). Constable Bunker's wife was Anne Martha Bunker and his children, some the same age as Abijah, were Joseph, Love, Milliet, Benjamin, James and Elijah Bunker. Joseph Bunker (b. 1666, Dover, NH; d.1719), uncle to Sarah and brother to John, married Mary Sarah Nute (daughter of James and Sarah Nute). They had one child, Mary (b. 24 June 1697) who married Clement Drew and had one child, Clement Drew, Jr.

DORCUS FIELD BUNKER was the child of ZECHARIAH and Sarah (Roberts) FIELD. It is from this family that the English lineage goes to 1040. Dorcus' siblings were Lt. Zachary, Stephen, Abigail, John, Mary and Daniel Field. Dorcas' father, Zechariah, was born during 1645 in Oyster River, York, Maine and died during 1712 in Oyster River, Maine. He was the child of Darby Field and Agnes Williams. Zechariah Field married twice – (1) Hannah (b. 21 June 1690; d. 1737) and (2) Sarah Roberts, the daughter of Lt. John and Abigail Roberts and the mother of Dorcus Bunker Field and her siblings John, Thomas, Abigail (Hall), Joseph and Hatevil Roberts.

The father of ZACHARIAH FIELD was DARBY FIELD. His parents were Darby and Agnes (Williams) Field. Zechariah Field's siblings were Elizabeth (Jones), Joseph, Mary (Woodman) and Sarah (Drew) Field. Darby Field was born 1610 in England. He died on 1 August 1651 in Strawberry Banks, Strafford, New Hampshire. Agnes Williams was born in 1616 in Boston, Lincolnshire, England and died during 1674 in Durham, Strafford County, New Hampshire. Darby Field's occupation was listed as a farmer and seller of wine.

The father of DARBY FIELD was JOHN FIELD JR. (b. 1579, St. Giles, Cripplegate, London, England; d. 1616, Boston, Lincolnshire, England) and Ellen Field (b. 1588; d. 1664, Boston, Lincolnshire, England) (parents Arthur Huchinson and Ellen Wright). The children of John Jr. and Ellen Field were Darby, Henry, Robert and Richard Field.

The father of JOHN FIELD JR. was the REVEREND JOHN FIELD, also known as John Felde, John the Elder, Reverend Field or "The Astronomer." John Field was born in 1519 and died on 26 March 1587. John Field was also known as the "Rector of Cripplegate." His wife's name was not known but his children were John Field, Jr., Reverend Theophilus Field and Nathaniel Field. Thomas Field is listed as a half-brother.

The father of REVEREND JOHN FIELD was WILLIAM FIELD JR. William Field Jr. was born in 1470 in Bradford, Yorkshire, England and he died during 1542 in East Ardsley, West Yorkshire, England. William Field Jr. married Anabella Rivers (m1) and Elizabeth (m2) Field. The children of William Field Jr. were Richard, Reverend John and Thomas Field.

The father of WILLIAM FIELD JR. was WILLIAM STRANGEWAYS FIELD SR. William Strangeways Field Sr. was born in 1400 in Bradford, West Yorkshire, England. He died on 1 April 1480. He married Katherine Field (b. 1420, Bradford, England; d. 1480). The children of William Strangeways Sr. and Katherine Field were William Field Jr. and John Field.

The father of WILLIAM STRANGEWAYS FIELD SR. was THOMAS DEL FELD (Field) JR. and his mother was Isabel Field (b. 1365, Bryn, Lancashire, England; d. 12 March 1429, Bradford, Yorkshire), the daughter of Henry Strangeways of Salford and Alice Strangeways. Isabel was first wife to Sir Thomas Gerald, Knight of Kingsley & Bryn, Earl of Lancaster and Member of Parliament. Sir Thomas Gerald and Isabel's children were Sir John Gerald of Kingsley and Joan Fifield, Heiress of the Vyne, b. 1385 (wife of Sir John Sandy's of Anders, son Sir Knight Walter Sandy's of Anders). Isabel's children with William Strangeways Field Sr. were Robert Field and William Strangeways Field.

The father of THOMAS DEL FELD JR. was THOMAS DEL FELD SR. Thomas del Feld Sr. was born in 1330 in Sowerby near Halifax, York, England. He died during 1391 in Bradford, Yorkshire, England. He married (m1) Matilda de la Feld (b. 1334, Sowerby, Halifax, England) and (m2) Anabel/Annabelle del Feld (b. 1333, Sowerby, Yorkshire; d. 1429, Bradford, Yorkshire). His children by Matilda were Agnes (b. 1361), Alice (b. 1363) John (b. 1363) and Richard (b. 1367) Field. His child by Annabelle del Felde/Field was Thomas del Felde/Field Jr. (b. 1360, Bradford, Yorkshire; d. 11 March 1429)

The father of THOMAS DEL FELD SR was JOHN DEL FELD. He was born in 1300 in Sowerby, Lancashire, York, England and died during 1391 in Sowerby, Lancashire, England where he is buried in Berkhampstead-St. Mary. The wife of John Del Feld was not known (b. 1282) but their children were Thomas del Feld, Sr., Ephraim Field, Anne Field, Sarah Field and William Field.

The father of JOHN DEL FELD was THOMAS DEL FELD. He was born during 1278 in Sowerby, near Halifax, York and died during 1322 in Sowerby near Halifax, York. His wife's name was not known but his children were Adam and John del Feld with a half-brother of Richard Del Feld.

The father of THOMAS DEL FELD was ROGER DE LA FELD. Roger de la Feld was born during 1240 in Sowerby, Yorkshire and he died during 1278 in Sowerby, Yorkshire. His wife's name was not known but his children were Richard and Thomas Del Feld.

The father of ROGER DE LA FELD was ROBERT DEL FELD. He was born during 1220 in Sowerby, Halifax, West Riding, Yorkshire. His only child was Roger De La Feld.

The father of ROBERT DEL FELD was ADAM DEL FELD. He was born during 1200. His only child was Henry Del Feld.

The father of ADAM DEL FELD was HENRY DEL FELD. He was born sometime near 1150 in England. His only child was John de la Feld.

The father of HENRY DEL FELD was JOHN DE LA FELD. He was born sometime circa 1090 in Alsace-Lorraine, Grenoble, Isere, Rhone-Alps. His only child was Hubertus del Feld.

The father of JOHN DE LA FELD was HUBERTUS DEL FELD. He was born during 1030 in Alsace- Lorraine, Grenoble, Isere, Rhone-Alpes, France. He died during 1092 in Chateau, Inanes, England. The father of Hubertus Del Feld was Unknown Comte De La Feld.

The father of HUBERTUS DEL FELD was the (UNKNOWN NAME) COMTE DE LA FELD. The Comte was born during 1018 in Chateau del la Feld, Colmar, Alsace, Lorraine, France. He died during 1040.

HENRY STRANGEWAYS OF SALFORD was father of Isabel Field and the grandfather to WILLIAM STRANGEWAYS FIELD and born 1337 in Lancashire, England where he died in 1385. Henry Strangeways married Alice Strangeways (b. 1340; d. 1377) and their children were Sir John Strangeways of Strangewycke and Isabel Field. By his mother's previous marriage to Sir Thomas Gerald, Henry Strangeways of Salford's siblings were Sir John Strangeways of Strangewyke and half brothers, John IV del Lyon, the Baron Fortevoit (b. 1314, Glamis, Scotland; d. 4 November 1382, Bahail Forrfashire, Scotland) and Knight Chamberlain of Scotland and Elizabeth and George de Lyons, Duke of Clarence.)

The father of ISABEL FIELD was HENRY STRANGEWAYS OF SALFORD.

The father of HENRY STRANGEWAYS OF SALFORD was THOMAS STRANGEWAYS OF SALFORD (b. 1297, Salford, Lancashire, England; d. 1346) Thomas Strangeways married ALICE LYONS STRANGEWAYS (Alice De St. Liz). The children of Thomas and Alice Lyons Strangeways were Sir John Strangeways of Strangewyche and Henry Strangeway of Salford.

ALICE LYONS (DE SAINT LIZ) STRANGEWAYS was born during 1300 at Warkworth Castle, Banbury, Northhamptonshire, England and died in 1374 in Warkworth, Banbury, Northhamptonshire. Alice Lyons' sister was Roland de Saint Liz. Her parents were William de Saint Liz of Warkworth (b 1274, Warkworth; d. 1313, Duddington) and Matilda De Sentis.

The PARENTS of THOMAS STRANGEWAYS were GEOFFREY STRANGEWAYS (b. 1270, Salford, Lancashire, England; d. 1346) and Sibel Strangeways.

HENRY STRANGEWAYS OF SALFORD'S wife was Alice (DE SAINT LIZ) Strangeway. Henry Strangeways of Salford and Alice (De Saint Liz) Strangeway's children were Isabel Field (wife of Thomas Del Feld Sr., mother of William Strangeways Sr.) and her brothers were Sir John Strangeways of Strangewyche and half-brother, John IV de Lyon (b. 1314; d. 4 November 1382, Scotland) Baron of Forlevoit, Knight, Chamberlain of Scotland

Alice De St. Liz married first John de Lyons III, the Baron of Fortevoit, Forgandenny and Droumgawen. Their child was John IV de Lyon, Baron of Fortevoit, Forgandenny and Droumgawen, Angushire. Alice Lyons then married Thomas Strangeways of Salford. ALICE (DE SAINT LIZ) (m. 1 LYONS) (m. 2) STRANGEWAYS' father was WILLIAM DE SAINT LIZ (DE SENLIS) OF WARKWORTH and her mother was Matilda De Sentis.

The father of ALICE LYONS STRANGEWAYS was WILLIAM DE SAINT LIZ (DE SENLIS) OF WARKWORTH. William de Saint Liz de Senlis of Warkworth (b. 1274; d. 1313, Huntington, Northamptonshire, England) was married to Matilda De Sentis. Their children were Alice Lyon Strangeways and Rowland de Saint Liz.

The father of WILLIAM DE SAINT LIZ (DE SENLIS) OF WARKWORTH was RICHARD DE SAINT LIZ OF WARKWORTH (b. 1243, Northhampshire; d. 1286). Richard de Saint Liz of Warkworth married Matilda (Maud) and had one child, William de Saint Liz, and a half brother, William Senlis.

The father of RICHARD DE SAINT LIZ OF WARKWORTH was SIMON V DE SENLIS DE ST. LIZ of WARKWORTH (b. 1218, Banbury, Northampshire; d. 1296, Huntingdon). He married Anne Bullstra (b. 1224; d. 1300, Banbury, Northumberland). The parents of Anne Bullstra were Richard (b. 1198; d. 1254) and Amica (b. 1172; d. 1235, Shropshire). Simon and Anne Senlis had children Richard and William Senlis.

The father of SIMON V DE SENLIS was SIMON IV DE SENLIS (de St. Liz). He was born between 1165 and 1181 in Banbury. He died during 1250 in Banbury, Northhampton.

The father of SIMON IV DE SENLIS was SIMON DE SENLIS III, 8TH EARL OF HUNTINGDON, 5TH EARL OF NORTHHAMPTON and Alice de Gaunt, Countess of Northhampton. Alice de Gaunt was the daughter of Gilbert de Gaunt, Earl of Lincoln & Rohese de Claire. Simon de Senlis III, 8th Earl of Huntingdon was born in 1145, Warkworth, Northhampton, died 1184, Huntington and was buried at St. Andrews priory.

The father of SIMON DE SENLIS III was, SIMON SENLIS II, 4th EARL OF HUNTINGDON AND NORTHHAMPTON (SIMON SENLIS, SIMON DE ST. LIZ, SIMON SAINT LIZ). He was born during 1098 and died in August during 1153; buried at Saint Andrews Priory, Northhampton, Northhamptonshire, England. The wife of Simon Senlis was Isabel (Elizabeth) de Beaumont. Isabel (Elizabeth) de Beaumont was the daughter of Sir Robert de Beaumont, Knight Earl of Leicester, Justicar of England and Amice (Uta) de Gael, Heiress of Breteuill, Countess of Leichester. Isabel de Beaumont siblings were Robert de Beaumont, 3rd Earl of Leichester, Hawaise de Beaumont, Countess of Gloucester and Margaret Beaumont.

The children of SIMON SENLIS II, 4TH EARL OF HUNTINGDON AND NORTHHAMPTON and Isabel de Beaumont were Isabel de Sentis (de St. Liz) and Simon de Sentis III, 8th Earl of Huntingdon; 5th Earl of Northhampton, Amise de Saint Liz, Hawise de Saint Liz, William de Saint Liz, Matilda de Senlis, Walthrop de Saint Liz and half-brother, Malcom IV, King of Scotland, House of Albanach.

The father of SIMON SENLIS II, 4TH EARL OF HUNTINGDON AND NORTHHAMPTON was SIMON I DE SENLIS. Simon I de Senlis was considered a crusader. He was born during 1066 in Capelle-les-Grands-Normandy, France and died during 1111 in La Chante Sur-Loire, Burgundy, France after returning from a pilgrimage to the Holyland. He was buried in Faches-Thumesnil, Nord-Pas de Callis. He married MATILDA/MAUD DE SENLIS (b. 1072, Northumberland, England; d. 23 April 1130, Scotland), Countess of Huntingdon. MATILDA/MAUD DE SELIS' parents were WALTHEOF, EARL OF NORTHUMBERLAND and Judith de Lens, Countess of Huntingdon. *Matilda married Simon I de Senlis, Earl of Huntingdon and David I, King of Scots. Matilda was the Countess of Huntingdon and Northhampton and Queen of Scotland.*

The parents of Matilda de Senlis were Waltheof Earl of Northumberland and Judith de Lens, Countess of Huntingdon. Matilda's siblings were Utred de Fitz Walthehof, Lord of Tyndale and Adelisa de Huntington. The father of Waltheof, Earl of Northumberland was Waltheof, Earl of Northumbria (b. 1045, Wallsend, England; d. 31 May 1076, St. Giles Hall, Winchester,

Hampshire – Beheaded for treason but "may have been innocent") (brother to Sybl FitzSiward, Queen b. 1009; d. 1070, Iona, near Elgin, Moran, Scotland and Osbean Bulax), whose father was Siward Biornsson (Sigurd the Dane), Earl of Northumbria (b. circa 1020, Denmark; d. 26 March 1055, England) and Comte de Northumberland by 1041, whose father was Beorn Berrson, Earl of Denmark (b.. circa 997; d. 1046, Chichester, England).

The children of Matilda de Senlis and Simon Senlis I were Simon de Senliz II (4ᵗʰ Earl of Huntingdon and Northhampton), Matilda de St. Liz, Waltheof del Liz and Henry, Earl of Huntingdon. **The children of Matilda Senlis and David I, King of Scots were Malcolm IV, King of Scotland** were daughters, Claricia Ingen Dabid (b. 1115, Kelso, Scotland; d. 1135, Scotland) and Hodierna Ingen Dabid.

David I, King of Scots, was born 1083 in Fordoun, Kincardinshire, Scotland. He was the son of Malcom III, Canmore, King of Scots and Saint Margaret, Queen of Scots. David I, King of Scots, had son Malcom IV, King of Scotland, House of Albounach with Matilda de Sentis, Countess of Huntingdon. He was brother to Edmund of Scotland MacMael, 1ˢᵗ Earl of Fife and brother to Duncan II, King of Scots.

The father of MALCOM IV, KING OF SCOTS was DAVID I, KING OF SCOTS, whose father was MALCOM III, KING OF SCOTS (b. 26 March 1031, Dunkeld, Perthshire; d. 13 November 1097, Alnwich, Northumbershire. Buried Dunfermilne Abbey). Malcom III was King of Scotland from 1058-1093. The father of MALCOM III KING OF SCOTLAND was DUNCAN I, KING OF SCOTS. He reigned from 1034-1040. *Source: Geni Genealogy.*

The children of THOMAS and Sarah (Bunker) PINKHAM (Generation 4) were:

~ ABIJAH THOMAS PINKHAM: Born 9 February 1734, Dover, NH. Married Rachel
    Huckins in 1753. American Revolutionary War Patriot. Died 3 March 1779,
    Durham, New Hampshire.

~Sarah Pinkham: Born 1735, Dover, New Hampshire.

~Joseph Pinkham: Born 1736, Dover, NH. Married (m1) Elizabeth Deering and (m2)
    Elizabeth Hayes. Died August 1819, Jackson, New Hampshire (American
    Revolutionary War Patriot) (Pinkham's Notch, New Hampshire).

Abijah's brother Joseph Pinkham (4), son of Thomas (3) and Sarah (Bunker) Pinkham, born 1736 in Dover, New Hampshire became a Captain in the American Revolutionary War. He married Elizabeth Deering (daughter of Clement Deering and Hannah Davis Deering) born 1740 prior to 1776. Joseph and Elizabeth Pinkham had one son, Joseph Deering Pinkham (b. 1762; d. 1837). After 1776 Joseph Pinkham married Elizabeth Hayes (b. 12 April 1741 Rochester; d. January 1814), daughter of Benjamin Hayes and Jane Snell Hayes). Thomas Davis, grandfather of Elizabeth Hayes deeded on 8 September 1763 land described as "one half part of all the lands where I the aforesaid Thomas Davis now dwell (Schneider & Rubin)." After the American Revolution, Joseph resided near Pinkham's Notch, New Hampshire. Joseph and Elizabeth's children (5) were George (b. 1777; d. 1822), Daniel (b. 1779; d. 1855), Rufus (b. 1780; d. 1858) and Elizabeth (b. unknown; d. unknown) Pinkham.

While Joseph Pinkham resided in New Hampshire, a 1789 document was found in Canada signed by a "John Johnson." John Johnson, perhaps a relation of Solomon Johnson, who named a son, John, and whose daughter, Julia V. Johnson, was the wife of Amos Phelps III, the brother of Elizabeth Phelps, wife of Comfort Carpenter Pinkham.

The document reads:

> Joseph Abijah Pinkham, Montreal 1789
>
> My Lord,
>
> The Land Board -- having taken the -- petition into consideration are of opinion that the settlement of tract a number of persons of the description of M. Austin (X for signature) his -- would be a great advantage and benefit to the Province, they therefore humbly submit the __ to your Lordship and have requested me a --- it. I am
>
> My Lord, your Lordship most obedient and most humble servant,
>
> John Johnson

> *(Amos Phelps III married Julia V. Johnson, daughter of Solomon Johnson)*

~<u>Mary Pinkham</u>: Born 1744.

Both Abijah Thomas and Joseph Pinkham (4), sons of Thomas Pinkham (3), became American Revolutionary soldiers with Joseph retaining the role of Captain. Thomas Pinkham lived a short life dying at age thirty-nine either before or after the birth of his last child, Mary (b. 1744). Both daughters of Thomas and Sarah Pinkham (Sarah and Mary) also died young. Thomas Pinkham was speculated not to be a Quaker.

The eldest son of Thomas Pinkham (3) was ABIJAH THOMAS PINKHAM (Generation 4). Abijah married Rachel Huckins (b. 15 March 1732, Oyster River, NH) in 1753. The Huckins family ancestors also signed the Dover Combination. Abijah was an American Revolutionary soldier in 1775. Here again the story also gets murky because Abijah is sometime claimed to be the son of Otis Pinkham and Abigail Tibbetts and grandson of John Pinkham (2). However, Abijah is not recorded in Friends Church records with the other Otis/Abigail children. Some historians claim because Abijah named his children some of the same names used in the Otis Family, he should be placed as the son of Otis Pinkham. Additionally, not only does Abijah Pinkham not appear in Friends records with the other Otis children but also, Otis has a recorded son born directly after Abijah proving the unlikely possibility of this relationship. As noted previously, Friends records are replete with mentions of members being disowned. Also, it is noted Thomas (3) does not have a devout relationship with the Quaker faith. Abijah is placed as the firstborn son of Thomas and Sarah (Bunker) Pinkham because Abijah's firstborn children were named Thomas (after his father) and Sarah (after his mother, Sarah Bunker). He is, therefore, the grandson of Richard (2) and Elizabeth Pinkham.

RACHEL HUCKINS PINKHAM, Wife to Abijah (4) Pinkham:

Abijah Pinkham married Rachel Huckins (b. 15 March 1732; d. 10 November 1818) on 11 January 1753. Abijah's great-grandfather was Dover Combination signer, Richard Pinkham (1) as was Rachel Huckins' great-grandfather, Robert Huckins, who also signed the Dover

Combination (*Source: New England Historical & Genealogical Registrar 1913-1915, Henry Winthrop Hardin, MA, past law professor of Cornell and Columbia. Copyright 1916 UESRY Private Printed by Henry Winthrop Harden*). The marriage of Richard Pinkham's great-grandson Abijah Pinkham (Pinkham Generation 4) and Robert Huckins great-great-granddaughter Rachel Huckins (Huckins Generation 5) is significant because both sides of the family had ancestors who were the first settlers to Dover, New Hampshire: Richard Pinkham (1) and Robert Huckins (1).

ROBERT HUCKINS (Huckins Generation 1) was born in Devonshire, England. He immigrated to Dover, New Hampshire prior to 22 October 1640 and is one of the forty-two signers of the Dover Combination, like Richard Pinkham (1).

Until the end of the French Indian War all New Hampshire settlements were near the coast. In 17_3 the "great" road was built from Durham through to Barrington, Barnstead and Gilmanton. By the 6th generation, the Huckins family went east of Toronto to Whitby, Ontario while this Pinkham branch (Richard1Richard2Thomas3Abijah 4Samuel5Samuel6Comfort7) crossed into Canada from Vermont to Stanstead, Quebec in 1800 then moved to Ontario by 1842 after the English-French War in Quebec.

Robert Huckins (1)'s wife's name is unknown but his children were (Generation 2): JAMES (b. 1655, Oyster River, NH, deceased at massacre of 1689; killed by Indians at Old River - Pikes Journal Register, vol. 33, pg. 96; Belknap History p. 138).), who married Sarah Burnham (the daughter of Robert and Frances Burnham b. 1651, Oyster River, NH; d. 31 December 1673), and Sarah (b. 1654, Oyster River, NH; d. 14 October 1704), who married James Chelsley (son of Phillip and Sarah Chelsley b. 16 July 1675; d. before 1699). (*Pikes Journal Register, Vol pg.156*), Huckins. Lt. James Huckins (2) was taxed in 1664, listed as being a constable in 1676, a miller and one of two "selectmen." After James Huckins (2) died, Sarah Burnham Huckins married Captain John Woodman on 17 October 1700. *Source: Quints Dover, Hoyt's Old Family of Salisbury & Amesbury, p. 33 & p. 366.*

Lt. James and Sarah Huckins children were (Generation 3) ROBERT (b. 1672, Oyster River, NH), James (died in massacre) and Sarah (b. 12 Dec. 1674; d. 14 October 1704) Huckins.

It is noted Lt. James Huckins (2) had a garrison house on the outskirts of Oyster River, NH. In August of 1689 the Indians killed and "slew" him and seventeen other men while they were working in the field of Widow Joseph Coe. The Huckins' Garrison House was defended against Indians by women and two boys, one of whom was Robert Huckins (3). The Indians killed three or four children then carried away the "inmates" (women) and boys. One of the boys, "doubtless" Robert Huckins (3), escaped the next day (*Source: Mather's Magnolia, App. Art. Vi, Belknap History, New Hampshire, Vol. 1, page 205.*). Lt. James Huckins' widow, Sarah, was recovered at Fort Androscoggin after a year of captivity. "She is not mentioned in James Huckins' will dated 20 December 1705, deeded 16 April 1675 by William Beard which suggested a former marriage to a daughter of William and Elizabeth Beard."

Robert Huckins (3) (b. 1672) married Welthen Thomas in 1692. Robert Huckins was a yeoman and miller. Welthen married again (m2) in 1727 to John Gray. Welthen Thomas was the daughter of James and Martha (Goddard) Thomas and born in Dover, NH (*Source: NH Deeds, Vol 17, pp. 53, 55; New Hampshire State Papers, p. 149*). Robert Huckins rebuilt the garrison house and in 1701 had the mill on Huckins' brook. In 1698, it is historically noted that the "eldest son and heir of James Huckins, the only son of Robert Huckin's, "deceased" conveyed 6 acres on Cocheo Marsh which had been granted to Robert Huckins in 1648. (*Source: New Hampshire Deeds, vol. 6, p. 206*) In 1705, he had the administration upon the estate of "Robert Huckins, his grandfather (*Source: New Hampshire State papers, vol. 31, p. 545.*)." He was first "selectman" then assessor and finally constable in Dover, NH. He was baptized on 17 January 1719.

Robert and Welthen Huckins children (Generation 4) were all born in Oyster River, NH: Mary (born abt. 1693), Hannah (born abt. 1695), ROBERT (Robert -1, James – 2, Robert -3) (b. 14 October 1708 Oyster River Parish, NH; d. before 1777), May (b. 15 May 1724), Lt. Job, Hannah (b. 1728), Samuel (born abt. 1730) and Jonathan Huckins. Robert Huckins (4) married first Meriboh Jackson (m1), daughter of William and Mary Jackson then Sarah Snell (m2), daughter of Samuel Snell, born in Barrington, NH. Robert Huckins (4) was Durham, NH Constable in 1740 and Nottingham Constable from 1757-1765. He received "40 acres" as per his father (Robert Huckins – 3) will on the other side of the old garrison house in Oyster River, NH. In 1757 Robert Huckins (4) sold the land to Dr. Joseph Attinson and bought 50 acres of land in Nottingham. *Source: New Hampshire Deeds, Vol. 2, p. 33.*

The children (Generation 5) of Robert and Mariboh (Jackson) were Mary (baptized 14 December 1729) *(Source: NH Registrar, Vol. 33, p. 346)* and RACHEL Huckins.

Mary Huckins married on 24 November 1754 Samuel Serbes (b. 10 Aug. 1710, Dover, NH) of Barrington who was a blacksmith and the son of William and Deborah Serbes. The child of Samuel and Mary Serbes was Samuel of Strafford, NH who was born in 1758. He was a farmer and soldier in the American Revolutionary war. Samuel Serbes, Jr. married Anna Foss (daughter of Ichabod and Hannah Foss, b. Barrington, NH; d. Gilmanton, NH) and Moses of Barnstead and Gilmanton who was a merchant who married unknown Daniels.

Rachel Huckins (b. 15 March 1732; d. 10 Nov. 1818) (Huckins Generation 5) married (according to Reverend John Adam's records) Abijah Pinkham (Farmer, b. 9 Feb. 1734; d. 3 March 1779) (Pinkham Generation 4) of Durham, New Hampshire on 11 January 1753.

ABIJAH THOMAS (4) and Rachel (Huckins Generation 5) PINKHAM'S children (Generation 5) (Huckins Generation 6) were all born in Durham, New Hampshire. The seven children include: Thomas Pinkham (b. June 1755; married Sarah Ballard; d. 26 May 1811, Woodstock, NH.), Sarah Pinkham (b. 1757; married 13 January 1776 Robert Williams of Barrington), SAMUEL (b. 11 May 1760; married Dorothy Ordway; d. 1830, Stanstead, Quebec), Abijah (b. 22 July 1763; married on 11 December 1783 Sarah Spencer born 23 October 1763; d. 8 July 1815, Durham, NH), Anne (b. 1766; married on 15 February 1798 to John Jenkins), Abigail (b. 1773; m1 Ephraim/m2 Libby; d. 30 August 1852 Lowell, MA) and Paul (b. 1776; m. Susanna Green on 12 September 1789). It is from Samuel Pinkham (b. 1760, Durham, NH; d. 1830, Stanstead, Quebec) we enter Canada during 1800 with Generations 5 (Samuel) and 6, twenty years after Richard Pinkham (6) of Nantucket (1777).

ABIJAH THOMAS PINKHAM (Generation 4) (b. 9 February 1734, Dover, NH; d. 3 March 1779, Durham, NH) was a gentleman farmer, trader and landowner in Durham, New Hampshire. The name, Abijah, means "God" in Hebrew. Abijah Pinkham also served in the American Revolutionary War. He lived a short life like his father, Thomas, as he passed away at age forty-five years old and left a will dated 16 February 1779. He bequeathed to his wife Rachel half his estate if she remained a widow and only one-third if she remarried, as law of that time permitted. Abijah bequeathed to his firstborn son, Thomas, all lands in Durham and sixteen acres in Colley's Marsh plus one sixteenth of a sawmill near the grist mill. To his second son, SAMUEL, then aged nineteen and when he reached age twenty-one, Abijah bequeathed money, fifty acres of unimproved land in Gilmanton, NH or Barnstead, NH at "the discretion of his executor." Samuel also received Abijah's "Regimental Suit of Cloathing." To his son Abijah, Abijah Sr. bequeathed cattle, money and his "best holiday suit of apparel." Son, Paul, also received money and cattle and "a suit of decent everyday Cloaths." Daughter Sarah (wife of Robert Williams) received household furniture. Daughters Abigail and Anne Pinkham were to receive furniture and a cow at age eighteen. Legacies were also given to his grandson, Ballard, and granddaughters, Sarah and Mary. Thomas, the oldest son was the executor of the will in May of 1779. The account includes a receipt dating 10 May 1797 for 15 pounds – "For bringing up two children under Eage one Five year and half old, and the other three and four months at the death of my Father." (Schneider & Rubin)

The New Hampshire Revolutionary War Records state Abijah Pinkham enlisted on 6 September 1762 for military service as an Ensign in New Hampshire. He is then recorded on 5 November 1775 in the Revolutionary War Rolls of 1775-1783 for the state of New Hampshire.

The children (Generation 5) of ABIJAH THOMAS and Rachel (Huckins, daughter of Robert Huckins and Meriboh Jackson of New Hampshire) PINKHAM born Durham, New Hampshire were:

~Thomas Pinkham: Born: June 1755. Died: 26 May 1811, Woodstock, NH.

Married (m1) Sarah Ballard; (m2) Johanna Burnham.

Married (1) Sarah Ballard (d. March 1814). Child of Thomas and Sarah (5) Ballard was Ballard Pinkham (6) born 29 October 1774 who married Mary Flossom. Thomas Pinkham married (m2) Johanna Burnham (d. 27 March 1854). Children (Generation 6) of Thomas and Johanna Pinkham were Sarah (Sally) Pinkham (b. 13 March 1778; d. May 1847), Thomas Pinkham (b. 29 July 1780; m. 16 August 1804 to Peggy Vincent; d. 17 May 1851), Susannah Pinkham (b. 14 February 1782; m. September 1802 to Lt. Robert Mathes; d. 6 February 1858), Mary (Polly) Pinkham (b. 12 October 1784; d. 14 October 1784), Mary (Polly) Pinkham (b. 28 April 1787; m. August 1813 to Benjamin Folson of Walpole), Sophia Pinkham (b. 20 February 1798; m. 18 December 1806 to Elisha Locke), Timothy Pinkham (b. 20 February 1792; m. 23 August 1812 to Sally Garland; d. – drowned on 2 October 1850) and Pamela Pinkham (b. 6 February 1795; d. 25 December 1798).

Thomas Pinkham (6), son of Thomas and Johanna (Burnham) Pinkham:

New Hampshire Birth Records, Early to 1900: Thomas Pinkham
        Birth Date: 29 July 1790. Birthplace: Woodstock, Grafton, NH.
New Hampshire Marriage Record 1636-1947: Thomas Pinkham to
        Peggy Vincent. Marriage date: 16 August 1804. Marriage
        location: Durham, Stafford, New Hampshire.
1850 United States Census Woodstock, Grafton, New Hampshire:
        Thomas Pinkham. Thomas Pinkham age 70 born New Hampshire

with wife Margerie Pinkham age 67 born New Hampshire with Sarah Pinkham age 38 born New Hampshire and Janette George age 11 born NH.

1851 Death: Thomas Pinkham. Burial Place: Woodstock, Grafton, New Hampshire. Cemetery: Woodstock Cemetery. Death date: 6 May 1851. Birth date: 29 July 1780. *Source: FindAGrave*

The children (6) of Thomas and Peggy (Margaret) Vincent Pinkham were:
Pamelia Pinkham (b. 1805, Durham, NH)
Emeline/Sukey Pinkham (b. 7 January 1807, Peeling Grafton, NH)
Delilah Pinkham (b. 28 November 1809, Woodstock, Grafton, NH)
Sarah Pinkham (b. 1811, Woodstock, Grafton, NH)
Thomas Vincent Pinkham (b. 24 March 1814, Peeling, Grafton, NH)
Mary Pinkham (b. 17 February 1817, Peeling, Grafton, NH)
Rogers Pinkham (b. 3 March 1819, Woodstock, Grafton, NH)

New Hampshire Death Record 1654-1947: Sarah Pinkham, age 66 years and 10 days; born 1811, Woodstock, NW, daughter of Thomas and Margaret Pinkham. Single. Death date: April 1877. Location: Woodstock, New Hampshire.

New Hampshire Death Record 1654-1947: Pamelia Russell, 72 years, 3 months, 13 days born 1805, Durham, New Hampshire. Death date: April 1877. Location. Woodstock, New Hampshire. Married. Daughter of Thomas and Margaret Pinkham.

New Hampshire Death Record 1654-1947: Mary P. Smith, age 70 years; 3 days born 1817, Woodstock, NH, daughter of Thomas Pinkham and Margarette Vincent. Death date: 20 February 1887. Location: Woodstock, NH.

Timothy Pinkham (6), son of Thomas and Joannah (Burnham) Pinkham:

New Hampshire Marriage Record: 1812 Timothy Pinkham to Sally Garland. Location: Durham, Stafford, New Hampshire.

1830 United States Census Durham, Stafford, New Hampshire Census: Timothy Pinkham.

1850 United States Census New Market, Rockingham, New Hampshire: Timothy Pinkham, age 58 born 1792 New Hampshire. Wife Sarah (Sally Garland) Pinkham age 59 born 1791 New Hampshire.

Child of Timothy and Sarah (Sally Garland) Pinkham (7): William age 34 born 1816 New Hampshire with Mary Pinkham (wife) age 28 born 1822, New Hampshire. Grandson - Charles Pinkham (8) age 2 born 1848 NH.

~Sarah Pinkham: Born 1757. Married to Robert Williams on 13 January 1777 in

Barrington, VT.

~SAMUEL PINKHAM: Born 1760. Died 1830, Quebec. Story to follow.

~Abijah Pinkham: Born 22 July 1763. Married to Sarah Spencer. Children of Abijah and Sarah (Generation 6) were: Elizabeth Pinkham (b. 7 July 1784; m. 13 November 1800 to Ebenezer Cornell), Sally Pinkham (b. 8 July 1789; m. 28 November 1805 to Jonathan Fifield), Augustus H. Pinkham (b. 25 March 1791), John S. Pinkham (b. 25 December 1793; d. 11 October 1819), Margery Pinkham (b. 19 April 1796; m. 22 October 1822 to Reverend George Washington Russell; d. November year unknown in Woodstock, NH), Abigail Pinkham (b. 13 July 1799; m. 27 April 1820 to Joseph Russell of Woodstock, NH; d. February 1890), Pamelia Pinkham (b. 6 September 1805; m. 20 May 1833 to Peter Russell of Woodstock, NH – son of Joseph Russell and Mary Robb; d. 20 July 1877).

New Hampshire Marriage Record 1637-1947: Abijah Pinkham, age 20 born 1763 to Sarah Spencer, age 20 born 1763. Marriage Date: 11 December 1783. Marriage Location: Durham, Strafford, New Hampshire.

Children of Abijah and Sarah (Spencer) Pinkham (6):
        Elizabeth Pinkham (b. 7 July 1784, Durham, Strafford, NH)
        Sarah Pinkham (b. 8 July 1789, Durham, Strafford, NH)
        Augustus Pinkham (b. 25 March 1791, Durham, Strafford, NH)
        Margery Pinkham (b. 19 April 1796, Durham, Strafford, NH)

New Hampshire Death Record 1654-1947: Abijah Pinkham. Death date: 8 July 1815. Location: Durham, New Hampshire.
Record for Abijah Pinkham, son of Abijah and Rachel Huckins Pinkham.

~Anne Pinkham: Born 1766. Married to John Jenkins on 15 February 1798.

~Abigail Pinkham: Born 1773. Married (m1) Ephraim Smith and (m2) Reuben Libby. Died 30 August 1852, Lowell, MA. Children (6) Delilah Smith b. 12 April 1798, Wolfesburg, NH, Smith Libby b. 1802 and Abigail Libby.

~Paul Pinkham: Born 1776. Married to Susanna Green on 12 September 1789.

Abijah Thomas Pinkham is listed in the United States Revolutionary War Rolls 1654-1947 on 5 November 1775 as the military rank of Private for New Hampshire. His final rank was Sergeant for New Hampshire, service that notes his birth as 9 February 1734 in Dover, New Hampshire. His death is noted as 3 March 1779 in Durham, Strattford County, New Hampshire. He was a Private in Captain Smith Emerson's Company and is listed in the Hammond Rolls of the soldiers of the Revolutionary War, New Hampshire State Papers, Volume 14, Pages 234-235. (Source: NARA.) Abijah Pinkham was listed as residing in the city of Durham in the county of Strafford, New Hampshire. His spouse was recorded as Rachel Huckins.

SAMUEL PINKHAM (5) was the third child of Abijah and Rachel (Huckins) Pinkham. His father died when he was nineteen and, thus, he inherited land in Belknap County,

New Hampshire when he turned twenty-one. Samuel Pinkham (5) was given the choice of settling either at Barnstead (incorporated in 1727) or Gilmanton (incorporated in 1727), New Hampshire. Samuel chose the unimproved land in Gilmanton where he married Dorothy Ordway on 12 November 1783. Dorothy Ordway was born 17 July 1751 in Amesbury, MA. She was the daughter of Moses and Anne (Huntington) Ordway. Samuel and Dorothy Pinkham settled in Loudon, New Hampshire from 1783-7 before moving to Danville, Vermont in 1788. In 1800 they moved to No. 11, 9th Range of Stanstead, Quebec with most members of their family (Generation 6). Samuel Pinkham (5) died in Quebec in May of 1830. Dorothy (Ordway) Pinkham died in Quebec on 10 August 1850. Both Samuel and Dorothy are buried at the Quebec Anglican Church at Roxton and Milton.

Dorothy Ordway married Samuel Pinkham ("Marriages performed by Reverend Isaac Smith, Smith Meeting House, Gilmanton, NH, Belknap County, 1775-1817; Marriages performed in Gilmanton). Samuel Pinkham (5) was the son of Abijah (4) and Rachel (Huckins) Pinkham (Thomas – 3, Richard – 2, Richard – 1). The Smith Meeting House was the first church in that part of New Hampshire. A detailed record of the church is listed in a book titled, "*A Brief History of Smith Meeting House Gilmanton, New Hampshire*" by Edward J. Maher.

DOROTHY ORDWAY, Wife to Samuel (5) Pinkham: Paternal Ordway Genealogy

Dorothy Ordway was the daughter of Moses and Anna (Huntington) Ordway. She was born on 17 July 1759 (Amesbury births: "Tan Book" Topsfield Historical Society Topsfield, MA 1913). Dorothy Ordway married Samuel Pinkham (Marriages performed by Reverend Isaac Smith, Smith Meeting House, Gilmanton, NH, Belknap County, 1775-1817; Marriages performed in Gilmanton). Samuel Pinkham (5) was the son of Abijah (4) and Rachel (Huckins) Pinkham (Thomas – 3, Richard – 2, Richard – 1).

The Smith Meeting House marriage records list: "Samuel Pankham and Dorithy Ordway of Loudon, November 12, 1783"

Moses Ordway (Generation 4 Ordway) (James3John2James1) was one of the first settlers in Louden, NH. He married Anne (a) Huntington (Generation 4 Huntington). Both MOSES and ANNE (HUNTINGTON) ORDWAY were from Amesbury, MA. Moses Ordway was born on 11 April 1721. Anne Huntington was born on 15 March 1716. The married couple lived near a "yellow schoolhouse."

Cousins of Moses Ordway (4), Joses and Daniel Ordway, also moved to Louden, NH when the city was first settled. They were soldiers in the American Revolutionary War. Joses Ordway served in Captain John Abbott's company and in Major Gage's regiment. Daniel Ordway was in the foot company in Andover, MA.

The Generation 1 of the Ordway Family began when brothers Abner and James Ordway sailed from Tower Hill, England and settled in Watertown/Newbury, Massachusetts between 1635-40. James (1) Ordway married (m2) Ann(e) Emery, daughter of John Emery on 23 November 1648. Records show James (1) also married to (m1?) Sara Fitz but marriage date of 8 October 1654 might not be correct. Sara Fitz was the daughter of Robert Fitz and unknown who left his legacy to James (1) Ordway.

Abner Ordway married Sarah Brown, daughter of Stephen Brown of Newbury, MA, on 15 August 1656. Sarah Brown was the widow of Edward Dennis of Boston, MA. Sarah Brown was the daughter of Stephen Brown of Newbury, MA. Abner and Sarah Ordway did not have children.

James (1) and Anne (Emery) Ordway had ten children (Generation 2): Ephraim, James (father of Moses Jr.), Edward, Sarah, JOHN, Isaac, Jane, Hannah, unknown, Annie and Mary. James Ordway was recorded as being a farmer and an owner of boats.

The fifth child and fourth son of James and Anne Ordway was JOHN (2) Ordway who was born on 17 November 1658. He married in 1681 Mary Godfrey, the daughter of Peter Godfrey. The ten children of John (2) and Mary Ordway became Generation 3 of the Ordway family and included JAMES Ordway (3). James (3) Ordway (John2, James1) married Elizabeth Heath Haverhill on 8 December 1714.

The seven children (Generation 4) of JAMES (3) and Elizabeth Ordway were: James, MOSES (father of Dorothy Ordway), Elizabeth, twins – Elizabeth & Sarah, John and Benjamin Ordway.

Joses (4) Ordway was the fourth son and youngest child of James (Generation 3, James2, James1) and Mariboh (Morsey) Ordway born 15 June 1753. Joses Ordway was a solder in Captain John Abbot's company and in Major Gage's regiment of militia, including Burgoyne's surrender. Joses' brother Daniel (4) Ordway, also an American Revolutionary soldier, and his sister Persis (4) Ordway moved to Louden. Persis married cousin Moses Ordway Jr.

Joses Ordway was a farmer who married Lucy Chamberlain on 13 April 1794. Lucy Chamberlain was born on 16 March 1766 in Hopkintown, MA and was the daughter of Abiel and Lois (Whitney) Chamberlain. Lois Whitney was born in Hopkintown, Massachusetts on 5 October 1734. The children of Joses and Lucy Ordway (Generation 4) were: Lucy, Lois, Sophia, Abiel, John C., Susan and Harriet Ordway.

Dorothy Ordway was born between 1747 -1767 (17 July 1759) and church records list her burial as: Dorothy Odervy Pinkham, 14 August 1850 in Stanstead, Quebec with text listing "wife of Samuel Pinkham, aged 93, one of the earliest settlers." *Source: Stanstead Journal Vital Statistics,1845-1860, page 35.*

Dorothy Ordway was born in Amesbury, Essex County, Massachusetts. She was Generation 4 Ordway and Generation 6 Huntington. As stated previously, Moses Ordway married Anne (Anna) Huntington in December of 1746. Anne Huntington (Generation 5 Huntington) was born on 16 March 1716 in Amesbury, MA and died on 7 March 1779 in Louden, Merrimack, NH. The children of Moses and Anne (Huntington) Ordway were (Generation 5 Ordway): UNKNOWN (b. 24 July 1747), Sarah (b. 25 May 1751), Anna (b. 27 March 1751), Masha (b. 28 March 1753), Mary (b. 7 December 1754), Elizabeth (b.17 April 1751) and Dorothy (b. 17 July 1759) Ordway.

DOROTHY ORDWAY, Wife to Samuel (5) Pinkham: Maternal Huntington Genealogy

As stated previously, Dorothy Ordway was the daughter of Moses and Anna (Huntington) Ordway. She was born on 17 July 1759 (Amesbury births: "Tan Book" Topsfield Historical Society Topsfield, MA 1913). Dorothy Ordway married Samuel Pinkham (Marriages performed by Reverend Isaac Smith, Smith Meeting House, Gilmanton, NH, Belknap County, 1775-1817; Marriages performed in Gilmanton). Samuel Pinkham (5) was the son of Abijah (4) and Rachel (Huckins) Pinkham (Thomas – 3, Richard – 2, Richard – 1).

The Smith Meeting House marriage records list:

"Samuel Pankham and Dorithy Ordway of Loudon, November 12, 1783"

From the HUNTINGTON FAMILY ASSOCIATION: SIMON HUNTINGTON sailed in 1633 from

England to Massachusetts with wife, Margaret Barret, and children, including son from first wife, William Huntington. WILLIAM HUNTINGTON married Johanna Bayley and had son named John Huntington. JOHN HUNTINGTON married Elizabeth Hunt and had son named William Huntington. WILLIAM HUNTINGTON married Mary Goodwin/Mary Colby and had nine children including son Samuel Huntington. SAMUEL HUNTINGTON married Elizabeth Martin and had seven children including Anne Huntington (b.16 March 1716-17). ANNE HUNTINGTON married Moses Ordway of Amesbury, MA on 25 December 1746 and had six children including Dorothy Ordway (b. July 1759). Dorothy Ordway married Samuel Pinkham.

Anne Huntington is the descendant of SIMON HUNTINGTON who died on a voyage from England to America, and thus a member of the Huntington Family Association.

The text that follows is taken from "The Huntington Family in America – a genealogical memoir of the known descendants of Simon Huntington from 1633 – 1915" published by the Huntington Family Association of Hartford, CT in 1915, Press of the Hartford Print, Co. (Elihu Geer Sons) 16 State Street, Hartford, CT.

Prior to Simon Huntington and his son William Huntington arriving in America, four generations preceding them began with THOMAS HUNTINGTON and unknown who had three children, RICHARD, Thomas and Elizabeth. Richard (b. 1460) married in 1498 Alice Loring, the daughter of Simon Loring of Little Samford, England. Richard and Alice Huntington had five sons: Robert, CHRISTOPHER (b. 18 December 1500), John, Simon (died young) and Richard. Christopher married on 17 April 1537 to Elizabeth Bayley (Bailey), the daughter of George Bailey of London. Christopher and Elizabeth Huntington had GEORGE (b. 9 January 1538) and seven other sons and one daughter. George married on 5 August 1580 to Anne Fenwick, the daughter of Robert Fenwick. George and Anne Huntington had children: 1) Margaret (b. 11 May 1581; m. 27 January 1607), 2) Samuel (b. 16 February 1582, officer in the army of King Charles the first, 3) SIMON (our ancestor) (b. 7 August 1583) 4) George (b. 2 June 1585), 5) Andrew (b. 18 January 1587; m. June 1 to Elizabeth, daughter of William Rockwell) 6) Robert (b. 6 March 1589).

It is assumed Simon Huntingon (b. 7 August 1583) was married prior to his marriage to Margaret Baret on 21 June 1627 given his age because usually marriages at age forty-four were second marriages. Margaret was the daughter of Christopher Baret, the Mayor of Norwich, England. In 1633 Simon, Margaret, William, Christopher, Thomas and Simon Huntington sailed to America.

Simon Huntington's second wife, Margaret Barrett (Baret) Huntington and Huntington children arrived in Massachusetts in 1633. The text recorded states:

"Margaret Huntington, widow, arrived in 1633. Her husband Simon died by the way of smallpox. She brought __ children with her."

Widow Margaret Huntington (nee Barrett) married in 1635/6 Thomas Stoughton and moved to Windsor, Connecticut according to Roxbury, MA church records. Listed as the children of Margaret and Thomas Stoughton are: William (most likely Simon's child by his first wife), Christopher (b. 1628), Thomas, Simon (b. 1629/30) and Ann (Stoughton?) Huntington.

When Margaret (m2 Simon Huntington) Stoughton moved with her new husband to Windsor, Connecticut along with her children Christopher, Thomas, Simon and Ann, young William Huntington stayed in Massachusetts as he must have been between the age ten and eighteen and Margaret (Huntington) Stoughton was not his mother. The Massachusetts Bay Colony was a Puritan community that eventually allowed the settling across the Powwow and Merrimack Rivers. Amesbury, Massachusetts was settled in 1642. Salisbury Town Records list William Huntington as an inhabitant of New Town and one of thirteen people whose children were given 500 acres of land. He "removed" to west side of Powwow River as "ordered" on 26 December 1642. Described as "a religious and enterprising" man, he resided next to Thomas Hoyt in Pleasant

Valley on the banks of the Merrimac River. He also paid tax to support "Reverend William Worchester, the pastor of the First Church in Salisbury.

According to Salisbury records William Huntington (Generation 1) owned:

1. 1653: 1 acre and 92 rods of Beach Commons, Lot 55.
2. 1654: Inhabitant of New Town.
3. 1658: Oct 29 – "one of 13" given 500 acres. His son, John, inherits land.
4. 1660: "A township is granted to Willi Howntinton for his son."
5. 1661: One of 25 to whom lots are laid at Lion's Mouth.
6. 1662: April 1 – Drew 120 acres of land; March 1662-3, 30 acres "west of pond near children's land."
7. New Town, Nov. 18, 1663 – "Drew lots between Hamptonshire and Powow river in 1667, 12th month, 18th day drew lots in 4 places."
8. 1664: Bought of John Hoyt, Sr. land adjoining his Merrimac River property.

William (Generation 1) Huntington, son of Simon Huntington, married Joanna Bayley, daughter of John Bayley of Chippendale, England who was the great-grandson of George Bayley, the great-grandfather of Simon Huntington. John Bayley bequeathed, through her brother John Bayley Jr., Joanna Huntington and two of her children land located in Newbury by the Merrimac River.

Generation 2 of the Huntington family begins when John Huntington (b. "On Sunday last week of August 1643; d. 1729) was born to William Huntington (Generation 1) in Amesbury, Massachusetts. The children (Generation 2) of William and Joanna (Bayley) Huntington were (Generation 2): JOHN (b. Aug. 1643; d. 1729), James (b. unknown; d. 5 December 1646) and Mary (b. 8 May 1648, Amesbury; m.14 June 1667 to Joshua Goldsmith, son Jeramiah Davis Goldsmith – "…grandfather John Huntington and my Aunt Mary Goldsmith, widow, the bond pledging her maintenance.") Huntington.

John Huntington (Generation 2) married (m1) Elizabeth Hunt on 25 October 1665 and (m2) Elizabeth Blaisedel in 1686. John Huntington had a seat in the First Congregational Church in Amesbury and was also a constable. The children (Generation 3) of John and Elizabeth Huntington were: Hannah (b. 16 August 1666; d. 17 August 1666), Mary (b. 15 November 1667; m1 - Abraham Joyce, m2 Jeremiah Dow), Elizabeth (b. 1669; m. 22 May 1689 to Lt. Thomas Hoyt, Jr. – William Huntington lived on property next to Hoyts. Had 53 grandchildren, 121 great-grandchildren, 142 great-great grandchildren), Hannah (b. 19 November 1671; m. William Chandler on 29 November 1692), Sarah (b. 1 November 1672; d. 7 April 1708), Susannah (b. 4 February 1674; m. 20 December 1699 to Andrew Downey), William (m1 Mary Goodwin, m2 Mary Cobley, nine children, Executer of father, John Huntington's will.), SAMUEL (b. 7 April 1708; m. Elizabeth Marsh) and Deborah (b. 22 September 1687; m. 8 January 1713 to Edmund Elliot) Huntington.

The children of Samuel and Elizabeth Huntington are (Generation 4): Samuel (b. 13 January 1709/10, Elizabeth (b. 2 March 1711/12), John (b. 24 December 1714), ANNE (b. 16 March 1716/17, Amesbury; m. Moses Ordway of Amesbury, MA; d. 7 March 1779, Louden, Merrimack, NH), Jonathan (b. 20 February 1719/20), David (b. 2 February 1724/25. David was in the Company of Militia at Bunker Hill) and Jacob (b. 29 December 1726) Huntington.

Moses Ordway married December 1746 in Amesbury, Essex, MA, Anne Huntington (b. 16 March 16, 1716/17, Amesbury, MA). Born in Amesbury, MA, the children of Moses and Anne (nee Huntington) Ordway were (Generation 5 from William Huntington): Sarah (b. 25 May 1751), Anna (b. 27 March 1751, assumed), Masha (b. 28 March 1753), Mary (b. 7 December 1754), Elizabeth (b. 17 April 1757) and DOROTHY (b. 17 July 1759) Ordway.

In Gilmanton, NH, the church lists marriage records for: Samuel Pankham and Dorithy Ordway of Louden, November 12, 1783.

Church records list: Dorothy Odervy Pinkham burial 14 August 1850, Stanstead, Quebec - "wife of Samuel Pinkham, aged 93, one of the earliest settlers..." *Source: Stanstead Journal of Vital Statistics, 1845-1846, Page 35.*

Eliza Ordway (b. 17 April 1751; d. 14 March 1877) is buried at Reedsville Cemetery in Stanstead, Quebec. She was a sister of Dorothy Ordway and daughter of Moses and Anne Ordway.

The Huntington Family arrived in the Saybrook Colony, Connecticut after Margaret Huntington married Thomas Stoughton in 1635/6 and moved her family to Windsor, CT. Christopher Huntington, HALF-BROTHER to William Huntington of New Town, MA, arrived in the United States in Massachusetts with his mother and siblings. His father died of smallpox while on the voyage from England.

Christopher Huntington, brother to William Huntington, married Ruth Rockwell, daughter of William Rockwell on 7 October 1654. Christopher Huntington owned one-hundred acres of land and was "first townsman." In 1678, he was listed as being the town clerk, a post in which he succeeded Richard Bushnell. In 1685, he was one of twelve "patentees" of the town of Norwich. Christopher Huntington died in 1691 and was considered a pioneer of Norwich, Connecticut.

Christopher Huntington 1 to Christopher Huntington 2:

"...all that our one hundred acres of uplands and meadows which we hold in partnership as it was given to us by our honored father, Christopher Huntington as by his last will and testament..."

The children (Generation 2) of Christopher and Ruth (Rockwell) Huntington were: Christopher (b. 13 April 1653; d. 1654 - "lived 1 year 4 months"), Ruth (b. 13 April, 1653; d, 1654), Ruth (b. April 1658, Saybrook, CT; m. 26 March 1681 to Samuel Pratt of Saybrook; d.14 February 1683), CHRISTOPHER (b. 1 November 1660), Thomas (b. 18 March 1664), John (b. 15 March 1666), Susannah (b. Aug. 1668), Lydia (b. 1672) and Ann (b. 25 October 1675; m. to Jonathan Bingham, son of Thomas & Mary Rudd Bingham, Bingham (b. 15 April 1674). (Jonathan Bingham was the third of eleven children of Thomas Bingham, the Deacon of Windham Church) Huntington.

Christopher Huntington (Generation 2) was born 1 November 1660 and married (m1) Sarah Adgate (b. Jan. 1663), daughter of Deacon Thomas Adgate, (m2) Mrs. Mary Bushnell, widow of Richard Bushnell of Saybrook - mother to his first eight children who died during February of 1705 at age 42 and (m3) Mrs. Judith (Stevens) Brewster (widow of Jonathan Brewster, great-grandson to Elder Brewster, spiritual guide to Mayflower Pilgrims) on October of 1706.

The children (Generation 3) of Christopher (2) and Mary Huntington were: Ruth (b. 28 November 1682 – she is the mother of Dartmouth College founder Eleazar Wheelock), CHRISTOPHER (b. 12 September 1686), Isaac (b. 5 February 1688), Jabez (b. 26 January 1691), Matthew (b. 16 April 1696), Hezekial (b. 16 December 1696), Sarah (b. 5 January 1699-1700), Jeremiah (b. 15 December 1702; d. 1703), Judith (b. 10 September 1707), John (b. 14 November 1709), Elizabeth (b. 6 May 1712) and Jeremiah (b. 20 December 1715) Huntington.

Christopher (Christopher2, Christopher1) was born on 12 September 1686 and died 2 June 1730. He married (m1) Abigail (Abel), widow of Barnabus Lathrop. Abigail Abel (b. 16 March 1690; d. 27 May 1710) was the fifth daughter of Caleb and Margaret (Post) Abel. Christopher and Abigail Huntington had eight children. Christopher (2) married (m2) Elizabeth Ensworth of Canterbury, CT and they had one child who died 2 March 1734/5. Christopher (2) married (m3) Mary Brewster on 4 June 1740. They had no children. On 7 February 1750 Christopher (2) married (m4) Mrs. Mary Gaylord of Hebron, CT who died 14 March 1761.

Ruth Huntington, sister of Christopher Huntington (2), married Ralph Wheelock of Windham, MA on 8 January 1707/8. Ralph Wheelock was the son of Captain Eleazer Wheelock who was born in Mendon, MA in 1683. Ralph Wheelock was Deacon of Windham Church. The children of Ralph and Ruth Huntington (second cousins to Samuel Huntington) Wheelock were Elizabeth (b. 18 July 1704), Eleazer (b. 22 April 1711; d. 24 April 1779), Ruth (b. 25 May 1713), Abigail (b. 3 March 1717), John (b. 20 January 1720) and Sarah (b. 7 July 1725) Wheelock. Sarah Wheelock married on 21 December 1742 to James Bingham and had seven children including Jerusha Bingham (b. 15 October 1743) who married on 19 September 1769 to Rev. Samuel Kirkland. Their child was Dr. John Kirkland who became a President of Harvard University (1810-1828).

Eleazer Wheelock was born on 22 April 1711 on a 300-acre farm in Windham CT and was the child of Ralph and Ruth (Huntington) Wheelock. Eleazer Wheelock was the great –grandson of the first teacher of the first free school in the United States and graduated from Yale College in 1733 with distinction. He obtained a Doctor of Divinity degree from the University of Edinburgh. Eleazer Wheelock obtained a charter from King George II on 13 December 1739 and raised funds to educate Native Americans, money that eventually served as a foundation for Dartmouth College. Lord Dartmouth, a board of trustee member, opposed education of colonist' sons. Wheelock kept the donation, and named the Dartmouth College after Lord Dartmouth in Hanover, NH in 1771. Eleazer and Ruth Huntington's son, John Wheelock (second cousin to Anne Huntington, Generation 4 Huntington), was a member of the first Dartmouth graduation class. John Wheelock was the second president of Dartmouth College and served a forty-year term. Brothers Colonial Eleazer and James also graduated from Dartmouth College. Eleazer Wheelock's daughter, Ruth, became the wife of Reverend Dr. Allen (Patten) of Northhampton, a President of Bowdoin College.

Eleazer Wheelock married (m1) Mrs. Sarah Maltby, daughter of Reverend John Davenport of Stamford and their child was Ruth (b. 25 May 1713, m. Reverend Dr. William Patten of Hartford, CT). Eleazer also married (m2) Miss Mary Bridmade of Milford, CT. Eleazer and Mary Wheelock's children (second cousins to Anne Huntington) were: John (graduated in first class of Dartmouth 1771, second Dartmouth College president), Colonial Eleazer (Dartmouth College graduate), James (Dartmouth College graduate) and Abigail (b. 3 March 1717; m. Reverend Dr. Pomeroy of Hebron, CT, graduate of Dartmouth) Wheelock.

Huntington Family Synopsis:

Ann(e) Huntington: William Huntington, son of Simon Huntington (born 7 August 1583; m2 Margaret Barrett who was born 28 September 1595 on 21 June 1627 Norwich, England) who died 11 May 1633 "On Board Small Pox" with a burial in the Atlantic Ocean (parents: George Huntington; mother: Anne Fenwick b. 1548 London, England whose parents were Robert and Anne Fenwick) was brother to: Thomas Huntington, Christopher Huntington Sr., Ann Huntington and DEACON SIMON Huntington.

WILLIAM Huntington (1) became one of the first settlers of Amesbury, Massachusetts where a plaque states this fact in 1654. His son, JOHN (2), had a son, SAMUEL (3), whose daughter, ANNE (4) Huntington married Moses Ordway and whose child, Dorothy married Samuel Pinkham (Pinkham and Huntington Generations 5).

Deacon Simon's great-great grandson signed the Declaration of Independence. Deacon Simon Huntington II was born on 6 July 1629 in St. Andrews, Norwich, England. He died on 28 June 1706 in Norwich, CT. He was Deacon of the Congregational Church, a plantation owner, a Puritan and a revolutionary politician.

Deacon Simon II (1) Huntington married Sarah Clark (b. 24 June 1633, Saybrook, CT; d. 21 September 1721, New Haven, CT, daughter of John and Elizabeth Clark of Saybrook, CT) and had children (2): Mary Forbes, Sarah Tracy, Simon III Huntington, JOSEPH

Huntington, Samuel Huntington, Elizabeth Huntington, Elizabeth Sarah Backus, Nathaniel, Daniel and James Huntington.

JOSEPH (2) Huntington was born September 1661 in Norwich, CT and died 29 December 1747 in Windham, CT. He married Rebecca Adgate (b. 1 June 1666, Norwich, CT; d. 26 November 1748, Windham, CT, daughter of Deacon Thomas Adgate and Mary Bushnell. Deacon Thomas Adgate was from England, his father: Asahal Adgate 1594) and had children (3): NATHANIEL (b. 1 Sept. 1691, Norwich, CT; d. CT), Joseph II, Jonathan, David, Solomon, Sarah Wright, Mary Fitch and Rebecca Crane.

NATHANIEL (3) Huntington was a farmer and political activist who married Mehetabel Thurston (b. 8 June 1700, Colony of Rhode Island and Providence Plantation; d. 4 October 1781, Windham, CT) and had ten children (4): Reverend Nathaniel Huntington Jr., Abigail Kimball, Mehetebel Webb, GOV. SAMUEL HUNTINGTON, Captain Eliphalet Huntington, Reverend, Jonathan Huntington, Reverend Enoch Huntington, Sybell Eels and Elijah Huntington.

Governor Samuel Huntington (4) was cousin to Anne Huntington (4) and a signer of the Declaration of Independence. His biography includes: Jurist (lawyer), patriot in the American Revolution, delegate to the Continental Congress, Signed the Declaration of Independence and Articles of Confederation, President of the Continental Congress 1779-1781, Chief Justice of the Connecticut Supreme Court, 18th Governor of Connecticut from 1786 until his death on 5 January 1796.

DECLARATION SIGNER: **SAMUEL HUNTINGTON**

Samuel Pinkham received the option to inherit land in either Barnstead or Gilmanton, New Hampshire, and chose Gilmanton. Gilmanton, Belknap County, New Hampshire was incorporated in 1727. Named for the "Gilman" family as twenty-four members of that surname received grants by King George, other families received grants, as well. It is possible a grant is how Abijah Pinkham bequeathed Gilmanton land to his son, Samuel Pinkham. By 1790 the population of Gilmanton included more than two-thousand-five-hundred residents as it developed into one of the most populated towns in New Hampshire. Given Samuel Pinkham was a farmer, the increasing number of inhabitants was likely the reason for Samuel and Dorothy (Ordway) Pinkham's move from Gilmanton, New Hampshire to Danville, Vermont by 1788.

The original Gilmanton grant stipulated: "From the head of Barnstead, next to the town of Chichester; thence on the N. W. line to Winipissiokee Pond or the river that runs out of said Pond, and from the first place where it began, to run N. E. Six miles; then N. W. two miles; then due N. to Winipissiokee Pond; thence on said Pond and river to meet the first line; provided it does not entrench on any former legal grante." The charter was signed the 20th of May by His Majesty's Colonial Governor, John Wentworth. During the French War, several frontier towns were tried greatly by the raids of hostile Indians... and the settlement of Gilmanton was delayed for a series of years. In fact, there was not a permanent settlement until the close of 1761."(*Source: History of Merrimack and Belknap Counties, New Hampshire by J. W. Lewis & Co. Philadelphia, 1885. 1108 pgs. Transcribed by J. Brown at nh.searchroots page 785.*)

"In March of 1773, the Reverend Isaac Smith came into town, the second minister, and entered upon the pastorate of forty years (J. W. Lewis)." Reverend Isaac Smith married

Samuel Pinkham and Dorothy Ordway. The town of Barnstead was founded in 1727 and settled during 1764 primarily with people from Cape Cod's Barnstable, Massachusetts and Hempstead, New York, hence the name. The land was ideal for farming and situated south of the lakes region next to the town of Gilmanton.

Danville, Vermont was founded on 31 October 1786 by the Vermont legislature and by 1796 became the county seat for Caledonia County, Vermont. Originally named Hillsboro because of the topography, it was granted by New York. During 1785 fifty emigrants from New Hampshire and Massachusetts arrived. By 1789 over two-hundred settlers emigrated. As a farmer, the unpopulated lands surrounding Stanstead, Quebec likely appealed to Samuel Pinkham. Therefore, Danville's population growth may have been the impetus for the Samuel Pinkham family to move to Canada.

~SAMUEL PINKHAM:

Birth: 11 May 1760, Durham, Strafford Co., New Hampshire
           Father: Abijah Thomas Pinkham (b. 9 February 1734, Dover Neck, NH)
           Mother: Rachel Huckins (b. 15 March 1732, Oyster River, NH; d. 10 Nov 1818, NH)
Source: The Lineage of Sarah (Pinkham) Williams Beginning with her parents, Abijah Pinkham and Rachel Huckins by James F. Schneider & Holly Rubin. 2013.

1763 United States Census: SAMUEL PINKHAM, Rockingham County, 1763, New Castle Township. *Source: page 114, NH Early Census index.*

Revolutionary War Rolls, New Hampshire 1781 – West Point - SAMUEL PINKHAM, Private in Captain Timothy Emerson's Company.

Marriage: 11 November 1783, SAMUEL PONKHAM (Pinkham) to Dorithy Ordway of Loudon. *Source: "New Hampshire Marriage and Divorce Records 1659-1947; New England Historical Genealogical Society Citing New Hampshire Bureau of Vital Records, Concord, New Hampshire Marriages performed by Reverend Isaac Smith, Smith Meeting House.*

1790 United States Census: SAMUEL PINKAM (Pinkham), Danville, Orange, Vermont, Date –1790, Page – 195. Family members total – 7; Male head of family over age 16- 1; Male under 16 – 1 (Samuel); 5 – females. *Source: 1790 United States Census.*

Moved to Number 11, 9th Range, Stanstead, Quebec in 1800.

Source: *Forests and Clearings: The History of Stanstead County, Province of Quebec, with sketches of more than five hundred families by B. F. Hubbard*

"SAMUEL PINKHAM, b. in Durham, N. H., 11 May 1760. Married 1783 Dorothea Redxoay (Dorothy Ordway), a native of Amesbury, Massachusetts. They settled in Louden, N. H. and in 1788 removed to Danville, Vt., whence they removed to No. 11, 9th Range, in 1800..." "Theodosia Carpenter, m. Samuel FinJeham"

Stanstead, Quebec Settler's Monument: SAMUEL PINKHAM 1800

<u>1825 Lower Canada Census:</u> SAMUEL PINKHAM (3) lived with sons, Joseph and Abijah Pinkham. Widow Thankful Carpenter, the mother of Theodosia Carpenter who married Samuel Pinkham, son, b. 1787, of Samuel and Dorothy Pinkham, resided nearby Samuel and Dorothy (Ordway) Pinkham.

<u>1826 Sale</u> to son, Abijah Pinkham. *Source: Biblioteque et Archives Nationales du Quebec, Montreal, Quebec, Canada*

<u>Death:</u>   May 1830, Stanstead, Quebec *Source: undocumented*

<u>1850 Death</u> of Dorothy Ordway Pinkham, wife of SAMUEL PINKHAM, signed by son, Abijah Pinkham. *Source: The Drouin Collection, Montreal, Quebec*

<u>Dorothy Ordway Pinkham:</u>

<u>Birth:</u>   17 July 1759, Amesbury, Massachusetts *Source: Town and City Clerks of Massachusetts, Massachusetts Town and Vital Records 1626-1988*
<u>Father:</u> Moses Ordway
<u>Mother:</u> Anne (Huntington) Ordway

<u>Marriage:</u>   11 November 1783 to Samuel Pinkham
Source: *New Hampshire, Marriage and Divorce Records, 1659-1947, New England Historical Genealogical Society, Citing New Hampshire Bureau of Vital Records*, Concord, NH.

<u>Death:</u>   20 August 1850, Dorothy Ordway Pinkham, Stanstead, Quebec, Methodist Church *Source: Quebec, Canada, Vital and Church Records (Drouin Collection),* Montreal, Quebec

<u>The children of SAMUEL SENIOR and Dorothy (Ordway) Pinkham (Generation 6):</u>

1) <u>Betsy Pinkham Bachelder</u>: Born 22 May 1784. Died 1861, Rockingham County, NH. Married Jonathan Bachelder (b. 9 October 1776, Danville, Caledonia County, VT), son of Daniel Bachelder and Judith (Judah Jenkins). Jonathan Bachelder died 20 February 1842, Ruiter's Corners, Estrie Region, Quebec, Canada. (*Bachelder Family page 251*)
2) <u>Deborah Pinkham Williams</u>: Born 2 September 1785. Married Thomas Williams (son of Robert Williams and cousin, Sarah Pinkham Williams) on 2 January 1805 in Derby, Vermont, USA. *Source: Vermont Vital Records, 1760-1954*
3) <u>SAMUEL PINKHAM</u>: Born 5 August 1787, Louden, NH. Married Theodosia Carpenter (b. 18 November 1780, Westminster, VT; d. 9 March 1858, Stanstead, Quebec). Died 28 February 1857 Roxton/Milton (Anglican Church), Stanstead, Quebec, Canada.
4) <u>Sarah Pinkham Ruiter</u>: Born 20 April 1789, Danville, Caledonia County, VT. Married Thomas Ruiter (b. 30 May 1791, Caldwell Manor, Missisquoi, Quebec), son of John Ruiter and Sarah (Flyer) Ruiter. Died 29 March 1873 in Ruiter's Corner, Stanstead, Quebec, Canada.
3) <u>Mary Pinkham Lee</u>: Born 20 May 1791, Danville, VT. Married Ede Lee (b. 1 October 1791, Connecticut) in Stanstead, Quebec. Died in 1872, Stanstead, Quebec, Canada.

4) <u>James Pinkham</u>: Born 4 Feb. 1793, Danville, VT. Died 5 May 1813, Quebec.
5) <u>Joseph Pinkham</u>: Born 18 February 1795, Danville, VT. Married (m1) Sarah Moulton (b. July 1796, New Hampshire), daughter of William and Judith (Ladd) Moulton/(m2) Sarah Sawyer; m3 Jerusha Spencer. Died 8 August 1878, Worcester, Massachusetts, USA.
6) <u>Martha Pinkham Bartlett</u>: Born 18 December 1796, Danville, VT. Married Nathaniel Bartlett on 29 March 1818 in Stanstead, Quebec, Canada.
7) <u>Dorothy Pinkham Cushing</u>: Born 16 December 1798, Danville, VT. Married Manda Thurber Cushing, Esquire (b. 10 November 1798, Putney, Windham, VT) in December of 1829 in Stanstead, Quebec as 3rd wife. Died 16 May 1843, Stanstead, Quebec, Canada. Dorothy Pinkham Cushing is buried at Pleasant View Cemetery in Barnston, Estrie Region, Quebec. A daughter was born to Dorothy (age 33) on 2 December 1832 - Sarah E. Cushing. Sarah Cushing married Hamlton Peters and died at age 40 on 24 May 1872 in Lowell, Massachusetts where she is buried at the Lowell Cemetery.
8) <u>Abijah Pinkham</u>: Born 5 March 1802, Stanstead, Quebec. Married to Hannah Sleeper (b. 18 June 1805, Stanstead, Quebec; d. 14 October 1884, Stanstead, Quebec). Died 26 September 1886, Stanstead, Quebec, Canada. *Signed Dorothy Ordway Pinkham's death certificate.*

<u>Joseph Pinkham</u>: Born 18 February 1795, Danville, VT. Married (m1) Sarah Moulton (b. July 1796, New Hampshire), daughter of William and Judith (Ladd) Moulton; (m2) Sarah Sawyer; (m3) Jerusha Spencer. Died 8 August 1878, Worcester, Massachusetts, USA.

Joseph's nephew Comfort Carpenter Pinkham moved to Ontario, Canada with Moulton family members) (Joseph's mother, Dorothy Ordway Pinkham, was born 17 July 1759 in Amesbury, MA; Sarah Moulton's father, William Moulton born 1740 in Amesbury, MA) (Sarah Moulton - wife of Joseph Pinkham born 15 July 1796, Louden, NH; Joseph Pinkham's brother, Samuel Pinkham Junior, born 1787, Louden, NH).

<u>Married</u>: Sarah Moutton:

SARAH MOULTON, daughter of WILLIAM MOULTON (b. 6 March 1768, Amesbury, MA; died Quebec) and Judith (Ladd) Moulton who married 23 October 1791 in Loudon, Merrimack, New Hampshire. Recorded in 1825 Richelieu, Stanstead, Quebec Census. Father of <u>Sarah</u> <u>Moulton</u>, Harris Moulton, John Ladd Moulton and Louisa (Moulton) Rogers. Son of JOSEPH MOULTON.

Harris Moulton: Born 2 October 1793, Loudon, Merrimack, NH.
1825 Richelieu, Stanstead, Quebec Census;
Died 5 October 1847, Stanstead, Canada East (Quebec).
John Ladd Moulton: Born 9 July 1800, Quebec; Died 15 March 1843, Quebec.

JOSEPH MOULTON (b. 1740, Amesbury, MA) and unknown. Father of Sarah Moulton, <u>William Moulton,</u> Avery Moulton, Judith Moulton, Ruth Moulton JOSEPH MOULTON was son of William Moulton & Ruth (Emery) Moulton.

DEACON WILLIAM MOULTON (b. March 1698, Newbury, Essex, Massachusetts Bay; d. 23 November 1762, Amesbury, Essex, Massachusetts Bay)

M1 - Abigail (Webster) Moulton
Children m1: Abigail Moulton Bartlett, Benjamin Moulton
M2 - Ruth (Emery) Moulton. Married 24 April 1716, Newbury, Essex, MA
Children m2 - Ruth Moulton, Stephen Moulton, Mary Moulton Allen,
Jonathan Moulton and Joseph Moulton

WILLIAM MOULTON JR. Born 25 May 1664, Hampton, Rockingham, NH; Died 24
July 1732, Newbury, Essex, MA.
M1 - Abigail (Webster) Moulton; Married 27 May 1685, Newbury, MA
M2 - Sarah (Clark) Ordway; Married 1730
Father of Abigail (Moulton) Bartlett, William Moulton, Jonathan Moulton, Joseph
Moulton, Stephen Moulton

WILLIAM MOULTON. Born 1617, Ormesby, Norfolk, England; Died 18 April 1664,
Hampton, Rockingham, New Hampshire.
M1 - Margaret (Page) Sanborn; married abt. 1645, Hampton, Rockingham, New
Hampshire. Father of William Moulton, Jr.

Joseph Pinkham Records:

Tax Assessment: Ohio Tax Returns. Joseph Pinkham, 1820; Derby,
Derby Township, Pickaway, OH; 1840, Tate Township, Ohio, USA.

1825 Lower Canada Census: Joseph Pinkham, Stanstead, Richelieu.
Family of 10. (Joseph & Sarah; Amy, Ursula, Joseph H. Samuel, Clarissa,
dau. EAL-Judith, Lucius Moulton and James Smith Pinkham)

1830 Stanstead, Quebec Assembly School Records: Pupil list.

B.8.1 Gates - May 1830 (Children of Joseph Pinkham): Aurelia,
Clarissa, James (Smith), Judith, Julia (Julie-Ann), Lucius (Moulton)
and Ursula Pinkham (*with Dorothy Pinkham, daughter of Abijah
Pinkham*)

B. 8.2. Gates October 1830 (Children of Joseph Pinkham): Aurelia,
Clarissa, James (Smith), Judith, Julia (Julie-Ann), Lucius, Ursula
Pinkham (*with Dorothy Pinkham, daughter of Abijah Pinkham*).

Tax Assessment: Ohio Tax Returns. Joseph Pinkham, 1820--1831.
Derby, Derby Township, Pickaway, OH; 1840, Tate Township, Ohio, USA.

Ohio Tax Records, 1800-1850: J. P. Pinkham, Tax Assessment 1833,
Washington Township, Miami, Ohio, USA.

~Birth: 16 May 1836, *Louisa Maria Pinkham,* Grafton, Massachusetts.

~Death: 16 February 1837, *Louisa Maria Pinkham*, age 9 months. Death Place:
Grafton, Massachusetts. Parents: James and Sarah Pinkham. *Source:
Massachusetts, Town Clerk, Vital and Town Records, 1626-2001*

~ Birth*:* 5 December 1837*, William Wright Pinkham* born Grafton,
Massachusetts, son of James and Sarah Pinkham.

~ Birth: 11 December 1839, *Albert Henry Pinkham,* born Grafton,
Massachusetts, son of James and Sarah (Moulton) Pinkham.

~Death: *William Wright Pinkham* on 13 March 1840, last child of Joseph and
Sarah (Moulton) Pinkham. (*Albert Henry Pinkham youngest child*)

~Death: 22 November 1841, Grafton, Worcester, Massachusetts: Sarah
Moulton Pinkham born 15 July 1796, Louden, Hillsborough, NH.

Birth: Sarah Moulton. 15 July 1796, Louden, Hillsborough, New
Hampshire. Father: William Moulton. *Source: New Hampshire Birth Records, Early to 1900*

Death: 22 November 1841. Sarah Pinkham. Age 45. Birth year: 1796. Death
Place: Grafton, Worcester, Massachusetts. Spouse: Joseph Pinkham.
Source: Massachusetts, Town Clerk, Vital and Town Records, 1625-2001

Burial: Sarah Moulton Pinkham. Birth: 15 July 1796, Loudon, Merrimack
County, NH. Death: 22 November 1841 (Aged 45), Worcester, Worcester
County, Massachusetts. Burial: Pine Grove Cemetery, North Grafton,
Worcester County, Massachusetts. *Source: FindAGrave*

1841 Marriage (m2): Joesph Pinkham to Mrs. Sally (Sarah) Sawyer on 1
March 1841(1842) in Grafton, Massachusetts.

~Birth (m2): 22 March 1841, *George Edward Pinkham,* born Grafton,
Massachusetts, son of Joseph and Sarah G. Pinkham.

*George Edward Pinkham likely died after birth as Joseph and Sarah G.
Pinkham name second child, George, a year later.*

~Birth (m2): 12 April 1843, *George L. Pinkham.*

1847 Death of *George L. Pinkham:* Son of James (Joseph) and Sarah (m2) on 5
January 1847. Age 3 years, 8 months and 13 days. *Canker Rash.*

1848: Birth of *Albert S. Pinkham,* son of Joseph and Sarah (m2) Pinkham.

1848 Death of Sarah Pinkham (m2): Sarah, wife of Joseph age 44 on 11
September 1848. Born 1804, Warner, New Hampshire. *Consumption.*

1848 Death of Sarah Pinkham (m2): age 44 born 1804 in Warner, New
Hampshire. Died 11 September 1848 in Grafton, Massachusetts, the wife
of Joseph Pinkham. *Source: Massachusetts Death 1641-1913*

1849 Marriage (m3): Joseph Pinkham (age 60) to Jerusha Spencer of
Hartford, Connecticut. Date: 3 July 1849 Connecticut. "Third marriage
for Groom." *Source: Grafton Marriage, Birth, Death Records*

1849 Marriage: 3 July 1849. Marriage location: Grafton, Worcester,
Massachusetts. Joseph Pinkham age 60 born 1789 to Jerusha Spencer
age 45 born 1804.

Death: 20 February 1851 of *Albert S. Pinkham*, age 3 years, son of Joseph Pinkham in Worcester, Massachusetts. *Source: New Hampshire Gazette, 4 March 1851*

Tuesday, 15 June 1852, *Boston Herald*: "We learn from the Providence *Mirror*, that on Friday last a verdict of $1000 damages was rendered against Joseph Pinkham of New England Village, in Grafton, for breaking his marriage promise with Martha H. Hollbrook of Providence."

Friday, 18 June 1852, *The Congregationalist:* "A verdict of $1000 damages has been rendered in Providence against Joseph Pinkham for breaking his marriage promise with Martha H. Hollbrook of Providence."

3 July 1852, *The Flag of Our Union*: "Joseph Pinkham of New England Village, promised to marry Martha H. Hollbrook of Providence but afterwards, altered his mind, and was obliged to pay $1000 for his instability."

1855 United States Census Grafton, Worcester, Massachusetts: Joseph Pinkham. Birth year: 1795. Birthplace: Vermont, USA. Age: 60. With Jerusha Pinkham age 50 born Connecticut. Son Albert H. Pinkham age 15 born Massachusetts.

~Birth (m3): *Laura A. Pinkham born 1858 Wisconsin to Joseph and (m3) JerushaPinkham.*

1860 United States Census Windham, Windham, Connecticut: Joseph Pinkham. Age 65 born 1799 Vermont. With Jerusaha Pinkham age 57 born Connecticut & William Sexton age 10 born 1850 Connecticut.

1870 United States Census Windham, Windham, Connecticut: Joseph Pinkham. Age 75 born 1795 Vermont. Wife Jerusha Pinkham age 65 born Connecticut. Daughter Laura A. Pinkham age 12 born 1858 Wisconsin.

1878 Death: Joseph Pinkham age 83. Death Date: 8 August 1878. Death Place: Worcester, Massachusetts. Father's Name: Samuel. Mother's name: Loretta (Dorothy) Ordway. Parents born: New Hampshire. Birth year: 1795. Birth location: Danville, Vermont. Profession: Farmer. Death age: 83 years, 5 months, 20 days.

The children of Joseph and (m1) Sarah (Moulton) Pinkham (Gen 7):

(Grafton, Massachusetts records from *Grafton Birth, Marriage Death book*)

Amy Pinkham: Born abt. 1811- 1815, Quebec; Death unknown post 1870.

Amy Pinkham moved to Wisconsin with the same family as her cousin, J. Samuel Pinkham (son of Samuel Jr. and Theodocia Carpenter) - the Mason family. J. Samuel Pinkham and sons, Joseph and Cephus Pinkham, were listed with Betsy Higgens and her daughter Emily Mason in the same 1855 Union, Rock County, Wisconsin census. Joseph Pinkham also resided in Wisconsin by 1858 where his youngest child, Laura A. Pinkham (m3), Amy's half-sibling was born.

1870 Rutland, Dane, Wisconsin Census: Amy Pinkham, age 55 born 1815 Canada with the James T. Mason family in the 1870 Rutland, Dane County, Wisconsin - James T. Mason born 1796 Vermont.

Ursula S. Pinkham: Born 1817 QC; Baptized 1835, Stanstead, QC.

Marriage: 16 August 1849: Ursulla U./S. Pinkham. Age 32 born 1817. Father: Joseph Pinkham. Mother: Sarah Pinkham. Marriage Place: Grafton, Worcester, Massachusetts. Spouse: Reverend A. H. House. Age 37 born 1812, Nashua, New Hampshire. Parents: Frederick and Polly House. *Source: Massachusetts, Town Clerk, Vital and Town Records, 1626-2001.*

James Smith Pinkham: Born July 1821, Stanstead, Estrie Region, Quebec, Canada. Died 8 July 1884, Worcester, Worcester County, Massachusetts, Son of Joseph and Sarah (Moulton) Pinkham. *Source: FindAGrave*

Married: (m1) Mary Stratton born 17 December 1823.

Birth: 12 April 1843, *James Henry Pinkham*, son of James S. and Mary Pinkham (Grafton Birth book incorrectly lists this child as the son of Joseph and Sarah m2 Pinkham).

Death: 23 September 1843, *James Henry Pinkham*, son of James S. and Mary Pinkham. Birthplace: Grafton, Worcester, Massachusetts. *Source: Massachusetts Birth & Christenings 1639-1915* Burial: Worcester Rural Cemetery, Worcester, MA. *Source: FindAGrave*

Birth: 18 August 1844, *Charles Henry Pinkham*, son of James S. and Mary Pinkham of Grafton, Worcester, Massachusetts. *Source: Massachusetts, Town Clerk, Vital and Town Records, 1625-2001*

Birth: 15 February 1848, *Albert Sumner Pinkham*, son of James Smith and Mary (Stratton) Pinkham.

Death: Mary Stratton Pinkham (m1), 17 Oct. 1849 age 25. Buried: Worcester Burial Cemetery, Worcester, MA.

Married: (m2) (abt. 1850) Jane P. Smith born 6 September

1824, Princeton, Worcester County, Massachusetts, daughter of Cyrus and Prudence (Wilder) Smith.

Death: 20 February 1851, *Albert Sumner Pinkham*. Age 3 years 4 days (b. 15 February 1848). Father: James Pinkham. Mother: Mary Pinkham. Buried: Worcester Burial Cemetery, Worcester, MA *Source: Massachusetts Births 1841-1915*

Birth: (m2) June 1851, *Albert James Pinkham*, son of James Smith and Jane P. Smith Pinkham.

Death: (m2) 20 August 1852, *Albert James Pinkham*, age 1. Buried: Worcester Rural Cemetery, Worcester, MA. Son of James Smith and Jane P. (Smith) Pinkham

1865 Massachusetts State Census, Auburn, Worcester, MA: James S. Pinkham age 43 born 1822 Canada with wife J. P. Pinkham (Jane P.) age 40 born Massachusetts and son C. H. (Charles Henry) Pinkham, age 20 born 1844 MA, USA.

1880 United States Census, Worcester, Worcester, Massachusetts: James S. Pinkham age 58 born 1822 Canada. Married. Occupation: Carpet Dealer. Parents born: New Hampshire. With wife: Jane Pinkham age 55 born Massachusetts.

Death: 16 July 1884, James S. Pinkham, age 63 years and 8 days. Married. Occupation: Merchant. Birth year: 1821. Birthplace: Stanstead, Quebec, Canada. Father's name: Joseph Pinkham. Mother's name: Sarah (Moulton) Pinkham.

Death: 5 March 1901 (age 76), Jane P. (Smith) Pinkham. Age 76 years, 5 months 27 days. Wife of James Smith Pinkham. Son: Albert James Pinkham (1851-1852).

Joseph H. Pinkham: Born abt. 1822/1831, Quebec; Baptized 1849 St. Cecile de Milton, Quebec.

Marriage: 20 July 1851, Joseph H. Pinkham. Age 20 born 1831. Father's name: Jos Pinkham. Mother's name: Sarah Pinkham. Spouse: Clarrisa E. Gifford. Age 20 born 1831. Parents: Porter P. & Mary Gifford. *Source: Massachusetts Marriages, 1841-1915*

United States Civil War Soldiers Index, 1861-1865: Joseph Pinkham. Event place: Wisconsin. Military Beginning rank: Pirvate. Military ending rank: Private. Military Side: Union. Military Unit: 12th Regiment, Wisconsin Infantry. Military Company: K.

1875 Garden City, Blue Earth, Faribault, MN- Minnesota State Census: Joseph Pinkham born 1822 with wife Julie Anne Pinkham born 1835.

Children of Joseph and Julie Pinkham: (Charles & Joseph)
Alma J Pinkham
Albert Pinkham
Alice E. Pinkham

Naturalization: Joseph Pinkham 21 October 1880, District Court, Kearny County, Nebraska. Birthplace: Canada.

Death: 9 May 1883. Joseph Pinkham. Location: St. Paul, Ramsey, Minnesota. Cemetery: Oakland Cemetery.
Death: Jos. Pinkham born 1822 age 61, Ramsey, Minnesota, USA. *Source: Minnesota County Deaths*

Lucius Moulton Pinkham: Born 1823, Quebec, Canada. Died 16 April 1893, Worcester, Massachusetts, USA.

Marriage: 10 June 1847. Lucius M. Pinkham of Springfield age 24 born 1823. Parents: Joseph and Sarah Pinkham. Location: Grafton, Worcester, Massachusetts. Spouse m1: Caroline S. Fiske age 22 born 1825. Parents: Calvin & Martha Fiske. *Source: Massachusetts Marriages, 1841-1915*

1850 United States Census Chickpea, Hamden, Massachusetts: Lucius M. Pinkham born 1823, Canada with Caroline S. Pinkham.

1880 United States Census Newton, Middlesex, Massachusetts: Lucius M. Pinkham. Age: 58 born 1822 Canada. Occupation: Newspaper pub. Father's birthplace: Vermont. Mother's birthplace: New Hampshire. Wife: Caroline S. Pinkham age 54 born Massachusetts. *Source: United States Census, 1880*

Marriage: 21 March 1893. Lucius Moulton Pinkham. Parents: Joseph Pinkham and Sarah Moulton. Location: Newton, Middlesex, Massachusetts. Spouse (m2): Maria Jackson Hunt Hart. Parents: William H. Hunt & Sarah Wellington. *Source: Massachusetts Marriages, 1695-1910*

Death: 16 April 1893. Lucius Moulton Pinkham. Death location: Worcester, Worcester County, MA. Birth date: 1822. Cemetery: Worcester Rural Cemetery. "Age 71 years. Son of Joseph and Sarah Moulton Pinkham. In 1847

at Grafton, MA, he married first Caroline S. Fiske. On 23 March 1893 he married second Maria Jackson Hunt Hart."
Source: FindAGrave

Clarissa J. Pinkham: Born 1826, Quebec. Married 1846, MA.

Married: 20 September 1846. Clarissa J. Pinkham. Age 20 born 1826. Father: Joseph Pinkham. Mother: Sarah Pinkham. Marriage place: Grafton, Worcester, Massachuetts, USA. Spouse: Albert Sawyer. Age 23 born 1823. Parents: Elijah and Fanny Sawyer. *Source: Massachusetts Marriages, 1841-1915*

Judith L. (*E. A. L.*) Pinkham: Born 1834, Quebec. Married 24 December 1845: Judith L. Pinkham to Samuel O. White of Worchester, MA.

Aurilla-Susanna Pinkham: Baptized 1835, Stanstead, QC. Married to Daniel H. Knowlton on 31 January 1841 in Grafton, MA.

Julie-Ann Pinkham: Baptized 1835 Stanstead, Quebec. Married to Samuel Clough of Natick, MA on 30 September 1841 in Grafton, MA.

Louisa Maria Pinkham: Born 16 May 1836, Grafton, MA. Died 16 February 1837, Grafton, Massachusetts.

William Wright Pinkham: Born 5 December 1837, Grafton, MA. Died 13 March 1840, Grafton, Massachusetts.

Albert Henry Pinkham born 1839, Massachusetts.

Marriage: 1 September 1862. Albert H. Pinkham born 1839 age 23. Parents: Joseph and Sarah Pinkham. To m1 Annie J. Smart age 23 born 1840. Parents: John & Abbie Smart. *Source: Massachusetts Marriages, 1841-1915*

Death: Albert H. Pinkham. Age: 72. Death date: 28 May 1912. Death location: Jamaica Plain, Suffolk, MA. Birth year: 1840. Father's name: Joseph Pinkham. *Source: Massachusetts, Town Clerk, Vital and Town Records, 1626-2001*

Spouse: m2 Louisa A. Rines Pinkham. Death 27 September 1917. Gloucester, Essex, MA. Birth year: 1844. Spouse's name: Albert H. Pinkham. Parents: Osborne & Louisa P. Rines. *Source: Massachusetts State Vital Records, 1841-1920.*

The children of Joseph and (m2) Sarah (Sawyer) Pinkham:

George Edward Pinkham: Born 22 March 1841. Died 1841, Grafton, Massachusetts.

George L. Pinkham: Born 12 April 1842. Died January 1847, Grafton, Massachusetts.

Albert S. Pinkham: Born 1848. Died 20 February 1851, Grafton, Massachusetts.

The child of Joseph and (m3) Jerusha (Spencer) Pinkham:

Laura A. Pinkham: Born 1858 Wisconsin.

Abijah Pinkham: Born: 5 March 1802, Stanstead, Quebec. Married: 1824 Hatley, QC to Hannah Sleeper (*Bachelder Family pages 252 & 263*) (b. 18 June 1805, Stanstead, Quebec; d. 14 October 1884, Stanstead, Quebec). Baptized: 1835, Stanstead, Quebec. Died: 26 September 1886, Stanstead, Quebec.

1825 Lower Canada Census: Stanstead, Richelieu: Abijah Pinkham. Inhabitants: 5 (Abijah and Hannah Sleeper Pinkham; children: *Dorothy Pinkham*, Samuel Sleeper Pinkham born 1822, James Pinkham b. 1823)

From Stanstead Historical Society Archives 1931: ..."*June 9th, 1931 visted the school at Pinkham's Corner which consisted of 21 scholars under the instruction of Mrs. Julia Moulton. (6 in Alphabet, 4 in words of 1 or 2 syllables, 2 just commenced reading, 1 in Testament, 7 in English Reader, 3 studying geography, 3 studying Grammar, 3 just commenced writing). The school appears to be thriving under the care of a well qualified Teacher. The committee, Captain Davis, J. Bachelder and A. Pinkham were present and applauded the school...*"

1830 Appendix B. Assembly Schools Pupils List, Table B:

B. 8. 1. Gates May 1830: *Dorothy Pinkham* with children of Joseph Pinkham.

B. 8. 2. Gates October 1830: *Dorothy Pinkham* with children of Joseph Pinkham.

1835 Baptism Record: Wesleyan Methodist Stanstead: Abijah Pinkham. Father Samuel Pinkham; Mother: Dorothy Pinkham.

1871 Canada Census, Stanstead Plain, Stanstead, Quebec: A. Pinkham. Age 69. Born 1802 Quebec. Married. Nationality: English. Religion: W. Methodist. With Hannah Pinkham. Age 66. Born 1805 Quebec. Married. Nationality: English. Religion: Methodist.

1881 Canada Census, Stanstead Plain, Stanstead, Quebec: Abijah Pinkham. Age 79 born 1802 Canada. Married. Occupation: Farmer. Ethnicity: English. Religion: W. Methodist. Wife Hannah Pinkham age 75 born Canada.

Burial: Hannah Sleeper Pinkham. Born: 18 June 1805. Died: 14 October 1884 Stanstead, Estrie Region, Quebec. Cemetery: Crystal Lake Cemetery. *Source: FindAGrave.*

<u>Burial:</u> Abijah Pinkham. Born: 5 March 1802. Death date: 26 September 1886. Event Place: Stanstead, Estrie Region, Quebec. Cemetery: Crystal Lake Cemetery. *Source: FindAGrave*

<u>Children of Abijah Pinkham and Hannah (Sleeper) Pinkham</u> (Gen 7):

~Dorothy Pinkham: Born 1824. Attended school 1830 between ages 5-6.

~<u>Samuel Sleeper Pinkham:</u> Born 1826.

> <u>Marriage:</u> 1847, Stanstead, Quebec to Mary M. Ball. Location: Stanstead, Quebec. Religion: Congregational. Place of Worship: Congregational Church.
> <u>Baptized:</u> 1862, Stanstead, Quebec: Samuel Sleeper Pinkham.
> <u>Death:</u> 4 Jan 1892, age 66 years, buried Ruiter's Corner Cemetery.

> <u>Children of Samuel and Mary (Ball) Pinkham</u> born Quebec:
>
>> Samuel Pinkham (born 1849-1851/baptized 1862)
>> Samuel Clarence Pinkham
>>
>> Abigail Pinkham (born 1853)
>>
>> Albert Knight Pinkham (b. 1849-1854/Baptized 1862)
>>
>> Abijah Pinkham (born 1855/Baptized 1862)
>>
>> Katie Pinkham (born 1856)
>>
>> Edward Renfrew Pinkham (b. 1860-1/Baptized 1862)
>>
>> Harriet (Hattie) Jennie Pinkham (born abt. 1860-1864)
>>
>> Burton Pinkham (born abt. 1867-1868)

> <u>1871 Census of Canada</u>, Stanstead: Samuel Pinkham. Birth year 1826 Quebec. Age 45. Married. Religion: W. Methodist. Origin: English. Wife: Mary Pinkham age 41. Children: Samuel Pinkham age 22 (born 1849), Abigail Pinkham age 18 (born 1853), Albert Pinkham age 17 (born 1854), Edward Pinkham age 10 (born 1861), Burton Pinkham age 3 (born 1868), Katie Pinkham age 15 (born 1856) and Harriet Pinkham age 7 (born 1864).

Census record next family lists: Comfort Carpenter age 39 (born 1832) and wife Ann Elizabeth (age 39) with son William Carpenter age 6. Samuel Pinkham & Dorothy's son, Samuel Pinkham Jr. married Theodocia Carpenter born 1808 Quebec, daughter of Comfort Carpenter. Comfort Carpenter, son of Caleb Carpenter, was a nephew of Theodocia Carpenter who married Abijah Pinkham's bother, Samuel Pinkham Junior.

1881 Canada Census, Stanstead, Quebec: Samuel
Pinkham. Age 56 born 1825 Quebec. Married. Occupation:
Farmer. Ethnicity: English. Religion: W. Methodist. Wife:
Mary Pinkham age 52 born Quebec. Children born Quebec:
Clarence age 30 (born 1851), Hattie age 21 (born 1841),
Abijah age 26 (born 1855), Albert age 22 (born 1849),
Edward age 21 (born 1850), Jennie age 18 (born 1863) and
Burton Pinkham age 14 (born 1867).

1891 Stanstead, Quebec Census: Samuel Pinkham, age 69
b. 1822 - father. Wife Mary, age 61 - mother. With, son.
Son, Edwin Pinkham age 30 born 1861. Wife of Edwin,
Louisa age 31.

> Children of Edwin and Louisa Pinkham:
>
> Gracie Pinkham (born 1885)
>
> Mabel Pinkham (born 1890)
>
> Edwin Siblings: Allen V. Pinkham (born 1862)
>
> (Kate) Celane Pinkham (born 1856)
>
> Abijah Pinkham (born 1859)
>
> (*1891 Census records surname: Prickham*)

Burial for Samuel Pinkham: 1892, Rock Island, Quebec,
        Congregational Church Source: Drouin.

Burial: Samuel S. Pinkham. Event date: 1892. Event
        Place: Ruiter's Corners, Estrie Region, Quebec.
        Death date: 4 January 1892. Cemetery: Ruiter's
        Corner Cemetery. *Source: FindAGrave.*

Marriage of children of Samuel S. Pinkham and Mary M. Ball
        Edward R. Pinkham: Marriage 28 October 1882 to
                Elizabeth Salis. Farmer of Stanstead, QC (age
                22) born 1860. Son of Sam. S. Pinkham and
                Mary M. Ball.
        Vermont Town Clerk; Vital/ Town Records 1732-2005:
                Father: Saml S Pinkham/Spouse Mary M Ball.
                Children: Edward R. Pinkham. Other: Eliza
                Salis, Issac Salis, Melissa Salis.
        Albert K. Pinkham - Death of farmer age 41 born
                1862 Stanstead, QC. Death date: 1 October
                1903, Stanstead, QC. Death cause: Heart

failure. Son of Samuel Pinkham born
Stanstead and Mary Ball born Stanstead, QC.
Jennie Hattie Pinkham: marriage:
Vermont Town Clerk; Vital/Town Records 1732-2005:
Jennie Hattie Pinkham to Albron Irving Dixon.
Parents: Graham Dixon; Lydia Blanchard.
Father-in-law: Samuel Pinkham and Mary Ball.

~James Pinkham: Born 1823, Quebec. Died 5 May 1843, age 20. Buried:
Ruiter's Corner Cemetery, Quebec.

~*Mary Florence Pinkham:* Born abt. 1824. Baptized 1862, Stanstead, QC.

~Calvin Wilde Pinkham: Born 13 December 1826, Stanstead, Quebec.
Baptized 1838, Stanstead, QC. Married Susan Sleeper (*Bachelder
page 262*). Died 1 January 1901, Fond du Lac, Wisconsin, USA.

Baptism: 1838, Stanstead, Quebec.

Naturalization: Calvin W. Pinkham: 5 April 1859 Fond Du
Lac, Wisconsin, County Naturalization records 1807-
1992.
1860 United States Census, Fond du Lac, Wisconsin: C.
W. Pinkham. Age 32 born 1828 Canada. Wife: Susan D.
Pinkham age 32 born Canada. Son - William E. Pinkham
age 1 (born 1859) Wisconsin.
1870 United States Fond du Lac, Wisconsin census: C. W.
Susan, James B. Pinkham and Sarah Jane Pinkham, born
1864 WI.
1880 United States Census: Fond Du Lac, Wisconsin, w/
Calvin C, Susan D. & Burton.
1880 United States Census: Fond du Lac, WI w/ Calvin C.,
Susan D. & Susie Jane Pinkham and Burton.
Wisconsin Death Index, 1820-1907: Susan D.
Pinkham, 12 February 1896 Fond Du Lac, WI. Death
Record for Susan Davis (Sleeper) Pinkham: Born 23
January 1826 Stanstead, QC. Father: Ira D. Sleeper.
Mother: Polly Sleeper.
Death Record for Calvin Wilde Pinkham: Birth: 13
December 1826 (Stanstead, Quebec). Death: 1
January 1901 Fond du Lac, WI. Cemetery: Rienzi
Cemetery.

~Susie Jane Pinkham; Father Calvin Pinkham; C. W.
Pinkham, C. Pinkham. Mother: Susan D.
1870 United States Census Fond du Lac, WI w/ C. W.
Susan & James B. Pinkham, 1864 birth WI.

1880 United States Census Fond du Lac, WI w/
Calvin C., Susan D. & Burton Pinkham.
1905 (Married) Wisconsin
1905 United States Census Fond du Lac, WI w/
Louis, Marion, James Hintz.
Death 1942 California - 1 February 1942, Sausalito,
SF/Marin, CA: Susie Jane Adams born 10
May 1864, Fond Du Lac, WI. Father: Pinkham.
Mother: Sleeper. Husband: Octavian R.
Adams. Daughter: Mrs. Marian W. Heinz.
Address: 315 4th Street, Sausalito, CA.

~Loelah Pinkham Lee: Born 9 November 1830, Stanstead, QC. Baptized
1853, Stanstead, QC. Married 13 September 1850, Stanstead, QC.
Died 18 February 1905, Los Angeles, CA, USA. *Story to follow.*

~Georgiana Pinkham: Born 27 August 1844. Baptized 1845. Died 16 April
1845. (8 months). Buried Ruiter's Corner, Stanstead, Quebec.

~Louis-Abijah Pinkham: Born 1846, Stanstead, QC. Baptized 1847,
Stanstead, QC. Died 1 March 1847, Stanstead, Quebec.

~Abijah Pinkham, Jr.: Baptized 1852 or 1862, Stanstead, Quebec.

~George Lorin (L.) Pinkham: Born 1847, Stanstead, Quebec.

1867 Marriage, Stanstead, Quebec: George L. Pinkham to Ella P.
Sweet.

1881 Coaticook, Stanstead, Quebec Census: Geo. L. Pinkham,
age 34 born 1847 Quebec. Married. Occupation: Railway Agent.
Religion: Methodist. Wife: Ella T. Pinkham age 27 born USA.

Loehlah Pinkham Lee: (*Biography from various sources*)

Loehlah Pinkham (Generation 7 Pinkham) died in Los Angeles, CA. Father: (Generation 6)
Abijah Pinkham, brother to SAMUEL Pinkham (Generation 7 - Cousins Comfort Carpenter
Pinkham, b. 1811 Quebec and Loehlah Pinkham, b. 1830 Quebec) and Hannah Sleeper
(Bachelder Generation 10) Pinkham.

LOELAH PINKHAM was born on 9 November 1830 in Stanstead, Quebec and died on 18
February 1905 in Los Angeles, California. She is buried in Angelus Rosedale Cemetery on 1831
Washington Blvd near USC's University Place where she lived. She married Reverend John
Parker Lee who was born in Stanstead, Quebec on 15 January 1821 in Stanstead, Quebec and
died on 22 November 1910 in Los Angeles, California where she, her husband John Parker Lee
and her daughter Mackie Lee Morrill are buried. Her aunt, Mary Pinkham, married Ede Lee, a
member of the same Lee family.

According to the "Wesleyan University Record" (Middletown, Ct), John Parker Lee "took up
residence at University Place in 1890 and became minister of Trinity Church. During her lifetime
Loelah Pinkham Lee taught in departments of "music, modern language and arts."

Early Stanstead, Quebec settlers included both the Lee and Pinkham families. The Lee family is mentioned as Wesleyans in Stanstead historical records. John Parker Lee was born on 15 January 1821 in Stanstead, Quebec with twin Amanda Lee. They were the children of Elias and Rhoda (Morrill) Lee. Amanda Lee married Reverend Ebenezer Hobson who graduated from Wesleyan University, Middleton, CT in 1848 along with John Parker Lee. Reverend Ebenezer Hobson taught in Jasper, Alabama, during the Civil War.

Accounts from Wesleyan University and Wesleyan Church records include John Parker Lee biographies:

"John Parker Lee was born in Stanstead, Canada on 15 January 1821 and died in Los Angeles, California on 22 October 1910. He prepared for college and pursued a theology course at Newbury, VT and in 1844 he enrolled in the sophomore class at Wesleyan University, CT where he graduated in 1847. Mr. Lee went South and engaged in teaching, in which he had a calling for twenty years, a career of conspicuous success in Alabama and Mississippi. He was for six years a member of a firm of booksellers and stationers and in 1886-87 was Warden of the city of Atlanta. During 1900, he removed to Los Angeles to pass the evening of his days. He was a member of the Methodist Church of Canada until he went South when he identified with the Methodist Episcopal Church of the South, in which he remained until the end. He was ordained in the ministry in 1848 and was in frequent demand for occasional and special sermons. While living in Los Angeles, he was honored and beloved by the pastors and members of the Trinity Church where he made his home, as well as, by a host of other churches quickly came to know his work and words. His attachments were strong, his friendships enduring. He was married to Miss L. H. Pinkham of Stanstead, Quebec and is survived by three daughters: Ella, wife of Wesley W. D. Haven of Macon, Georgia, Mackie, wife of Herbert Morrill, and Rosa B. (Bell) Lee of Los Angeles."

John Parker Lee (biography) was born on 15 January 1822 in Stanstead, Quebec. 1847-8 - High school teacher in Summerfield, South Carolina. 1849 - Principal of Camden high school in Camden, South Carolina. 1850 - Teacher of Ancient Languages & Mathematics in Oak Bowery Female College, Alabama. 1851-2 - Teacher of Ancient Languages & Mathematics at Ashborn Masonic Female College, Alabama. 1853 - President of Ashborn Masonic Female College. 1854 - "Returned North for health." 1855 - Teacher of Mathematics at Tuskegee Female College, Alabama. 1850-60 - "Called to Stanstead" because of the death of his father. 1864 - Principal of Brookhaven College for Young Ladies, Mississippi. 1866-7 - Engaged in farming, Stanstead. 1870-76 - Principal of Stanstead Academy. 1876 - Member of the firm of J.W. Burke & Co. Publishers, Booksellers, Stationers, etc., Macon, Georgia, then sold old interest in company. 1877-81 was engaged in farming in Forsyth, GA.

John Parker Lee married Loelah Pinkham of Stanstead, Quebec on 19 September 1850. Their children (excluding Mackie Lee b. 31 March 1862) were listed in 1851 as: Ella (Loelah) Alabama, born on 15 November 1852; Emma America, born 30 March 1856 and Rosa Bell, born 19 July 1862. Their address, listed in the 1851 Wesleyan College records was: Cedar Lawn, Forsyth, Monroe County, Georgia.

The Lee Family settled in Connecticut in the mid 1600s ("Supplement to John Lee of Farmington, Hanford County, CT."). John Parker Lee graduated in 1847 from the Wesleyan University in Connecticut and was ordained a Methodist Episcopal minister in 1848. He became "Warden" of the city of Atlanta in1886-88. During the Civil War the Lee family (John Parker, Loelah and Ella) moved from the South back to Stanstead, Quebec. "In 1900, he removed to Los Angeles" where he became minister at the USC Trinity Methodist Episcopal Methodist Church (1900-1940) when it was located on Broadway/4th Streets in Los Angeles. Rev. John Parker and Loelah Lee "took up residence at University Place (USC) in 1890."

John Parker and Loelah Pinkham (Pinkham Generation 8) Lee's childfren (second cousins to Pinkham Generation 8) were (excluding "Emma America Lee b. 30 March 1856):

i.   Ella (Loelah) Alabama Lee born 15 November 1851 in Oak Bowery, Alabama; d. 21 July 1935 Bibb County, Georgia.
ii.   Mackie Lee born 31 March 1862 in Stanstead, Quebec; d. 28 March 1941, Los Angeles, CA.
iii.   Rosa B. (Bell) born 19 July 1869 in Stanstead, Quebec.

Ella Lee married Wesley W. Dehaven who had Canadian parents and was an architect in Macon, GA. Rosa Lee graduated from the Female College in Macon, GA where she studied music and painting. She moved to Los Angeles in 1899. Mackie Lee married Herbert L. Morrill in 1891. Mackie graduated at Fort Edward Institute with high honors. She was principal of the art department of the Tennessee Female College. Herbert L. Morrill's occupation was "commercial traveler." It is noted that Mackie Lee Morrill moved to Los Angeles by 1909 after the death of her mother. The child of Herbert L. Morrill and Mackie Lee Morrill was Lewis Lee born 12 June 1893 (Pinkham Generation 9). Like the Lee (Ede Lee, son of Ede Lee and Mary Pinkham) and Pinkham families, the Morrill family also settled Stanstead, Quebec in 1800.

In a book by Edan Hughes, "Artists in California 1786-1940" Mrs. Loelah H. Lee (Artist, Resident of Los Angeles in 1903), Rosa B. Lee (Artist, Resident of Los Angeles, 1909) and Mrs. Mackie L. Morrill (Artist, Resident of Los Angeles in 1909) are listed as early California Impressionist artists.

Loelah H. Pinkham Lee is buried at the Los Angeles Angelus Rosedale Cemetery with John Parker Lee and Mackie Lee Morrill (*Source: FindAGrave: 97817713*). The Angelus Rosedale Cemetery was founded in 1884 when Los Angeles population was 28,285. Los Angeles mayors and pioneers are buried at this historical cemetery.

Pinkham Generations 8 and 9 are buried at the Los Angeles, California Angelus Rosedale Cemetery in graves marked:
Loelah H. Lee 1830-1905
Rev. John P. Lee 1821-1910
Mackie L. Morrill 1862-1941

Most of the family of Samuel and Dorothy Pinkham left Vermont to reside in the No. 11, 9th Range of Stanstead, Quebec, Canada beginning in 1800 when the property was cleared (*Source: "Forests and Clearing of Stanstead County, Quebec: A History of 500 Families" by B. F. Hubbard*). Stanstead Plain, Quebec was created in 1769 by Canadian Governor Lord Dorchester and settled by Americans seeking farmland. In 1790 by Royal Enactment the Province of Quebec was divided into Upper and Lower Canada. In 1800 when Stanstead was settled. Samuel, then age forty, and his wife, Dorothy, moved to Quebec with their son Samuel (which some records incorrectly reported as "deceased"), Sarah (married Quebec-born Thomas Ruiter in Stanstead, Quebec), Mary (married Quebec-born Ede Lee), Martha (married Quebec-born Nathaniel Bartlett) and Dorothy (married Quebec-born Manda Thurber Cushing, Esq.) in Stanstead Quebec). Samuel and Dorothy Pinkham's youngest son, Abijah Pinkham (6), was born in Stanstead, Quebec in March of 1802. Betsey (Pinkham) Bachelder and her husband Jonathan also lived in Stanstead, but after his death in Stanstead in 1842 she left (perhaps, with a married child) and died in New Hampshire.

Among those families documented as the early settlers of Stanstead, Quebec is the Lee family whose faith was with the Wesleyan Church. Ede Lee is noted as marrying "AFary (Mary) Pinkham in 1810. Sarah Pinkham married Thomas Ruiter, son of Loyalist John Ruiter, on 30 May 1793. John Ruiter served in the British Army during the French War.   Being a firm loyalist, he left his country at the time of the American Revolution, then came to Canada, where he was afterwards, employed as an officer in the British Service. Captain John Ruiter married Sarah Flyer in 1789. They settled in Ruiter's Corner, Stanstead, Quebec in 1800 where his son, Thomas was born. Captain Ruiter was in the British Service as Captain in the War of 1812 and 1815. Moving to Stanstead, Quebec was likely American Revolutionary Patriot, Comfort Carpenter, and his wife, Thankful Canfield. Comfort and Thankful Carpenter "settled near the place now known as Smith's Mills in 1800." Mr. Carpenter built a sawmill that year, the first erected in the town. Comfort Carpenter, an American Revolutionary soldier, died on 15 April 1806 in Stanstead Plain, Quebec and his wife, Thankful (Kent) Carpenter died in Stanstead, Quebec in 1851. *Source: The History of Stanstead County Province of Quebec by B. F. Hubbard*

Comfort and Thankful Carpenter's children included Theodosia (who married Samuel FinJeham or Pinkham), Thankful (who married John Merrill), Caleb (who married Sarah Rogers), Charles (who married Eliza Eaton), Persia (who married Benjamin Tilton), Harry (who married E. Wright) and Harriet (who married Ebenezer Barry). Written in the text about the Stanstead families is a crop described as being harvested by "Abijah of Hampshire" (perhaps, Abijah Pinkham, son of Samuel of New Hampshire) with further text mentioning Caleb and Comfort Carpenter at the mill (*B. F. Hubbard*). Because the families were not Catholic, births were not recorded and much information regarding these families is unavailable. However, from this point on, this Pinkham branch (most of Generation 6 and Samuel Generation 5) remain in Quebec for generations.

Stanstead Plain was founded in 1796 by Johnson Taplin who arrived from New England looking for fertile farming land. Situated south-east of Montreal, the County of Missisquoi borders Derby, Vermont in the south, the County of Stanstead in the east, Sheffield in the north and the west by the County of Rouville and the Missisquoi Bay. Missisquoi translates to "the place of water birds" in Amerindan text. The county was comprised of the Lordship of Saint-Armand and the townships of Stanbridge, Dunham and Sutton. By 1831 the Missisquoi County population reached ten-thousand inhabitants primarily of British descent. By 1840 only ten-percent of the population were French Canadians. The land was ideal for farming corn, oats, rye and buckwheat. Mills for flour and sawing were many. The Lordship of Saint-Armand was granted to Nicolas Levasseur in 1746 but it was not until 1787 that it was acquired by Thomas Dunn. Dunham was the first county established in Lower Canada in 1796 with the township of Stanbridge founded during 1800 followed then by the town of Sutton which was founded during 1802.

Birth and marriage records in the Eastern Townships were rarely legal documents. Traveling New England clergymen would perform weddings known as, "Marriage Smuggling," as well as, baptisms. American clergy would carry out religious services while visitng their families in Quebec. Since these American clergy could not legally register the marriage, baptisms or burials they presided over in Quebec, few records exist in Canadian Eastern Townships. Therefore, many early settlers have Eastern

Township generational gaps given lack of verifiable documents to prove family history.

The county of Stanstead in the "Townships of the East - Cantons de l'Est (Eastern Townships)" was bordered in the west by the county of Potton, to the east by Barnston, to the north by the County of Hatley and to the south with the American border and town of Derby, Vermont. Though colonized in 1800, the county of Stanstead was established in 1827. The county produced superior wheat from land irrigated by the Memphremagog lakes, as well as, Massawippi, Coaticook and Magog rivers. By 1831, the county population of ten-thousand could be broken down per person/city with 84 inhabitants of Bedford, 2,221 residents of Barnston, 1,170 living in Bolton, 1,600 residents Bolton, and 4,226 individuals living in Stanstead.

Stanstead elected Marcus Child and Ebenezer Peck as deputies in 1829, individuals who favored of the Papineau rebellion against the British, including restricting the selling goods by Britain in Lower Canada. At that time, Richard Freiligh (Freilighsburg) and Ralph Taylor were elected deputies of the county of Bedford (where the Amos Phelps and Samuel Pinkham Jr. familes resided during 1825 and 1831) both Loyalists (to the Crown). When the 1834 Ninety-Two Resolutions passed in Montreal, the Stanstead Plain assembly confirmed loyalty to the British Crown while the Holland Mills assembly affirmed support for Papinaeu. Between 1834 and 1837 the county of Missisquoi was the most Loyalist-predisposed township, while the townships of Dunham and Stanbridge took a reformer stance, in contrast to Sutton, Saint-Armand and villages of Phillipsburgh and Freilighsburgh which were Loyalist centers. Struggle continued until 1838 the when government insisted upon allegiance to the Queen. Organized on 4 July 1837, considered Independence Day in the United States of America, the rejection of the Ninety-Two Resolutions took place in Stanbridge. Among concerns were lordship tenure and immigration, as well as, ethnic tensions between British settlers and the French Canadians. On 6 December 1837, eighty rebels from the United States moved into Loyalist territory near Saint-Armand. The Missisquoi Volunteers defeated the Patriots without British assistance. From this point, the townships lost Loyalist allegiance, and the "Townships of the East (Eastern Townships)" began growth of a French-Canadian population. Following 1837 during the Quebec dispora, many Phelps and Pinkham familes from this line moved back to the United States, or in the Comfort Carpenter Pinkham line's case, to the Province of Ontario, Canada.

Stanstead, Quebec today is known as a town in the Memphremagog Regional County Municipality in the Esrie Region of Quebec, located on the Canada-United States border across from Derby Line, Vermont. The Derby Line-Stanstead Border crossing connects Main Street, Derby line with Quebec Route 143 Stanstead and is one of two local crossings between two towns (Beebe Plain - Beebe border crossing) on the Vermont-Quebec border. Prior to merging, the towns of Stanstead Plain, Beebe and Rock Island were known as "les trois villages (the Three Villages)" because they connect at borders.

Brothers Joseph Pinkham and Abijah Pinkham, sons of Samuel and Dorothy Pinkham, are noted in the Land Petitions of Lower Canada. Abijah Pinkham made an 1830 land petition (item #69825) and Joseph Pinkham (m. Sarah Moulton) the same year (item # 69828). A local newspaper noted on 9 June 1831, a "school at Pinkham's corner consisted of 21 scholars under the instruction of Miss Julia Moulton where the students learned alphabet, words of two syllables, reading, Testament, English reader, Geography and Grammar." "The school appears to be a thriving, flourishing condition, and under the care of a qualified Teacher. The committee, Captain -- J. Bachelder and A. Pinkham (*Abijah Pinkham*) were present and applauded the school." *Source: Stanstead Historical Society*

SAMUEL PINKHAM (Generation 6), son of Samuel and Dorothy Pinkham, married Theodosia Carpenter (born 18 November 1780, Westminster, Windham, VT) in Stanstead, Quebec. The only mention of the event takes place in the "Forest and Clearing" text where the Pinkham name is spelled FinJeham, not Pinkham. It is likely Samuel Pinkham Junior, married Theodosia Carpenter shortly after arriving in Stanstead as his child, Comfort Carpenter Pinkham (whose son, John, in his marriage records his father as, Comfort Carpenter), was born in 1811 and named for Theodosia's father, Comfort Carpenter who died in 1806. The Carpenter family history originates from the Plymouth Colony. Comfort Carpenter, Comfort Carpenter Pinkham's grandfather, likely served in the Old French and Indian Wars (Fort George, Rhode Island in 1757, in Colonel Harris' regiment in 1760 and as ensign in Captain Peck's company in 1761), but also as an American Revolutionary Solder whose likely rank was Private (Comfort Carpenter, *Connecticut*, USA, Continental Troops. Listed in the US Revolutionary War Pension and Bounty-Land Warrant Application files of 1800 for Connecticut). His wife, Thankful Kent, also had early Puritan genealogical roots from Massachusetts. Comfort Carpenter arrived in Stanstead, Quebec with his brother, Amos Carpenter, an American Revolutionary Patriot who died in Stanstead, Quebec.

The Carpenter family has an equally early American history worth noting. Like Richard Pyncombe, William Carpenter (1) was born in 1575 in England and arrived in the United States with his son William (2), William's (2) wife and four children on the sailing ship, *Bevis*, in 1638. William (1) died shortly before 1644 in Rehoboth, Massachusetts. William Carpenter (1) was born in Newtown, Shalbourne Parish, Wiltshire, England. By 1608 he was a leaseholder of Westcourt Manor, Shalbourne near the Wiltshire Hampshire border. William was the age of 62 when he left England for America. William Carpenter (2) was born in 1605 in Wiltshire. He married Abigail Brandt, daughter of John and Alice Brandt on 28 April 1625 in Shalbourne Parish, now Wiltshire, England. The children of William and Abigail Carpenter were John Carpenter (Christened on 8 October 1626 in Shalborne Parish, *Bevis* Passenger), Abigail Carpenter (Chr. 31 May 1629) in Shalborne Parish, *Bevis* Passenger), William Carpenter (Chr. 6 April 1634, Shalborne Parish, *Bevis* Passenger), Samuel Carpenter (Chr. 1 March 1636; d. April 1936, Shalbourne Parish), Samuel Carpenter (Born abt. 1638 Weymouth, Norfolk, MA – his mother, Abigail was pregnant while on the *Bevis*), Hannah Carpenter (b. 3 April 1640, Weymouth, Norfolk, MA) and Abiah Carpenter (b. April 1643 Weymouth, Norfolk, MA). Because the Massachusetts Bay Colony required church membership, records list the Carpenter family as founding members of the Rehoboth (Newman) Congregational Church. William Carpenter (2) was one of the fifty-eight founding members and buried in the Old Rehoboth Cemetery. Historians have not proved earlier evidence of the Carpenter religious affiliation but it is confirmed the family were "certainly not Baptists" like other Carpenters in New England (the William Carpenter family of Rhode Island). Captain William (2) Carpenter and his five sons became known as the "Family of Heroes" because over 300 of the male descendants served in the American Revolutionary War – more than any other American family.

Theodocia Carpenter (and Comfort Carpenter Pinkham) are descendants of WILLIAM (1) (2) whose son was Lt. Samuel Carpenter born in Weymouth, Norfolk in 1663 and died in 1737 in Rehoboth, MA. SAMUEL CARPENTER (1) married Patience Ide in 1683 and died in 1737. Samuel and Patience had a son named TIMOTHY CARPENTER (2) (born 17 October 1686; d. 23 November 1769) who married Experience Chaffee (b. 24 March 1682, Rehoboth, Bristol County, MA; d. 19 April 1754, Rehoboth, Bristol, MA). Timothy and Experience Carpenter had five children: Jedidiah Carpenter (b. 15 December 1696, Rehoboth, MA), Althea Carpenter (b. 17 August 1714, Rehoboth, MA; d. 5 May 1736), Timothy Carpenter Jr. (b. 25 October 1721, Rehoboth, MA; d. 22 December 1795, Rehoboth, MA), Samuel Carpenter (b. 8 April 1725; d. 7 August 1752) and AMOS CARPENTER (3) (b. 12 February 1715; d. 13 September 1787). Amos Carpenter married Mary Phoebe Gould (b. 1724, Gloucester, Essex, MA; d. 12 October 1792, Westminster, VT) on 13 April 1746. Amos and Mary Carpenter had nine children born in Westminster, Vermont: Abnel B. Carpenter (b. 1752; d. June 1810), Amos Carpenter (born abt. 1756; d. in Stanstead, Quebec), Polly Carpenter (b. 1763; d. 30 July 1813 Dalton Coos, NH), Daily Carpenter (born abt. 1764; d. Charlestown, Sullivan, NH), Sally Carpenter (born abt. 1766; d. Gennesse Flats, NH), Pamelia Carpenter (born abt. 1768; d. 1786), Squire (born abt. 1772), Roswell Carpenter (born abt. 1774; d. 1854, Northfield, VT) and COMFORT CARPENTER (4) (born abt. 20 August 1763, Westminster, VT; d. 15 April 1806, Stanstead Plain, Estrie Region, Quebec) (Siblings noted with alternate names - Betsey and Caleb).

Comfort Carpenter married Thankful Kent on 22 March 1777. Comfort and Thankful Carpenter had nine children (GEN5 Carpenter): THEODOSIA CARPENTER (b. 1780 Westminster, Windham, VT; d. 1858 Stanstead, Quebec), Persis Carpenter (b. 1788; d. 1789), Thankful Carpenter (b. 1792), Caleb Carpenter (b. 1795; d. 1862, Stanstead, Quebec), Charles M. Carpenter (b. 1797; d. 1862), Harry Carpenter (b. 1802), Horace, Harriet and Persis (2) Carpenter. The (Theodosia-Generation 5) (Comfort's siblings Amos, Polly, Betsey and Caleb) Carpenter and (Samuel-Generation 6) Pinkham families lived in the United States (New Hampshire, Massachusetts and Vermont) from 1640 onward until descendants moved to Quebec during 1800. Samuel Pinkham Junior's marriage to Theodocia Carpenter was the only marriage between these two families for these specific NH Richard Pinkham-MA Samuel Carpenter family lines.

Amos Carpenter, Comfort Carpenter's brother, verifiably was an American Revolutionery Soldier with a soldier rank for the state of Vermont. He was born on 12 February 1715 in Rehoboth, Bristol County, Massachusetts. His service was with Goodrich in the Rolls of the Soldiers of the Revolutionary War 1775-1780 (page 266) (Source: NARA). The service description is: Captain Michael Gillson, Major Elkannah Dav Militia, 1780. Amos Carpenter, and likely brother, Comfort Carpenter, were Patriots in the American Revolutionary War and brothers who moved to the Eastern Townships together.

While reviewing Land Petitions of Lower Canada, 1764-1841, the wife of Comfort

Carpenter, Widow Thankful Carpenter is listed in 1821-1822 (*item #14946*). Comfort Carpenter's brother, Amos Carpenter, is listed in 1792-1795 (*item #14909*) and 1821-1822 (item #14910). Comfort's son, Caleb Carpenter, is noted in 1801-1802 (*item #14915*), 1802 (*item # 14916*), 1807-1825 (item #14917) and 1809 (*item #14918*).

In an 1825 Township of Stanstead, Quebec census, the families that Pinkhams married into resided near one another. Those individuals included Hiram Sleeper, Caleb Carpenter (brother of Comfort Carpenter) (family of 5), Samuel Ruiter (married Pinkham relations), Abijah Pinkham (family of 5), Samuel Pinkham (family of 3), Joseph Pinkham (family of 10), Widow Thankful Carpenter (2 females under age 14, one female age 14-19, one male age 20-40 single, and one female age greater than 40), Amos Carpenter (brother of Comfort Carpenter) and Joseph Carpenter. An 1851 obituary for Thankful Carpenter reads: "*Thankful died suddenly in this town on the 20th ult. Thankful, widow of Comfort Carpenter who came to this town on the first of the present century, buiit and occupied the first mills in town ofr about 6 years when death removed him, living with the charge of a family, exposed to the privations and obstacles incident to the first settlers which were admirable surmounted and sustained by her, who, for a full half century, has been esteemed as a king obliging neighbor and tender affectionate wife.*" Listed as Thankful Kentfield or Canfield. Comfort Carpenter's estate was administrated by Joseph Pride, Record page 72, Volume 5. As a *foot note - "After the above was put in type, Lucius Carpenter informed the writer that the actual location of the sawmill alluded to as having been build by his grandfather, Comfort Carpenter, was at what was known as Mack's Mills - sometimes called Mack's Hollow - about one mile south of Tomifobia Village. The site was the foundation of the present sawmill, which in the past century and more, has passed through several hands including ownership by Daniel Mack, from whom the locality took its name.* Source: Lepitre, Log Cabin Chronicles

It is recorded: "The Stanstead head of one branch of the family represented by Lucius E. Carpenter of Tomifobia, was Comfort Carpenter, said to have been one of seven Carpenters who moved from the States to Stanstead in 1800. Comfort settled near what is now known as the Tomifobia, formerly Smith's Mills, as per Forest and Clearings (B. F. Hubbard): "built a sawmill that year, the first erected in town." "He came with his wife, Thankful Canfield and family, from Westminster, Vermont. Nine children were born of this union, two of which died young, the others were Theodocia m. Samuel Pinkham; Thankful m. John Merrill; Caleb m. Sarah Rogers; Charles m. Elizabeth Eaton; Persis m. Benjamin Tilton; Harry m. Edith Wright; Harriet m. Ebenezar Wright. Four other children, brothers and sisters of Comfort, who moved and settled in Stanstead were Amos Carpenter m. Elizabeth Lane; Polly Carpenter m. Peter Little; Betsey Carpenter m. James Andrews and Caleb Carpenter, also two nieces, Sarah Carpenter m. Asa Hasting and Phoebe Carpenter, who m. Henry Rider. It is said that 46 members of this family served in the American Revolutionery War.

Caleb (Carpenter), the eldest son of Comfort (b. 1795) married Sarah Rogers in 1819. The children of Caleb and Sarah (Rogers) Carpenter were: Laura Jane, William, Mary, Norris, Julia, Aurelia, Comfort and Edward Granville Carpenter. Comfort Carpenter (b.1831; d. 29 August 1908; Buried Ruiter's Corners) married Ann Elizabeth Kilburn in 1859. The children of Comfort and Ann Elizabeth (Kilburn) Carpenter were William K.

(born 1865; died 1942), Lucius E. (born 1867) and Sarah E. (born 1874) Carpenter. Lucius E. Carpenter, born 1867, married Carrie Lunderville in 1902. The child of Lucius E. and Carrie (Lunderville) Carpenter was Gordon K. Carpenter born 1904 (*same year of birth as Robert Earlby Pinkham*) who married Mona Agnes Fonniais (sp?) in 192-. Lucius E. Carpenter was for several years secretary-treasurer of Stanstead Township, and has been Secretary-Treasurer of the Protestant School Commissioners of the Stanstead Township. The lineal descent of the Carpenters dates from the year 1261, placed in Switzerland, a little later but before 1300, one named John is found in England. The American head of the family was William (Carpenter), b. 1655, the twelfth generation of descent from the Swiss founder of the family." *Source: Lepitre*

Samuel Pinkham Junior is recorded in the Actes de Notarie 1799-1845 of Leon LaLanne. These records were reviewed for guardianship of Amos Phelps III and Elizabeth Phelps, if their mother had passed, as well as, information regarding Lot 9, Range 2 Stanbridge where both Amos Phelps Junior/"the younger" and Diadama Long Phelps resided. The record is image #144 of the records for Missisquoi, Quebec, Canada. Samuel Pinkham signed as a witness for a document that read:

> *6 July 1808 - This is done and passed at Armond, in the County of Bedford in the house of Joel Ackley in the foremorn of the sixth day of July in the year of our Lord one-thousand-eight-hundred and eight in the presence of Samuel Pinkham Junior and David Vaughn who with the said, William Wightman, the said notary have herewith subscribed their names and presences -- by first duly and according to the law. Samuel Pinkham, Jr. (Signed) and David Vaughn, William Wrightman, John Baker, James Martingdale. 4th Range, Stanbridge.*

This document was image 141 of 3,183. There was not a record for Phelps between 6 July 1808 and August 1808 although a record number 144 (image 008138784) was reviewed for Phelps Jr. notation in search for an 1813 will by Amos B. Phelps Junior.

~SAMUEL G. PINKHAM (JUNIOR):

Birth: 5 August 1787, Louden, New Hampshire
        Father: Samuel Pinkham (b. 11 May 1760, Durham, NH; d. May 1830, Stanstead, Quebec)
        Mother: Dorothy Ordway Pinkham (b. 17 July 1759; d. 20 August 1850, Stanstead, Quebec)

Marriage: 1809 Stanstead, Quebec to Theodosia Carpenter
    Source: Forest and Clearings, the history of Stanstead, County, Province of Quebec with 500 families. By B. F. Hubbard
"Comfort Carpenter married Thankful Canfield. They settled in Stanstead near the place now known as Smith's Mill in 1800. Mr. Carpenter built a saw mill that year, the first erected in town. He died in 1806, she died in 1815. Their children were: (entry 206) Theodosia, m. Samuel Pinkham..."
    2) Deaths 1815 – 1879, St. Francis Church, Volume 1: Theodosia Carpenter, CONJ (Spouse) Samuel Pinkham, *Source: d. 3-09-1858, Congregational, Canton, Stanstead*

Death: 1 March 1857, Stanstead, Quebec

The children of Samuel and Theodosia (Carpenter) Pinkham (Generation 7):

1) Caleb Pinkham: Born 13 March 1810, Quebec. Married (m1) Mary Downing 1829 in Quebec and (m2) Deborah Veal 1880 in MN. Moved to Geauga County, Ohio in 1831, Wisconsin in 1855 and Milles Lac, Minnesota in 1862. Died 5 August 1889, Milles Du Lac, Minnesota, USA. *Children (m1): Josephus (Cephus) (b. 1828/29 Quebec), Comfort (b. 1831 Quebec), Huldah (b. 1834 OH), Henry (b. 1837 OH), Phebe (b. 1840 OH) and Caleb Jr. (b.1845 OH) Pinkham.*

2) Comfort Carpenter Pinkham: Born 1811, Quebec. Married Elizabeth Phelps 1832, Quebec. Moved to Durham County, Ontario prior to 1842. Died 1855, Clarke County, Ontario, Canada. *Children (first four born Quebec; last five Ontario): Cynthia (b. 1832), Elect(r)a (b. 15 March 1834), Mary (b. 1836), Edwin A. (b. 1840-1841,) Willard (b. 1841-1842), John Wesley (b. 1845), Jane (b. 1850), Samuel (b. 6 April 1852) & Charles (b. 11 June 1855) Pinkham.*

3) Huldah Pinkham Warren: Born abt. 1815, Quebec. Married 1831, Abbotsford, Quebec (to Seth Warren – *Marriage certificate signed by Sam G. Pinkham and "Betsy" Phelps. Next church entry, on same day, for husband's nephew's baptism - signed by Sam G. Pinkham and Jeremiah Phelps*). Moved to Geauga, Ohio in 1831. Died post 1880, Painesville, Lake, Ohio, USA. *Children: Emily, Huldah Jane, Emma, Alice and David C. Warren.*

4) James O. Pinkham – Born 1816, Quebec. Married Mathilde Tetreau-Duchame 1842, St. Pie, QC. Died 3 June 1902, Tewkesbury, MA, USA.

5) J. Samuel Pinkham: Born abt. 1825-1826 Quebec. Married (*m1*) Domitilde Chartier 1844 Quebec/ (*m2*) Betsy Higgens (born 11 October 1814, Quebec), daughter of Benjamin & Mary Higgens of Canada); d. 6 March 1901, Evansville, Wisconsin). Moved to Wisconsin in 1855. Died 1879, Union, Rock County, Wisconsin, USA. Children: (m1) Samuel (b. 1844, NY) Joseph (b. 1846, Quebec) and Cephas (b. 1847, Quebec) Pinkham.

6) Joseph Abijah Pinkham: Born 16 May 1827, Quebec. Married Rosina Chartier (Born abt. 1832, Quebec) in 1850. Moved to Mower, MN with Jeremiah Phelps family. *Children: Mary (b. 1849 Quebec; d. Madera, CA), Rosina (b. 1851 Quebec), Sarah Ann (b. 1853 Quebec), Samuel (b. 1855, Wisconsin), Theodocia (b. 1858 MN; d. Madera, CA), Henry (b. 1863 MN), Matilda (b. 1865 MN), Aaron (b. 1867 MN) & Charles (b. 1869 MN) Pinkham.* Died 19 January 1909 (*birth: 16 May 1827*), Madera, Madera County, California, Calvary Cemetery, Madera, California. *Source: FindAGrave*

7) Samuel Pinkham III: Born abt. 1828-1830, Quebec. Married Louisa Hill 1887 Mower, MN. Died 13 September 1887, Mower, Minnesota, USA.

1808 Sale of Land by Samuel G. Pinkham. Leon LaLanne, Acts de Notarie, Quebec.

1825 Lower Quebec Census, St. Cesaire, Bedford, Quebec – SAMUEL PINKHAM – family of 7; resided near the Amos, Jeremiah and Oliver C. Phelps families. *Source: Library and Archives Canada, Public Archives, Ottawa, Ontario.*

This census states the Samuel Pinkham Junior family is comprised of seven members. Noted in this census would be parents Samuel and Theodocia with children Caleb, Comfort, Huldah, James O. Pinkham and an unknown Pinkham daughter or J. Samuel Pinkham.

1831 Lower Canada St. Cesaire, St. Hyacinthe, Census – SAMUEL PINKHAM farmer (cultivateur) living alongside Amos, Jeremiah and Oliver Phelps families. *Source: Library and Archives Canada, Public Archives, Ottawa, Ontario*

This census states Samuel Pinkham Junior's family is comprised of eight members, and Samuel is a Farmer. Samuel and Theodocia are parents with six children: two daughters one over age 14 (Huldah) and one under age 14 (unknown); a son age 14-16 (James O. b. 1816), two children 5-14 (b. 1818-1825) (unknown daughter & J. Samuel b. 1825), two children five and under (b. 1826-1831) (Joseph Abijah b. 1827) (Samuel III b. 1828-1831). Comfort (b. 1811/age 20) missing from census record; m. 1832.

1842 Lower Canada Census, Milton, Shefford – SAMUEL PINKHAM, farmer. Number of Inhabitants: 7. (*Listed next to Harry Carpenter; Theodocia (Carpenter) Pinkham's brother.*). *Source: Library and Archives Canada*

Note: This is a family of seven. Samuel and Theodocia (Carpenter) Pinkham resided next to the Jeremiah Phelps family, the uncle of Elizabeth Phelps, wife of son Comfort Carpenter Pinkham who is listed in the 1842 Newcastle, Ontario census with a family of 7. Son Caleb Pinkham married in 1829 and by 1838 moved to Ohio. Daughter Huldah Pinkham Warren married in 1831 then moved to Ohio as her husband had property there by 1829. Son James Pinkham married during 1842 Matilde Tetreau-Duchame. Samuel Pinkham III was single and J. Samuel Pinkham married 1844. Son Joseph Abijah Pinkham married 1849, therefore was single in 1842. Likely there was a daughter Pinkham (born abt. 1818-1823) whose name is unknown. This is a census record for parents Samuel Junior and Theodocia (Carpenter) Pinkham with children James Pinkham and his wife (Mathilde Tetreau-Duchame) or an unknown Pinkham daughter, J. Samuel Pinkham, Joseph Abijah Pinkham and Samuel III Pinkham.

Death: 1 March 1857, Stanstead, Quebec, "Samuel Pinkham, the son of the late Samuel Pinkham of Stanstead, Quebec." Buried Roxton and Milton, Quebec, Anglican Church. *Source: Drouin Collection, Montreal, Quebec, Canada, Institut Genealogique Drouin.*

~Theodocia Carpenter Pinkham:

Birth: 18 November 1780, Westminster, Vermont
          Father: Comfort Carpenter (b. 20 August 1763; d. 15 April 1806, Stanstead, Quebec)
          Mother: Thankful Kent (Canfield) Carpenter (b. 22 March 1763; d. 1851, Stanstead, Quebec)
          (*Name listed as both "Theodosia" and "Theodocia" on records.*)

Source: *A Genealogical History of the Rehoboth Branch of the Carpenter Family in America* by Amos Bugbee Carpenter, Amherst, MA, 1898 - American Genealogical-Biographical Index (ABBI) – Theodosia Carpenter (Volume 25, Page 271).

<u>Vermont Warnings Out:</u> Vol. 2: Southern Vermont by Alden M. Rollins. Picton Press
  Camden, ME Windsor County – Hartford (p. 58):

"26 Mar 1807 Carpenter, Theodosha"

A "Warning Out" was a civil matter which emanated from the town council then
presented to the person(s) in question by the sheriff or constable. Typically, warnings
out were not followed by expulsion but instead a formal record noting the town would
not accept financial responsibility for person living there who were not admitted
inhabitants and had little or no need of support. Often, they were sent back to their
town of origin. The "Hazard Index" of New York Yearly Meeting (Vermont Monthly
Meetings included) did not note any Comfort Carpenter family members. In the
<u>Vermont Warnings Out: Vol. 1: Northern Vermont</u> book by Alden M. Rollins, on ("p.
351)" page 256 of Orange County, Vermont dated "14 September 1809," the "Merrill,
John Jr. and family" were "warned out." Theodocia's sister, Thankful Carpenter, was
the wife of John Merrill, Jr. To be "warned out," one had to be Quaker, but zero Quaker
birth records have been located for Theodocia Carpenter.

<u>Marriage:</u> 1809, Stanstead, Quebec to Samuel Pinkham
    Source:*"Forest and Clearings, the history of Stanstead County, Province of Quebec with 500 families."* By B. F. Hubbard:

*"Comfort Carpenter married Thankful Canfield. They settled in Stanstead near
the place now known as Smith's Mill in 1800. Mr. Carpenter built a saw mill that
year, the first erected in town. He died in 1806, she died in 1815. Their children
were: (entry 206) Theodosia, m. Samuel Pinkham…"*

<u>Death:</u> 9 March 1853, Canton, Stanstead, Quebec

<u>The children of SAMUEl JUNIOR and Theodocia (Carpenter) PINKHAM (Gen7):</u>

1) <u>Caleb Pinkham:</u> Born 13 March 1810, Quebec. Married (m1) Mary Downing
        1829/(m2) Deborah Veal. Died 5 August 1889, Milles Du Lac, MN, USA.
2) <u>Comfort Carpenter Pinkham:</u> Born 1811, Quebec. Married Elizabeth Phelps
        1832 Quebec. Died 1855, Clarke County, Ontario, Canada.
3) <u>Huldah Pinkham Warren:</u> Born abt. 1815, Quebec. Married 1831, Abbotsford,
        Quebec (to Seth Warren – *marriage certificate signed by Sam Pinkham &
        "Betsy" Phelps)*. Died post 1880, Painesville, Lake, Ohio, USA.
4) <u>James O. Pinkham:</u> Born 1816 Quebec. Married Mathilde Tetreau-Duchame
        1842, St. Pie, QC. Died 3 June 1902, Tewkesbury, MA, USA. *Source: MA Wills
        & Probates*
5) <u>J. Samuel Pinkham:</u> Born abt. 1825-1826, Quebec. Married (m1) Domitilde
        Chartier 1844 QC/(m2) Betsy Higgens. Died 1879, Union Rock, WI, USA.
6) <u>Joseph Abijah Pinkham:</u> Born 6 May 1827, Quebec. Married Rosina
        Chartier 1849, QC. Died 29 January 1909, Madera, Californa, USA.
7) <u>Samuel Pinkham III:</u> Born abt. 1828-1830, Quebec; Married Louisa Hill 1887
        MN, USA. Died 13 September 1887, Mower, Minnesota, USA.

<u>Death:</u> 9 March 1858 in Canton, Stanstead, Quebec *Source: Death 1813-1879 Saint-Francois Church Records* Theodosia Carpenter. Conj – Samuel Pinkham (spouse)

Samuel Pinkham Junior (Father of Comfort Carpenter Pinkham) and Amos Phelps family members (likely the widow of Amos Jr., mother of Elizabeth Phelps) resided next to one another in Quebec 1825 & 1831 census locations. In addition, the family siged baptismal and marriage documents together. The marriage of Comfort Carpenter Pinkham and Elizabeth Phelps was the only union between the two families.

1) <u>1831 Lower Canada Census: St. Cesaire, St. Hyacinthe, Quebec:</u> Thomas Phelps (Amos Phelps), Jeremie Phelps, Oliver Phelps and Samuel Pinkham.
2) <u>1831 Huldah Pinkham marriage to Seth Warren:</u> Marriage document signed by **brother – Betsy Phelps** and father, Samuel Pinkham (**Sam G. Pinkham**). Next record was baptism for Seth Warren's brother, Oliver Warren's child signed by: **Sam G. Pinkham** (Samuel Pinkham) and **Jerimiah Phelps.**
3) Phelps/Pinkham families moved to Ohio together: Jeremiah Phelps and Abijah Joseph Pinkham (brother of Samuel Pinkham) moved to Minnesota.
4) <u>Huldah Pinkham Warren (sister of Comfort Carpenter Pinkham) moved to Ohio where both A. Phelps and E. Phelps resided</u>. *Source: 1870 Ohio Census.*
5) <u>Comfort Carpenter Pinkham's brother, Caleb Pinkham (named for mother's brother, Caleb Carpenter) moved from Quebec to Ohio in 1850.</u> *Source: 1850 United States Census, Munson, Geauga, Ohio.* Caleb Pinkham's children named for brother, Comfort, and sister, Huldah, Pinkham. Listed along with Alfred Phelps. 1880 Census lists father – Samuel Pinkham as correctly born in Vermont.
6) <u>1870 Census of Maquoketa,</u> Iowa: Amos Phelps (brother of Elizabeth Phelps): born Canada; parents born: Vermont – Amos Phelps born January 1786, VT.

Since no birth records for Samuel & Theodocia Carpenter Pinkham children exist in the Eastern Townships of Quebec, proof Comfort Carpenter Pinkham was brother to Caleb, Huldah, Samuel and Abijah Pinkham can be determined from the following documents:

1) Caleb Pinkham was named for Theodocia's brother, Caleb Carpenter (b. 1795). Brothers Comfort Carpenter, Caleb Carpenter and Amos Carpenter (*American Revolutionary War status confirmed*) moved to Stanstead, Quebec in 1800. Caleb Carpenter was also the name of Theodocia Carpenter's uncle. *Source: 500 Settlers of Stanstead by B. H. Hubbard*
2) Caleb Pinkham in 1850 United States Census: Geauga, Ohio. Children named for siblings: Comfort Pinkham and Huldah Pinkham. *Source: 1850 United States Census.*
3) Caleb Pinkham in 1860 United States Census: Clayton, Crawford, Wisconsin. Between1865-1869 brother Joseph Abijah Pinkham and family moved to Clayton, Wisconsin from Mower, Minnesota where they had resided alongside the Jeremiah Phelps family.
4) Caleb Pinkham in <u>1870 United States Census:</u> Minnesota – state where Jeremiah Phelps and his Uncle Joseph Abijah Pinkham settled in 1850.

5) Caleb Pinkham in <u>1880 United States Census</u>: Princeton, Mille Lacs notes: Father (Samuel Pinkham) born Vermont (*wrong - born Louden, NH*) mother (Theodocia Carpenter) born Massachusetts (*wrong - born Westminster, VT*).

6) Huldah Pinkham married 1831 to Seth Warren in Abbotsford, Quebec with document signed by father (Samuel Pinkham), "Sam G. Pinkham" and brother (Comfort Pinkham), 'Betsy Phelps," Comfort Pinkham's wife in 1832.

7) Huldah Pinkham Warren, with Seth Warren, husband, in 24 June 1870 Geauga, Ohio Census: Born 1816 in Lower Canada (Quebec).

8) Huldah (Pinkham) Warren – <u>1880 United States Census</u>: Painesville, Lake, Ohio. Widower living with child, Emily Cadeau. Listed as mother-in-law age 63 (born 1817). Parent's birthplace: Massachusetts – where (grandmother) Dorothy Ordway Pinkham was born.

9) Abijah Joseph Pinkham in <u>1860 United States Census</u>: Austin, Mower, Minnesota (same location as Jeremiah Phelps). Age incorrect. Children named for parents: Samuel and Theodocia Pinkham.

10) Joseph A. Pinkham in <u>1865 Minnesota State Census</u>: Lyle, Mower, Minnesota. Children: Samuel born 1855 and Theodocia Pinkham.

11) Mower Minnesota Courthouse Deeds: (Joseph) Abijah Pinkham 17 May 1859/2 January 1863. This is the city where Jeremiah Phelps' family moved.

12) Joseph Pinkham - <u>1870 United States Census</u>: Clayton, Crawford, Wisconsin. Birthplace: Canada. Parents of foreign birth (*incorrect but residing in Quebec*). Children named for parents: Samuel & Theodocia Pinkham.

13) Abijah Pinkham - <u>1900 United States Census</u>: Clayton, Crawford, Wisconsin. Marriage year 1850 (prior to move to Minnesota); Years married: 50. Age 72 – birth May 1837.

14) Samuel Pinkham – S. Pinkham – <u>1855 Wisconsin State Census</u>: Number of males: 4; number of females – 6. Foreign born (Canada)- 0.

15) Carpenter Family: Source: Forest & Clearings – History of Stanstead County, Quebec by B. F. Hubbard Mention of Caleb Carpenter – Uncle and brother of Theodocia Carpenter Pinkham who named her eldest son, Caleb Pinkham; Brother Caleb Carpenter had son, Comfort Carpenter (b. 1831; d. 1908, Quebec).

16) Map of Stanstead, Quebec/Derby, Vermont border: Tomifobia River where Carpenter MIll existed and Pinkham Brook/Pinkham Cemetery (until 1960).

1825-31 Canadian censuses for the Eastern Townships of Quebec, there are six Pinkham surnames listed, five related to this line. Unrelated was a Thomas Pinkham listed in 1831 at Bonaventure to Point au Maquereau, Bonaventure, Quebec, Canada. Related were: Abijah Pinkham (son of Samuel and Dorothy Pinkham) residing (1825) in Stanstead, Richelieu, Quebec, Samuel Pinkham and Dorothy Pinkham residing (1825) in Stanstead, Richelieu, Quebec, Joseph Pinkham (son of Samuel and Dorothy Pinkham) residing (1825) Stanstead, Quebec, Samuel Pinkham (son of Samuel and Dorothy Pinkham) residing (1825 & 1831) St. Cesaire, Bedford, Quebec (alongside the Amos Phelps Sr., Jeremiah Phelps and Oliver C. Phelps families) then Samuel Pinkham Junior residing (1842) Milton, Shefford, Quebec next to the Jeremiah Phelps family. Likely other children were born (and died) between the birth of James O. Pinkham (1816) and J. Samuel (born abt. 1825-1826) as Abijah Joseph (born 1827) and Samuel

51

III (born 1828-1830) were likely the youngest children. Since no birth records for the children of Samuel Junior and Theodocia (Carpenter) Pinkham were found, it is assumed at least one unknown daughter was born between 1817-1824.

Children of Samuel Pinkham Junior and Theodocia Carpenter were named for various family members. Caleb Pinkham was named for Theodocia Carpenter's brother/uncle. Comfort Carpenter Pinkham was named for Theodocia Carpenter's father, Comfort Carpenter. Joseph Abijah was named for American Revolutionary Patriot and great-grandfather Abijah Pinkham and Samuel Jr.'s brother, Joseph, while Samuel Pinkham III was named for his grandfather and father, Samuel Pinkham (Senior and Junior).

An early Quebec record listed only nineteen Pinkham first names: Abijah, Annie Laura (Coates), Caleb (son of Samuel and Theodosia, b. 1810; married Mary Downing; d. 1889), Charles (Austin), COMFORT (son Samuel and Theodosia, b. 1811; m. 1832 Elizabeth Phelps), Edgar, Emma Maud, Ephraim, George Lorin, Hannah (wife of Abijah, son of Samuel and Dorothy b. 1802), Huldah (sister of Comfort, daughter of Samuel and Theodosia), Isaac N., Isaac William, Kate Ledoh, Lillie M., Mary (wife of Caleb), Mary Ann, Samuel (father of Comfort), Scottina Mary and William John. Samuel and Theodocia (Carpenter) Pinkham daughter(s) were likely included in this list.

The children of SAMUEL JUNIOR and Theodocia (Carpenter) PINKHAM born Quebec and their children's family members were (Generation 7):

~Caleb Pinkham (1):
    Birth: 13 March 1810, Quebec, Canada
    Marriages:
        M1 Mary Downing (b. 1808, Vermont; d. 1878, Minnesota, USA)
        M2 Deborah Ann Veal (b. 1834, Indiana; d. 1923, Minnesota, USA)
    Death: 5 Aug 1889, Mille Lacs County, Minnesota, USA
        Buried: Oak Knoll Cemetery, Mille Lacs County, Minnesota, USA

        Marriage: M1 – Caleb Pinkham; Spouse – Mary Downing; Event – Marriage; Marriage Year – 1829; Marriage location – Abbotsford, Quebec; Religion – Protestant; Place of Worship – Protestant. *Source: Drouin.*

        "On tenth day of March eighteen hundred and twenty-nine Caleb Pinkham of Rougemont Farmer Bachelor and Mary Downing of the same place Spinster by me, Joseph Abbot, Missionary of __ District." Signed by Caleb Pinkham and Mary Downing – by mark.

        Married at the Anglican Church of the St. Paul d'Abbotsford, District of Montreal, Quebec
            Married 18 March 1829 – Farmer of Rougemont – to Mary Dowling of Rougemont, Spinster. Married at Anglican Church of St. Paul d/Abbotsford, Quebec, Canada.

The children of Caleb & Mary (Downing) Pinkham (Generation 8):

Josephus (Cephas) Pinkham (b. 1 December 1829; d. 12 Aug 1921 WI)
Comfort Pinkham (b. 1831, Quebec; d. 1887, MN)
Huldah Pinkham Pickett (b. 1834, Geauga, OH; d. MN)
Henry Pinkham (b. 1837, Geauga, OH; d. 1907, IA)
Phoebe Ann Pinkham Crook (b. 1840, Geauga, OH; d.1872, MN)
Caleb J. Pinkham (b. 1845, Geauga, OH; d. 1926, MN)

Geauga County was originally part of the French colony of Canada (New France) which was ceded in 1763 to Great Britain and renamed the Province of Quebec. In the late 1700s, the land became part of the Connecticut Western Reserve in the Northwest Territory and was purchased by the Connecticut Land Company in 1795. Geauga County was founded on 1 March 1801. The first settlement was Burton, Ohio made up of three Connecticut families in 1795. The Connecticut Land Company included fifty-seven proprietors, one of whom was Oliver Phelps. Members of the Samuel Pinkham family (Caleb Pinkham and Huldah Pinkham Warren) born Quebec lived in Ohio alongside the Amos Phelps family born Norwich, Connecticut.

Ohio Tax Records, 1800-1850: Captain Pinkham. Date: 1827. 120 acres on Western Reserve. (Unconfirmed is whether this Pinkham is a distant relation and a reason why Caleb Pinkham and Huldah Pinhkam Warren moved to Ohio.)

Ohio Tax Records: 1838-1850:
> 1838-1852 Fowlers Mill, Munson Township, Geauga, Ohio Tax Assessment: Caleb Pinkham. *Source: Ohio Tax Records, 1800-1850*
> 1840 Burton, Burton Township, Geauga, Ohio Tax Assessment: Caleb Pinkham. *Source: Ohio Tax Records, 1800-1850*
> 1843-1845 Fowlers Mill, Munson Township, Geauga, Ohio: Caleb Pinkham. *Source: Ohio Tax Records, 1800-1850*
> 1846-1847 Fowlers Mill, Munson Township, Geauga, Ohio: Caleb Pinkham. *Source: Ohio Tax Records, 1800-1850*
> 1848-1850 Fowlers Mill, Munson Township, Geauga, Ohio: Caleb Pinkham. Source: Ohio Tax Records, 1800-1850

(Munson, Geagua, Ohio land total: 77 acres. Page 115. Listed with Alfred Phelps.)

1850 United States Federal Census: Caleb Pinkham; Name – Caleb Pinkham; Age – 40; Birth year – abt. 1810; Birthplace – Canada; Home in 1850 – Munson, Geauga, Ohio, USA; Gender – Male; Family number – 173; Household Members: Caleb Pinkham (Age 40); Mary Pinkham (Age – 41), Cephas (Josephus – born Quebec) Pinkham (Age 21), Comfort Pinkham (born Quebec) (Age 18); Huldah Pinkham (born Ohio) (Age 16); Henry Pinkham (born Ohio) (Age 13); Pheba A. Pinkham (born Ohio) (Age 10) and Caleb Pinkham (born Ohio) (Age 5). *Source: 1850 Census, Munson, Geauga, Ohio*

Notes on Wiota, Wisconsin: Wiota, Lafayette. The town was founded when Alexander Hamilton's son discovered ore during the 1820s.

<u>1855 Wisconsin Census</u>: Caleb Pinkham. Event Place – Wiota, Lafayette, Wisconsin. Number of White Males – 3. Number of White Females – 2. *Source: Wisconsin State Census, 1855*

1858 Homestead Entry Land Grant dated 1 June 1858 – Cephas Pinkham. Mineral rights for Lafayette County, Minnesota. Signed by Samuel W. Pinkham, brother or nephew to Caleb Pinkham.

<u>1860 Crawford, Wisconsin Census</u>: Caleb Pinkham. Census date: 4 August 1860. Location: Clayton, Crawford, Wisconsin. Name: Caleb Pinkham, Age 50 born 1810 in *Vermont*, Male, White, Farmer, Value of Real Estate: 600. Value of Personal Assets: 50, Place of birth: *Vermont*. Name: Mary Pinkham, Age 52, White, Female, Place of Birth: Vermont. Name: Caleb, Age 15, Male, White, Place of Birth: Ohio. *Source: NARA page 144, Wisconsin 1860 Crawford Census*

1860 Clayton, Crawford County, Ohio Census: J. Samuel Pinkham, age 33 (b. 1827). Listed with wife Betsey (age 41 – born 1819), children: H – male age 22, Emily age 18, Jane age 16 & Joseph, male age 14. Brother of Caleb Pinkham, son of Samuel G. Jr. and Theodocia (Carpenter) Pinkham.

<u>1861-1865 United States Civil War Index</u>: Wisconsin - (Stephen Pinkham) (William P. Pinkham), (Samuel Pinkham), Cephas Pinkham, Comfort Pinkham and Caleb Pinkham.

<u>1861-1865 Private, Union in US. Army, Navy & Marine Corps from Mills Lacs, Minnesota</u>: Caleb Pinkham: Name: Caleb Pinkham. Family #: 42. Rank: Private. Company: K. Start date: 17 October 1861; End date: 16 July 1865. Term: 3 years, 8 months, 29 days. *Source: NARA*. (son: Caleb Pinkham- b. 1845. Age 1861 – age 16/ Caleb Pinkham Sr. - b. 1810. Age 1861 – 51)

<u>1862 Minnesota Homestead Patents</u>: Caleb Pinkham in the Minnesota, Homestead and Cash Entry Patents, Pre – 1908: Name: Caleb Pinkham; Land Office: Taylors Falls; Document Number – 153; Total acres – 160; Misc. Doc. NR: 241; Signature: Yes; Canceled Document – No; Issue Date – 5 February 1872; Mineral Rights Reserved: No; Metes and Bounds - No; Statutory Reference – 12 Stat. 392; Multiple Warrantee Names – No; Act of Treaty – 20 May 1862; Multiple Patentee Names – No; Entry Classification – Homestead Entry Original; Land Description: 1 SW 4TH PH No37 N 27 W28; *Source: United States Bureau of Land Management, Minnesota, Homestead and Cash Entry Patents, Pre-1908*

1862 Homestead Entry 20 May 1862: Comfort Pinkham. 162 acres, Taylors Falls, MN. Land next to father, Caleb Pinkham.

<u>1870 United States Census</u>: Caleb Pinkham; Name –Caleb Pinkham; Event type – Census; Event year – 1870; Event Place – Minnesota, United States; Gender – Male; Age – 60; Race – White; Race – W; Birth year (estimated) – 1809-1810; Birthplace – Canada; Page number – 3; Household – Caleb Pinkham (M – 60 –

Canada); Mary Pinkham (F – 63 – Vermont). *Source: United States Census 1870, NARA.*
Listed alongside son, Comfort Pinkham.

1870 United States Census: Comfort Pinkham (son of Caleb & Mary Pinkham, next entry on record): Comfort Pinkham, age 29, Farmer, Land owner, born in Canada; Althea, age 27, Keeping House, born New York; Althea, age 15, female born Wisconsin; Orville (Orin) age 12 born Wisconsin; Theodora age 10, female born Wisconsin: James, age 5, Male born Wisconsin.

Pinkham-Veal Wedding: *"Mr. Caleb Pinkham, aged 70 years, and Miss Deborah Veal, aged 45, were declared man and wife by Justice Nokes on Sunday evening. Mr. Pinkham is a hale old gentleman and will make a good a husband as most men a score of years younger."* *Source: MN local newspaper*

1880 United States Census: Caleb Pinkham; Name – Caleb Pinkham; Event – Census; Event Date – 1880; Event Place – Princeton, Mille Lacs, Minnesota, United States; Gender – Male; Age – 70; Marital Status – Married; Race – White; Race – W; Occupation –Farmer; Relationship to head of household – self; Birth year – 1810; Birthplace – Canada; Father's birthplace – Vermont, US; Mother's birthplace – Massachusetts. Household: Caleb Pinkham, self (M – 70- birth place – Canada; Deborah Pinkham, wife (F, 45, birthplace Ohio), and Minnie Gay – other (F – 4 – birthplace Minnesota). *Source: United States Census 1880*

Minnesota State Census 1885: Caleb Pinkham; Name: Caleb Pinkham; Event Place – Princeton, Mille Lacs, Minnesota; Age – 75 years; Birth year – 1810; Birthplace- New York; Race – White; Race – White; Gender – Male; Volume – Traverse, Mille Lacs, Pines, Benton; Household: Caleb Pinkham (M – 75 years – Birthplace – New York); Debbie Pinkham (F – 46 years – birthplace – Indiana). *Source: Minnesota State Census, 1885*

United States Census of Union Veterans and Widows of the Civil War, 1890 – Caleb Pinkham: Name – Caleb Pinkham; Event type – Census; Event Date – 1890; Event place – Mille Lacs, Minnesota, United States.

Death: 5 August 1889 Mille Lacs County; Minnesota, USA. Caleb Pinkham; Event type: Burial; Event date – 1889; Event Place – Princeton, Mille Lacs, Minnesota, United States; Birth date - 13 March 1810; Death date – 5 August 1889; Cemetery – Oak Knoll Cemetery. *Source: FindAGrave*

United States Civil War and Later Pension Index: Caleb Pinkham; Name: Caleb Pinkham; Event type – Pension; Event date – 12 July 1926; Event Place – United States; file name – 17787443.

References for the children of Caleb and Mary (Dowling) Pinkham:

~Josephus (Cephas) Pinkham – Born 1 December 1828, Lower Canada
Death: 12 August 1927, Wisconsin, USA
Immigration year (1900 Census): 1845 – Age 17
(M1) 16 March 1851 Illinois to Sarah (Sally) Keene (b. 1829 New York)
(M2) 9 Sept 1885 WI to Lydia A. Fulip (b 1850 Wisconsin)

Source *FindAGrave* lists Josephus "Cephus" Pinkham as being born 1 December 1828 in Ontario, Canada. If true, then brothers Caleb and Comfort Pinkham may have moved to Ontario together with the Comfort Pinkham family being the only known descendants of Samuel and Theodocia Pinkham to remain in Canada. Caleb and Huldah Pinkham moved to Ohio while Comfort Pinkham moved to Ontario, Canada in 1842. "J. Samuel" moved to Wisconsin by 1855, Joseph Abijah and "Samuel III," moved to Minnesota and James O. went to Massachusetts. Speculation remains whether Samuel III signed his name on Caleb Pinkham's son, Cephas Pinkham's mineral rights document by 1858.

> Marriage Record: Cephus Pinkham to Sally Keene. Marriage date: 16 March 1851. Marriage Place: McHenry, Illinois.

> Birth: Frank Pinkham. Birth date: 29 February 1852 Illinois. Father's name: Cephas Pinkham. Mother's name: Sarah Kerns.

> Birth: *William Pinkham born 1853, Wisconsin.*

> 1855 Wisconsin State Census: Cephus Pinkham. Event Place: Wiota, Lafayette, Wisconsin. Number of White Males: 3; Number of White Females: 1. *Source: Wisconsin State Census, 1855.*

> Birth: *Isaac Samuel Pinkham (m1) born 26 Dec 1857, Wiota, WI. Went by "Samuel" Pinkham rather than Isaac.*

> *1858 Homestead Entry Land Grant dated 1 June 1858 – Cephas Pinkham. Mineral rights for Lafayette County, Minnesota. Signed by **Samuel W. Pinkham**. Caleb Pinkham: 1862 MN Mineral rights and land grants. Unconfirmed: Was Samuel W. Pinkham, Cephas' uncle?*

> United States Civil War Soldiers Index: Cephas Pinkham. Private, Wisconsin. Military Unit: 33rd Regiment, Wisconsin Infantry. *Source: NARA*

> 1860 United States Census: Alphus Pinkham (Cephus) Pinkham. Event Place: Clayton, Crawford, Wisconsin. Age – 30; Birth year – 1857. Household of Alphus (Cephus) age 30 born Canada East (Quebec), wife Sarah Pinkham age 31 born New York and children *Frank Pinkham age 9 born Illinois*, William Pinkham age 7 *born Wisconsin 1853* & Samuel Pinkham age 3 born Wisconsin 1857. *Source: United States Census 1860, NARA* Prior entry for brother, Comfort Pinkham, his wife, Cinderella, and children Alta, Orin and Theodocia Pinkham.

1862 Homestead Entry 20 May 1862: Samuel W. Pinkham.
Bureau of Land Management. 162 acres in St. Cloud, Minnesota.

Land was given as per military service. Caleb Pinkham, and his son, Comfort Pinkham also had Homestead Entry on same date in Minnesota:

> *Birth: Joseph Pinkham (m1) born 1861, Wisconsin.*

> *1862 Homestead Entry 20 May 1862: Comfort Pinkham. 162 acres, Taylors Falls, MN. Land next to father, Caleb Pinkham.*

United States Civil War Soldiers Index 1861-1865: Cephus Pinkham.

1870 United States Census: Cephas Pinkham: Birth year 1829-1830 born Canada age 40. Wife – Sarah Pinkham age 41 born New York. Children: William Pinkham age 16 born 1854; Isaac Pinkham age 13 *born Wisconsin 1857*; and Joseph Pinkham age 9 *born Wisconsin 1861.* Source: 1870 US Census, NARA

1875 Wisconsin State Census: Cephus Pinkham. Event Place – Wiota Town, Lafayette, Wisconsin. Number of White Males – 4; Number of White Females – 2. Source: Wisconsin State Census, Wisconsin State Historical Society, Madison

> *Birth: Dora Pinkham (m1) born 1871, Wisconsin.*

1880 United States Census: Cephas Pinkham. Event Place: Wiota, Lafayette, Wisconsin. Age 50, born 1830 in Canada. Married. Farmer. Parent's birthplace: Father/Mother – Canada. Wife: Sarah Pinkham age 51 born New York and daughter, Dora age 9 born United States. Source. NARA

1885 (m2) Marriage of Josephus Pinkham (Cephas Pinkham) – Name – Cephas Pinkham; Event – Marriage; Event Date – 9 September 1885; Event Place – Darlington, Lafayette, Wisconsin, US; Race – White; Birthplace – Lower Canada; Father's Name – Caleb Pinkham; Mother's Name – Mary Downing; Spouse's Name – Lydia A. Fulp; Spouse's Gender – Female; Spouse's Race – White; Spouse's Birthplace – Wisconsin; Spouse's Father's Name – Samuel Fulp; Spouse's Mother's Name – Rachel Smith. Source: Wisconsin County Marriages 1836-1911 Darlington, Lafayette, Wisconsin, United States, Wisconsin Historical Society, Madison

> *Birth: Mary Pinkham (m2) born 1888, Wisconsin.*

> Marriage: William Pinkham to Mary Southerland. Event Date - 27 February 1889 Darlington, Lafayette, Wisconsin. USA.
> Father: Cephas Pinkham. Mother: Sarah Kerns. Spouse's

father: George Southerland. Other: Eliza Brown. Spouse: Mary Southerland.

Marriage: Dora M. Pinkham to D. Charles O' Rourke. Event Date - 4 May 1891 Monroe, Green, Wisconsin. Dora M. Pinkham, born Wiota, Wisconsin. Parents: Spouse's father – Cephas Pinkham. Spouse's Mother – Sarah Kerns. *Source: Wisconsin, County Marriages, 1836-1911, Wisconsin Historical Society, Madison*

1890 Land Grant for Samuel W. Pinkham. St. Cloud, Minnesota. 160 acres. Signed with Cephus Pinkham (Not Isaac Samuel Pinkham born 1857).

1900 United States Census: Cephus Pinkham. Event Place – Wiota Town, Lafayette, Wisconsin. Age – 71 born in Canada. Parent's birthplace: Father/Mother –Canada. Wife, Lydia A. Pinkham, age 50 born Wisconsin. Daughter – Mary Pinkham age 13 born Wisconsin. *Source: 1900 US Census NARA*

1905 United States Census: Cephas Pinkham. Event Place – Wiota, Lafayette, Wisconsin. Age 75 born 1830 Canada. Parents birthplace: Father/Mother – Canada. Married. Head of Household. Wife – Lyda Pinkham age 55 born US. Daughter Mary age 18 born US. *Source: Wisconsin State Census, 1905, State Historical Society, Madison*

1920 United States Census: Cephas Pinkham. Event Place –Blanchard, Lafayette, Wisconsin, United States. Age 91, Married, Head of Household. Proprietor of farm. Born 1829 Canada. Immigration year: 1845. Parent's birthplace: Father/Mother – Canada. Wife – Lydia A. Pinkham age 69 born Wisconsin. Daughter Mary Pinkham age 32 born Wisconsin. *Source: NARA*

Death: Josephus Pinkham. Alias: Cephas. Birth Date – 1 December 1828 (*Lower Canada not Ontario, Canada*). Death date: 12 August 1927 (age 98) Woodford, Lafayette, County, Wisconsin. Burial: Old Argyle Cemetery, Argyle, Lafayette County, Wisconsin. *Source: FindAGrave*

1940 United States Census: Issac C. Pinkham (*not "S" for Samuel*). Age 84 born 1856 Wisconsin. Widowed. Event place: Cadiz, Green, Wisconsin. Last place of residence: Rural, Green County, WI. With son: Charles A. Pinkham born 1914 Wisconsin and his wife, Ronatta Pinkham age 29 born WI.

Death: Isaac Samuel Pinkham. Burial place: Argyle, Lafayette, Wisconsin. Cemetery: Old Argyle Cemetery. Death date: 30 August 1943. Birth: 26 December 1857 Wisconsin. *Source: FindAGrave*

~Comfort Pinkham - Born 1831, Quebec. Death: 1887, Minnesota, USA.

Marriage: 24 July 1853 – Comfort Pinkham. Event Date: 24 July 1853.
Event Place: Wiota, Lafayette, Wisconsin. Spouse's Name:
Cinderella Norton.

Birth: *Orrin Pinkham 1858, Clayton, Crawford, Wisconsin.*

Birth: *Theodocia Pinkham 1860, Clayton, Crawford, Wisconsin.*

1860 United States Census: Comport Pinkham (Comfort Pinkham):
Name: Comport Pinkham; Event type – census; Event date -
1860; Event place – Clayton, Crawford, Wisconsin, United States;
Gender – Male; Age – 29; Race – White; Birth year - 1831;
Birthplace - Canada East; Page -153; Household : Comport
Pinkham – Male-Age 29 - Birthplace – Canada East; Altha Pinkham
– Female – Age 26 – birthplace – New York; Orrin Pinkham – Male
– Age 2 – birthplace – Wisconsin; Theodocia Pinkham – Female –
Age 0 – Birthplace – Wisconsin. *Source: United States Census 1860*

*Entry following is for brother, Cephus Pinkham, wife, Sarah, and children
Frank, William and Samuel Pinkham.*

Franklin, Sauk County in the State of Wisconsin 30 August 1860 Census:
Comfort Pinkham. Name: Comfort Pinkham. Age: 30. Male.
Farmer. 300 acres of farmland owned. Born: Canada West
(*actual: Canada East*). *Married within the year*. Listed with:
Salomon Prickham (Samuel), Male. Age – 16 b. 1844. Born:
State of New York. Wife Altha was born New York - is this her
brother Salomon?

Note: "Samuel W. Pinkham" signed land grants with Cephus Pinkham.

United States Civil War Soldiers Index 1861-1865: Comfort Pinkham.
Private; Military Side – Union; Military State – Wisconsin – 7th
Regiment Infantry. *Source: United States Civil War Soldiers Index, 1861-1865*

United States Civil War Soldiers Index 1861-1865 - Comfort Pinkham.
Event Place: New York, United States. Event Place: New York.
Event Beginning Rank: Private. Military side: Union. Military Unit:
76th Regiment, New York Infantry. Military Company: C. Note:
See also 7 Wisconsin Volunteers.

1862 Homestead Entry 20 May 1862: Comfort Pinkham. 162 acres,
Taylors Falls, MN. Land next to father, Caleb Pinkham.

Birth: *James Pinkham b. 1865, Clayton, Crawford, Wisconsin.*

1870 United States Census: Comfort Pinkham. Name: Comfort
Pinkham; Event Year – 1870; Event Place – Minnesota, United
States; Gender – Male; Age – 39; Race – White; Occupation –
Farmer; Birth year – 1830-1831; Birthplace – Canada; Household:
Comfort Pinkham – Male – Age 39 - Birthplace – Canada; Altha
Pinkham – Female – Age 27 – Birthplace – New York; Orin
Pinkham – Male – Age 15 - Birthplace – Wisconsin; Theodore
(Theodosia) Pinkham – Female – Age 10 – Birthplace – Wisconsin;
James Pinkham – Male – Age 5 (born 1865) – Birthplace –
Wisconsin. *Source: United States Census, 1870. NARA*

1875 Minnesota Census: Comfort Pinkham. Name: Comfort Pinkham;
Event Place – Milo, Mille Lacs, Minnesota; Age – 43; Birth Year –
1832; Father's birthplace – Canada; Mother's birthplace – Canada;
Race – White; Gender – Male; Household – Comfort
Pinkham/M/birthplace – Canada; Ammarica Pinkham/F/birthplace –
New York; Altha Pinkham/F/Birthplace Wisconsin; Theodosia
Pinkham/F/birthplace Wisconsin; James Pinkham/M/Wisconsin.
*Source: Minnesota State Census, 1875; Volume McLeod, Martin, Meeker and Mille Lacs Country,
State Library and Record Service, St. Paul*

1880 United States Census: Comfort Pinkham. Comfort Pinkham age
49 born 1829 Canada, Farmer. Wife: Aurilla Pinkham age 40 born
1840 New York with son James Pinkham age 14 born 1866
Wisconsin and son Ovrin Pinkham age 22 born 1858 Wisconsin.
Source: United States Census, NARA

United States General Index to Pension Files: Comfort Pinkham. Event:
Pension. Event Date: 1883. Event Place – Minnesota, US.
Beneficiary's Name: Ammarilla Pinkham. *Source: United States General Index
to Pension Files, 1861-1934*

United States Civil War and Later Pension Index: Comfort Pinkham.
Name: Comfort Pinkham; Event Type – Pension; Event Date – 25
May 1885; Event Place – Wisconsin, United States; Military
Regiment – 7; Military Unit – Infantry; Military Rank – -; Shipping
Company – 1; File Name – 21111720. *Source: United States Civil War and Later
Pension Index, 1861-1917, NARA*

1885 Minnesota State Census: Comfort Pinkham. Location: Blue Hill,
Sherburne, Minnesota. Comfort Pinkham age 55, Born abt. 1830
Canada. Wife: Amerilla Pinkham age 51 born Virginia 1834 and
James W. Pinkham age 19 born Wisconsin 1866. *Source: Minnesota State
Census, 1885*

1916 Death of Altha Cone – Father: Comfort Pinkham. Name –
Altha Cone;   Gender – Female; Death date – 12 January 1916;
Death place – Foreston, Mille Lacs, Minnesota; Age – 61; birthdate
– 27 April 1854; Race – White; Father's Name: Comfort Pinkham;

Mother's name – Emmerella Northen. *Source: Minnesota Deaths and Burials,* `
1835-1990

Son: <u>Orin Pinkham</u>: <u>1895 Minnesota State Census</u>: Foreston
Village, Milles Lac, Minnesota: Orin Pinkham born 1883
Wisconsin. With wife, Lydia age 32 born Minnesota.
Children: Warren J. Pinkham age 12 Minnesota, Roy L.
Pinkham born 10 Minnesota and Nettie Pinkham born 8 MN.

Warren Pinkham b. 1865 WI son: <u>Warren James Pinkham</u>:
<u>1905 Minnesota State Census, Princeton Township,
Mills Lacs</u>: Warren Pinkham born 1883 Minnesota.
Father born Wisconsin. Mother born South Dakota.
<u>1942 United States WW2 Draft</u>: Warren James
Pinkham, Age 58. Date: 27 Apritl 1942. Birthdate: 5
June 1883 Blue Hill, MN. Height: 5'5". Employer:
Son Line Railroad.
<u>Death</u>: Wife of Warren Pinkham: Alma E.
Pinkham. Age 67 born 1895 Sweden. Death
date: 26 November 1952. Burial: Hennepin,
Minnepolis, MN. Spouse: Warren J. Pinkham.
Parents: Claus Samuelson and Christine M.
Gustafson.
<u>Death</u>: Warren J. Pinkham: Burial: Hennepin,
Minneapolis, MN. Cemetery: Hillside Cemetery.
Death date: 1965. Birth: 1883.

~<u>Huldah Pinkham Pickett</u>: Born 1834, Ohio.

1850 United States Census, Wiota, Lafayette County Wisconsin:
Nelson Picket age 20 born 1830 New York, with Hiram,
Harriet, John, Louisa, Charles and Augustine Picket.

<u>Marriage</u>: 23 October 1853. Nelson Picket born New York. Father:
Hiram Picket. Mother: Louisa Picket. Spouse: Huldah Pinkham.
Father Caleb Pinkham. Mother: Mary Pinkham. Marriage Place:
Cadiz Green, Wisconsin, United States. *Source; Wisconsin Marriages, 1836-*
1920

<u>1855 Wisconsin Census</u>: Nelson Pickett, Wiota, Lafayette, Wisconsin.

<u>1860 United States Census</u>: Wiota, Lafayette, Wisconsin. Hulda Pickett
born 1834 Ohio with Nelson Pickett and children: George, Mary,
Phebe and Byron Pickett.

United States Civil War Soldier's Index, 1861-1865; Wisconsin:
Nelson Pickett.

<u>1870 United States Census</u>, Wiota, Lafayette County, Wisconsin. Nelson Picket born 1830 New York with Huldah Picket born 1835 Ohio and George, Mary, Phebe, Bryan and Henen Picket.

1875 Wisconsin State Census: Nelson Picket, Wiota, Lafayette, WI.

<u>1880 United States Census</u>, Wiota, Lafayette County, Wisconsin. Nelson Picket, born 1830 New York. Spouse: Hulda Picket. With Keenen C., Louise, Urilla, Utilla & Hiram Picket.

<u>1890 United States Census of the Union</u>: Nelson Pickett. Wiota, Lafayette, Wisconsin.

<u>1910 United States Census</u>: Jordan, Green, Wisconsin. Nelson Picket born 1830 New York. Spouse: Huldah Pickett. With Grant Picket.

<u>Married</u>: Hiram Pickett born Lafayette County, Wisconsin. Marriage of Hiram Pickett born Lafayette, County, Wisconsin. Father: Nelson Pickett. Mother: Huldah Pinkham. Marriage date: 28 October 1895. Marriage Place: Monroe, Green Wisconsin. Spouse: Julia Ableman, born Lafayette County, Wisconsin. Father: Christian Ableman. Mother: Emma Dennse.

<u>Wisconsin Marriages</u>: Nelson Pickett; Spouse: Huldah Pinkham. For children: Byron Pickett to Camie Bell Way; George Pickett to Rosina Campbell; Hiram Pickett to Julia Ableman; Urilla Pickett to Charles Miller; Mary E. Pickett to Ezekial Schultz and Hattie Pickett to Peter D. Ableman.

Nelson Pickett, father <u>Wisconsin Death Records, 1867-1907</u>. Spouse: Hulda Pickett. Son: George Pickett.

Death of Nelson Pickett: 2 June 1910, age 80 (born 28 November 1829). Monroe, Green County, Wisconsin. Burial: Old Argyle Cemetery, Lafayette County, Wisconsin.

From cemetery records: Nelson Picket born 28 November 1829 in Spafford, Onondaga County, New York, the son of Hiram and Harriet (Pulsipher) Picket. He was one of six siblings. He married Hulda Pinkham on 23 October 1852 in Cadiz, Green County, Wisconsin. They were parents of twelve children: George, Mary, Phebe, Byron, Heenan, Sarah, Louise, Utilla, Urilla, Hiram, Grant and Harriet Pickett.

Of Huldah Pinkham, if buried here with Nelson there is no stone or markings that she is. Source: FindAGrave

~Henry Pinkham: Born 1837, Ohio. Died 2 April 1907, Goldfield, Iowa.

1859 Marriage of Henry Pinkham: Name: Henry Pinkham; Event type –
Marriage; Event date – 27 September 1859; Event place – La
Crosse, Wisconsin, United States; Gender – Male; Birthplace –
Ohio; Father's name – Caleb Pinkham; Mother's name – Mary
Pinkham; Spouse's name – Miranda Abigail Oviatt; Spouse's
gender – Female. *Source: Wisconsin, County Marriage, 1836-1911, La Crosse, Wisconsin,
United States, Wisconsin Historical Society, Madison*

1860 United States Census: Henry Pinkham. Event Place: Argyle,
Lafayette, Wisconsin. Age 24 born 1836 Ohio. Wife – Miranda
Pinkham age 22 born Ohio. Son William Pinkham age X month
(under age 1) born Wisconsin. *Source: United States Census: 1860. NARA*

1862 Iowa, Records of Persons Subject to Military Duty - 1862-1910.
Henry Pinkham age 37. Event Place: Eagle Grove, Wright, Iowa.

1870 United States Census: Henry Pinkum (Pinkham). Event Place:
Adams, Green, Wisconsin. Age 33 born 1836-1837 Ohio. Wife:
Miranda Pinkum age 32 born Ohio. Pinkham children born in
Wisconsin: Wallington age 10; Ellen age 8, Abigail age 6; William
age 4; Henry age 2. *Source: United States Census, 1870, NARA*

1880 United States Census Liberty, Wright County, Iowa: Henry
Pinkham. Age 42 born 1838 Ohio, Wife Miranda Pinkham age 42
born Ohio. Children: Wellington Pinkham born 1860 Wisconsin
with Pinkham siblings born Wisconsin -- Ellen born 1862, Abigail
born 1867, Sherman age 14 born 1866 & Henry age 12 born 1868
plus children born Iowa - Royal age 4 born 1876 and Edith age 2
born 1878.

1885 Iowa States Census, Liberty, Wright, Iowa: Henry Pinkham. Age 47
born 1838. Wife, Miranda. Children: Wellington age 24, Abbie age
20, Sherman age 18, Henry age 15, Royal age 9 and Edith age 5.

Death: Henry Pinkham. Age 69. Death: 2 April 1907. Location:
Goldfield, Wright County, Iowa. Married. Birthplace: Ohio.
Occupation: Farmer.

Iowa Deaths & Burials: Henry Pinkham. Age 69. Death: 2 April 1907.
Burial: 4 April 1907. Death Place (original): Liberty. Death
Location: Goldfield, Iowa. Birthdate: 1 August 1837 Ohio.
Occupation: Farmer. Father's name: Caleb Pinkham. Mother's
name: Mary Downing.

Children of Henry and Miranda Pinkham:

Iowa, County Marriage: Marriage date: 21 December 1897.
Marriage Location: Humbolt, Iowa. <u>Henry Clay Pinkham</u> Age 31
born 1866. Father's name: Henry Pinkham; Mother's name:
Miranda Ovatt. Spouses name: Elizabeth Florence Hinton.
Spouse age: 23 born 1874. Spouse's parents: Simon V. and
Elizabeth Hinton.

Daughter born to <u>Henry C. Pinkham</u>: Nellie Fern Pinkham born 15
September 1898 in Iowa. Father's name: Henry C. Pinkham.
Mother's name: Elizabeth Hinton.

Daughter Ellen Pinkham. Marriage: <u>Iowa County Marriages</u>: 18
October 1882, Goldfield, Wright County, Iowa. Ellen E. Pinkham to
W. H. Overbaugh age 33 born 1849 Ohio, son of Charles N.
Overbaugh and Eliza J. Davigans. Ellen E. Pinkham age 21 born
1861 Wisconsin. Father: <u>Henry Pinkham</u>. Mother: Miranda
Oveatt.

Death: <u>Henry Clay Pinkham</u>. Burial: Goldfield, Wright
County, Iowa. Cemetery: Glenwood Cemetery. Death date:
26 May 1945. Birth date: 15 November 1867. *Source: FindAGrave*

Obituary: (*Source: <u>Goldfield Chronicle</u>*) - *Services for H. C. Pinkham. Prominent Wright County
Died Wednesday Following Two Years of Failing Health and Illness. Henry C. Pinkham,
age 86, one of Wright Counties first citizens, died early Wednesday morning at his
home in Goldfield following two years of failing health. Funeral Services have been set
for Saturday at 2:30 in the Methodist Church with the Rev. Frank C. Green in charge.
Burial will be at the Goldfield Cemetery. Mr. Pinkham was born in Wisconsin in 1867
but resided most of his life in Wright County and the Goldfield area. He lived for about a
year as a youth in Nebraska. He also operated a drug store in Livermore for a short
time, and in Goldfield, too.*

*Life of Service: Mr. Pinkham's life has been one of public service, dedicated to the
building of a better community and country. He served for 24 years as Supervisor of
Wright County. He was active and instrumental in the development of the extensive
county drainage system and had a great part also in putting every Wright county farm
on an all-weather road. Mr. Pinkham has a part in developing the drainage system from
30 drainage ditches in the county to 234. His road record is just as startling in the
increase of miles. He served for 18 years on the Goldfield school board, on the official
board of the Methodist church, on the board of the Farmers Elevator Co. He also
headed the Red Cross and promoted the Old Settlers picnic in Goldfield for many years.*

*Few men have had so active and prominent part in the growth and development ot this
country. It is impossible to list all his many good deeds and accomplishments both in
public office and private life. Always his outlook was optimistic and progressive. He*

tempered this optimism with good judgement and thereby achieved a reputation for himself that will be undying.

He is survived by his wife and one son, Glenn, both of Goldfield, and a sister, Mrs. Ellen Overbaugh, 91 of Spokane, Washington. He was preceded in death by a daughter and a brother, Wellington, who died last year.

Mr. and Mrs. Pinkham celebrated their Golden wedding anniversary at their home on Sunday, December 21, 1947, being honored with more than 200 guests.

Out-of-town relations attending: Mr. & Mrs. Allan Herrick; Mr. & Mrs. James Stewart of Des Moines; Mr. & Mrs. Charles Pinkham, Cedar Falls: Mr. & Mrs. Ed Bygness; Mrs. Fern Klasse Renwick; Dr. Lon Overbaugh and son Mitchell, S. D.: Mr. Lake Hinton, Lake Park; Mr. and Mrs. Dowell Hinton, Round Lake, MN; Mr. and Mrs. Harry Hinton and daughter, Worthington, MN; Mrs. Victor Bargman, Rodman; Mr. & Mrs. Vane Graham, Conrad; Mrs. Eddie Donweilter; Mr. and Mrs. Burns and granddaughter; Mr. and Mrs. B. J. Anliker, Mrs. Elizabeth Anilier, West Bend.
Source: *Eagle Grove Eagle*, Eagle Grove, Iowa, Thursday, June 3, 1954

Wellington Pinkham: 1895 Iowa Census: Wellington Pinkham. Age 34 born 1861. Event place: Wright, Iowa. 1910 United States Census: Liberty, Wright County, Iowa: Wellington Pinkham. Age 49 born 1861 Wisconsin. Parents born Ohio. Wife Nellie age 35 born Wisconsin. Children born Iowa: Margie age 13 born 1897 and Josephine age 6 born 1904.
Death: 1944 Iowa.

~Phebe Ann Pinkham Crook: Born – 3 August 1840, Geauga, Ohio. Death – 13 January 1872, Mille Lacs, Minnesota. Cemetery: Milo Cemetery. Source: FindAGrave
Husband Geroge Crook died 27 July 1900 Princeton, Mille Lacs, MN. Children likely: Lillian Alfreda Crook, Comfort Crook, Hannah Crook & Samuel Crook. Phebe Pinkham Crooks named children for uncles Comfort and Samuel.

~Caleb Pinkham, Junior: Born 10 July 1846, Geauga, Ohio.
Death: 22 June 1926, Princeton, Mille Lacs, MN.
(Buried with father, Caleb Pinkham).
(M1) Elvira Slater (b. 1838, New York).
(M2) On 29 Dec. 1910 to Grace Orton (b. 1886, MN).

United States Civil War Soldiers Index 1861-1865: Caleb Pinkham.

1870 United States Census: C. J. Pinkham. Age 25 born 1844-1845 Ohio. Wife – Elvira Pinkham age 32 born New York. Child: Harriet Pinkham age 3 born Minnesota. Source: *United States Census, 1870 NARA*

1875 Minnesota State Census: Caleb Pinkham. Event Place: Princeton, Mille Lacs, Minnesota. Age – 30. Birth year – 1845. Father's birthplace – Canada. Mother's birthplace – Canada. Wife – Elvira Pinkham born New York. Step-sons – William Slater, Charles Slater & Dewitt Slater. Children: Hattie E. Pinkham and Melina A. Pinkham born Minnesota. *Source: 1875 Minnesota State Census NARA*

1880 United States Census: Caleb Pinkham. Event Place – Princeton, Mille Lacs, Minnesota. Age – 35, Married. Farmer. Born 1845 Ohio. Parent's birthplace -Vermont (Lower Canada). Wife: Elvira Pinkham age 47 born New York. Step-son –D. C. Slater age 15 born Minnesota. Pinkham daughters born Minnesota: Hattie, age 12, Melinda, age 8, Jessie age 4. *Source: 1880 US Census, NARA*

1885, Minnesota State Census: Caleb Pinkham. Event Place: Princeton, Mille Lacs, Minnesota. Age 39 years. Born 1846 Ohio. Wife: Elivra Pinkham age 52 born New York. Daughters born Minnesota: Hattie age 18, Lunnie age 13, and Jessie age 9 Pinkham. *Source: Minnesota State Census 1885 Traverse, Mille Lacs, Pine, Benton State Library record*

1900 United States Census: Caleb Pinkham. Event Place: Greenbush & Princeton Townships, Princeton Village, Mille Lacs, Minnesota. Caleb Pinkham, head of Household, age 55 born Ohio July 1845. Marriage year – 1865. Parent's birthplace (Canada) – Vermont. Wife – Elvira Pinkham age 68 born New York. Nephew – Warren Pinkham age 17 born Minnesota. Servant – Grace Orton age 15 born Minnesota. *Source: United States Census, 1900, NARA*

Nephew "Warren Pinkham born 1883 Minnesota." Likely the son of Henry Pinkham, as brother's Josephus and Comfort Pinkham's children born WI.

1905 Minnesota State Census: Caleb J. Pinkham. Event Place – Princeton Township, Mille Lacs, Minnesota. Age 60 born Ohio 1845. Father's birthplace – Vermont; Mother's birthplace – New Hampshire. *Source. Minnesota State Census, 1905*

Marriage: 29 December 1910 – Caleb J. Pinkham of Custer County, Minnesota to Grace Orton of Custer County Minnesota. Event Place: St. Paul, Ramsey, Minnesota. *Source: Minnesota Marriage, 1849-1950*

1920 United States Census: Caleb Pinkham. Event place – Minneapolis Ward 8, Hennipin, Minnesota. Caleb Pinkham, head of household age 74, married born 1846 Ohio. Renter. Parent's birthplace – Vermont (Canada). Wife – Grace Pinkham age 34 born Minnesota. Children – Edith J. Pinkham age 7 born Nebraska. Grace A.

Pinkham age 3 born Minnesota. Caleb A. Pinkham age 1-12 months born Minnesota. *Source: United States Census 1920, NARA*

Death: 11 June 1926: Caleb Jr. Pinkham. Name – Caleb Jr. Pinkham; Gender – Male; Death Date – 22 June 1926; Death Place – Minneapolis, Hennepin, Minnesota; Age – 80; Birth date – 1846; Marital status – Married; Spouse's name – Grace; Father's name – Caleb Pinkham; Mother's name – Mary Downing. *Source: Minnesota Deaths and Burials, 1835-1990, Minnesota*

Burial: Caleb J. Pinkham. Birth Date – 10 June 1845. Death Date: 22 June 1926. Event Place – Princeton, Mille Lacs, Minnesota. Cemetery: Oak Knoll Cemetery. *Source: FindAGrave*

After moving from Quebec to Geauga, Ohio, a city founded by the Phelps family, with sister, Huldah Pinkham Warren (Seth Warren), the Caleb Pinkham family moved to Wiota, Wisconsin in 1855 before settling in Mille Lacs, Minnesota by 1861. Caleb Pinkham's son, Josephus Pinkham, and daughter Huldah Pinkham Pickett remained in Wiota, Wisconsin as did his brother, J. Samuel Pinkham and cousin, Calvin Pinkham, the son of Abijah and Hannah (Sleeper) Pinkham. Joining Caleb Pinkham in Mille Lacs, Minnesota were sons, Comfort Pinkham and Caleb Pinkham, Jr. plus daughter, Phebe Pinkham Crook. Caleb's nephew, Huldah Pinkham Warren's child, moved to Fillmore, Minnesota by 1880, as did his brother, Comfort Pinkham's son, Edwin Pinkham. Samuel and Theodocia's son and Caleb's brother, Joseph Abijah Pinkham, moved from Quebec to Minnesota with the Jeremiah Phelps family then moved to 1900 California.

Caleb Pinkham's sons, Josephus, Comfort and Caleb Jr., all married women born in New York, and Comfort was recorded residing in the 1860 alongside census "*Samuel Pinkham, age 16 born 1844 New York.*" Comfort Pinkham enlisted with both the Wisconsin military and New York Militia during the Civil War. The New York connection is unconfirmed. Josephus Pinkham married Sarah Kerns (b 1829, NY), Comfort Pinkham married Cinderella Norton (b. 1834, NY) and Caleb, Jr. married Elvira Slater (b. 1838, NY). *Samuel (W.) Pinkham b. 1844 New York listed in 1860 census with Comfort Pinkham. Samuel W. Pinkham signed land grants with Cephus and Caleb Pinkham. Whether NY-born Samuel W. Pinkham was Samuel III's son is unproven.*

The grandchildren of Caleb and Mary (Dowling) Pinkham (Generation 9) were:
Children of Josephus Pinkham:

Frank Pinkham	(b. 29 February 1852 IL)
William Pinkham	(b. 1853 WI)
Isaac *Samuel* Pinkham	(b. 26 December 1857 WI)
Joseph Pinkham	(b. 1861 WI)
Dora Pinkham	(b 1871 WI)
Mary Pinkham (m2)	(b. 1888 WI)

Children of Comfort Pinkham:

Orrin Pinkham	(b. 1858 WI)
Theodocia Pinkham	(b. 1860 WI)

James Pinkham	(b. 1865 WI)

Children of Henry Pinkham:

Wellington William Pinkham	(b. 1859 WI)
Ellen Pinkham	(b. 1862 WI)
Abigail Pinkham	(b. 1864 WI)
Sherman William Pinkham	(b. 1866 WI)
Henry Pinkham	(b. 1868 WI)
Royal Pinkham	(b. 1876 IA)
Edith Pinkham	(b. 1878 IA)

Children of Caleb, Jr. Pinkham:

Harriet Pinkham	(b. 1867 MN)
Melina Pinkham	(b. 1872 MN)
Jessie Pinkham	(b. 1876 MN)
Edith J. Pinkham (m2)	(b. 1913 NE)
Grace A. Pinkham (m2)	(b. 1917 MN)
Caleb A. Pinkham III (m2)	(b. 1920 MN)

~COMFORT CARPENTER PINKHAM (2) (Generation 7): (*Story to follow siblings*)

Born abt.   1811, Quebec

Married: 1832 to Elizabeth Phelps (b. 1812) in Freilghsburg, Quebec at the Holy Trinity Anglican Church

Death: Estimated during 1855, Clarke County, Ontario, Canada

The children of Comfort and Elizabeth (Phelps) Pinkham (Generation 8) were Cynthia, Electra, Mary, Willard, Edwin, John Wesley, Phebe Jane, Samuel and Charles W. Pinkham.

~Huldah Pinkham Warren (3) (Generation 7):

Birth: Born abt. 1815, Quebec. Married Seth Warren 1831, Abbotsford, Quebec.

Huldah Pinkham's birth year varied per record. In 1831 if she was born 1813 she would have been age 18 at marriage date. Brother Comfort Pinkham was born 1811.

Marriage: 1831: Name: Huldah Pinkham. Spouse: Seth Warren, Marriage year – 1831. Marriage location: Abbotsford, Quebec. Religion – Protestant (Anglican). Place of worship: Protestant (*Anglican*). *Source: Drouin*

"On the sixteenth of November one thousand eight hundred and thirty-one, Seth Warren, Bachelor from _ and Huldah Pinkham, Spinster, both of major age … in marriage in the presence of her father and his brother." Signed by: Seth Warren, Huldah Pinkham, Oliver Warren, **Betsy Phelps** and **Sam G. Pinkham**. Location: Abbotsford, St. Hyacinthe, Quebec.

While document states "in presence of her father and his brother (Oliver Warren)," it is signed by Comfort Carpenter Pinkham's 1832 wife– *Betsy Phelps* – and Sam G. Pinkham, Huldah Pinkham's father.

Death: Post 1880, Painesville, Lake County, Ohio, USA

The Children of Huldah Pinkham and Seth Warren (Generation 8):
> ~Emily Warren: Born 1836/1837, Canada. Died 26 October 1920, Painesville, Lake County, Ohio. Married Joseph Caddoo 1865. Immigration year to Ohio – 1869 (From 1920 United States Census – Parents born: Canada. Children: Minnie Caddoo Becker (b. 1870; d. 1950) & Robert Caddoo (b. 1886; d. 1921).
> ~Huldah Jane Warren: Born 1850. Marriage Huldah Jane Warren to Addison Gooden. Date: 21 May 1850, Lake, Ohio, USA.
> ~Emma Warren: Born 1851 – Malbaie, Bas Canada.
> ~Alice Warren: Born 1852.
> ~David C. Warren: Born 1862 Fillmore, Minnesota. S. K. Warren – birth of son, David C. Warren: Mother's name: Huldah Warren Father's name – S. K. Warren. 1882 Fillmore Minnesota.

(Brother, Caleb Pinkham, named daughter, Huldah Pinkham, after his sister, Huldah.)

> Seth K. Warren, husband of Huldah Pinkham:
> Ohio Tax Records 1826, 1827, 1828, *1829**, 1830, 1831, 1833
> *1829** Ohio City Land Tax Records: Name: Seth Warren; Event Place – Salem Township, Ashtuabula, Ohio; Taxation Type – City Land; Event date – 1829. *Source: Ohio Tax Records, 1800-1850, Ohio Genealogy Society.*
> 1830 Salem Township, Ashtabula, Ohio County Land Grant – Seth Warren *Source: Ohio Tax Records, 1800-1850.*
> 1831 Salem Township, Ashtabula, Ohio County Land Grant – Seth Warren. *Source: Ohio Tax Records, 1800 – 1850.*
> 1833 Conneaut Township, Ashtabula Ohio County Land Grant – Seth Warren. *Source – Ohio Tax Records, 1800-1850.*

1851 Quebec Census: Seth Warren, Milton-Shefford, Quebec. Age 49 born 1812 Bas. Canada, Married.

Moved to Fillmore, Minnesota between 1851 and 1862 (son born 1862 MN).

1870 United States Census: Huldah Warren. Name – Huldah Warren; Event type – census; Event place – Ohio, United States; Gender – Female, Age – 54; Race – White; Birth year – 1815-1816; birthplace – Canada. Household: Seth Warren – Farmer – birthplace Lower Canada – birth year 1810-1811 – Age 59; Huldah Warren – birthplace Lower Canada – birth year 1815-1816 – Age 54. *Source: United States Census, Ohio, NARA*

1870 Ohio Census – Chardon, Geauga, Ohio – Joseph Caddoo age 34 born
1836 Canada, wife Emily (Warren) Caddoo age 33 born 1837 Canada
with Alice Warren age 18 born 1852 Canada.)
(Joseph Caddoo – Naturalization Ohio 1874. Born Canada)

(Seth Warren died between 1871 and 1880.)

1880 United States Census: Huldah Warren. Name: Hulda Warren; Age – 63; Birth
year – abt. 1817; Birthplace – Canada; Home in 1880 – Painesville, Lake, Ohio;
Race – White; Gender – Female; Relation to Head of House – Mother-in-law;
Marital Status – Widowed; Father's birthplace – Massachusetts; Mother's
birthplace – Massachusetts. (Not Quebec). Household members: Joseph
Caeddoo, age 46; Emily Caeddoo, age 44; Minnie Caeddoo, age 9; Hulda
Warren, Age 63. *Source: 1880 United States Census, NARA*

Possible Caeddoo misspelling: Cadeaux. Emily Warren Cadeaux – b.
1836. (1861 Quebec Census: Emily Warren, Event Place – Milton,
Shefford, Quebec; Age – 24, Birth year – 1837; Birthplace – Bas. Canada;
Marital Status – Single; Religion – E. *Source: Quebec Census 1861, Public Archives QC*

1920 United States Census, Painesville, Lake County, Ohio – Joseph Caddoo
age 87 born Canada and wife Emily Caddoo age 85 born Canada and son
Robert Caddoo age 34 born 1886 Ohio.

Death: Emily Warren Cadoo d. 26 October 1920, Painesville, Lake
Country, Ohio, USA.
Death: Joseph Caddoo buried Evergreen Cemetery, 1922
Painesville, Lake, Ohio. d. 3 April 1922. *Source:* FindAGrave Wife
Emily Warren Cadoo 1837-1920; married 1865).

Married: Minnie Caddoo, daughter of Emily Warren Caddoo, to
Samuel Becker. The daughter of Minnie Caddoo and
Samuel Becker was Nellie H. Becker who married 7
December 1922 to Newman Rocco.

Death: Seth A. Warren d. 1 April 1919, Ashtabula, Ohio, USA

~James O. Pinkham (4) (Generation 7) – Born 1816, Quebec. Married 1842,
Mathilde Tetreau-Duchame, St. Pie, Quebec. Died 3 June 1902, Tewkesbury,
Massachusetts, USA. *Source: MA Wills & Probates.*

There are no confirmed records of James O. Pinkham until his Massachusetts death.
Rehoboth Carpenter ancestors of Comfort Carpenter, the father of Theodocia
Carpenter, cofounded the original colony. Uncle Joseph Pinkham resided in Grafton,
MA. James O. Pinkham is recorded as being a farmer near Haverhill, Massachusetts
where he died at age 86. His parents are listed as "Samuel and Theodocia" born
Canada. James O. Pinkham was born in Canada but his parents parents were not.

Although little is known about James O., his brother, J. Samuel Pinkham married Domitilde Chartier, a relation to Rosina Chartier, the wife of brother Joseph Abijah Pinkham who moved to Mower, Minnesota. James O. Pinkham married Mathilde Tetreau-Duchame in 1842 prior to his brother J. Samuel's 1844 marriage at the same location. The children born to Mathilde and James O. Pinkham were likely James Pinkham (b. 1845 Quebec) and Charles A. Pinkham (b. 1851 Quebec), as well as, a Samuel Pinkham who died 1866 Quebec. James O. Pinkham married in St. Pie, Quebec by 1842, then moved to Minnesota as did his younger brother, Joseph Abijah Pinkham along with the Jeremiah Phelps family and youngest brother Samuel III.

St. Pie, QC Marriage records:
1842 St. Pie, QC   m.   James Pinkham   Mathilde Tetreau-Duchame
1844 St. Pie, QC   m.   J. Samuel Pinkham   Domitilde Chartier

The children *speculated* of James O. and Mathilde (Tetreau-Duchame) Pinkham:

~James Pinkham- Born 1845, Canada.
1875 Red Wing City, Goodhue, Minnesota State Census:
        James Pinkham born 1845 Canada.

~Samuel Pinkham: Born abt. 1847-1850; d. 1866, Quebec.

~Charles A. Pinkham: Born 1851, Canada.
Marriage: 10 October 1873 - Charles A. Pinkham to Ella G.
        Palver. Location: Faribault, Minnesota, USA.
1875 Blue Earth City, Faribault, Minnesota State
        Census: C. A. (Charles A. Pinkham). Wife: Ella
        Pinkham born Wisconsin with *G. B.* Pinkham.
1876 Birth: Harriet M. Pinkham. Birth Date: 6 May 1876.
        Location: Blue Earth City Township, Faribault,
        Minnesota, USA. Father: Charles A. Pinkham.
        Mother: Ella G. (Palver) Pinkham.
1880 United States Census Blue Earth City, Farabault, MN:
        Charles A. Pinkham, Wife: Ella J. Pinkham, Hattie
        Pinkham born 1876 Minnesota.
1880 Blue Earth City Faribault, Minnesota census: Chas. A.
        Pinkham. Age 29 born 1851. Married. Occupation:
        Hotel Keeper. Father's birthplace: *New Hampshire*.
        Mother's birthplace: *New Hampshire*.

From baptismal records Quebec: The children of James and Mathilde Pinkham
        1849 St. Cecile de Milton   Joseph Pinkham
        1849 St. Cecile de Milton   Marie-Matilda Pinkham
        1850 St. Cecile de Milton   Charles Pinkham

Brother "J. Samuel" Pinkham's sons were Josephus and Cephus Pinkham. Samuel G. Pinkham Jr.'s brother, Joseph Pinkham, had moved to Massachusetts by 1839. Curious is a record for Charles E. Pinkham (b. 1850; d. 12 November 1931 Springfield, MA) as the father is listed: Caleb Pinkham. Caleb Pinkham from this line did not have a son named Charles. Likely Joseph and Marie-Matilda Pinkham were children born different years after 1842 or the wife of James Pinkham (Marie Mathilde) was baptized.

Death: James O. Pinkham. Death date: 3 June 1902. Death Place: Tewkesbury, Massachusetts. Father's name: Samuel. Mother's name: Theodocia. Age 86 years. Birth year: 1816. Country born: Canada. Parent's born: Canada. Occupation: Farmer. *Source: Massachusetts Deaths, 1841-1915*

~J. Samuel Pinkham (5) (Generation 7): Born abt. 1825-1826, Quebec. Died 1879, Union, Rock County, Wisconsin, USA.

Married (m1) Domitilde Chartier in 1844 (at least two children born)/(m2) Betsy Higgens. Son Joseph Pinkham, born 1846 Quebec, named for uncle (J. Samuel age 19); son Cephas Pinkham born 1847 (J. Samuel age 20). Domitilde Chartier likely died 1847.

The initial "J" possibly was incorrect on the marriage record as on the Wisconsin death record as it changes to, "B." "Joseph" could not have been his first name because his brother Joseph Abijah was named as such, nor was it "James," as another brother was "James O." Even more curious, is the youngest child of Samuel Junior and Theodocia (Carpenter) Pinkham was named Samuel and recorded as Samuel Pinkham III in Mower, Minnesota, the same city his brother, Joseph Abijah Pinkham, had moved with the Jeremiah Phelps family. Adding to the mystery is a Samuel W. Pinkham.

St. Pie, Quebec Marriage records:
1842 St. Pie, QC   m.   James Pinkham   Mathilde Tetreau-Duchame
1844 St. Pie, QC   m.   J. Samuel Pinkham Domitilde Chartier

Brother, Joseph Abijah Pinkham, married Rosina Chartier (sister or relation of Domitilde Chartier). A son, Samuel Pinkham born New York in 1844, was perhaps the oldest child of Samuel and Domitilde (Chartier) Pinkham. Sons born 1846 and 1847, include one named for uncle, Joseph Pinkham.

1855 Wisconsin State Census: S. Pinkham: Name – S. Pinkham; Event Place - Union, Rock, Wisconsin; Number of white males – 4; Number of white females – Foreign Born – 9. *Source: Wisconsin State Census 1855, Wisconsin State Historical Society, Madison.*

Uncle Joseph Pinkham lived in Wisconsin during 1858 where youngest child (m3) was born. Cousin Amy Pinkham, eldest child of Joseph Pinkham and m1, resided with Mason family relations in Wisconsin during 1870.

1860 United States Census: Samuel Pinkham (Born 1827). Age 33.
     Resided near eldest brother Caleb Pinkham listed on same census page – Caleb Pinkham age 50 (Born 1810), his wife Mary and son, Caleb Junior age 15 born

Ohio. Samuel Pinkham family – farmer. Wife – Betsy age 47 (Born abt 1813 born Canada East). Pinkham children born Lower Canada: Halow Mason, male age 22, *Emily Mason age 18 borrn 1842 Quebec,* Jane Mason age 14 born 1846 Quebec, <u>Joseph Pinkham</u> - *not Mason,* age 14 born 1846 Quebec, Olivia age 11, <u>Cephas Pinkham</u> - *not Mason,* age 13 born 1847 Quebec, Charles Mason, age 10 and, Mary Mason, age- 8. *Source. United States Census 1860, NARA.* If Samuel W. Pinkham born New York 1844 and the eldest child of Samuel and Domitilde, he would have been age 16 in 1860 and is missing from Wisconsin census.

Note surnames are incorrect and a mix of Higgens, Pinkham and Mason individuals.

The Quebec/Vermont Pinkham - Higgens - Mason family connection is not defined but on 30 October 1850 Michael Mason was naturalized in Wisconsin *(Source: Wisconsin, County Naturalization Records, 1807-1992).* Charles Mason, listed in Samuel Pinkham's 1860 Wisconsin census, is noted in a Pine Valley, Clark, Wisconsin marriage record for 10 March 1879 as marrying Delaphane Delane and defined as born in Canada, as well as, an American citizen whose father was Michael Mason and mother was Clemans Mason. Neither Mason parents were listed on the 1860 Samuel Pinkham census while the children of Michael Mason were, and Emily Higgens (daughter of Betsy Higgens?) married Edward Mason, also not listed on the census. Interestingly, the Mason 1870 Rutland, Dane County, Wisconsin census lists Amy Pinkham, Joseph Pinkham's daughter born 1815.

> <u>1870 Rutland, Dane, Wisconsin Census</u>: *Amy Pinkham,* age 55 born 1815 Canada with the James T. Mason family in the 1870 Rutland, Dane County, Wisconsin - James T. Mason born 1796 Vermont.
>
> Emily Higgens Mason is listed as wife of Edward Masson in the 1860 census record. Higgens-Pinkham family members were given her married surname from Edward Masson.
>
> From <u>1880 Leon, Waushara, Wisconsin Census</u> record: Household of Edward Masson: Age 47 born France. *Emily J. Masson, wife born Canada age 38 born 1842 Canada* with daughter *Eliza Jane Masson* born 1860 Canada, son Hiram Masson age 15 born 1865 Canada and Anna M. Masson age 0 born Canada (Wisconsin).
>
> <u>Marriage</u>: (Cephne) Cephus Pinkham. Marriage date: 23 November 1869. Marriage location: Union, Rock, Wisconsin, USA. Father's name: Samuel Pinkham. Mother's name: *Forgotten* Pinkham. Spouse's name: Emmeline Richardson. Spouse's father's name: Ozro Richardson. Spouse's Mother's name: Emmeline Richardson. (*Likely, "Forgotten" was "Domitilde Chartier" who died shortly after Cephus' birth.*)
>
> <u>United States Civil War Soldier's Index,1861-1865</u>: (Josephus) Cephas Pinkham. Event date: 1861-1865. Event Place: Wisconsin. Military rank beginning: Private. Military Final Rank: Private. Military side:

Union. State or Military term: Wisconsin. Military Unit: 33rd Regiment, Wisconsin Infantry. (*Age 18 if enlisted 1865*).

United States Civil War Soldier's Index 1861-1865: Joseph Pinkham. Event date: 1861-1865. Event Place: Wisconsin. Military rank beginning: Private. Military Final Rank: Private. Military side: Union. State or Military term: Wisconsin. Military Unit: 12th Regiment, Wisconsin Infantry. (*Age 19 if enlisted 1865*).

United States Civil War Soldier's Index 1861-1865: Stephen Pinkham, Samuel Pinkham, Joseph Pinkham, Cephas Pinkham and William P. Pinkham. (*Unconfirmed is if this is J. Samuel with sons: Joseph and Cephas plus Stephen and William P. Pinkham, sons m2 B. Higgens.*)

1870 United States Census: Josephus Pinkham (Cephas); Joseph Pinkham. Event Place: Union, Rock, Wisconsin. Age: 25. Born 1845. Birthplace: Canada. *Sons of Samuel Pinkham, Joseph and Cephas Pinkham, were noted with last name of "Mason" on 1860 Census.* Household: Josephus (Cephas) Pinkham, male, age 25 born Canada. W. Pinkham, female age 19 born Vermont. Brother, Joseph Pinkham (not Mason), age 26 born Canada and Ellen Richardson, female age 5 born Wisconsin.

1879 Death of Samuel B. Pinkham: Birth: Unknown. Death: 1879 Wisconsin, USA. Burial: Old Baptist Cemetery, Union, Rock County, Wisconsin. *"In a list of Details for Decorating Soldiers Graves for Memorial Day 1884 by T. L. Stephen, G. A. R. Post' S. B. Pinkham was listed at Union Cemetery." This is broken stone is located just to the left of Elizabeth Higgens Pinkham, her stone reads: wife of Samuel Pinkham. On Memorial Day 20, 2016 the Adjuct of the American Legend concurred with the marking of the grave with a flag holder and American flag. In addition, a newspaper account which appeared in the Evensville Review on 12 May 2010, page 23, Column 1 follows: In review 130 years ago (1880), the only child, son of widow Pinkham, of Union Village, age two, was drowned in a cistern near the house Monday forenoon. The mother is almost frantic with grief. She has lost two children before, and less than a year ago she lost her husband by being buried in a well he was digging. She feels now as though her cup of sorrow was 'full.' This account places Samuel's death at 1879."* Source: FindAGrave

Initial, "B" likely incorrect as per other "Samuel Pinkhams" were transcribed with incorrect initials. J. Samuel Pinkham's middle name was Samuel. Whether he had a son in New York (Samuel Pinkham b. 1844) remains unproven along with why did this individual resided at age sixteen with Caleb Pinkham's son, Comfort Pinkham. Also unconfirmed is whether his name was B. Samuel.

1880 Census Rutland, Dane, Wisconsin: Eliza (Betsy Higgens) Pinkham born 1815. With Jane Mason, her daughter, and John S. Mason, Frank Hartley.

1900 Evansville, Union, Rock, Wisconsin Census: Elizabeth Pinkham. Birth: October 1813, Canada East (Quebec). Immigration 1855. With Jane Mason, Emily Bullock.

Death of Betsy Pinkham, wife of Samuel Pinkham: Death – Elizabeth Higgens Pinkham. Event Date – 1901. Event place – Evansville, Rock, Wisconsin. Gender – Female. Age – 87. Marital Status – Widowed. Occupation – Housekeeper. Birth Date – 11 October 1814. Birth Year – 1814. Birthplace – Canada. Burial Date – 6 March 1901. Burial Place – Union, Rock, Wisconsin. Father's Name - Benjamin Higgens. Father's birthplace – Canada. Mother's Name – Mary Higgens. Mother's Birthplace – Canada. Spouse's Name – Samuil Pinkham.

> *Benjamin Higgens - 1825 Dunham, Bedford Quebec Census:*
> *Number of inhabitants: 9. Father of Elizabeth Higgens.*
> *Benjamin Higgens - 1842 Farnham, Shefford Quebec Census:*
> *Farmer; Number of inhabitants: 6.*

~ Joseph Abijah Pinkham (6) (Generation 7):

Birth: Born 6 May 1827, Quebec; Married Rosina (Chartier) Pinkham in 1849. Died 29 January 1909, Madera, California, USA.

The first-born children of Samuel and Theodocia (Carpenter) Pinkham are noted via repeated census birth year notation: Caleb Pinkham born 1809; Comfort Carpenter Pinkham 1811. Siblings, James O. Pinkham and Huldah Pinkham were born between the years 1813 and 1817. James O. Pinkham's death record list a birth year of 1816 while Huldah's birth year varied per record. Joseph Abijah was not named, "James" as per his brother, James O. Pinkham born 1816. However, his California death record notes "James" not "Joseph" as his first name, and a birth year of 1827.

1849 St. Cecile de Milton marriage: Joseph Pinkham to Rosalie Chartier

At St. Cecile de Milton, (Abijah) Joseph and Marie (Rosalie Chartier) may have been baptized (or these were the names of James and Mathilde Pinkham's children):
      1849 St. Cecile de Milton baptized: Joseph Pinkham
      1849 St. Cecile de Milton baptized Marie-Matilda (*Rosalie*) Pinkham

Proof Joseph Abijah and Rosina (Chartier) Pinkham moved with Jeremiah Phelps family can be found in the book:

> "Early Days in Cedar City" by Ethelmae Eylar Carter (Our Family History 1958): Jeremiah and Mary Phelps and families) … Next came Welcome Osborne and family, also Joshua Welch and Abijah Pinkham with their families…"

"EARLY DAYS IN CEDAR CITY: In regard to the early days in Mower County, my wife (Hannah Phelps) and I drove from Burlington, Racine County, Wisconsin, with a team of horses, to find a home in the territory of Minnesota. We arrived at David Chandler's farm October 13, 1856. In the spring of that year I was married to Hannah Phelps, daughter of Jeremiah and Margaret Phelps, who moved to Mover County, from Burlington, Wisc., with the following families: Thomas Bonnallie, George and William Phelps, Diadamy and Mary Phelps, and John Watkins anf family, composed of eight sons and daughters. John Phelps had preceded them and was on the ground with Eben Merry and family. David and John Chandler, John Osborne and family, Caleb Stock and a Mr. Smith. The last two named with John Phelps composed the mill company. Next came Welcome Chandler and family, also Joshua Welch and Abijah Pinkham with their families. These with a Mr. McKee and Means comprised the neighborhood settlement in the winter of 1856-57. In the spring came Welcome Chandler and Andrew Gemmel and their families. Before my wife and I arrived, Caleb Stock and Mary Watkins had spent their honeymoon. After their marriage, John Phelps went back to Racine County, Wisconsin and there married Miss (Julia) Lyons, which made another very valuable addition to our young but growing society. Then Timothy Goslee won the affection of Ann Watkins. These three were the first on the list of marriages of Cedar City. Cedar City mill was pushed to completion and began grinding in due time. But, alas the June freshet took the pioneer mill down with its rapid current and our young city grew no more and like many western towns ceased to live."

Note: Welcome Chandler married Jeremiah and Margaret Phelps' daughter, Amy Phelps. This marriage record was signed by Huldah Pinkham, the sister of Joseph Abijah Pinkham who married Seth Warren.

1859-1863 Mower, Minnesota County Courthouse Records:
    (Grantee) PINKHAM, Abijah. 17 May 1859. (Grantor) Joshua Welsh. Book of
           Deeds, page 98.
    (Grantor) PINKHAM, Abijah, 17 May 1859. (Grantee) Sanford Tanner. Book C of
           Mortgages, page 412 (or 415).
    (Grantor) PINKHAM, Abijah & wife. 2 January 1863. (Grantee) Andrew Gemmel.
           Book F of Warranty Deeds, page 232.
    (Grentee) PINKHAM, Abijah & wife. 1 April 1863. (Grantor) Sanford Tanner.
           Book C, Satisfaction of Mortgage, page 415.

1860 United States Census: (Joseph) Ubijak (Abijah) Pinkham: Event Type – Census;
    Event Date – 1860; Event Place - Town of Austin, Mower, Minnesota, United
    States; Age – 30; Race – White; Birth year – 1830; Birthplace – Canada;
    Occupation – Farmer; Household - (Joseph) Ubijak (Abijah) Pinkham age 30
    (Born abt. 1830 – Canada), Rosina Pinkham age 28 (Born abt. 1832, Canada),
    Mary Pinkham age 11 (Born abt. 1849 – Canada), Rosina Pinkham age 9 (Born
    abt. 1851) Sarah Ann Pinkham age 7 (Born abt. 1853 – Canada), Samuel
    Pinkham age 5 (Born abt. 1855 Wisconsin), Docia – Theodocia age 2 (Born abt.
    1858 – Minnesota). *Source: United States Census, 1860.*

Children of Joseph Abijah and Rosina Pinkham: Mary (b. 1849 Quebec), Rosina (b. 1855 Quebec), Sarah Ann (b. 1853 Quebec), Samuel (b. 1855 Wisconsin), Theodocia (b. 1858 MN), Henry (b. 1863 MN), Matilda (b. 1865 MN), Aaron/Michael C. (b. 1867 MN), and Charles (b. 1869 MN). (9 children living) 1865 Census lists John Pinkham (death date unknown). Michael Cole Aaron "Mike" Pinkham was born 4 July 1865 MN.

1861 Census, Lyle, Mower County, Minnesota: Joseph A. Pinkham. Household:
    Joseph A. Pinkham, Rosina Pinkham and children: Mary, Rosina, Sarah Ann,

Samuel, Theodocia, Henry and John Pinkham. *Source: Minnesota Sate Census: 1865, State Library & Records, St. Paul, MN.* Named children Samuel and Theodocia for parents.

1865 Minnesota State Census: Lyle, Mower, Minnesota - Joseph A. (Abijah) Pinkham household: Joseph A. Pinkham, Rosina Pinkham, Mary Pinkham, Rosina Pinkham, Sarah Ann Pinkham, *Samuel Pinkham, Theodocia Pinkham*, Henry Pinkham, John Pinkham. *Source: Minnesota State Census 1865 Lyle, Mower, Minnesota, State Library & Records Service, St. Paul.*

The Joseph Abijah Pinkham family moved to Clayton, Crawford, Wisconsin between 1866 and 1869. By this point, his brother, Caleb Pinkham had moved to Minnesota. Brother Samuel Pinkham continued to reside in Union, Rock, Wisconsin with nephew, Josephus Pinkham while niece, Huldah Pinkham Picket resided in Wiota, Wisconsin.

1869 Marriage of Rosina Pinkham: Event date: 2 January 1869. Event Place: Crawford, Wisconsin. Marriage of Aaron Copas to Rosina Pinkham.

United States Civil War Soldiers Index: Joseph Pinkham. Private. Military Side: Union. State: Wisconsin. Military Unit – 12th Regiment, Wisconsin Infantry. *Source: NARA*

1870 United States Census: Wisconsin, United States: Joseph Pinkham; Name: Joseph Pinkham; Event place - Wisconsin; Gender – Male; Age – 50; Race – White; Birth year – 1819-1820; Birthplace – Canada; Household of Joseph Pinkham age 50 (Born abt. 1819, Canada), Rosina Pinkham age 36 (Born abt. 1834, Canada), Mary Pinkham age 19 (Born abt. 1851, Canada), Sarah H. Pinkham age 16 (Born abt. 1854, Canada), Samuel Pinkham age 13 (Born abt. 1857, Canada), Thodiar - female (Theodocia) Pinkham age 11 (Born abt. 1859, Minnesota), Henry Pinkham age 8 (Born abt. 1863, Minnesota), Matilda age 5 (Born abt. 1865, Minnesota), Aaron (Michael C.) Pinkham age 3 (Born abt.1867, MN), Charles Pinkham age 1 (Born abt. 1869, Wisconsin). *Source: 1870 US Census, NARA*

1875 Wisconsin State Census: A. Pinkham. Event Place – Clayton, Crawford, Wisconsin. Number of White Males: 3. Number of White Females: 4.

1880 World Vital Records: Biga, Pinkham (Abijah Pinkham). Residence: Clayton, Crawford, Wisconsin. Male; Farmer; Parents: Father – Canada; Mother – Canada. Household: Biga Pinkham (self) - Age 52; wife – Rosina Pinkham age 40; son – Henry Pinkham age 17; daughter – Matilda Pinkham age 14; Son – Michael Pinkham age 12 (born 1868 MN).

1895 Wisconsin State Census: 1895: J. A. Pinkham. Event Place: Clayton Town, Crawford, Wisconsin. Number of Males: 1. Number of Females: 1. Birthplace: British America: 2.

1900 United States Federal Census: Abija Pinkham. Name: Abija (Abijah) Pinkham. Age: 72. Birthdate: May 1837 (1827). Birthplace – Canada. Home in 1900s:

Clayton, Crawford, Wisconsin. White. Male. Head of Household. Married to Rosina Pinkham. Marriage Year: 1850. Years married: 50. Father/Mother's birthplace – Canada. Owner of House. Owner of Farm. Household members: Abija Pinkham age 72, Rosina Pinkham age 66. Abijah Pinkham is a farmer who owned 81 (?) acres. Rosina Pinkham had 9 children with 7 living.

This 1900 census records daughter Theodocia Copas (with husband Sanford Copas) above the Abijah Pinkham listing and follows with son, Mike (Michael C.) Pinkham. All are farmers.

<u>1905 Wisconsin, State Census:</u> A. Pinkham. Name: A. Pinkham. Census Date: 1895. Residence County: Crawford. Residence State: Wisconsin. Locality: Clayton. Household members: A. Pinkham (no age listed).

Son, Michael C. Pinkham moved to California prior to 1904 where his child, Bertha Pinkham was born in 1906. Daughter Theodocia (Pinkham) Copas moved to Madera, California between March of 1908 and the 1910 Madera, California census. Daughter Mary (Pinkham) Townsend moved to Madera by 1910. Joseph Abijah Pinkham visited or moved to Madera, California by 1909 where he died on 29 January 1909 at age 82 (born 1827 Quebec). He was buried at Madera, California's Calvary Cemetery (Block 15, Row 1, Plot 67) and the funeral home was listed as, Jay's Chapel. The California Death Index, 1905-1939 incorrectly lists his name as "James" and states "James A. Pinkham, male, age 82, death date - 1909, death place - California, birth year - 1827. Joseph Abijah Pinkham, son of Samuel Jr. and Theodocia (Carpenter) Pinkham was born 1827 in Stanstead, Quebec, Canada; died 1909 in Madera, California, USA.

> <u>1909 Californai Death Index:</u> James A. Pinkham. Death date: 1909. Birth
> year: 1827. *(Joseph Abijah Pinkham)*

> <u>Madera, California Cemetery:</u> James Pinkham. Death date: 29 January 1909.
> Funeral Home: Jay Chapel. Cemetery (Madera, CA): Calvary.
> *(Joseph Abijah Pinkham)* (Lavina Pinkham, wife of son, Michael Pinkham,
> is buried at Calvary Cemetery on 15 February 1915.

<u>Children of Joseph Abijah & Rosina Pinkham (Generation 8):</u>
>> Mary Pinkham Townsend (b. 1849, Quebec)
>> Sarah H. Pinkham Copas (b. 1854, Quebec)
>> Rosina Pinkham Copas (b. 1855, Quebec)
>> Samuel (K.) Philip Pinkham (b. 14 April 1857, Quebec)
>> Theodocia Pinkham Copas (b. 1865, Quebec)
>> Henry Pinkham (b. 1863, Mower, Minnesota)
>> Matilda Pinkham (b. 1865, Mower, Minnesota)
>> Aaron Michael Cole Pinkham (b. 1867, Mower, Minnesota)
>> Charles Pinkham (b. 1869, Mower, Minnesota)

~Mary Pinkham Townsend: <u>Marriage</u> 18 January 1871. Spouse's name: Mary Pinkham. Spouse's parents: Spouse's father: Abija Pinkham. Spouse's mother: Rosina Pinkham. Marriage Place: Crawford, Wisconsin. Name: Thomas Townsend. Father's name: James Townsend. Mother's name: Jemina Townsend.

<u>1875 Wisconsin Census</u>: Courtland, Columbia, Wisconsin: Mary Townsend. Number of females: 1. Number of males: 2.

<u>1880 United States Census</u>, Clayton, Crawford, Wisconsin: Mary Townsend. Female age 28 born 1852 Canada. Parent's birthplace: Canada. Wife of Thomas Townsend age 28 born 1852. Farmer. Father's birthplace: Kentucky. Mother's birthplace: Ohio. Townsend children born Wisconsin: Rosana (Rosina) age 7 born 1873, Walles C. age 3 born 1877 and Thederia (Theodocia) Townsend age 1 born 1879.

<u>1900 United States Census</u> Clayton Town, north side Soldiers Grove Village, Crawford, Wisconsin: Mary Townsend. Age 55 born August 1845 Canada French (Quebec). Married 30 years; marriage year 1870. Number of children living: 5. Number of children born: 6. Parent's born: Canada France. Husband: Thomas C. Townsend age 54 born Ohio. Children of Thomas and Mary (Pinkham) Townsend born Wisconsin: Thedosia age 12 born 1888, Francis (son) age 21 born 1897, Rosa Bell age 12 born.

> <u>Marriage</u> (Wisconsin 1836-1930): Dosha Townsend (Docia - Theodocia) to Eugene Carrell, son of Charles and Mary Carrell. Parents: T. C. and Mary Townsend.

<u>1910 United States Census</u> Township 3, Madera, California: Thomas C. Townend. Age 72 born 1838 Ohio. Parents born Kentucky. Wife: Mary Townend, age 60 born Canada.

> <u>Death</u>: Thomas C. Townsend. Age 70 born 1851. Death Place: Madera, California. Burial Place: Arbor Vitae Cemetery, Madera, California. Death date: 30 May 1921. Birth date: 1851. *Source: California Death Index 1905-1939; FindAGrave*

<u>Death</u>: Mary C. Townsend. Age 65 born 1851. Death date: 6 January 1916. Death place: Madera, California. *Source: California Death Index 1905-1939*

<u>Death</u>: Mary C. Townsend. Birth: 1850. Age: 66. Burial: Arbor Vitae Cemetery, Madera, California, USA. *Source: FindAGrave*

Death (Wisconsin 1867-1907): Sarah P. Townsend Bell.
Parent: Mary M. Townsend

~Rosina Pinkham: Marriage 2 January 1869. Rosina Pinkham.
Marriage to Aaron Copas. Marriage Place: Crawford, Wisconsin.

1870 United States Census Clayton, Crawford, Wisconsin. Rosina
Copas. Birth year 1852. Age: 18. Birthplace: Canada. Head of
household: Avron Copas. Age: 22. Birth year: 1848.
Birthplace: Ohio. Child of Rosina and Avron Copas: Henry
Copas age 0 born 1870.

1880 United States Census Clayton, Crawford, Wisconsin. Rosina
Copas. Age 25 born 1855 Canada. Married. Parents born
Canada. Husband: Aaron Copas. Age 31 born 1849 Ohio.
Farmer. Parents born Pennsylvania.

1900 United States Census Clayton, Crawford, Wisconsin: Rosina
Copas age 48. Birthdate: August 1852. Birthplace: Canada F
(Quebec). Number of living children: 9. Mother of how many
children: 16. Copas children born Wisconsin: Henry age 31 born
1869. Samuel age 29 born 1871, Rosetta age 17 born March
1883, Mike age 10 born 1890, Mary age 8 born 1892, Oscar age 5
born 1895 and Dorabell age 3 born 1897.

1910 United States Census Clayton, Crawford, Wisconsin: Rosina
Copas born 1852 Canada, age 58. Marital status: Widowed. Head
of household. Parents born: Canada. Copas children: Oscar age
16 born 1895, Henry age 41 born 1869, Charles age 25 born 1885,
Dora age 13 born 1897, Mike age 20 born 1890 and Mary age 18
born 1892.

1920 United States Census Crawford, Wisconsin: Rosina Copus.
Age 67 born 1853 Canada. Widowed. Relationship to head of
household: Mother. Parents born Canada. Head of Household:
Henry J. Copus. Age 50 born 1870. Single. Father born Ohio.
Mother born Canada. Michael Copas age 30 born 1890, Charles
Copas age 34 born 1886. With William Copus age 7 born 1913.

1930 United States Census Clayton, Crawford, Wisconsin. Rosina
Copus. Age 76 born 1854 Canada. Widowed. With sons: Henry
Copus age 60 born 1870 and Charles Copus age 46 born 1884.

Death: Rosina Pinkham Copus. Born: 20 August 1852 Quebec.
Died: June 1939 Crawford County, Wisconsin. Burial: Mook
Cemetery, Rolling Ground, Crawford County, Wisconsin.

Source: *FindAGrave* - Children of Rosina Pinkham Copus - Henry Copus 1868-1944; Samuel P. Copus 1871-1954, Charles Copus 1884-1952, Michael E. Copus 1888-1974, Mary Copus Copenhefer 1892-1966, Oscar Warren Copus 1894-1972, Dora Belle Copus Coleman 1896-1968.

~Sarah Ann Pinkham Copas: Born 10 June 1855. Death 31 December 1924. Burial: Mook Cemetery, Rolling Ground, Crawford, WI.

Immigration year: 1867 (Minnesota)

Married: 1877 to Henry Copas

1880 United States Census Clayton, Crawford, Wisconsin. Sarah A. Copas. Married. Age 24 born 1856 Canada. Wife. Parents born Canada. Husband: Henry Copas age 30 born 1850 Ohio. Farmer. Married. Parents born Pennsylvania.

1900 United States Census Clayton, Crawford, Wisconsin. Sarah Copas age 44 born January 1856 Canada France. Parent born Canada. Married 1877. Number of children: 5. Husband: Henry Copas age 55 born Ohio. Children of Henry and Sarah (Pinkham) Copas born Wisconsin: Anna Copas age 19 born 1881, Samuel Copas age 16 born 1884 and Pearley E. Copas (son) age 14 born 1883.

1910 United States Census Clayton, Crawford, Wisconsin. Sarah M. Copas. Age 55 born 1855 Canada. Parents born Canada. Married to Henry Copas age 65 born 1845 Ohio. Children of Henry and Sarah (Pinkham) Copas: Dalia Copas, George R. Copas, Ann Copas (age 27 1883 born Wisconsin), Sam Copas (age 25 born 1885 Wisconsin) and Pearl Copas (son) (age 23 born 1887 Wisconsin).

1920 United States Census Crawford, Wisconsin: Sarah Copus. Age 66 born 1854 Canada. Immigration year: 1867. Married. Parents born Canada. Head of Household (son) Samuel Copus. Single. Age 37 born 1883 Wisconsin. Father's birthplace: Ohio. Mother's birthplace: Canada.

Death: 24 December 1924. Sarah Ann Pinkham Copas. Born 10 June 1855. Burial: Rolling Ground Cemetery, Crawford, WI, USA.

~Samuel Philip Pinkham: Born 14 April 1857, QC. Married: March 1878. Marriage: Samuel Pinkham to Susan Frilda Copas; Crawford, Wisconsin. Parents: Joseph Abijah Pinkham/Roina

(Rosina) Pinkham. *Source: Wisconsin County Marriages, 1836-1911, Wisconsin Historical Society Madison.* Sister, Theodocia Pinkham, married John Copas.

Marriage: Samuel K. Pinkham 24 March 1878, Crawford, Wisconsin. Father: Abijah Pinkham. Mother: Rosina Pinkham. Spouse: Susan Frida Copas. Spouse's Father: John Copas. Spouse's Mother: Eva Copas. *Source: Wisconsin County Marriages, 1836 – 1911, Wisconsin Historical Society, Madison*

1880 United States Census Clayton, Crawford, Wisconsin. Family of Henry Copas age 30 born Ohio with wife, Sarah A. age 24 born Canada and children born Wisconsin: Dora age 3, George age 2 and Frank Copas age 0. Family of Sanford Copas age 24 born Ohio, brother of Henry Copas. Wife of Sanford Copas Docia (Pinkham) Copas, age 20 born Wisconsin, and daughter Mary M. Copas age 3 born Wisconsin. With Samuel Pinkham, brother of Theodocia Pinkham Copas, age 22 born Wisconsin, and his wife, Susan Frida Copas age 18 born Wisconsin, sister of Henry and Sanford Copas.

1900 United States Census Clayton, Wisconsin: Samuel (Dinkham) Pinkham. Born April 1857 Minnesota. Parents - Father born Canada; Mother born Canada. Wife Susan Pinkham born June 1860 Wisconsin. Parents - Father born Virginia; Mother born Ohio. Married 1879 to Samuel Pinkham.

Children of Samuel and Susan (Copas) Pinkham:
Adam Pinkham (b. 1886 Wisconsin)
Eve Pinkham (b. 1886 Wisconsin)
Varney Pinkham (b. 1890 Wisconsin)
Erving Pinkham (b. 1894 Wisconsin)
Mary Pinkham (b. 1897 Wisconsin)
Elizabeth Pinkham (b. 1899 Wisconsin)

Marriage of Mary Pinkham to Delbert Orick (born 1895 Wisconsin) to Mary Pinkham Oreck (born 1897 Wisconsin).

2 July 1905 Marriage of Eva Pinkham (father: Samuel Pinkham – parents Joseph Abijah & Rozina Pinkham): Name – Thomas Dobson; Event date – 2 July 1905; Event place – Bell Center, Crawford, Wisconsin, United States; Gender – Male; Marital Status – Single; Race – White; Birthplace – Grant County, Wisconsin; Father's name – Thomas Dobson; Mother's name – Ellen Edwards; Spouse's

name – Eva Pinkham; Spouse's Gender – Female; Spouse's race – White; Spouse's birthplace – Clayton, Wisconsin; Spouse's Father's name – Samuel Pinkham; Spouse's Mother's name – Susan Copas; Note: PR Name: Jr.;
Source: Wisconsin, County Marriage, 1836-1911; Wisconsin Historical Society, Madison

1905 <u>Wisconsin State Census</u>: Samuel Pinkham age 48 born 1857 Minnesota parents born Canada. Wife Susan (Copas) Pinkham age 44 born Wisconsin. Daughter Eva Pinkham age 18 born 1887 Wisconsin, Son Warren Pinkham age 13 born 1892 Wisconsin, Irvin Pinkham age 11 born 1894 Wisconsin, Mary Pinkham age 9 born 1902 Wisconsin, Elizabeth age 6 born 1899 Wisconsin and Mother-in-Law; Eva A. Copas age 82 born Ohio.

1920 <u>United States Census</u> Clayton, Crawford, Wisconsin: Samuel Pinkham, age 62 born 1858 Wisconsin. Parents born Canada. With wife, Susan (age 57 born Wisconsin), son Erving Pinkham (age 26 born 1894 Wisconsin), daughter Elizabeth Pinkham (age 20 born 1900 Wisconsin), daughter Mary Orick (age 23 born 1897 Wisconsin) and her husband Delbert Orick (age 25 born Wisconsin).

1930 <u>United States Census</u> Clayton, Crawford, Wisconsin: Samuel Pinkham, age 73 born 1857 Minnesota. Widowed. Parents: Born Canada. With son - Ervin Pinkham age 36 born 1894 Wisconsin and wife Olivia age 38 born Wisconsin.

<u>Death</u>: Samuel Philip Pinkham. Event Date: 1935. Event Place: Rolling Ground, Crawford, Wisconsin. Birth date: 14 April 1857. Death: 5 July 1935. Cemetery: Mook Cemetery.
Source: FindAGrave

FindAGrave information is not accurate. Samuel Phillip Pinkham: Birth 14 April 1857 Austin, Mower County MN - Theodocia Pinkham, Samuel's sister was born 1859 in Austin, Mower County, MN. Samuel was born 1857 Quebec not Wisconsin or MN.

~<u>Theodocia Pinkham Copas</u>: Born 1859, Austin, Mower County, MN. Death: 1937, Madera, California, USA.

4 October 1877 <u>Marriage</u> of Theodocia Pinkham (Name: Theodoria (Theodosia) Pinkham; Event – Marriage; Name: Sanford Copas; Event Date – 14 October 1877; Event Place – Crawford, Wisconsin; United States; Father's Name – John Copas; Mother's name – Abijah E. Copas; Spouse's name – Theodoria Pinkham; Spouse's Gender – Female; Spouse's father's name – Abija (Joseph Abijah) Pinkham;

Spouse's Mother's name – Rozina Pinkham. Source: Wisconsin County Marriages, 1836 – 1911, Wisconsin Historical Society, Madison. Brother, Samuel Pinkham, married Susan Frida Copas.

1880 United States Census Clayton, Crawford, Wisconsin. Family of Henry Copas age 30 born Ohio with wife, Sarah A. age 24 born Canada and children born Wisconsin: Dora age 3, George age 2 and Frank Copas age 0. Family of Sanford Copas age 24 born Ohio, brother of Henry Copas. Wife of Sanford Copas, Docia (Pinkham) Copas, age 20 born Wisconsin, and daughter Mary M. Copas age 3 born Wisconsin. With Samuel Pinkham, brother of Theodocia Pinkham Copas, age 22 born Wisconsin, and his wife, Susan Frida Copas age 18 born Wisconsin, sister of Henry and Sanford Copas.

> Marriage: 2 February 1898: Mary A. Copas born Clayton, Crawford, Wisconsin, daughter of Sanford and Theodocia Copas to George B. Bell, son of T. B. and Margaret A. Bell. Event place: Richwood, Richland, Wisconsin.

1900 United States Census Clayton town, south side, Crawford, Wisconsin. Sanford Copas born September 1854, married 21 years to Theodocia Pinkham Copas born 1858 age 43 married 21 years with Copas children: Joseph born June 1885, Minnie born September 1890, Emily born August 1892 and Christopher born October 1895.

Theodocia Pinkham Copas married Sanford Copas, and as per the 1900 census, had been married for 21 years. She was born October 1858, now age 42 and had 7 children, 6 living. Sanford Copas was born Ohio with parents born Pennsylvania. He was a farmer owning approximately 83 acres. Theodocia was born Minnesota with parents born Canada.

Next entry is for parents: Abijah Pinkham and Rosina with brother Mike (Aaron) Michael C. (Cole) Pinkham family.

1905 Wisconsin State Census Clayton, Crawford, Wisconsin: Theodocia Copas, age 40 born 1865 Minnesota, parents both born Canada. Wife of Sanford Copas, age 53 born Ohio. Children of Sanford and Theodocia Copas born Wisconsin: Joseph Copas age 21, Minnie Copas age 16, Emily age 13, John age 11 and George age 9.

1905 <u>Marriage</u>: Minnie Copus, daughter of
Theodosia and Sanford Copus born Clayton to John
Dahlberg, son of August and Caroline Dahlberg born
Richwood. Marriage date: 8 October 1905. Event
Place: Tavera, Richland, Wisconsin.

Son Joseph Henry Copas born March of 1908 in Wisconsin,
therefore the family moved to California between April 1908-1910.

<u>1910 United States Census</u> Township 3, Madera, California.
Head of Household: Sanford Copus age 55 born Ohio.
Wife, Theodosia Copus age 51 born Minnesota. Children:
Johnie A. Copus, age 13 born Wisconsin. George S. Copus,
age 11 born Wisconsin. Grandson Joseph H. Dolward
(Dalberg) age 2 born Wisconsin (likely son of Minnie Copus
Dalberg).

<u>1930 United States Census</u> Millview, Madera, California. Head
of household Sanford Copus age 75 born Ohio with
Theodocia Copus age 71 (born 1859) Minnesota with sons
John Copus age 36 born Wisconsin and Joseph Copus age
22 born Wisconsin.

<u>California Death Index</u>: Theodosi C. Copus, age 78. Death 5
December 1937, Madera, CA, USA. (Born abt. 1859)
Certificate number: 79296. Burial: Arbor Vitae Cemetery,
Madera, Madera, California.

<u>Obituary for Theodosia Catherine (Pinkham) Copas</u>. *Source: FindAGrave*

Birth: 1859 Minnesota; Death: December 1937 age 77-78.

"Mrs Sanford Copas Summoned by Death:

*Mrs. Theodosia Catherine Copas, 78 was claimed by death
Sunday morning at 8:20 o'clock at her home on Magnolia
avenue, after a long period of illness. She leaves her
husband, Sanford, four sons, Joe, John and George of
Madera, and Chris of Wisconsin; three daughters; Mrs.
Emma Pedrino of Madera and Mrs. Mary B. Bell and Minnie
Martin of Wisconsin; 23 grandchildren and 24 great-
grandchildren. Funeral services will be held from the chapel
of the R. S. Jay Mortuary Tuesday afternoon at 2 o'clock.
Internment will be at the Arbor Vitae Cemetery. "*

<u>Death of Sanford and Theodocia Copas Children in California</u>:

1940 Death: Johnie Abijah Copas. Event date: 21 January 1940. Event place: Madera, California, USA. Birth: 25 September 1895 Wisconsin. Father's name: Copus. Mother's name: Pinkham.

1957 Death: George Sanford Copus. Event date: 28 September 1957. Event Place: Contra Costa, California, USA. Birth: 2 September 1897 Wisconsin. Father's name: Copus. Mother's name: Pinkham.

1982 Death: Emily Theodocia Enos. Event date: 8 July 1982. Birth: 26 November 1891 Wisconsin. Father's name: Copus. Mother's name: Pinkham.

1989 Death: Joseph Henry Copas. Event date: 21 September 1989. Birth: 22 March 1908 Wisconsin. Mother's name: Pinkham.

~Henry Pinkham: Born 1863, Austin, Mower County, Minnesota.

23 July 1882 Marriage of Henry Pinkham to Johannah Mook – Crawford Wisconsin. Parents: (Joseph) Abijah Pinkham/Lavina Pinkham. *Source: Wisconsin, County Marriages, 1836-1911, Wisconsin Historical Society, Madison.*

~Matilda Pinkham: Born 1865 Wisconsin. Married: Dobbs. Died 10 June 1886. Burial: Rolling Ground, Crawford, Wisconsin. Cemetery: Saint Phillips Catholic Cemetery. *Source: FindAGrave*

~Aaron Michael Cole "Mike" (Michael C.) Pinkham: Born July 1866, Mower, (Born 4 July 1865) Minnesota. Death: 26 July 1942 Crawford, Wisconsin.

Married Lavina Johnson, born October 1865 in Wisconsin.

1900 United States Census: Clayton Town, South Side, Crawford, Wisconsin: Mike Pinkham. Married 10 years to Lavina (Johnson). He was born July 1866 Minnesota. The children of Mike and Lavina Pinkham were Rosina age 8 born 1891, Joseph H. age 5 born November 1894, John H. age 3 born September 1896 and Thomas Pinkham age 1 born 1898. Mike Pinkham was a farmer born July 1866 Minnesota. Parents born Canada - English.

Record listed below father and mother, Abjiah and Rosina Pinkham, and sister, Theodocia Copas with Sanford Copas family.

Left Wisconsin during 1904 for California.

86

1910 United States Census: Township 3, Madera, California: Michael C. Pinkham. Head of household born 1866 Minnesota. Spouse: Lavina Pinkham born 1867 Wisconsin; parents born Ohio. Children: Phebe R. (Rosina) Pinkham age 17 born 1893 Wisconsin, Joseph L. Pinkham age 15 born 1895 Wisconsin, John H. Pinkham age 13 born 1897 Wisconsin and Bertha Pinkham age 6 born 1904 California.

Father's death: James A. Pinkham (Joseph Abijah): Birth year: 1827. Death date: 1909. Age 82. *Source: California Death Index, 1905-1939* Madera Calvary Internment: Pinkham, James Abijah; Block 15, Row 1; Plot 67; Cemetery - Calvary; Death date - 29 January 1909. Also, noted: Lavina M. C. Pinkham: Block 8/Lot 167, Plot A, Calvary. Date of birth - 28 October 1866; Death - 15 February 1915.

Wife's death: Lavina Pinkham: Birth - 28 October 1866; Death - 15 February 1915, age 48. Burial: Calvary, Madera, Madera, California. Madera Cemetery notes: Parents: Isreal Johnson and Phebe Copus both of Ohio; born 1866, Nativity, Wisconsin. The funeral home is listed as Jay's Chapel.

Father of Lavina Johnson: Isreal Johnson:
1870 United States Census: Isreal Johnson: Isreal Johnson age 48 born Ohio with spouse, Phebe Johnson age 40 born Ohio. Children born Wisconsin: Richard age 15, Henry age 12, Eva A. age 9, Rebecca age 7, *Lavina age 5*, Phebe age 3 and Israel Johnson age 0.
1885 Wisconsin State Census, Clayton, Crawford, Wisconsin: Isreal Johnson: Military rank: Private. Military Service Place: Wisconsin.
Isreal Johnson: Death date: 25 March 1890, Crawford, Wisconsin. *Source: Wisconsin Death Index, 1820-1907*

1920 United States Census, Township 3, Madera, California: John Pinkham born 1898 Wisconsin with Bertha Pinkham born 1904 California, Joe Pinkham born 1895 Wisconsin and Thomas Pinkham born 1898 Wisconsin. Children of Michael Pinkham. *Mother Lavina Pinkham died February 1915.*

1930 United States Census, Howard, Madera, California: Michael Pinkham with spouse: Vina Pinkham.

1930 United States Census, Madera, California: Thomas Pinkham (son of Michael and Lavina Pinkham) with spouse Aline Pinkham. Children: Rosalie Pinkham born 1928 California and Helen M. Pinkham. Rosalie Pinkham born 1928 - daughter of Thomas Pinkham and Alene Pinkham, with sister Helen M. Pinkham: Residence 1930 Madera, California; 1940 Sacramento, California.

<u>1930 United States Census</u> Chowchilla, Madera, California: Joseph H. Pinkham born 1896 Wisconsin (Son of Michael and Lavina Pinkham)

<u>Michael C. (Cole) Pinkham (Aaron) "Mike" Pinkham</u>: Death 26 July 1942, age 77, Crawford, Wisconsin. Buried: Mook Cemetery, Rolling Ground, Crawford County, Wisconsin. Birth: 4 July 1865 Minnesota.

<u>~Samuel Pinkham III (7) (Generation 7)</u>:

<u>Born abt</u>: 1828-1830, Quebec

<u>Death</u>: 14 September 1887, Mower, Minnesota, USA

Samuel III likely moved to Mower, Minnesota after brother Joseph Abijah Pinkham. Samuel Pinkham III was a child of Samuel Junior and Theodocia (Carpenter) Pinkham born between the years 1828 and 1830. Proof of his birth year is unattainable, but confirmed by 1825 and 1831 Quebec census records of which he was not listed in 1825, but recorded in 1831. If he was "about 50" (as per his obituary) then he was born during this period. Theodocia Carpenter Pinkham would have been nearing age fifty when he was born although his age, at death is listed is noted as unconfirmed. Records list this individual as Samuel Pinkham III, which would only be the case if Samuel Junior was the father. As with Caleb Pinkham's son, Josephus, who named a child "Issac Samuel," then census records mix the use of "Issac" and "Samuel," likely "J. Samuel's" first name began with the letter "J" but he went by "Samuel." Samuel III did not note his middle name and moved to Mower, MN with his brother, Joseph Abijah, who is buried as, "James A. Pinkham" although his brother was named, "James O. Pinkham."

<u>Grand Army Muster Rolls, Austin, Mower, Minnesota, USA</u>: Samuel Pinkham, born 1831 Canada; Farmer; Age 53. Date: 31 March 1884.

<u>1869-1940 Minnesota, Grand Army of the Republic Membership</u>: Samuel Pinkham, Military Service, Austin, Minnesota, USA. Age: 53.

<u>1884 United States Pension</u>: Samuel Pinkham; Name – Samuel Pinkham; Pension; Event Date - 1884; Event Place - Minnesota; Beneficiary: Louisa Pinkham. *Source: United States General Index to Pension Files, 1861 – 1934. 1917*

<u>13 July 1887 Marriage</u>: Samuel Pinkham; to Louisa Hill; Mower, Minnesota, US. *Source: Minnesota, County Marriages, 1860-1949*

Mower County Historical Society, Austin, Minnesota – marriage certificate: PINKHAM, Samuel married Louisa Hill – 13 July 1887 in Lyle, MN. Minister Reverend W. E. Stanley. Page 8; Column 1.

Mower County Courthouse Death Records: Pinkham, Samuel, City of Austin (MN). Date of Death – 13 September 1887.

Mower County Death Transcript – 14 September 1887: Pinkham, Samuel. Death: 11 September 1887. *Age 50 years old (born 1837).* Cause: Sudden Death: strychnine poisoning.

Mower County Transcript (Newspaper), Wednesday, September 14, 1887. Caption: *Sudden Death – Samuel Pinkham died very suddenly at his home between Cedar River and M & N track Sunday morning at half past eleven o'clock. Mr. Pinkham had been a resident of Mower county about twenty years. He was about 50 years old (abt. 1827) and leaves a wife to whom he had been married about two months.*

The coroner held an inquest on the remains Monday afternoon and the verdict was that the deceased came to his death from strychnine administered by his own hand. It could not be determined whether he took the poison with the intention of self-destruction or whether it was an overdose of the drug taken as a medicine. It was shown that he was addicted to the use of laudunnum and other dangerous drugs.

The remains will be buried today by the G. A. R. Post, of which organized the deceased was a member.

United States Census of Union Veterans and Widows of the Civil War, 1890 – Samuel Pinkham, spouses name – Louisa Pinkham; 1890; Event place: Austin, Mower, Minnesota, United States. *Source United States Census of Union Veterans and Widows of the Civil War, 1890; NARA.*

"Old Soldiers Buried in Austin, MN Cemeteries" – 30 May 1913 – **Samuel Pinkham, III** Calvary.

Notation of Samuel Pinkham III confirms father was Samuel Pinkham Junior, son of Samuel Pinkham, Senior, and mother was Theodocia Carpenter, daughter of Comfort Carpenter.

~COMFORT CARPENTER PINKHAM (7): Marriage 1832 to Elizabeth Phelps.

Birth: Born abt. 1811, Quebec, son of Samuel and Theodosia (Carpenter) Pinkham.

Marriage: 13 March 1832, Freilighsburg, Quebec, Holy Trinity, Anglican Church

"On this thirteenth day of March one-thousand eight hundred and thirty-two, Comfort Pinkham of the Parish of St. Cesaire and Elizabeth Phelps, spinster of Stanbridge, both of major age, were married after publication of the Banns in presence of the subscribing witnesses." Signed by: James Reid, Minister. Comfort Pinkham, Elizabeth Phelps, Amos Phelps and Julia V. Phelps." <small>Source: Drouin</small>

COMFORT CARPENTER PINKHAM (7) has no recorded birth which was not unusual given the only recorded births in Quebec were those of Catholic babies during the early 1800s. When traveling American clergy did record births, marriage and deaths, they were not legal in Canada. Comfort Pinkham's 1832 marriage to Elizabeth Phelps took place at the Anglican Church, Holy Trinity, Freilighsburg, Quebec where his father, Samuel Pinkham (6) was buried. The text reads: *On the thirtieth day of March one thousand and eighteen hundred and thirty-two, Comfort Pinkham, Bachelor of the Parish of St. Cesaire and Elizabeth Phelps, Spinster of Stanbridge both of major age were married after publication in the presence of witnesses. Signatures read: Thomas __, Comfort Carpenter Pinkham, Elizabeth Phelps, Amos Phelps and Julia Phelps.* The digitized document lists Comfort's name as, Campart, a likely combination of his first name, Comfort, with his middle name, Carpenter. Although birth records and parentage cannot be confirmed for Elizabeth Phelps, one can conclude her brother was Amos Phelps III because both he and his wife were witnesses who signed the marriage record. Amos and Julia Phelps' 1830 marriage record from the Anglican Church in Philipsburg, Quebec reads: *On this thirtieth day of December one thousand eight hundred and thirty, Amos Phelps, Bachelor and farmer of Stanbridge and Julia VP Johnson, Spinster, both of Stanbridge both of major age were married after publication. Witnesses signing the document were: Caleb Tree, Betsy Sweet.* Jeremiah Phelps' son, Amos Phelps, was baptized in the Anglican St. Stephen Church during 1825.

The parents of Elizabeth Phelp cannot be proven by birth record but likely she was the second child of Amos Phelps Jr./"the younger" who was born while her father fought in the War of 1812. Amos B. Phelps Jr. was born in Rutland, Vermont, the eldest son of Amos Senior and Diadama (Long) Phelps. His brother, Luman B. Phelps, born in Rutland, Vermont, also fought in the War of 1812 and married Hannah Briggs on 11 June of 1812 in Rutland, Vermont. It likely Amos B. Phelps Jr. married prior to 1809.

Before Elizabeth Phelps married Comfort Pinkham, Amos Phelps III, Elizabeth Phelps' brother, married a Julia V.P. Johnson (b. 1810, Montepelier, VT). Amos and Julia then had many children baptized in Quebec – Sarah Margaret Phelps (b. 1840), Eliza (named for sister Elizabeth) A. Phelps (b. 1843) and Orville Phelps (b. 1850). During 1856, the family moved to Maquoketa, Iowa. However, Orville Phelps, their son, stayed in Quebec and did not move to Iowa until 1886 when he was thirty-six years old. From this Phelps line (Amos III and Elizabeth Phelps), four Phelps children were married at the Anglican Church, Holy Trinity in Freilghsburg, Quebec, the same church where Comfort and Elizabeth Pinkham were married in 1832. Comfort and Elizabeth (Phelps) Pinkham's son, Charles Pinkham (8), born Ontario, Canada, is baptized there, as well.

Most of Samuel and Dorothy Pinkham's children moved to Quebec from Vermont. Of Samuel and Theodosia's Pinkham's children, all moved after 1830 to the United States except Comfort Carpenter Pinkham who moved to Ontario, Canada by 1842. Luman B. Phelps, the brother of Amos B. Phelps, Elizabeth Phelps Pinkham's father, also moved to Ontario by 1830 as his first wife, Hannah Phelps died in that province during 1830. Two of the Amos Phelps named sons (of half-brother, Eldad Phelps, and Oliver Cromwell Phelps) also moved to work in Ontario as laborers (in 1851/1861 census) like Comfort Carpenter Pinkham did in 1842.

Caleb Pinkham married Mary Downing on 10 March 1829 in the Anglican Church of St. Paul d'Abbotsford in Quebec, Canada. His first children (Generation 8), Josephus and Comfort (named for his brother and grandfather, Comfort) were born in Quebec. Caleb and Mary Pinkham then moved to Ohio with sons Josephus and Comfort in 1835 where children, Henry, Huldah (named for his sister Huldah Pinkham Warren who also moved to Ohio), Caleb (for uncle, Caleb Carpenter) and Phebe Ann Pinkham were born. When Mary died, Caleb married Deborah Ann Veal in Mille Lacs County, Minnesota at age seventy while his bride was age forty-five.

Comfort (7) and Elizabeth Pinkham had at least three children (Generation 8) born in Quebec. Cynthia A. Pinkham was born in 1832 in Quebec, Elect(r)a Pinkham was born 13 March 1834 in Quebec and Mary Pinkham born 1835 in Quebec. The birth location of Edwin A. Pinkham is not confirmed, however Comfort and Elizabeth Pinkham moved to Ontario, Canada ("Upper Canada" from 1791-1841 then "Canada West" from 1841 - 1867) by the 1842 Newcastle, Durham County census which records a family of seven. Willard Pinkham, then the youngest child, was born between 1841 and 1842. Edwin's birth would be after 1836 and prior to 1841 in Quebec or Ontario, likely 1840-1841.

During 1837-8 there was a rebellion of French against English in Quebec which may have been the reason Comfort and Elizabeth Pinkham left Quebec for Ontario. While son Willard Pinkham could have been born in Ontario during 1842, the first confirmed son born 1845 Ontario was named for the Methodist founder, John Wesley. Comfort and Elizabeth (Phelps) Pinkham's Ontario born children were *Willard*, John Wesley, Jane Phebe, Samuel (named for Comfort's father) and Charles. W. Pinkham.

Comfort Carpenter Pinkham Analysis:

The analysis will prove Comfort Carpenter Pinkham was the son of Samuel Pinkham Junior and Theodosia (Carpenter) Pinkham.

There is no direct evidence available to connect Comfort Carpenter Pinkham to his parents Samuel Pinkham Junior and Theodosia Carpenter. The search for proof was conducted in many Eastern Townships of Quebec, Canada including Stanstead, Stanbridge, Milton, Freilighsburg and St. Cesaire, as well as, in Clarke, Durham County, Ontario, Canada. In these areas both land and court records were searched for without success. However, as there was only one Pinkham family who emigrated to Stanstead, Quebec in 1800, any such Pinkham surname recorded in Lower Canada during this period related to this line. As for Theodocia Carpenter, her father, Comfort Carpenter, and his brother Amos Carpenter, were original settlers of Stanstead in 1800. Tax records were searched (FHC #971.4 R4a) but nothing significant was found. The Eastern Township Quebec genealogist at American Ancestors was consulted and confirmed there were no birth records in this remote area of Quebec. Fortunately, the Notarial records of Leon LaLanne (available at *Family Search*) were written in English, rather than French, however, within these documents, only one record for Samuel G. Pinkham was found which listed a property purchase in 1808 but zero family proof. The Stanstead Genealogy Society did not have any birth records for Pinkham, Carpenter nor Phelps families and confirmed birth records for the Eastern Townships began after 1820. The Stanbridge Historical Society was also consulted since Elizabeth Phelps was noted as a "Spinster of Stanbridge" when she married Comfort Pinkham, but only records post 1835 were archived. The Durham County, Ontario Historical Society was also consulted and resulted in Elizabeth Phelps Pinkham's newspaper death notice. All vital records were searched for but no post 1820 birth documents were found in the Montreal Drouin Collection. Tax and court records for the Eastern Townships of Quebec were limited, written mostly in French, and the surname of Pinkham was not found. Records for the Eastern Townships were searched by DAR genealogists on their trip to Salt Lake City, but none found. Historical societies in Lower Canada were consulted but no information was found. Historic newspapers from Canada were searched but little was found except a few obituaries post 1820. Pinkham, Carpenter and Phelps family Bibles were searched for, but none found. The GRC was checked for associated names, but none were recorded. The Ontario History - Upper Canada Pioneer Research website also had zero proof of the names of Samuel and Theodocia Carpenter Pinkham's children born post 1809 in Quebec, Canada.

Despite lack of birth records, census records prove Comfort Carpenter Pinkham's 1811 Eastern Township birth. For instance, the 1825 Lower Canada Census in St. Cesaire, Quebec lists his father, Samuel Pinkham and his family living next to Phelps family members (Amos Senior, Jeremiah and Oliver C.). This information is confirmed by his marriage which notes Comfort Carpenter Pinkham as a "Bachelor of St. Cesaire." The book, "The History of Stanstead" by B. F. Hubbard in 1874, proves the marriage between Samuel Pinkham Junior and Theodocia Carpenter. The Drouin Collection listed an 1832 marriage record for Comfort Carpenter Pinkham to Elizabeth Phelps signed by witnesses Amos and Julia V. Phelps, Elizabeth Phelps' brother and sister-in-law. The marriage record of Huldah Pinkham, Comfort Carpenter Pinkham's sister, to Seth Warren, was signed by witness Betsy Phelps, Comfort Pinkham's future wife. The United States Census 1870 Clayton, Crawford County, Wisconsin (p. 402A) proves Caleb Pinkham, elder brother of Comfort Carpenter Pinkham, named children for his siblings – Comfort and Huldah Pinkham. The Mille Lacs County, Minnesota census notes the same children names, as do censuses taken in Claridon, Geauga County, Ohio (p 136B) and 1860, Clayton Crawford County, Wisconsin (p 735). The Austin, Mower County, Minnesota (p. 440) census proves Comfort Carpenter Pinkham's brother, Joseph Abijah Pinkham, moved from Quebec to Minnesota with the Jeremiah Phelps (son of Amos Phelps, Senior) family followed by Samuell III. The 1850 Munson, Geauga County, Ohio census (p. 185A) confirms siblings, Caleb Pinkham and Huldah Pinkham Warren, moved to an Ohio Phelps founded town. The death record for James O. Pinkham (Obit; MA death records, *Ancestry*) stated his parents were Samuel and Theodocia (Carpenter) Pinkham, thus proving the parentage of Caleb, Comfort Carpenter, Huldah, James O., J. Samuel, Joseph Abijah and Samuel III Pinkham.

Samuel Pinkham Junior's wife was Theodosia Carpenter who was the daughter of Comfort Carpenter. Proving family line via onomastics, they named their son Comfort Carpenter Pinkham for Theodocia's father, Comfort Carpenter. They named their eldest son, Caleb Pinkham, for Theodocia Carpenter's uncle and brother, Caleb Carpenter. Amos Carpenter, and likely Comfort Carpenter, fought in the American Revolutionary War then moved from Vermont to Stanstead, Quebec, Canada during the early 1800s.

The 1832 marriage record of Comfort Pinkham and Elizabeth Phelps noted their marriage in Frelighsburg, Quebec, Canada. The Frelighsburg Historical Society was consulted for Pinkham family information but none was found. Comfort Carpenter was listed on the marriage record as being a, "Bachelor of St. Cesaire," a title proven by Samuel Pinkham Junior's 1825 and 1831 St. Cesaire census records that confirm the family resided next to the Amos Phelps Senior, Jeremiah Phelps and Oliver C. Phelps families. Elizabeth Phelps was listed as being a "Spinster of Stanbridge," the same location where in 1825 "Widow H. (A.)" resided near Amos B. Phelps Jr.'s brother, Luman B. Phelps, and half-brother, Eldad Phelps with his son, Michael Phleps. The marriage record of Comfort Pinkham and Elizabeth Phelps was signed by Amos and Julia V. Phelps. This Amos Phelps III was Elizabeth Phelps' brother. Tracking Amos and Julia V. (Johnson) Phelps, it is learned they named their daughter, Elizabeth Ann Phelps (born Stanbridge 1843) likely after Amos Phelps III's sister, Elizabeth Phelps Pinkham, who moved from Quebec to Ontario prior to 1842. The 1825 census proved the only Pinkham family of seven residing in St. Cesaire was Samuel and Theodocia Pinkham with their children, Caleb, Comfort, Huldah, J. Samuel and James O. Pinkham. The 1831 census noted a family of eight resided in St. Cesaire: Samuel and Theodocia, Comfort, J. Samuel, James O., Joseph Abijah and Samuel III. The eighth individual was likely a daughter, name unknown, or unmarried Huldah Pinkham. The Samuel Pinkham Junior family was listed next to the Amos Phelps Senior, Jeremiah Phelps and Oliver C. Phelps families making it possible for Comfort Carpenter Pinkham, son of Samuel Pinkham Junior to meet their grandchild and niece, Elizabeth Phelps. Residing in Stanstead was Samuel Pinkham Senior and his wife Dorothy (Ordway) Pinkham with his sons, Abijah and Joseph Pinkham families. Abijah and Joseph Pinkham were the sons of Samuel Pinkham Senior and brothers to Samuel Pinkham Junior as stated in the book, The History of Stanstead County. The Samuel G. Pinkham Junior family remained in St Cesaire from 1825 until 1831, then the parents are listed in 1842 Milton, Shefford, Quebec again near the Jeremie B. Phelps family. During the 1825 and 1831 census records, the presumed children of Samuel and Theodosia (Carpenter) Pinkham fit listed age groups. The Samuel G. Pinkham Junior family were the only members of the Samuel Pinkham Senior family living in St. Cesaire, Quebec as Samuel Senior and Dorothy (Ordway) Pinkham with sons, Joseph (until he moved to Grafton, MA, USA) and Abijah Pinkham, and their families, resided in Stanstead, Quebec.

The 1831 marriage record of Huldah Pinkham was signed by Samuel Pinkham Junior, her father (Sam G. Pinkham) and Betsy Phelps, who later married Huldah's brother, Comfort Carpenter Plnkham. On the next page of the church document was baptism of Huldah's husband's (Seth Warren) nephew (brother Oliver Warren's son) also signed by

Samuel G. Pinkham, Comfort and Huldah Pinkham's father, and Jeremiah Phelps, the uncle of Elizabeth Phelps and brother to Amos B. Phelps Junior. This record, like the 1825 and 1831 St. Cesaire censuses, connects the Samuel Pinkham Junior and Amos Phelps families prior to Comfort Pinkham and Elizabeth Phelps's 1832 marriage.

Caleb Pinkham, Comfort Carpenter Pinkham's older brother, migrated to Geauga, Ohio before 1850, as did Huldah Pinkham Warren, his sister, who resided in the adjacent township. Huldah Pinkham Warren remained in Ohio, whereas Caleb moved to Clayton, Crawford County, Wisconsin one-hundred-and-six miles from his brother J. Samuel in Union, Rock, WI. Joseph Abijah Pinkham moved to Clayton, Crawford, WI after Minnesota while Caleb Pinkham migrated from Geagua, Ohio to Clayton, Crawford, Wisconsin then Mille Lacs, Minnesota. Uncle Joseph Pinkham, brother of Samuel Junior, resided in Wisconsin during 1858 before returning to Grafton, Massachusetts. Samuel Pinkham III died in Austin, Mower, Minnesota where Joseph Abijah Pinkham had initially resided after Quebec. James O. Pinkham died in Massachusetts, USA.

The repeated naming pattern is very strong in the Pinkham family. Caleb was the name of the son of Comfort and Thankful (Kent) Carpenter, Theodocia's brother, as well as, Comfort's brother. Caleb Pinkham then named his children after his younger siblings - Comfort and Huldah. Abijah, Samuel and Theodosia were also first names used repeatedly in this family line. Comfort Carpenter Pinkham also named son, Samuel, for both his father and grandfather. Additionally, the name "Abijah" is found in this Pinkham family because, Abijah Pinkham was the father of Samuel Pinkham, Senior. Descendants in the Samuel and Theodocia (Carpenter) Pinkham are repeatedly given the first names, Samuel, Theodocia, Abijah, Huldah, Caleb and Comfort.

The 1842 Canada East census records Samuel Pinkham Jr. living in Milton, Shefford County, Quebec where he is a farmer with a family of seven. At this point, some of his children would have moved away - Caleb and Mary Pinkham to Ohio, Huldah Pinkham and Seth Warren to Ohio and Comfort and Elizabeth Pinkham to Ontario, Canada. Likely the family of seven for Samuel Pinkham Jr. were Samuel and Theodocia and sons, James Pinkham (m. 1842 to Mathilde Tetreau-Duchame), the wife of James Pinkham or a Pinkham daughter, J. Samuel Pinkham, Joseph Abijah Pinkham and Samuel Pinkham III. An 1842 Newcastle, Ontario census noted Comfort Pinkham as a laborer in a household of seven which would be Comfort and Elizabeth (Phelps) Pinkham with children Cynthia, Elect(r)a, Mary, Edwin and Willard Pinkham. Elizabeth Phelps Pinkham's uncle, Jeremie B. Phelps is recorded in the 1842 Canada East Milton, Shefford, Quebec census with a family of 15 which might have included his brother, Oliver Cromwell Phelps and wife, as "Oliver C." is not recorded locally but never moved away from the Province of Quebec. Harry (*Henry*) Carpenter, Theodocia Pinkham's brother and family also resided at the same location. Elizabeth Phelps' Pinkham's brother, Amos Phelps III, is recorded in the 1842 Durham, Missisquoi census as having a family of seven and living alongside his wife, Julia V. Johnson Phelps' brother, John Johnson and Caleb Carpenter, Theodocia's brother, whose son was Comfort Carpenter.

The 1842 Clarke, Newcastle, Durham, Ontario census noted the other Stanbridge, Quebec families. Included with the Comfort Carpenter Pinkham family were Quebec Moulton and Carpenter families. Samuel Pinkham Jr.'s brother, Joseph Pinkham, married Sarah Moulton whose family originated in Amesbury, Massachusetts where Dorothy Ordway, the mother of both Samuel Junior and Joseph Pinkham, was born.

A pattern of working as a "laborer" (likely building of railroads) existed with Comfort Pinkham and Amos Phelps named individuals. In the 1842 Canada West census, Comfort Pinkham is listed alone as a laborer in Newcastle, Ontario, Canada. In 1851 Canada West census, the son of Eldad Phelps, Amos Phelps, is listed alone as a laborer in Oxford, Ontario, Canada. In the 1861 Canada West census, Amos Phelps, the son of Oliver C. Phelps is listed alone as a laborer in Frontenac, Ontario, Canada. To support their families financially, these sons of Samuel Pinkham Jr., Eldad Phelps (son of m1 and Amos Phelps Sr.) and Oliver C. Phelps (son of m2 and Amos Phelps Sr.) would work on the extensive railroad projects during this period in Ontario, Canada.

Comfort Carpenter Pinkham was named after his mother's father who was Comfort Carpenter. When Comfort Pinkham married Elizabeth Phelps in 1832, Samuel Pinkham Jr. was the only Samuel Pinkham Senior son residing in St Cesaire, thus proving the parentage to the "Bachelor of St. Cesaire." Most children of Samuel Pinkham Junior migrated to the United States except Comfort, who instead moved to Ontario, Canada, perhaps with Luman Phelps, Betsy Phelps' uncle (brother to Amos Phelps Junior/"the younger"), whose first wife died in Ontario (Luman Phelps married again, a record noted by a letter, and moved to Michigan by 1840) and Quebec Moulton/Carpenter families. Many members of the Samuel Pinkham Junior family moved to the United States with members of the Amos Phelps' families. These include, Amos B. Phelps, son of Jeremiah B. Phelps (who died in Santa Rosa, California by 1903) and Joseph Abijah (incorrectly noted at "James Abijah" on his California death certificate) Pinkham, given both these individuals moved to California. "James" (Joseph) Abijah Pinkham, who died in Madera, California in 1909, is noted in *FindAGrave* as the son of Samuel and Theodocia Pinkham. The 1842 Milton, Shefford, Quebec Census confirmed the Samuel Pinkham Junior family resided in the same township vicinity as the Jeremiah Phelps family as was recorded in both 1825 and 1831 St. Cesaire, Quebec census records.

As stated previously, a marker for this Pinkham line is the use of first names Comfort, Caleb, Huldah, Theodocia, Samuel and Abijah for their offspring to honor family members. Comfort Carpenter Pinkham was named for his mother's father, while his father, Samuel Pinkham Junior was named to honor his father, Samuel Pinkham Senior. Elizabeth Phelps' brother, Amos Phelps III was named for his father, Amos Phelps Junior/"the younger," and he for his father, Amos Phelps Senior, who was named in honor of a grandfather named, Amos Phelps. Not only was Samuel Pinkham Junior listed St Cesaire during 1825 & 1831, his family resided next to the Amos Phelps Senior, Jeremiah Phelps and Oliver C. Phelps families and his children moved to the United States with Phelps family members. In conclusion, the naming pattern of Samuel Pinkham's children, prove Comfort Carpenter Pinkham indeed is a son of Samuel Pinkham and Theodosia Carpenter Pinkham.

Children of Comfort Carpenter and Elizabeth (Phelps) Pinkham (Generation 8):

Cynthia Pinkham Wright – Born abt. 1832, Quebec. Married 1849 to Alfred Wright. Died 21 September 1879, Ontario, Canada.

Electa Pinkham Eddy – Born 15 March 1834, Quebec. Married Hiram Eddy 1854/5; Died 12 May 1916, Ontario, Canada. (*Electa* or *Electra*)

Mary Pinkham Coons – Born abt. 1835, Quebec. Married Coons; Moved to Minnesota. Death abt. 1875, Ashland, Dodge County, Minnesota, USA.

Edwin A. Pinkham- Born abt. 1840-1841, Quebec. Prior to 1867 moved to Dodge, Minnesota. Married May 1867 Catherine Campbell. 1900 moved to North Dakota, USA; Death: Post 1905 Eugene, Oregon, USA.

Willard Pinkham - Born abt. 1841-1842, Quebec/Ontario. Death unknown.

JOHN WESLEY PINKHAM – Born 20 September 1845, Clarke, Ontario; M1 Emma Harris/M2 Sarah Ann Irwin/M3 Margaret Elsworth. Died 28 October 1924, Oshawa, Durham County, Ontario, Canada.

Jane Phebe Pinkham Harris – Born 1850, Ontario. Married William Harris; Died 12 February 1919, Clarke, Durham, Ontario, Canada.

Samuel Pinkham – Born 6 April 1852, Ontario. Married 26 March 1872 to Margaret McLean. Died 6 July 1906, Kindersley, Saskatchewan, Canada.

Charles Pinkham– Born 11 June 1855, Manvers, Ontario. Married Lavina Corey of Quebec on 27 July 1881 in Lowell, Massachusetts, USA. Naturalized US Citizen on 21 November 1893 in Lowell MA, USA. Death undetermined post 1916.

COMFORT CARPENTER PINKHAM: Born 1811, Quebec; Grandson of Comfort Carpenter and descendant of Abijah Pinkham (4) (American Revolutionary War Patriot).

1842 Upper Canada Census: COMFORT PINKHAM, Labourer, Clarke, Newcastle, Durham County, Ontario, Canada. *Source: Library and Archives Canada, Public Archives of Canada, Ottawa, Ontario*

This record notes family of 7: COMFORT PINKHAM, Elizabeth (Phelps) Pinkham and children: Cynthia (b. 1832 QC), Elect(r)a (b. 1834 QC), Mary (b. 1835 QC), Edwin (b. 1836-1840 *Quebec or Ontario*) and Willard (b. 1841-1842 *Quebec or Ontario*)

Other 1842 Clarke, Newcastle, Durham County, Ontario, Canada settlers from Quebec included: John Carpenter (farmer, born Vermont), Joseph Moulton (Farmer, family of 6), Jno Moulton (Farmer, family of 13), Anson Moulton, Hiram Moulton (born 1798 Vermont; married 26 March 1846 Newcastle, Durham County, Ontario). Deaths in Orono, Durham included Wealthy Moulton Hall (b. 1808), Vesta Moulton Smith (b. 20 May 1810) and Mary Moulton Gamsby (b.

1806). Comfort Pinkham's mother was Theodocia Carpenter; his uncle married Sarah Moulton whose father, William Moulton, settled in Stanstead, QC by 1825.

1842 Lower Canada Census Milton, Shefford: Samuel Pinkham: Number of Inhabitants: 7. Samuel G. Pinkham Jr. with wife Theodocia (Carpenter) Pinkham, James Pinkham and wife, J. Samuel Pinkham, Joseph Abijah Pinkham, Samuel Pinkham III. Resided next to Jeremiah Phelps family.

1848 Census of Newcastle District: COMFORT PINKHAM, Living 1848 Clarke Township, Durham County, Province of Ontario. Family of 7 - Comfort & Elizabeth with children (*Cynthia Pinkham born 1832; age 16 in 1848 married 1849 Alfred Wright*), Electra, Mary, Edwin, Willard and John Pinkham, *Source: Clarke, Hope, Alnwick, Cramahe, Haldimand, Hamilton, South Monaghan; Provincial Archives of Ontario, Toronto*

Canadian Genealogy Index, 1600s-1900s: COMFT PINKHAM (Comfort Pinkham), Living, 1850, Clarke Township, Durham County, Province of Ontario. *Source:1851 Census for Newcastle District: Cartwright Clarke, Hope, Manvers.*

1851 Canada West Census: Family of PINKHAM, COMFORT. Farmer: Age 41; Elizabeth Comfort, age 42; Electra Comfort age 18; Mary Comfort age 16; Edwin Comfort age 11; Willard Comfort age 9; John Comfort age 7; Jane Comfort age 1. Last name, "Pinkham" transposed to, "Comfort." Should be Comfort Pinkham *Source: 1851 Census, Canada West, Durham County, Clarke Township.* Surname, ages and birth years listed are incorrect.

References:
> Marriage 23 March 1872 from the Victoria News: Vol.23, Pg. 419.- Samuel Prickham, 20, farmer, Clark, Ontario, same, s/o COMFORT & Elizabeth, married Margaret McLean, 19, Travers, Ireland, Clark, d/o Matthew and Selina. Witness Florence Uylott and L.E.G.G. Smithett both of Lindsay, March 23, 1872, Lindsay. *Source: Victoria News, 1872*

> 26 March 1872 Marriage of Samuel Pinkham: Samuel Pinkham, Born abt. 1852 Clarke, Ontario married Margaret McLean on 26 March 1872 in Victoria, Ontario, Canada. Last name spelled: Prickham. Samuel Prickham of Clark, Farmer. Names of parents; COMFORT PRICKHAM and Elizabeth Prickham. *Source: Ontario, Toronto, Canada "Registrations of Marriage, 1869-1928*

> Marriage (M2) on 20 November 1872; From the Victoria News: Vol. 23, Page. 399 – John Pinkham, 27, widower, farmer, Clark, Ops, s/o COMFORT & Elizabeth, married Sarah Ann Irwin, 19, Mariposa, same, d/o Robert and Mary J. Witness Eretus Smith and William Galbraith, both of Mariposa, 20 November 1872, Mariposa. *Source: Victoria News, 1872*

> Marriage (M2) on 20 November 1872: From Ontario County Marriage Registrar, 1858-1869. John Pinkham; Marriage; Date: 20 Nov 1872;

Event Place: Victoria, Ontario, Canada; Age – 27; Birth year – 1875; Birthplace – Clarke; Father's Name – COMFORT PINKHAM; Mother's Name birth year – 1853; Spouse's birthplace – Mariposa; Spouse's Father's Name – Robert Irwin; Spouse's Mother's Name – Mary J. Irwin. *Source: Ontario County Marriage Registers, 1858-1869. Victoria, Ontario, Canada; Archives of Ontario Toronto*

20 November 1872 Marriage of John Pinkham: John Pinkham, Widower, Farmer, Age 27, born 1845 of Mariposa, Victoria, Ontario, Canada, Parents: Father- COMFORT PINKHAM /Mother: Elizabeth Pinkham. Married Sarah Ann Irwin (spelled Iravin). *Source: Ontario Marriages 1869-1927 Archives of Toronto*

1875 Minnesota Deaths: Mary (Pinkham) Coon, Female, Death date: 9 June 1875; Death Place – Ashland, Dodge County, Minnesota; Age- 98/Birthdate - 1777 (Actual age: 40/ born 1835); Race – White; Marital Status – Married; Father's name: COMFORT PINKHAM; Father's birthplace Canada; Mother's Name- Elisabeth, Mother's birthplace – Canada). *Source: Minnesota Deaths & Burials, 1835-1990 citing Ashland, Dodge County, Minnesota*

1875 Ashland, Dodge, Minnesota State Census: Edwin Pinkham. E. A. Pinkham age 34 (born 1841/2 Quebec) born Canada; father born Canada; mother born Canada. *Source: Minnesota State Census, 1875*

11 November 1877 Baptism of Charles Pinkham, Freilighsburg, Quebec, Methodist Church. *"Charles son of COMFORT PINKHAM and Elizabeth Phelps his wife was born in the township of Manvers, Province of Ontario on the eleventh day of June one thousand eight hundred and fifty-five and was baptized on the eleventh day of November one thousand eight hundred and seventy-seven in the presence of subscribing witnesses by H. Cairns, Minister."* *Source: Drouin*

United States Census, 1880: Edwin A. Pinkham. Edwin A. Pinkham age 37 born 1843 born Canada; father born Canada; mother born Canada. *Source. United States Census, 1880*

27 July 1881 Marriage of Charles W. Pinkham: Charles Pinkham born 11 June 1855 in Ontario, Canada married Lavina A. Corey (born 1852 Quebec to parents Luther and Huldah A. Corey) in Lowell, Massachusetts. Parents: Father – COMFORT; Mother – Elizabeth). *Source: Massachusetts Vital Records 1840-1915 New England Historic Genealogical Society, Boston, Massachusetts*

Minnesota State Census, 1885: Edwin A. Pinkham. Edwin A. Pinkham age 41 born 1844 Canada; father born Canada; mother born Canada. *Source: Minnesota State Census, 1885*

1891 Census: "Eletra Eddy" (Electra Eddy), Female, Widow, birth year – 1834, birthplace – Quebec, Religion – Methodist, French-Canadian – No; Father's birthplace – Quebec; Mother's birthplace – Quebec.

Province - Ontario, District - Durham West, Subdistrict – Clarke, Household members: Harvey W. Eddy age 28, Eletra Eddy, Age 57.
Source: Year 1891 Census, Library and Archives, Canada – Place Clarke, Durham West, Ontario

1891 Census of Canada: John Pinkham; Gender – Male; Marital status - Married; Age – 45; Birth Year – abt. 1846; Birthplace – Ontario; Relation to Head of Household – Head; Religion – Methodist; French-Canadian – No; Spouse's name – Sarah A. Pinkham; Father's birthplace – Quebec; Mother's birthplace – Quebec; Province – Ontario; District number – 100; District – Ontario North; Subdistrict – Brock; Household Members: John Pinkham (Age 45), Sarah A. Pinkham (Age 37), Minnie Pinkham (Age 17), Lawrence Pinkham (Age 15), Harriet Pinkham (Age 13), Elizabeth Pinkham (Age 11), Annie Pinkham (Age 9), Milton Pinkham (Age 6), John W. Pinkham (Age 4). *Source: 1891 Canada Census Brock, Ontario North, Ontario. Library and Archives Canada, Ottawa, Ontario*

1900 United States Census (Pelican Township, Otter Tail, Minnesota): Edwin E. Pinkham (son of Edwin A. Pinkham). Age 28 born Minnesota. Father (Edwin A. Pinkham's)'s birthplace: Canada Fr. (France – Quebec); Mother's birthplace Canada Eng. *Source: United States Census, 1900*

1911 Census of Canada for John Pinkham: Name: John Pinkham, married, born 1846 age 45, religion – Methodist. French-Canadian: No. Father's birthplace: Quebec. Mother's birthplace – Quebec, District: Ontario North. Sub-district: Brock.

12 May 1916 Ontario Deaths – Eddy, Electra, 84 years, May 12, 1916, Clarke Township, Orono. Housewife. Widow. Father: PINKHAM, COMFORT. *Source: Archives of Ontario, Toronto, Canada*

12 May 1916 Death Record: Electa Eddy (Electra Pinkham Eddy). Death 12 May 1916, Clarke County, Durham, Ontario, Age 84, Burial Place: Orono, Father: COMFORT PINKHAM. *Source: Ontario Deaths, 1869-193, Archives of Ontario, Toronto*

Marriage (M3) on 5 July 1917: John Wesley Pinkham; age – 71; birth year abt. 1846; birthplace – Ontario, Canada; Marriage date – 5 July 1917; Marriage place – Ontario, Canada; Father – CARPENTER PINKHAM; Mother Betsey Phelp; Spouse – Margaret Elsworth. *Source: Archives of Ontario, Toronto, Ontario, Canada, Registrations of Marriages.*

~Elizabeth Phelps Pinkham: Married to COMFORT CARPENTER PINKHAM

Born: 1812, Stanbridge, Quebec (Sibling– Amos Phelps III, Born abt. 1809-1810)
      Father: Amos Phelps Jr. (b. January 1786, Rutland, Vermont)
      Mother: Unknown/ *"Widow H./A." (b. in Vermont)*

Marriage: 13 March 1832, Freilighsburg, Quebec, Holy Trinity, Anglican Church.

"On this thirteenth day of March one-thousand eight hundred and thirty-two, COMFORT PINKHAM of this parish of St. Cesaire and ELIZABETH PHELPS, spinster of Stanbridge, both of major age, were married after publication of the Banns in presence of the subscribing witnesses". Signed by: James Reid, Minister. Comfort Pinkham, Elizabeth Phelps, Amos Phelps and Julia V. Phelps."
Source: Drouin

<u>Death:</u> 17 September 1883, Orono, Ontario, Canada. *"Mrs. C. Pinkham, age 71 years."*

Elizabeth Phelps Pinkham Analysis

This analysis will prove Elizabeth Phelps is the daughter of Amos Phelps Junior/"the younger," grandchild of Amos Phelps Senior and Diadama (Long) Phelps and sister to Amos Phelps III born 1809 Stanbridge, Quebec.

Elizabeth Phelps' 1812 birth is not noted by any documentation in the Eastern Townships of Quebec but consistently recorded as "1812 Quebec" in census records after 1840. She married Comfort Carpenter Pinkham, born 1811 in Quebec, at the Frelighsburg Anglican Church where she was noted as "a Spinster of Stanbridge." A parent did not sign her marriage certificate (father Amos B. Phelps Junior died 1813; mother Widow "A" Phelps likely died post 1825) as her brother, Amos Phelps III, and his wife, Julia V. (Johnson) Phelps, were witnesses.

Based upon onomastics, Elizabeth Phelps Pinkham, was the daughter of unknown and Amos Phelps Junior/"the younger," the eldest son of Diadama (Long) Phelps and Amos Phelps, who was born in Rutland, Vermont during January of 1787.

Amos Phelps III, who signed the marriage license of his sister, Elizabeth Phelps, "Spinster of Stanbridge," was born in 1809/1810 Quebec, when Amos Jr., son of Amos Sr. and Diadama Long Phelps, would have been age twenty-four. Amos Phelps III noted on Iowa census records his parents were, "born in Vermont," which is likely since sibling members of this line (Eldad m1, Pheba m1, Luman m2) married their spouses in Franklin, Vermont. It also proves that Amos Phelps Junior, born 1786 Vermont was the father of Amos Phelps III because the children of Amos Phelps Sr. and Phebe (m1) were born in Connecticut while the children of Amos Phelps and Diadama Long (m2) were born in Rutland, Vermont - Amos B. Phelps Jr. (b. 1786 Rutland, VT) and Luman B. Phelps (b. 1876 Rutland, VT; married VT 1812, first child a daughter not named Elizabeth) and Jeremiah, Selinda and Oliver C. Phelps born Rougemont, Quebec.

Amos Phelps III, Elizabeth Phelps' brother, died in Maquoketa, Iowa, and shared his burial plot with Benejah Phelps (whose father, John Phelps, founded a Quaker settlement in upstate New York), the son of John Phelps (#3748 – Phelps Family; b. 1802 South Hero, Vermont) and grandson of Benajah Phelps (#1595 Phelps Family; b. 1775 Goshen, CT). The Phelps family tended to settle nearby one another in locations they pioneered. "Our Family History" by Ethalmae Eyler Carter recorded John Phelps as Amos Phelps Senior's father. The name, "Amos" was given to the first-born males in this line, thus confirming the naming pattern for Amos Phelp Junior/"the younger" to his son born 1809-1810 - Amos Phelps III. Amos and Julia V. (Johnson) Phelps, named their daughter, Elizabeth, likely for his sister, Elizabeth Phelps Pinkham.

Individuals with Phelps surnames existed in both Vermont and the Eastern Townships of 1800 - 1832 Quebec. However, only children from the Amos Phelps line named their offspring, "Amos." When tracking the Amos Phelps children in 1800-1840 Quebec, in the 1825 Bedford-Stanbridge census the child from Amos Phelps' first wife, Phebe (m1), Eldad Phelps and "Carman"/Luman Phelps, son of Diadama Long Phelps (m2) resided in Stanbridge with a Widow "H." (most likely "A." Phelps/Amos Phelps Junior/"the younger") and her daughter who was the same age as Elizabeth Phelps would have been while Amos Phelps Senior and Diadama (Long) Phelps resided in St. Cesaire (1831 Census) with (m2) sons, Jeremiah, and Oliver Cromwell Phelps (alongside the Samuel Pinkham Jr. family). In all, there were zero "Amos" Phelps sons listed with the other early Quebec Phelps families making the name of, "Amos," a predominate marker recording descendants for this specific Phelps line.

Six individuals named "Amos Phelps" resided in the 1800-1850 Eastern Townships of Quebec:
1) Amos Phelps, "Senior" (b. 31 March 1750, Hartford, CT; d. 1831, Rougemont, St. Hyacinthe, Quebec). Married: (m1) 1770 Connecticut to Phebe (b. 1750, CT; d. VT); (m2) 1790, Franklin, Vermont to Diadama Long, daughter of Samuel Long & Martha (Brewster) Long (b. 14 January 1763, Coventry, CT; d. 9 March 1837, Rougemont, Quebec).
2) Amos B. Phelps Junior/ "the younger:" (born January 1786, Rutland, VT) Son of Amos Phelps Senior and Diadama (Long) Phelps. Children: Amos Phelps III (b. 1809-1810); Elizabeth Phelps Pinkham (b. 1812). Died October 1813 during the War of 1812. Parents of Amos Phelps III were recorded in Iowa census – "born in Vermont." *(Son of Amos Senior and m2 Diadama Long Phelps)*
3) Amos Phelps: (Born abt. 1805, Quebec) Son of Eldad and Abigail (Tree) Phelps. 1825 Quebec Lower Canada Census for Eldad Phelps – One son, age 18-20. Moved to Crawford, Illinois prior to 1830. Recorded in 1830 and 1840 Crawford, Illinois, United States Census with one son age 5-10 (born 1825-1830). This Amos Phelps' son is listed in 1851 Canada West Oxford County census as Amos Phelps, age 26 (born 1825) with wife Elizabeth Phelps age 18 and son C. J. Phelps age two. The 1861 Canada West Frontenac census lists the grandson of Eldad Phelps, Amos Phelps, as age 32 born 1829 *(Grandson to Amos Senior and Phebe m1 Phelps)*
4) Amos Phelps III: (born 1809-1810, Stanbridge, Bedford, Quebec) Son of (based upon onomastics) Amos Phelps Junior/"the younger" and unknown. Married Julia V. Johnson in Phillipsburg, Quebec 13 December 1830. 1831 Quebec Census – family of 2 with Samuel Johnson (father of Julia V.) listed in Stanbridge. He and his wife signed the marriage document for his sister, Elizabeth Phelps, in 1832. In 24 November 1855 Amos Phelps was listed in the Militia of Stanbridge, Missisquoi, Quebec. By 1860 he moved to Maquoketa, Iowa where he resided with wife, Julia V. Johnson, and children.

He died 14 March 1891 in Maquoketa, Iowa, USA. Amos and Diadama Phelps' daughter, Selinda Phelps McRae, born 1794 in Rougemont, Quebec, moved with her husband to Waterloo, Black Hawk, Iowa, where she died in 1888. Selinda Phelps McRae was the aunt of Amos Phelps III. *(Grandson to Amos Senior and m2 Diadama Long Phelps)*

5) Amos B. Phelps: (Born 25 June 1825, Quebec; died 24 February 1903, Santa Rosa, CA, USA) Son of Jeremiah and Margaret (Collins) Phelps. Baptized 1825 Chambly, Quebec (Anglican). Married Maria C. Lyon in Quebec. Moved to Racine, Wisconsin in 1855. Amos Phelps became a naturalized American citizen on 21 April 1857 in Illinois. *(Grandson to Amos Senior and m2 Diadama Long Phelps)*

6) Amos Phelps: (Born 1 June 1827, Quebec; died 10 January 1893, Quebec) Son of Oliver Cromwell and Mary Josette (Roi) Phelps. Baptized in Abbotsford with his grandmother, Diadama (Long) Phelps as witness. Resided in Quebec until his death. *(Grandson to Amos Senior and m2 Diadama Long Phelps)*

Amos Phelps Senior immigrated to Quebec during 1793. A land sale on 8 July 1807 was made by Diadama Long Phelps, who resided at Richelieu, Shefford County, for Lot 9, Range 2, Stanbridge (60 acres on Pike River). Son, Amos Phelps Junior/"the younger," was also listed as residing at Lot 9, Range 2, Stanbridge which confirms the family relationship. Elizabeth Phelps, born 1812 is listed as being, a "Spinster of Stanbridge," on her marriage record to Comfort Carpenter Pinkham. Likely, the Widow of Amos Phelps, Junior/"the younger" lived on Amos Phelps Junior's property with their two children, Amos III & Elizabeth Phelps, until she died.

Amos Phelps Senior purchased Lot 11, Range 2 (100 Acres) in 31 March 1802 which he gave to his son (m1 marriage), Eldad Phelps, who was born 1783 in Connecticut. Two months later, this property is sold for 300 Spanish dollars. That Amos Phelps Senior purchased property for his children was verified by this record.

Amos Phelps Junior/"the younger" purchased land on 7 June 1807: Sale by George Ross to Amos Phelps, "the younger" – LOT 9, RANGE 2, STANBRIDGE – 2 acres on the northeastern bank of the Pike River for 100 Spanish dollars. This purchase proves Amos Phelps Junior/"the younger," was a resident of Stanbridge, Quebec. This land was not sold and likely remained Phelps' land during Elizabeth Phelps' birth and childhood.

One year later prior to September 1808, both Amos Phelps Senior and Amos Phelps Junior/"the younger," are noted as filing a bond: "Bond by Amos Phelps, senior and JUNIOR, to George Ross for 10 pounds in an assault and battery charge against Sam Bickford & Abner Bickford."

After 1808 there is no notation of Amos Phelps Junior/"the younger" in Stanbridge, QC. Amos Phelps Junior possibly married in Vermont then had children born in Stanbridge, Quebec - Amos (b. 1809-1810) and Elizabeth Phelps (b. 1812). Perhaps, his wife died after being listed as a "Widow" in the 1825 census as there is no mention her in either 1829 or 1831 marriage documents or the 1831 census (whereas there is a Widow Carpenter, the wife of Comfort Carpenter, Theodocia Carpenter Pinkham's mother).

It is noted Geauga County, Ohio was originally part of the French colony of Canada (New France) and was ceded to Great Britain in 1763 then renamed the Province of Quebec. In the late 1700s the land became part of the Connecticut Western Reserve in the Northwest Territory and was purchased by the Connecticut Land Company in 1795. Geauga County was founded on 1 March 1801. The Connecticut Land Company included 57 proprietors, including Oliver Phelps. Caleb Pinkham, son of Samuel Pinkham, and his sister, Huldah Pinkham (Seth) Warren, siblings of Comfort Carpenter (who married Elizabeth Phelps) Pinkham settled in Geauga, Ohio in 1838 – perhaps with Amos Phelps III who moved to Iowa. That the Phelps and Pinkham families moved together to different locations connects the Samuel Pinkham and Amos Phelps families.

In 1812 Amos B. Phelps, father to Elizabeth Phelps born that year, enlisted Swift's New York Miltia, representation that covered Vermont and New York. He died in October of 1813 whereas his brother, Luman B. Phelps, who also enlisted in June of 1813, returned to Quebec. There are no will or land record documents noted in Quebec Notarial Leon LaLanne records for the period 1812-1813 to confirm the inheritance of Amos B. Phelps Junior's widow or children, Amos III and Elizabeth Phelps.

After her father's death, the only listing of Elizabeth Phelps is at age 14 in the 1825 Stanbridge census with a "Widow H." or, given many misspellings on the census including "Carman" for "Luman," with her mother, "Widow A." (Amos Jr.) Phelps. She then married into the Pinkham family who resided alongside her grandparents (Amos and Diadama Phelps) and uncles (Jeremiah and Oliver Phelps) in both the 1825 and 1831 St. Cesaire, Quebec censuses. Given she is noted as a "Spinster of Stanbridge" means likely she resided at the property of her father in Stanbridge until she married. Jeremiah Phelps moved to Minnesota with Comfort Carpenter Pinkham's brother, Joseph Abijah Pinkham and he is noted in the 1842 Milton, Shefford, QC census with the family initial of "B." - Jeremie B. Phelps (m2 Rutland, Vermont-born sons of Amos Sr. and Diadama Long Phelps: Amos B. Phelps Jr. and Luman B. Phelps).

St. Cesaire, where Samuel Pinkham Jr., Amos Sr., Jeremiah and Oliver C. Phelps' families resided during 1825 and 1831 census reports, was located twenty-two miles from Stanbridge and thirty-one miles from Freilighsburg. St. Cesaire was also located seventy miles from Stanstead, Quebec. That Eldad, Luman and Widow "A." (Amos Jr.) Phelps resided in Stanbridge confirms Elizabeth Phelps, "Spinster of Stanbridge," met Comfort Carpenter Pinkham, "Bachelor of St. Cesaire," while visiting uncles Jeremiah and Oliver C. Phelps and grandparents, Amos Senior and Diadama (Long) Phelps.

Thus, while there are no birth records for Elizabeth Phelps, she was the grandchild and descendant of Diadama (Long) Phelps because:

1) Amos Phelps, Elizabeth Phelps' brother, signed her marriage document onomastically relating her to the Amos and Diadama (Long) Phelps family line. Amos Phelps III, was the son of Amos Phelps Junior/"the younger" and unknown born in Quebec 1809 when Amos Phelps was age 24 (Elizabeth Phelps was born when Amos Phelps Junior/"the younger" was age 26 in 1812.).
2) Amos Phelps Junior/"the younger" resided at the Phelps' property in Stanbridge where later Elizabeth Phelps, "Spinster of Stanbridge," likely lived with her brother (1825 census recorded: *blank* Phelps & Widow "H." Phelps) rather than St. Cesaire where the Samuel Pinkham Junior family resided nearby Amos Phelps Senior and sons Jeremiah and Oliver C. Phelps, the fact of which confirmed a connection between the Samuel Pinkham and Amos Phelps families.
3) Amos Phelps III (born 1809-1810), grandson of Amos and Diadama (Long) Phelps, was brother to Elizabeth Phelps Pinkham (born 1812), as he not only signed her 1832 marriage license, but also named his daughter, Elizabeth, after his sister.

The possibility for Elizabeth and Amos Phelps to be children of Luman Phelps, born 1787, is unlikely because Luman Phelps married Hannah Briggs (b. 1795, Connecticut) on 11 June 1812 in Vermont – the year of Elizabeth Phelps' birth, and their verified first-born child was "Amy Phelps" was born in Stanbridge, Quebec in 1814. Luman Phelps is recorded as living alongside the "Widow H." Phelps family in 1825; likely his brother Amos B. Phelps' widow and daughter, Elizabeth Phelps. Another connection exists between this Phelps branch and the children of Samuel & Theodocia (Carpenter) Pinkham. Luman and Hannah (Briggs) Phelps' daughter, Amy Phelps (b. 26 September 1814, Stanbridge, Quebec) married Welcome Chandler, and the witness was Oliver Warren. Oliver Warren was the brother of Seth Warren, Huldah Pinkham's – Comfort Carpenter Pinkham's sister - husband.

The 1842 Lower Canada Milton, Shefford, Quebec census recorded Samuel Pinkham Junior as a farmer housing seven Inhabitants and listed next to Harry (*Henry*) Carpenter, brother of Theodocia Carpenter Pinkham. Brother to Amos B. Phelps Junior, Jeremiah Phelps, is also listed in 1842 Lower Canada Milton, Shefford census with the "B." family initial as: Jeremie B. Phelps. By this point, Samuel and Theodocia's son, Caleb Pinkham, had married in 1829 and moved to Ohio by 1838. Their daughter, Huldah Pinkham Warren, married in 1831 then moved to Ohio. As Comfort and Elizabeth (Phelps) Pinkham were recorded in the 1842 Newcastle, Durham, Canada, West census with a family of seven, the 1842 Milton census confirms Pinkham-Phelps ties continue given the Samuel and Theodocia Pinkham family lived alongside Jeremiah Phelps' family (Elizabeth Phelps' uncle and cousins). The connection between the Amos Phelps-Samuel Pinkham family is documented by 1825, 1830 and 1842 Quebec census records as Comfort Carpenter Pinkham's parents, Samuel Junior and Theodocia (Carpenter) Pinkham family resided next to the Jeremiah Phelps' family even after Comfort Carpenter and Elizabeth (Phelps) Pinkham moved to Ontario, Canada.

To restate, Elizabeth Phelps was the daughter of Amos Phelps Junior/"the younger," a fact confirmed by a land sale made on 8 July 1807 by Diadama Long Phelps, who resided at Richelieu, Shefford County, Lot 9, Range 2, Stanbridge (60 acres on Pike

River) which connects Shefford County with Amos Phelps III and Elizabeth Phelps as their father, Amos Phelps Junior/"the younger," was listed as residing at Lot 9, Range 2, (Richelieu), Shefford County, Stanbridge thereby solidifying the family relationship. Elizabeth Phelps, born 1812 is listed as being, a "Spinster of Stanbridge," on her marriage record to Comfort Carpenter Pinkham. Milton was also located in Shefford Country, where both Jeremie B. Phelps and Samuel Pinkham Junior were recorded as farmers by the 1842 Quebec census.

In conclusion, based upon onomastics and other factors, the father of Elizabeth Phelps born 1812 Stanbridge, Quebec, Canada (and Amos Phelps III, b. 1809-1810 Stanbridge, Quebec, Canada) is Amos Phelps Jr./ "the younger," the eldest son of Amos and Diadama (Long) Phelps born January 1786 in Rutland, Vermont, USA.

Pinkham – Phelps Family Connections:
Elizabeth Phelps (daughter of Amos "the younger" and Unknown Phelps) and Comfort Carpenter Pinkham, son of Samuel Junior and Theodocia Carpenter (daughter of Comfort Carpenter and Thankful Wilcox) Pinkham left Quebec for Ontario prior to 1842. Children born before 1842 Ontario census were: Cynthia (b. 1832); Elect(r)a (b. 1834); Mary (b. 1835); Edwin (b. 1840-1841) and maybe Willard (b. 1842) Pinkham. The marriage between Comfort Carpenter Pinkham and Elizabeth Phelps was the only one between Phelps/Pinkham families although the families lived alongside one another and moved from Vermont between 1795 and 1800 to Quebec then returned to America post 1830s. The Samuel Pinkham Junior and Amos Phelps Senior families prove the connection of Elizabeth Phelps to the Amos Phelps and Diadama (Long) Phelps line:

1) Caleb Pinkham: (born 13 March 1810, Lower Canada) Eldest son of Samuel and Theodocia (Carpenter) Pinkham. Moved to Phelps-founded Geauga, Ohio in 1855 then Wisconsin and Minnesota where he purchased land. He was named for his Uncle Caleb Carpenter and named his children after his siblings: Comfort and Huldah Pinkham, as well as, after himself, Caleb Pinkham Junior.

2) Huldah Pinkham: (born abt. 1815, Stanstead, Quebec) Eldest (surviving) daughter of Samuel and Theodocia (Carpenter) Pinkham, who married Seth Warren, "in presence of her father and brother." The marriage document was signed by Seth Warren, Huldah Pinkham, Oliver Warren, BETSY PHELPS, and Sam G. Pinkham on 16 November 1831. That the document was not signed by Comfort Carpenter Pinkham, "the brother," but instead, "Betsy Phelps," proves the Amos Phelps/ Samuel Pinkham families were intertwined. The document following this marriage record lists a baptism for Oliver Warren Carpenter ("Carpenter" is the surname of American Revolutionary War Solider, Amos Carpenter, the uncle of Theodocia Carpenter, mother of Comfort Carpenter. Theodocia named her son after her father – Comfort Carpenter Pinkham) which is signed by JEREMIAH PHELPS, SAM G. PINKHAM, and Seth Warren, again connecting the Pinkham and Phelps' families: "...*On this sixteenth day of November one thousand eight hundred and thirty-one, Oliver Warren Carpenter, born on the twentieth day of September one thousand eight hundred and thirty-one was baptized in the presence of family and witnesses* – Thomas Johnson

Warren, Oliver Warren, SAM G. PINKHAM, JEREMIAH PHELPS and Harriet unknown." Oliver Warren and Seth Warren were brothers. Seth Warren married Huldah Pinkham, Comfort Pinkham's sister/daughter of Sam. G. Pinkham.

Seth and Huldah (Pinkham) Warren moved to Ashtabula, Ohio during the 1830s.

3) Joseph Abijah Pinkham: Son of Samuel and Theodocia (Carpenter) Pinkham. He left Quebec and settled in the same town as Jeremiah Phelps, son of Amos & Diadama (Long) Phelps. Abijah is named for his great-grandfather Abijah Pinkham who served in the American Revolutionary War and was his father, Samuel Pinkham's grandfather. Abijah purchased land in Mower County on 17 May 1859 and sold property the same property. He also sold property on 2 January 1863 and purchased property on 1 April 1863. He is listed in the 1860 Austin, Mower, Minnesota census along with his wife and children, including two named after his parents: Docia (Theodocia) born 1851 and Samuel born 1855. The Abijah Pinkham family moved to Wisconsin in 1875 with his children – Samuel Pinkham (born 14 April 1857, Quebec) and Theodocia Pinkham (born 1865 Mower, MN). Jeremiah Phelps moved to Mower, Minnesota with his family in 1857 and died in 1909 Madera, California after residing there since 1904.

4) Amos Phelps: (born 1809/1810, Quebec) Son of Amos Phelps Jr./ "the younger," moved to Maquoketa, Iowa by 1860. Selinda Phelps McRae, daughter of Amos Phelps Senior and Diadama (Long) Phelps, moved to Waterloo, Black Hawk, Iowa after her 1817 marriage (March 1817, All Saints, Missisquoi, Quebec) to Christopher McRae. Amos Phelps III was Selinda Phelps McRae's nephew. Benajah Phelps, son of John Phelps, who is listed in the Rutland 1790 Vermont census alongside Amos Phelps, Sr, is buried in the Iowa cemetery plot owned by Amos Phelps III, son of Amos Phelps Jr./"the younger" who died in 1813.

5) Amos Phelps: (born 1823; baptized 1825) Son of Jeremiah and Margaret (Collins) Phelps. Lsted in the Phelps Family Newsletter of February 1985 as **Amos B. Phelps**, from "Phelps Family Papers 1851-1864 item 33, University of Michigan, William L. Clements Library, Ann Arbor, MI. 20 letters from Amos B. Phelps dated 1851-1854 describe his experience as prospector during the Gold Rush in Placerville (El Dorado County). Amos B. Phelps (1824 -) (P3682), WRONG FATHER LISTED – SHOULD BE JEREMIAH PHELPS *#1569 Alexander, #521* Amos, #165 John, #47 Joseph, #24 Timothy, #14 William. PROVES: **Amos B. Phelps** was named after **Jeremiah Phelps' brother: Amos B. Phelps Junior/"the younger"** who died in 1813 during the War of 1812. In the 1842 Milton Shefford Quebec census, Jeremiah Phelps is listed as, "Jeremie B. Phelps", confirming the family line repeated usage of the initiall "B" with brothers, Amos B. Phelps Junior and Luman B. Phelps.

When Elizabeth Phelps, daughter of Amos Phelps Jr./"the younger," married Comfort Carpenter Pinkham, the son of Samuel Pinkham Junior, two families who had lived alongside one another during 1825 and 1831 (*1842*) Quebec census records (Samuel Pinkham Jr., Amos Phelps Sr., Jeremiah Phelps and Oliver Cromwell Phelps) were genealogically connected. While Joseph Abijah Pinkham, son of Samuel Pinkham Jr., moved with Jeremiah Phelps' family to Austin, Mower, Minnesota by 1858, the marriage of Comfort Carpenter Pinkham to Elizabeth Phelps was the only one between Samuel Pinkham Senior and Amos Phelps Senior familes.

~Elizabeth (Betsy) Phelps Pinkham, daughter of Amos Phelps Jr./"the younger" (b. 1786, Rutland, VT) and unknown.

Born: 1812, Stanbridge, Quebec, Canada

Daughter of Amos Phelps Junior/"younger," (b. 1786, Rutland, VT) and unknown. Sister to Amos Phelps III (born 1809-1810) who signed her marriage document. Marriage lists her as, a "Spinster of Stanbridge." Son, Charles Pinkham, born in Ontario, was baptized at Frelighsburg Anglican Church in Quebec where he named parents: Comfort Pinkham & Elizabeth Phelps.

Marriage: 13 March 1832 **Elizabeth Phelps** to Comfort Carpenter Pinkham. Witnesses: Amos & Julia V. Phelps. Location: Frelighsburg, Quebec, Anglican Church, Holy Trinity. *Source: Drouin*

Death: 17 September 1883, Orono, Ontario, Canada

"Died: PINKHAM, C. – At Orono, September 17th, **Mrs. C. Pinkham**, age 71 years. 21 September 1883." *Source: Canadian Statesman (Bowman, Ontario)*

References of Elizabeth Phelps Pinkham:
1) 1851 Census of Canada West (Ontario), Durham County: **Elizabeth Comfort** age 42. *(Age 39-years if born 1812)*. Last name for family: Comfort. Pinkham is listed as the first name of Comfort Pinkham (b. 1811 – correct age of 41), so entire family is listed with a surname of, Comfort. Religion: Methodist (named their son, John Wesley, after founder).
2) 1861 Census of Canada, Clarke, Durham County, Ontario: **Elizabeth Pinkham** age 50 (Born abt. 1811, **Widow**) with sons, Samuel Pinkham age 9, and Charles Pinkham, age 6. Listed next to daughter Cynthia Pinkham Wright (b. 1832, Quebec) and her husband, Alfred Wright with their 9 children. Separate entry on census page for Willard Pinkham, age - 18 (Born abt. 1843).
3) 1871 Census of Canada, Durham West, Ontario: **Elizabeth Pinkham,** age 58, abt. 1812, **Widowed**. Listed with sons, Samuel Pinkham (Age – 18) and Charles Pinkham (Age – 17).
4) 20 November 1872 – Marriage pf John Pinkham to Sarah Ann Irwin in Mariposa, Victoria, Ontario. Parents of Groom: Father – Comfort Pinkham; **Mother: Elizabeth Pinkham**. *Source: Ontario Marriages 1869-1927*
5) 26 March 1872 – Marriage of Samuel Prickham (Pinkham) to Margaret McLean, Victoria, Ontario. Parents of Groom: Father – Comfort Prickham (Pinkham); Mother **Elizabeth** Prickham **(Pinkham)**. *Source: Ontario Marriages 1869 – 1927*
6) 1881 Canada Census: Clarke, Durham West, Ontario: **Elisabeth Pincombe, age 68 born (1813) Quebec.** Pinkham misspelled, Pincombe.

Listed with daughter Jane Pinkham Harris and husband, William Harris with 4 Harris children including Elizabeth O. Harris age 5.

7) 11 November 1877 Baptism at Frelighsburg, Quebec Church for Charles Pinkham (born 11 June 1855 in township of Manvers, Ontario) - ..."**Charles, son** of Comfort Pinkham and **Elizabeth Phelps, his wife...**"

8) 27 July 1881 Marriage of Charles W. Pinkham to Lavina A. Corey (born Quebec) in Lowell, Massachusetts. Groom's Father: Comfort; Groom's **mother: Elizabeth.**

9) 5 July 1917 marriage of John Wesley Pinkham to Margaret Elsworth. Marriage place: Ontario. Groom's father: Carpenter Pinkham; Groom's **mother: Betsy Phelp.**

To determine Elizabeth Phelps' parentage, researching the Amos Phelps family was necessary to conclude the father of Elizabeth Phelps, and her brother, Amos Phelps III, was Amos B. Phelps Junior/"the younger," the eldest son of Amos Phelps Senior and (m2) Diadama (Long) Phelps.

~Amos B. Phelps Junior / "the Younger" Analysis:

This analysis will prove Amos Phelps Junior/"the younger" was the son of Amos Phelps Senior and Diadama (Long) Phelps, as well as, the father of Elizabeth Phelps (born 1812) and her older brother, Amos Phelps III (born 1809/1810).

There is no direct evidence to prove Amos Phelps Junior, also known as, "the younger," was son of Amos Phelps Senior and Diadama (Long) Phelps, but he is listed in a 1790 Rutland, VT census and in documents in the Eastern Townships of Quebec between the years 1790 and 1812 that prove he existed. The search for specific birth and marriage licenses, as well as, land grants or court records took place in Stanbridge, Quebec, Milton & St. Cesaire in Bedford Country, Quebec and Clark, Durham Country, Ontario, Canada. The Eastern Township Quebec Genealogist at American Ancestors was consulted and confirmed there were no birth records in this remote area of Quebec between 1790 and 1820. Although the Eastern Township of Quebec's Notarial records (Actes de Notarie, 1799-1845) of Leon LaLanne were written in English, there were no records that specifically mentioned Amos Phelps Jr./"the younger" was born in Rutland, Vermont, married in Stanbridge, Quebec or Vermont, left behind a widow named "A" Phelps or was father of Amos Phelps III and Elizabeth Phelps. The Stanbridge and Stanstead Historical Society had few records prior to 1830 as did the Drouin Collection which lists both Amos Phelps III marriage to Julia V. Johnson (born Vermont) in 1829 and Elizabeth Phelps marriage to Comfort Carpenter Pinkham in 1832 Freilighsburg, Quebec. *Family Search* and *Ancestry*.com records do not list much for this branch of the Phelps family nor did historical societies or newspapers for Lower Canada. Bible records for Pinkham and Phelps were searched unsuccessfully. The family book, "Our Family History," by Ethalmae Eylar Carter notes there were other family members not listed, thus my research into the Amos Phelps Junior/ "the younger" line. The Jackson County Genealogical Chapter of Maquoketa, Iowa provided information about Amos Phelps III and his Iowa descendants. A 1985 "Phelps Family Newsletter" verified the naming pattern using the initial, "B" for Amos B. Phelps Jr./"the younger (War of 1812 enlistment) with the Amos Phelps family as brothers and nephew - Jeremie B. Phelps (1842 Milton, Shefford Quebec census), Luman B. Phelps (War of 1812 enlistment) and Amos B. Phelps (son of Jeremiah Phelps) - all include the letter "B" as a middle initial.

The first mention of Amos Phelps and Diadama (Long) Phelps is found in the 1790 census of Rutland, Vermont. The family: Amos Phelps Jr. was listed as one of four males under age 16 which included Oliver-Cromwell Phelps (m1) age 9, Eldad Phelps (m1) age 7, Amos Phelps Junior (m2) age 4 (born January 1786) and Luman Phelps (m2) age 3 (born December 1787). The two youngest boys were the children of Diadama Long Phelps (m2) – Amos Phelps Junior and Luman Phelps. The Phelps family then moved to Stanbridge, Quebec in 1793 where a street was named, "Rue Phelps." The Carter book noted: Amos Phelps Senior was the son of John Phelps. This fact is useful since Amos Phelps Junior's son, Amos Phelps III, moved to Iowa and purchased a cemetery plot in which the grandson of Benajah Phelps and son of John Phelps, Benejah Phelps, was buried. Amos Phelps III was grandson of Amos Phelps Senior (born 1750 Simsbury, CT) not Benajah Phelps (born 1770 Goshen, CT).

Quebec land grants recorded a sale by Diadama Long Phelps and her son, Amos Phelps Junior/"the younger," which proved they both resided at the same residence and were, therefore, family members. The sale which took place on July 8, 1807, was by Moses Hunkins (Huckins) of Stanbridge, Quebec.

The *spelling of the last name, "Hunkins" was incorrect and was "Huckins," a New Hampshire family whose ancestors signed the Dover Combination like Comfort Carpenter Pinkham's relation, Richard Pinkham, then moved from Quebec to Ontario, Canada during the 1840s like Comfort and Elizabeth (Phelps) PInkham. Rachel Huckins married Abijah Pinkham, Samuel Pinkham Senior's parents.*

The sale notes: JULY 8, 1807 – Sale by Moses Hunkins of Stanbridge to Diadama Phelps (maiden name – Long), wife of Amos Phelps residing in Richelieu, Shefford Country LOT 9, RANGE 2 STANBRIDGE… On "7 January 1807 a sale is noted by George Rose to AMOS PHELPS, THE YOUNGER, LOT 9 RANGE 2 (STANBRIDGE) took place for 2 acres on the northeasterly bank of the Pike River for 100 Spanish dollars." Diadama Long purchased 60 acres on the Pike River, west boundary of the east bank for 300 Spanish dollars. That son, Amos Phelps Junior/"the younger" resided at the same address as his mother Diadama Long Phelps is proven by these two transactions and confirms that both the mother, Diadama (Long) Phelps and her son, Amos Phelps Junior/"the younger," lived at the same location in Stanbridge, Quebec.

Prior to 20 September 1808 it is noted: "a bond by **Amos Phelps, Sr. and Jr.** to George Ross for 10 pounds in an assault and battery action, Amos Phelps, senior and junior, enter a complaint against Sam Bickford and Abner Bickford (Signed by both Amos Sr. and Amos Jr.)." This entry proves the father of Amos Phelps Junior/"the younger" was Amos Phelps Senior, whose wife (m2) was Diadama (Long) Phelps, mother to Amos Jr.

After this 1808 document, Amos Phelps is not recorded until he enlisted to serve in the War of 1812. The document reads: "Amos B. Phelps born in Rutland Vermont in the year of 1786 enlisted for the War of 1812 in the New York, Vermont District – Swift's New York Militia." Amos Phelps Junior's brother, Luman B. Phelps, enlisted for the same NY/VT regiment in June of 1813 but returned to the Eastern Townships. Amos B. Phelps Junior died 19 October in 1813. His daughter, Elizabeth Phelps, was born in 1812. Whether Amos B. Phelps Junior married in Vermont during 1809 prior to the birth of son, Amos Phelps III, remains unconfirmed.

A search was made to conclusively find the marriage document between Amos Phelps Jr./ "the younger" during most likely 1808 and 1809, but nothing was found in Vermont. If the marriage took place by traveling American clergy in Quebec, it was not legally noted. Brother Luman Phelps' second marriage was confirmed by a hand-written letter. However, recorded documents prove Pheba Phelps (m1) married Simon Tree in Franklin, Vermont (1810), Eldad Phelps (m1) married Abigail Tree in Franklin, Vermont (1805) and Luman Phelps (m2) married Hannah Briggs in Franklin, Vermont (June 1812). Thus, it is likely since Amos Phelps III noted on his Iowa census his parents were both "born in Vermont" that Amos Phelps Junior/ "the younger" married (via letter) in (Franklin) Vermont prior to Amos Phelps III birth in 1809-1810 Stanbridge, Quebec.

1825 Stanbridge, Quebec census records are replete with mistakes including, "Carman," a translation for the name, "Luman," Phelps near, in the same census page, a "Widow H." which was likely a misspelled or phonetically misspoken (aye "A" to aye-ch "H") for the initial of Amos Phelps "the younger" – Widow "A." Phelps. This widow had a daughter who was between age of thirteen and fourteen years old which fits the age of Elizabeth Phelps born 1812 Stanbridge, later noted in her marriage document of 1832 as a "Spinster of Stanbridge." Elizabeth Phelps was also listed in the marriage document of her future husband, Comfort Carpenter Pinkham, sister's marriage as a witness signing her name as – Betsy Phelps. The shortened name, "Betsy" is noted in her son, John Wesley Pinkham's third marriage document in 1917 when his states his father was "Comfort Carpenter" and his mother was, "Betsy Phelp." The Pinkham and Amos Phelps families resided near one another (as proven by 1825, 1831 and 1842 census records) and members of both families (Jeremiah Phelps family with the Joseph Abijah Pinkham family went to Minnesota) (Amos Phelps III and Selinda Phelps McRae moved to Iowa) (Huldah Pinkham Warren and Caleb Pinkham moved to Geauga, Ohio founded by Phelps families) moved together back to the United States after 1840, as well. That Elizabeth Phelps was a member of the this specific (Amos) Phelps family is confirmed by her relationship to the Pinkham family of which only one settled as founders of 1800 Stanstead, Quebec (Samuel Pinkham Senior).

Tracking the surname Phelps in the Eastern Townships of Quebec between 1800 and 1820, along with the one Pinkham family (Samuel and Dorothy Ordway Pinkham) and their children – specifically, Samuel Pinkham Junior m. Theodocia Carpenter (Caleb, Comfort Carpenter, Huldah, James O., J. Samuel, Joseph Abijah and Samuel III Pinkham), this Pinkham family line is defined onomastically by the first name of Samuel, and by the fact Theodocia Carpenter's father was Comfort Carpenter, the name of her second born son. The first-born son was named for Comfort Carpenter's brother and son, Caleb Carpenter. Like Abijah Pinkham, Comfort Carpenter likely fought in the American Revolutionary War then moved to Stanstead, Quebec with his four Carpenter siblings. In the Amos Phelps family, one recognizes most children of Amos Phelps Senior, named a son, Amos, for their father. By highlighting this fact, it conclusively proves Amos Phelps Junior/"the younger" named his son, Amos Phelps III to honor his father and this son signed the marriage document of his only sibling, Elizabeth Phelps, in 1832. Amos Phelps III also named his daughter, Elizabeth born in 1843 Stanbridge, Quebec, after his sister, Elizabeth Phelps (born 1812, Stanbridge, Quebec).

The Amos Phelps family consisted of children from two marriages including Eldad (m1) Phelps, whose sons are not noted name-wise specifically but likely Michael and Amos Phelps. However, an 1825 census only lists two males recorded – Eldad (age 40-60) and son between the age 18 and 25. It is assumed this eldest son was named, Amos Phelps who later moved in 1830 to Illinois and was born between the years 1805-1807. Amos Phelps III born 1809 would have been age sixteen in this census and listed his parents as born in Vermont in later Iowa censuses. This verifies Eldad (m1) born in Connecticut, was not Amos Phelps III's father but the father of Amos Phelps born 1805-1807 who moved to Illinois in 1830. Luman Phelps married in 1812 Franklin, Vermont prior to his enlistment in the War of 1812. His children born from his first wife were all females with his eldest child named, Amy Phelps. Jeremiah Phelps married Margaret Collins in 1819 Quebec and named his firstborn son, Amos Phelps born 1 June 1825. This Amos Phelps moved to Wisconsin then later California where he is recorded in a Phelps family newsletter as, Amos B. Phelps. Oliver Cromwell Phelps, named for a half-brother (m1) who died prior to 1803, married Josette Roi and named his firstborn son, Amos Phelps, born 1 June 1827. This Amos Phelps remained in Quebec until his death. The birthdates for these children prove Amos Phelps Junior/"the younger" must be the father of Amos Phelps III (born abt. 1809/1810). It is also possible Amos Phelps Junior married in Vermont as did his half-siblings and siblings.

Proof Amos B. Phelps Jr. who enlisted in the War of 1812 was the son of Amos Phelps, Senior was found in letters by the son of Jeremiah Phelps, a prospector in Placerville, California during the Gold Rush years of 1850-1854. The letters, archived at the University of Michigan, denote an: Amos B. Phelps. Likely, Jeremiah Phelps named his son, "Amos B. Phelps," to honor not only his father, but also his deceased brother, Amos B. Phelps Junior, who died during the War of 1812 in October of 1813.

Onomastics plays a role in confirming the Amos Phelps family line as the naming pattern for "Amos" only takes place within Amos Phelps Senior descendant families. This name of the father can be used to distinguish this family line from other Quebec family lines (filiation). Also, Amos Phelps III named his daughter (born 1843 Stanbridge), Elizabeth, after his sister Elizabeth Phelps (born 1812 Stanbridge), as per familial naming patterns.

Tracking Amos Phelps III born 1809 in the 1831 Quebec census, one learns he resided on "Clergy Reserve" land near his father-in-law Solomon Johnson, who resided in

Vermont at the same time as Amos Phelps Senior. Figuring out how this was given to him proved unsuccessful as per questions to the "Clergy Reserve" expert at Bishops University in Quebec. Perhaps, he inherited it from his father, Amos Phelps Junior because his uncle, Luman Phelps is noted in an 1820 land record as selling "clergy reserve" land. It is likely Diadama (Long) Phelps gave "clergy reserve" land to her sons Amos B. Phelps Junior and Luman B. Phelps. In any case, Amos Phelps III, the son of Amos Phelps Junior/ 'the younger," resided in Quebec with his wife Julia V. (Victoria) Johnson as noted in 1831 census (where he and his wife resided next to her father) and near her brother, Sir John Johnson, in the 1842 census. Amos Phelps III is also listed in Stanbridge military records of 1850. During the French Rebellion, many families left Quebec. Amos and Julia V. (Johnson) Phelps moved to Iowa where it is noted in census record Amos Phelps III's father was "born in Vermont" and mother was "born in Vermont" while he was born in Quebec. Also, listed are his children, Elizabeth Ann Phelps, born Stanbridge, Quebec, named, most likely, for his sister, Elizabeth Phelps Pinkham. Their son, Orville, connects the family to the 1850 Quebec and 1855 Maquoketa census as the name in Quebec is mistakenly written – Philps.

The son of Amos Phelps Junior, Amos III, purchased a plot in Maquoketa, Iowa where a Connecticut Phelps relation, Benajah Phelps, was buried. Amos Phelps III's daughter, Elizabeth Ann Phelps, married a lawyer, and their son became a Nebraska Senator.

Because of lack of records, the most significant proof of Amos Phelps' relation to his mother, Diadama Long, is the sale of land in which they both reside at the same location: LOT 9, RANGE 2, STANBRIDGE. By tracking the children of Amos Phelps Senior, his son, Amos Phelps Junior, must be the father of Amos Phelps III born 1809 Quebec, the elder brother of Elizabeth Phelps born 1812 who signed her 1831 marriage document along with his wife, Julia (Johnson) Phelps. That both Amos B. Junior and Luman B. Phelps enlisted in the same War of 1812 regiment proves a further familial relationship, especially since following the death of Amos Phelps Junior, both Eldad Phelps (half-brother/m1) and Luman ("Carman") (brother/m2) Phelps reside alongside a "Widow H." (or "A.") Phelps who had a young daughter the same age Elizabeth Phelps would have been given she was born 1812. The naming pattern for "Amos" Phelps is for Amos Phelps Senior. All "Amos Phelps" named individuals are accounted for and prove Amos Phelps III born 1809 was the son of Amos Phelps Junior/"the younger" the first-born son of Diadama (Long) Phelps. Furthermore, Amos Phelps III, born 1809 Quebec, listed his parents as "born in Vermont" in Iowa census records. The Carter family history book notes John Phelps was the father of Amos Phelps. Amos Phelps III purchased a plot in Iowa where the son of a different John Phelps, Benajah Phelps, was buried connecting both Amos Phelps III (born 1809) and Elizabeth Phelps (born 1812) again to the Amos Phelps family.

Amos Phelps Junior/"the younger" was born 1786 in Rutland, Vermont to Amos Phelps, Senior and Diadama (Long) Phelps. He married likely in Vermont to a Vermont-born individual (unknown) and had two children born Stanbridge, Quebec – Amos Phelps III (born 1809) and Elizabeth Phelps (born 1812) - before dying in the War of 1812 in October of 1813. His ancestor was Amos Phelps born 1709 Simsbury, CT, USA.

Documents proving Amos Phelps Junior/"the younger" biography:

1) Heads of Families at the First Census of the United States taken in the Year 1790 – Vermont.
2) Amos Phelps Arrival Date to Quebec, Canada 1793. *Source: Canada National Archives Declaration of Aliens, Lower Canada 1794-1811*
3) "Our Family History" by Ethelmae Eylar Carter – Minneapolis, MN 1958.
    a) 1790 census – Amos Phelps Junior about age 3.
    b) 7 January 1807 – Sale by George Ross to AMOS PHELPS THE YOUNGER LOT LOT 9 RANGE 2 STANBRIDGE…
    c) 8 July 1807 – Sale by Moses Hunkins (Huckins) of Stanbridge to Diadama Phelps (maiden name "Long"), wife of Amos Phelps, residing at Richelieu, Shefford County LOT 9 RANGE 2 STANBRIDGE…
    d) Prior to 20 November 1808 – Bond by AMOS PHELPS SR. and JR. to George Ross for 10 pounds in an assault and battery action. AMOS PHELPS SENIOR and JUNIOR enter a complaint against Sam Bickford and Abner Bickford (Signed by both AMOS SR. and AMOS JR.).
    e) Amos Phelps Senior is the son of John Phelps as per Norfolk, Connecticut Land Records volume 9, page 278 dated 6 March 1812 and recorded 14 May 1812 – Amos Phelps of Stanbridge in the county of Worster (*incorrect*) in the Province of Lower Quebec, Canada Kingdom of Great Britain… sells land to Jedediah and Jeremiah W. Phelps both of Norfolk… land which was set off to him by his father's will. THIS ESTABLISHES AMOS PHELPS (SENIOR) AS THE SON OF JOHN PHELPS of Norfolk.
4) War of 1812 Registration: AMOS B. PHELPS. 2 Regiment (Swift's) New York Militia. Rank: Private. Military District #9=Vermont and New York.
5) 2 Swift's New York Militia – AMOS B. PHELPS: Sick 9 September to 9 October 1813; Died: 19 October 1813.
6) United States Registers of Enlistments in the US Army: LUMAN B. PHELPS. Enlistment date: 1 June 1813.
7) 1866 Land Patent awarded Jeremiah Phelps (122 acres in Minnesota) for being in the New York Militia Regiment, the same military unit as brother, Amos B. Phelps.
8) 1842 Milton, Shefford County, Quebec census lists: Jeremie B. Phelps family with the Samuel Pinkham Junior family (likely Samuel G. Pinkham Junior, wife, Theodocia Carpenter Pinkham, Joseph Abijah Pinkham, James O. Pinkham, J. Samuel Pinkham, Samuel Pinkham III and likely an unknown daughter or spouse of son). Also noted was the initial "B" which Amos B. Phelps Junior, Luman B. Phelps, Jeremie B. Phelps, and Jeremiah Phelps' son, Amos B. Phelps, use as their middle name signature.
9) Amos Phelps Junior/"the younger," son of Amos Phelps Senior (b. 1750) and (m2) Diadama (Long)Phelps: Born: January 1786, Rutland, VT. (two children – Amos B. Phelps. & Luman B. Phelps born before 1790 Vermont marriage).

10) Married: Unknown Phelps (*Note: Wm B. Phelps m. Orilla Ward on 24 January 1809 at Berkshire, VT. The initial, "B" is used on both Amos B. Phelps Junior. and Luman B. Phelps' War of 1812 registration, as well as, Amos B. Phelps, son of Jeremiah B. Phelps*).

11) "Our Family History" by Ethelmae Eylar Carter confirms the Phelps and Samuel & Theodocia Pinkham families moved to United States together: (Page 1) *"Next came... Abijah* (Joseph) *Pinkham with their families..."* (1855, Mower, Minnesota, USA).

12) Amos Phelps Sr. (named for ancestor Amos Phelps) (born 1750) has Connecticut-born children baptized with m1 – Phebe Phelps: Martha, Charlotte, Oliver-Cromwell and Eldad Phelps (baptized 1 June 1783, CT) and Rutland, Vermont and Quebec-born children not baptized with m2 - Diadama (Long) Phelps: Amos B. Phelps Junior (b. January 1786, Rutland, VT), Luman B. Phelps (b. 2 December 1787 in Rutland, VT), Jeremiah B. Phelps (b. 9 June 1794 Rougemont, Quebec), Selinda Phelps (b.1799 Rougemont, Quebec) and Oliver Cromwell Phelps (b. 1803 Rougemont, Quebec).

13) Quebec Land/Bond Records (*Source: Sweetsburg Archives*) (Carter): January 7, 1807: Sale by George Ross to Amos Phelps the younger Lot 9 Range 2 (Stanbridge) 2 acres on the northeasterly bank of the Pike River for 100 Spanish dollars.

14) July 8, 1807: Sale by Moses Hunkins of Stanbridge to Diadama Phelps (M2 – maiden name, "Long"), wife of Amos Phelps residing at Richelieu, Shefford Co, Lot 9 Range 2 Stanbridge – same address as Amos Phelps Junior/"the younger" in January 1807 entry. Son of *Amos Senior & Diadama (Long) Phelps.*

15) Prior to Sept. 1808: Bond by Amos Phelps, Senior and Junior, to George Ross for 10 pounds in an assault & battery action, Amos Phelps, senior and junior, enter a complaint against Sam Bickford & Abner Bickford (Signed by both Amos Sr. and Amos Jr.).

16) Amos Phelps Junior owned land (Lot 9 Range 2, where mother m2 Diadama Long Phelps resided) near brothers: "Eldad (m1) Phelps and Luman (m2) Phelps of Stanbridge – Lot 4 Range 1.

17) Aug 23, 1820. Notary at St. Armand, Bedford, District Montreal, Province Lower Canada – *Luman Phelps (married Hannah Briggs) of Stanbridge to William Briggs. $125 paid by William Briggs. Luman Phelps doth cede, sell, transfer and quit all the rest and remainder yet to come and unexpired of the term of 21 years commenced on Jan. 2, 1809 – Lot 1 Range 2 (a clergy reserve) 100 acres (same signature as on 2 December 1808 sale).*

18) Feb. 24, 1821: *Deed of sale by Eldad Phelps (married Abigail Tree) to Lyman Tree for $500, as the same was unto him conveyed by Amos Phelps on 6 May 1807.*

19) 1825 Phelps Stanbridge, Bedford, Quebec Census: (A) Phelps listed next to, Eldad Phelps and Carman (Luman) Phelps of Stanbridge, Quebec – speculation: Amos Phelps III with sister, Elizabeth Phelps and mother. Amos Phelps Sr. and brothers Jeremiah & Oliver C. Phelps listed at St. Cesaire, Stanbridge, Quebec.

20) Phelps family Franklin, Vermont Marriages – then reside - Stanbridge, Quebec – 58-mile distance: 1790: Amos Phelps to Diadama Long Phelps;1805 -Elidad

Phelps (m1) to Abigail Tree; 1810-Pheba Phelps (m1) to Simon Tree; 1812-Luman Phelps (m2) to Hannah Briggs Phelps who died in Ontario 1830.

21) Eldad & Carman (transposed name of Luman, Eldad Phelps' half-brother) Phelps are listed on same 1825 Stansbridge Census page. Transposed on same 1825 Stanbridge, Quebec Census was: Widow "H." Phelps and daughter alongside Eldad Phelps. Amos Phelps Junior/"the younger's" wife, "Widow "H." would be "ah-ye" if pronounced with an accent and spelled phonetically. Likely, the 1825 Stanbridge Quebec census listing was transposed for Widow "A." Phelps with daughter, Elizabeth Phelps living alongside Eldad Phelps and his son, Michael Phelps and family.

22) Documentation of Elizabeth Phelps Pinkham noted as "Spinster of Stanbridge in 1832 as per her marriage record to Comfort Carpenter Pinkham, "Bachelor of St. Cesaire."

23) 1842 Milton, Shefford County, Quebec Census record lists "Jeremie B. Phelps" as living alongside the Samuel Pinkham Junior family of 7. That Jeremiah Phelps included the "B." initial as did his brothers, Amos B. Phelps Junior/"the younger" and Luman B. Phelps notes family relationship to the children of Amos Phelps Senior and Diadama (Long) Phelps.

24) Amos B. Phelps, the son of Jeremiah Phelps, is noted in a Phelps Family newsletter with the same initial, "B". This son was likely named for Jeremiah Phelps brother, Amos B. Phelps Junior, who died during the War of 1812, as well as, grandfather, Amos Phelps Senior.

25) Sons of Amos Phelps Senior - Eldad Phelps, Amos B. Phelps Junior, Jeremiah Phelps and Oliver C. Phelps - named sons, Amos, in honor of their father, Amos Phelps, Sr. That Amos Phelps III, the son of Amos Phelps Jr., whose parents were born in Vermont and signed his sister's marriage license, plus is buried with a Phelps related child, Benajah Phelps, son of John Phelps, proves the relationship between Amos Phelps III, the brother of Elizabeth Phelps Pinkham.

Connected to the Rutland, Vermont-born son, Amos Phelps Jr./"the younger" and Amos Phelps Sr. family are the children (Pinkham Generation 8) of Comfort Carpenter and Elizabeth (Phelps) Pinkham who were Amos B. Phelps "the younger's" grandchildren:

Cynthia Pinkham Wright – Born abt. 1832, Quebec. Married 1849 to Alfred Wright. Died 21 September 1879, Ontario, Canada.

Electa Pinkham Eddy – Born 15 March 1834, Quebec. Married Hiram Eddy 1854/5. Died 12 May 1916, Ontario, Canada. (Electra)

Mary Pinkham Coons – Born 1835, Quebec. Married Coons. Moved to Minnesota near Uncle Caleb Pinkham. Died 1875, Ashland, Dodge County, Minnesota, USA.

Edwin A. Pinkham – Born 1840-1841, Quebec. Prior to 1867 moved to Dodge, Minnesota. Married 1867 Catherine Campbell. 1900 moved to North Dakota, USA. Died post 1905, Eugene, Oregon, USA.

Willard Pinkham - Born 1841-1842, Quebec/Ontario. Death unknown.

JOHN WESLEY PINKHAM – Born 20 September 1845, Clarke, Ontario. M1 Emma Harris/M2 Sarah Ann Irwin/M3 Margaret Elsworth. Died 28 October 1924, Oshawa, Durham County, Ontario, Canada.

Jane Pinkham Harris – Born 1848, Clarke Township, Durham County, Ontario. Married William Harris. Died 12 February 1919, Clarke Township Durham County, Ontario, Canada.

Samuel Pinkham – Born 6 April 1852, Ontario. Married 26 March 1872 to Margaret McLean. Died 6 July 1915, Kindersley, Saskatchewan, Canada.

Charles W. Pinkham– Born 11 June 1855, Manvers, Ontario. Married Lavina Corey of Quebec on 27 July 1881 in Lowell, Massachusetts, USA. Naturalized US Citizen on 21 November 1893 in Lowell MA, USA. Death unknown post 1916.

Therefore, the grandfather to the children of Comfort and Elizabeth (Phelps) Pinkham was War of 1812 Patriot, Amos Phelps Junior/"The Younger."

Amos Phelps Jr./ "the younger," son of Amos Senior and Diadama (Long)Phelps

Born: January 1786, Rutland, VT. Son of Amos Phelps (b. 1750, CT) & (M2) Diadama (Long) Phelps (two children – Amos B. Phelps. & Luman B Phelps born before 1790 marriage).
Married: Unknown Phelps (born Vermont)
Children: Amos Phelps III (b. 1809) and Elizabeth (Phelps) Pinkham (b. 1812)
Died: 19 October 1813, War of 1812. Private in NY/VT Militia.

"Our Family History" by Ethelmae Eylar Carter confirms the Phelps and Samuel & Theodocia Pinkham families moved to United States together: (Page 1) *"Next came… Abijah* (Abijah Joseph) *Pinkham with their families…"* (1855 Mower, Minnesota, USA).

Amos Phelps Senior (named for ancestor Amos Phelps) born 1750 has Connecticut-born children confirmed with M1 – Phebe Phelps: Martha, Charlotte, Oliver-Cromwell and Eldad Phelps (baptized 1 June 1783, CT) and Rutland, Vermont and Quebec-born children with – M2 Diadama Long: Amos Phelps Junior (b. January 1786, Rutland, VT), Luman Phelps (b. 2 December 1787, Rutland, VT), Jeremiah Phelps (b. 9 June 1794 Rougemont, Quebec) Selinda Phelps (b.1799, Rougemont, Quebec) and Oliver Cromwell Phelps (b. 1803, Rougemont, Quebec).

Quebec Land/Bond Records (*Source: Sweetsburg Archives*) (Carter):

January 7, 1807: Sale by George Ross to **Amos Phelps the younger** Lot 9 Range 2 (Stanbridge) 2 acres on the northeasterly bank of the Pike River for 100 Spanish dollars.

July 8, 1807: Sale by Moses Hunkins of Stanbridge to **Diadama Phelps** (M2 – maiden name, "Long"), **wife of Amos Phelps** residing at Richelieu,

Shefford Co, **Lot 9 Range 2 Stanbridge** – same address as Amos Phelps the younger in January 1807 entry. Son of *Amos & Diadama Phelps.*

Prior to Sept. 1808: Bond by Amos Phelps, **Senior** and **Junior**, to George Ross for 10 pounds in an assault & battery action, **Amos Phelps, senior** and **junior**, enter a complaint against Sam Bickford & Abner Bickford (Signed by both **Amos Sr.** and **Amos Jr.**).

Amos Phelps Jr. owned land near brothers – Luman Phelps & (half-brother) Eldad Phelps: "Eldad (M1) Phelps and Luman (M2) Phelps of Stanbridge – Lot 4 Range 1."

War of 1812 Registration: **Amos B. Phelps:** 2 Regiment (Swift's) New York Militia. Rank: Private. Military District #9, Vermont and New York.

*Brother, Luman **B. Phelps**, joined Vermont unit on 1 June 1813. An 1866 Land Patent was awarded Jeremiah Phelps for 122 acres of Minnesota land, a result of serving as a member of the New York Militia, the same regiment as his brother, Amos B. Phelps Jr.*

.

Aug 23, 1820. Notary at St. Armand, Bedford, District Montreal, Province Lower Canada – *Luman Phelps (married Hannah Briggs) of Stanbridge to William Briggs. $125 paid by William Briggs. Luman Phelps doth cede, sell, transfer and quit all the rest and remainder yet to come and unexpired of the term of 21 years commenced on Jan. 2, 1809 – Lot 1 Range 2 (a clergy reserve) 100 acres (same signature as on 2 December 1808 sale).*

Feb. 24, 1821: *Deed of sale by Eldad Phelps (married Abigail Tree) to Lyman Tree for $500, as the same was unto him conveyed by **Amos Phelps** on 6 May 1807.*

1825 Phelps Stanbridge, Bedford, Quebec Census: (A) **Phelps** listed next to, Eldad Phelps and Carman (Luman) Phelps of Stanbridge, Quebec – speculation: Amos Phelps III with sister, Elizabeth Phelps and mother. Amos Phelps Senior and brothers Jeremiah & Oliver C. Phelps listed at St. Cesaire, Stanbridge, Quebec.

Phelps family Franklin, Vermont Marriages – then reside - Stanbridge, Quebec – 58-mile distance:

1790: Amos Phelps to Diadama Long Phelps
1805: Elidad Phelps (m1) to Abigail Tree
1810 Pheba Phelps (m1) to Simon Tree
1812: Luman Phelps (m2) to Hannah Briggs Phelps
(Hannah Briggs Phelps died in Ontario 1830)

Eldad & Carman (misspelled name of Luman, Eldad Phelps' half-brother) Phelps are listed on same 1825 Stansbridge census page. Transposed on same 1825 Stanbridge Quebec census was: Widow "H." Phelps and daughter alongside Eldad Phelps. Amos

Phelps Jr./"the younger's" wife, "Widow "H." would be "ah-ye" if pronounced with an accent and spelled phonetically. Likely, the1825 Stanbridge Quebec census listing was transposed for "Widow A. (Amos Junior) Phelps with daughter, Elizabeth Phelps living alongside (m2) Luman Phelps, (m1) Eldad Phelps and his son, Michael and family.

Documentation of Elizabeth Phelps Pinkham noted as "Spinster of Stanbridge in 1832:

<u>1851 Canada West Census</u>: Family of Pinkham Comfort, Farmer: age 41, **Elizabeth Comfort**, age 42, Electra Comfort age 18, Mary Comfort age 16, Edwin Comfort age 11, Willard Comfort age 9, John Comfort age 7, Jane Comfort age 1. Last name, "Pinkham" transposed to Comfort." *Source: 1851 Census, Canada West, Durham County, Clarke Township.*

<u>1861 Ontario Census</u>: **Elizabeth Pinkham**, Female, age 50, Widow, Religion: Methodist, Home in 1861 Clarke, Durham, Canada West. Living with sons: Willard Pinkham (Willerd Pinkham) Pinkham (age 18, Laborer, birth year 1843, single, Christian), Samuel Pinkham, age 9, and Charles Pinkham, age 6, Pinkham. Listed nearby is daughter Cynthia Wright with husband Alfred and two children Charles and Lilly). *Source: Library & Archives, Canada, Ottawa, Ontario Canada, Census Returns for 1861.*

<u>1871 Ontario Census</u>: **Elizabeth Pinkham**, Widow, Religion: Church of England, Age (typed as 50/Abt. 1821) Born 1812, Age 58, Durham West, Ontario, Clarke County: Household members: Elizabeth Pinkham 58, Samuel Pinkham age 18, Charles Pinkham age 17. *Source: Library and Archives, Canada Census of Canada 1871*

<u>1881 Ontario Census</u>: Elisabeth Pincombe – F/68y/Quebec (sex/age/birthplace). As listed in the household of William Harris, husband of daughter, Jane Pinkham Harris. William Harris; age 36 years; birthplace – Ontario; Marital status – Married; Occupation – Farmer; Ethnicity – English; Religion – C. Methodist; Head of household name – William Harris; Event place – Clarke, Durham West, Ontario, Canada; Household: William Harris (Male/36 years old/Birthplace – Ontario), Jane Harris (Female;/33 years old/Birthplace – Ontario), Lucy J. Harris (Female/9 years old/Birthplace – Ontario), Elisabeth O. Harris (Female/5 years old/Birthplace – Ontario), William A. Harris (Male/3 years old/Birthplace – Ontario), **Elisabeth Pincombe (Female/68 years old/Birthplace – Quebec.)** *Source: Canada Census 1881, Library & Archives Canada, Ottawa, Ontario.*

<u>Death</u>: 17 September 1883. Died: PINKHAM – At Orono, September 17th, **Mrs. C Pinkham**, aged 71 years. *Source: Orono News, 1883*

<u>References</u>:
<u>1870 United States Census - Minnesota</u>: Edwin Pinkham: Birth year: 1842-1843; Birthplace – Canada, Occupation: Farmer, Household: Edwin Pinkham (M, 27, Canada), Catherine Pinkham (F, 26, Canada), **Elizabeth Pinkham** (F, 1, Minnesota), Marty Pinkham (F, infant, Minnesota).

*First-born child named after mother, Elizabeth Phelps Pinkham. *Source: United States Census, 1870, Minnesota; NARA.*

Marriage 23 March 1872 from the Victoria News: Vol.23, Pg. 419.- Samuel Prickham, 20, farmer, Clark, Ontario, same, s/o Comfort & **Elizabeth,** married Margaret McLean, 19, Travers, Ireland, Clark, d/o Matthew and Selina. Witness Florence Uylott and L.E.G.G. Smithett, both of Lindsay, March 23, 1872, Lindsay. *Source: Victoria News, 1872*

26 March 1872 Marriage of Samuel Pinkham: Samuel Pinkham, abt. 1852 Clarke, Ontario married Margaret McLean on 26 March 1872 in Victoria, Ontario, Canada. Last name spelled: Prickham. Samuel Prickham of Clark, Farmer. Names of parents; Comfort Prickham and **Elizabeth Prickham.** *Source: Ontario, Toronto, Canada "Registrations of Marriage, 1869-1928*

Marriage (M2) on 20 November 1872; From the Victoria News: Vol. 23, Page. 399 – John PINKHAM, 27, widower, farmer, Clark, Ops, s/o Comfort & **Elizabeth,** married Sarah Ann IRWIN, 19, Mariposa, same, d/o Robert and Mary J. Witness Eretus Smith and William Galbraith, both of Mariposa, November 20, 1872, Mariposa. *Source: Victoria News, 187.*

Marriage (M2) on 20 November 1872: From Ontario County Marriage Registrar, 1858-1869. John Pinkham; Marriage; Date: 20 Nov 1872; Event Place: Victoria, Ontario, Canada; Age – 27; Birth year – 1875; Birthplace – Clarke; Father's Name – Comfort Pinkham; Mother's Name - **Elizabeth Pinkham**; Spouse's name – Sarah Ann Irwin; Spouse's Age – 19, Spouse's birth year – 1853; Spouse's birthplace – Mariposa; Spouse's Father's Name – Robert Irwin; Spouse's Mother's Name – Mary J. Irwin. *Source: Ontario County Marriage Registers, 1858-1869. Victoria, Ontario, Canada; Archives of Ontario, Toronto.*

20 November 1872 Marriage of John Pinkham: John Pinkham, Widow Farmer, Age 27, born 1845 of Mariposa, Victoria, Ontario, Canada, Parents: Father- Comfort Pinkham /Mother: **Elizabeth Pinkham.** Married Sarah Ann Irwin (spelled Iravin). *Source: Ontario Marriages 1869-1927 Archives of Toronto*

Minnesota State Census, 1875: Edwin Pinkham. Event Place – Ashland, Dodge, Minnesota. "E". "A." Pinkham, age 34 born Canada; father born Canada, **mother born Canada**. *Source: Minnesota State Census, 1875*

1875 Minnesota Deaths: Mary (Pinkham) Coon, Female, Death date: 9 June 1875; Death Place – Ashland, Dodge County, Minnesota; Age- 98/Birthdate - 1777 (Actual age: 40/ born 1835); Race – White; Marital Status – Married; Father's name: Comfort Pinkham; Father's birthplace Canada; Mother's Name- **Elisabeth**, Mother's birthplace – Canada). *Source: Minnesota Deaths & Burials, 1835-1990 citing Ashland, Dodge County Minnesota*

11 November 1877 Baptism of Charles Pinkham, Freilighsburg, Quebec, Methodist Church. *"Charles **son of** Comfort Pinkham and **Elizabeth Phelps** his wife was born in the township of Manvers, Province of Ontario on the eleventh day of June one thousand eight hundred and fifty five and was baptized on the eleventh day of November one thousand eight hundred and seventy-seven in the presence of subscribing witnesses by H. Cairns, Minister."* Source: Drouin

1800 United States Census: Edwin A. Pinkham. Event place: Courtland, Kansas, USA. Age 37, born 1843 Canada. Father: Born Canada. **Mother: Born Canada**. Source: United States Census, 1880

27 July 1881 Marriage of Charles W. Pinkham: Charles Pinkham born 11 June 1855 in Ontario, Canada married Lavina A. Corey (born 1852 Quebec to parents Luther and Huldah A. Corey) in Lowell, Massachusetts. Parents: Father – Comfort; **Mother – Elizabeth).** Source: Massachusetts Vital Records 1840-1915 New England Historic Genealogical Society, Boston, Massachusetts

Minnesota State Census, 1885: Edwin A. Pinkham. Event place: Pelican Rapids, Otter Tail, Minnesota. Age 41 birth year estimated 1844 Canada. Father: Born Canada. **Mother: Born Canada.** Source: Minnesota State Census, 1885

1891 Census: "Eletra Eddy" (Electra Eddy), Female, Widow, birth year – 1834, birthplace – Quebec, Religion – Methodist, French-Canadian – No; Father's birthplace – Quebec, **Mother's birthplace – Quebec.** Province - Ontario, District - Durham West, Sub-district – Clarke, Household members: Harvey W. Eddy age 28, Eletra Eddy, Age 57. Source: Year 1891 Census, Library and Archives, Canada – Place Clarke, Durham West, Ontario.

1891 Census: Samuel Pinkham, Married, Age 36, Birth year – 1855, Ontario, Head of Household, Religion – Methodist, French-Canadian – No, Spouse's Name: Margaret Pinkham, Father's birthplace – England (?), **Mother's birthplace – Quebec**, Province – Ontario, District – 121/Victoria South, Sub-district – Verulam, Household members: Samuel Pinkham age 36, Margaret Pinkham age 35, Albert Pinkham age 17, Earnest Pinkham age 14, Ida Pinkham age 13, Maud Pinkham age 9, Fanny Pinkham age 7, Charles Pinkham age 5. Source: 1891 Census, Library and Archives Canada, Census Place – Verulam, Victoria South, Ontario

1891 Census of Canada: John Pinkham; Gender – Male; Marital status – Married; Age – 45; Birth Year – abt. 1846; Birthplace – Ontario; Relation to Head of Household – Head; Religion – Methodist; French-Canadian – No; Spouse's name – Sarah A. Pinkham; Father's birthplace – Quebec; **Mother's birthplace – Quebec**; Province – Ontario; District number – 100; District – Ontario North; Sub-district – Brock; Household Members: John Pinkham (Age 45), Sarah A. Pinkham (Age 37), Minnie Pinkham (Age 17), Lawrence Pinkham (Age 15), Harriet Pinkham (Age 13),

Elizabeth Pinkham (Age 11), Annie Pinkham (Age 9), Milton Pinkham (Age 6), John W. Pinkham (Age 4). *Source: 1891 Canada Census Brock, Ontario North, Ontario, Library and Archives Canada, Ottawa, Ontario*

Marriage (M3) on 5 July 1917: John Wesley Pinkham; age – 71; birth year – abt. 1846; birthplace – Ontario, Canada; Marriage date – 5 July 1917; Marriage place – Ontario, Canada; Father – Carpenter Pinkham; **Mother: Betsey Phelp**; Spouse – Margaret Elsworth. *Source: Archives of Ontario, Toronto, Ontario, Canada, Registrations of Marriages, 1869-1928*

To verify the parents of Elizabeth Phelps Pinkham born 1812 Stanbrdige, Quebec, and her brother Amos Phelps III born 1809-1810 Stanbridge, Quebec, research upon the Phelps family took place regarding that surname in the Eastern Townships of Quebec, Iowa, Minnesota and Wisconsin, all places where Quebec Pinkhams from the Samuel Pinkham, Sr. line moved, as well. A detailed account of each Phelps Eastern Township forename is listed on page 221 of this book.

Phelps Family:

Amos Phelps (Senior), son of John and Thanks (Wilcox) Phelps
Born: 31 March 1750, Simsbury, Hartford County, CT
Married: (m1) Phebe, Norfolk, CT; (m2) Diadama Long, Franklin, VT
Died: 1830 (-1832), Amos Phelps, the senior died at Saint-Hyacinthe, Monteregie Region, Quebec and is buried at Saint Paul's Anglican Church Cemetery. (Source: *FindAGrave*).

"The Phelps Family of America" by Judge Oliver Seymour Phelps: "#1167. IV. Amos, b. 31 Mar.,1750, removed to Vernon, then to Canada."

31 March 1750 birth – **Amos Phelps**, Simsbury, CT. Father: John Phelps.
Source: Connecticut Births & Christenings, 1649-1906.

AGBI index: **Amos Phelps** – Record of Connecticut Men in military & naval service during Revolutionary War 1775-1783.
1787   VT Census: **Amos Phelps** of Rutland, VT
1790   Marriage of **Amos Phelps** to Diadama Long, Franklin, VT
1790 United States Census: **Amos Phelps** of Rutland, VT
1791-1799   Land Petition of Lower Canada, **Amos Phelps** (#69102)
1792-1797   Land Petition of Lower Canada, **Amos Phelps** (#69104)
1793   Immigration List for **Amos Phelps**, family of 8 *Source: Canada Archives*
1795   Land Petition of Lower Canada, **Amos Phelps** (#69100)
            Rejected by Quebec Land Committee on 3 August 1795
1810   **Amos Phelps** – Sale – Saint Hyacinthe, Quebec
1825 Lower Canada Census -Bedford, St. Cesaire, St. Hyacinthe, Quebec
            Census: **Amos Phelps** – age 60 and upward with wife, Diadama Phelps alongside sons, Jeremiah Phelps & Oliver C. Phelps (and Samuel Junior & Theodocia Pinkham).

(1830 – Death of **Amos Phelps** b. 1750, Simsbury, CT. Saint-Hyacinthe, Monterregie Region, Quebec – father of Amos Jr./ "the younger," Luman, Selinda, Jeremiah & Oliver C. Phelps with wife m2 Diadama Long and Martha, Phebe, Oliver C. and Eldad Phelps with (m1) Phebe. *Source: FindaAGrave.*

1831 <u>Lower Canada Census</u> – St. Cesaire, St. Hyacinthe – Thomas (Amos) **Phelps**. Occupation – Rentier (living off income). Number in family – 3; One male over age 60, one female over age 45; one child age 5-14. Living alongside: Samuel Pinkham (family of 5; farmer) with brothers Jeremiah Phelps (family of 9; farmer) and Oliver Phelps (family of 8; farmer). Amos Phelps Junior/"the younger's" daughter, Elizabeth Phelps, "Spinster of Stanbridge," married Samuel Pinkham's son, Comfort Carpenter Pinkham.

Disputed:	The below record is Amos Phelps III, son of Amos Phelps Jr./"the younger" not Amos Phelps Sr. Amos Phelps Senior and Diadama (Long) Phelps lived alongside sons, Jeremiah Phelps and Oliver C. Phelps with Samuel Pinkham Jr. family. Amos Phelps Senior's name was misspelled to: Thomas. He resided in St. Cesaire, St. Hyacinthe. Amos Phelps III, son of Amos Phelps Jr./ "the younger," and wife, Julia V. Johnson, resided in Stanbridge near sister - Elizabeth Phelps "Spinster of Stanbridge"
1831	Canadian Genealogy Index, 1600s-1900: **Amos Phelps** Event: Living. Year: 1831. Place: Stanbridge Township. Province: Quebec. Source: extracts from the 1831 Census of Stanbridge Township, Missisquoi County, Quebec

<u>married to</u>:

Diadama Long Phelps, daughter of Samuel and Martha (Brewster) Long
<u>Born</u>:   14 January 1763, Coventry, Tolland Country, Connecticut. Daughter of Samuel Long and Martha Brewster. *Source: Edmund West*
<u>Married</u>: 1790 to Amos Phelps, Franklin, VT, USA
<u>Died</u>:   9 March 1837, Abbotsford, Monteregie Region, Quebec, Canada
<u>Buried</u>: Saint Paul's Anglican Church Cemetery

Samuel Pinkham Junior and Amos Phelps Senior families resided alongside one another in Quebec as recorded by 1825, 1831 and 1842 census lists. Samuel Pinkham Junior was born in New Hampshire during 1787 almost the same year as Amos Phelps Junior, who was born in Rutland, Vermont during 1786. It is likely these two individuals were friends, and the daughter of Amos Phelps Junior, even if he passed away during the War of 1812, Elizabeth (Betsy) Phelps, would meet Comfort Carpenter Pinkham, the son of Samuel Pinkham Junior. The marriage of Comfort Carpenter Pinkham, and Elizatbeth Phelps was the only one between Amos Phelps - Samuel Pinkham lines.

1825 and 1831 Quebec Census Records: Amos Phelps with sons Luman (*Carman*) (m2 Diadama Long), Eldad (m1 Phebe), Jeremiah (m2 Diadama Long) & Oliver Cromwell (m2 Diadama Long) Phelps - and grandson Amos Phelps III, the son of Amos Phelps Junior/"the younger" – with Samuel Pinkham Senior and sons Samuel (& Theodocia Carpenter) Pinkham, Joseph Pinkham and Abijah Pinkham.

Record Reference:

Phelps 1825 Quebec Census: (blank first name = A; possibly Amos III age 15) Widow A. (Amos Jr.) Phelps (and Elizabeth), Eldad (m1), Carman (Luman) (m2) – brothers and Amos Junior's widow living in Stanbridge, Bedford, Quebec. Residing in St. Cesaire, Bedford, Quebec: Amos Senior (Family of 2), Jeremiah (m2) and Oliver C. (m2) Phelps.

Pinkham 1825 Quebec Census: Abijah Pinkham, Samuel Pinkham Senior (m. Dorothy Ordway) and Joseph Pinkham living in Stanstead, Richelieu, Quebec with brother/son Samuel & Theodocia (Carpenter) Pinkham living at St. Cesaire, Bedford, Quebec with Phelps family Amos Sr., Jeremiah and Oliver Phelps plus Carpenter brothers (of Theodocia).

Phelps 1831 Quebec Census: Thomas Phelps (Amos); Rentier family of 3, married male over age 60, married, female over age 45; chlld age 5-14. Listed with sons, Jeremiah Phelps (family of 9; farmer) and Oliver Phelps (family of 8) plus Samuel Pinkham (family of 8; farmer).

Pinkham 1831 Quebec Census: Samuel Pinkham (family of 8); farmer; Samuel Jr., Theodocia, (Comfort), James O., J. Samuel, Joseph Abijah, Samuel III, daughter, plus son's wife, lived next to Jeremiah Phelps, Amos Phelps and Oliver Phelps. Religion for Pinkham/Phelps: Anglican.

Huldah Pinkham marriage 1831: Seth Warren. Daughter of Samuel & Theodocia (Carpenter) Pinkham married Seth Warren. Document signed by "Betsy Phelps" (likely friend and same age) and "Sam G. Pinkham." Next document is the nephew of Seth Warren, brother Oliver Warren's son – baptism record signed by both "Sam G. Pinkham" and Jeremiah Phelps. *Source: Protestant Church, Abbotsford, Quebec, Drouin Collection.*

1819 Marriage Record for **Jeremiah Phelps** to Margaret Collins confirms Jeremiah Phelps signature. Bachelder family records: Samuel Pinkham Junior's sister, Betsy Pinkham, married Jonathan Bachelder – preceded marriage certificate of Jeremiah Phelps to Margaret Collins.

Amos Phelps Family: Research to confirm Elizabeth Phelps (born 1812 Stanbridge, Quebec) and Amos Phelps (born 1810) were the children of Amos Phelps, Jr. born Rutland, Vermont in 1786.

Historical references from:

Phelps Family & Their English Ancestors by Oliver Seymour Phelps – Author notes
city as: Stonebridge, CW (Canada West). Actual location name: Stanbridge,
Quebec (Canada East)

Our Family History by Ethelmae Eylar Carter. Re: John & Charlotte (Phelps) Chartier-
Carter families – "*assumed other members of family existed…*"

("Eastern Township 1800-1850 Quebec Phelps Forename List from Abner B. to William
Pitt" found on page 221)

AMOS PHELPS, son of John (American Revolutionary War soldier in Captain Lyman's
Simsbury, CT army) and Thanks (Wilcox) Phelps was born at Simsbury, Connecticut on
31 March 1750. The Amos Phelps family moved to Rutland, Vermont then Quebec,
where "Rue Phelps" in Stanstead, Quebec is named for this Phelps line.

Individuals named "Amos" Phelps were mainly from the Amos Phelps b. 1750 CT line.
AMOS PHELPS b. 1809 is brother to ELIZABETH PHELPS b. 1812. This Phelps line:

AMOS PHELPS III: b. 1809, Lower Canada/Quebec (sister Elizabeth Phelps b. 1812
Stanbridge, Quebec), Canada; m. Julia V. Johnson 1829, Philipsburg, Quebec,
Canada; d. 21 March 1891, Maquoketa, Iowa, USA

AMOS PHELPS JR.: b. 1786, Rutland, VT; father Amos moved to Quebec, Canada
1793; d. 19 October 1813, USA.

AMOS PHELPS SR.: b. 21 March 1750, Simsbury, CT, USA; m1 Phebe in Norfolk, CT;
m2 Diadama Long 1785-1789 in Franklin, VT; d. 1831, Rougemont, Quebec,
Canada.

JOHN PHELPS: b. 20 July 1724, Simsbury, CT; m. Thanks (Thankful) Wilcox; d. 11
February 1812, Norfolk, CT, USA.

AMOS PHELPS: Born after 1 April 1708, Simsbury, CT; m. Sarah Pettibone; d. 11 June
1777, Simsbury, CT, USA.

JOSEPH PHELPS JR.: b. 20 August 1667, Windsor, CT; m. Mary Case; d. 20 January
1780, Simsbury, Hartford, CT, USA.

JOSEPH PHELPS: b. 13 November 1638, Crewkerne, England; m. Hannah Nash; d. 5
March 1684, Simsbury, CT.USA.

WILLIAM PHELPS: b. 19 August 1599, Crewkerne, Somerset, England; m1 Anne/m2
Mary (Elizabeth) Phelps; d. 1672, Windsor, Harford, CT, USA. Buried:
Founders Monument, Palisado Cemetery, Windsor, Hartford, CT. Noted as
Magistrate, Farmer and Landowner.

Amos Phelps:

Born: 31 March 1750, Simsbury/Turkey Hill, Connecticut, s/o John & Thanks Phelps

Married: M1 – Phebe (Born abt. 1750) in (?) (Connecticut) 1770
M2 – 1790 Franklin, VT to Diadama Long, daughter of Samuel Long &
Martha Brewster (b. 14 January 1763, Coventry, Connecticut; d. 9 March
1837, Rougemont, Quebec) (*MAYFLOWER DESCENDANT*).

The children of Amos & Phebe Phelps as baptized at Christ Church, Norfolk, CT:

1   Martha Phelps (Baptized 18 September 1774)
2   Charlotte Phelps (Baptized 6 September 1778)
3   Oliver Cromwell Phelps, (Baptized 29 April 1781; Died prior to 1803)
4   Eldad Phelps (baptized 1 June 1783)
    NOTE: 1831 Lower Canada Census, Stanbridge. Not Elizabeth/Amos Phelps father because Eldad Phelps was born in Connecticut.

Christ Church records note regarding the Hatch and Frisbie families – *"He (David Hatch) was dismissed from the church, Norfolk first, to go to Vermont about 1787 with others by the name of Phelps and Frisbie."*

In the "History of Rutland County, Vermont" by Smith and Rann, page 339, a "Freeholders in 1780" list includes Amos Phelps.   The term "Freeholder" meant ownership interest in real property – clear estate – with an uncertain duration. Freeholder: "To my wife for her lifetime, and then to my son, John…" – as it was unpredictable the lifetime of the wife or son. Given the uncertainness of the term there was no definitive date – it did not include leases that would expire nor ownership interest. In some old records land ownership was a certain size, or value. However, only "freeholders," owners of clear estate, could vote and hold office.

While in Rutland, VT, Amos Phelps did not join a church nor baptize his (m2) children born in Vermont. When married to first wife, Phebe, the children (Martha, Charlotte, Eldad and Oliver Cromwell Phelps) were baptized in Connecticut.

There are nine Amos Phelps land transactions in Rutland, VT, but land deeds state, Amos, "of Rutland." His wife's name does not appear on the deeds and in only one deed is a child listed (Charlotte Phelps signed deed). The Amos Phelps family lived in northern Rutland near the Pittsford line.

West Parish Congregational Church records begin in 1789. East Parish Records begin in 1796. Only one Phelps record exists in East Parish: 17 March 1790, Miny Phelps to Aaron Watkins (marriage record; West Parish Congregational Church; Church Records book 1; pg. 133). Likely "Miny" was Martha Phelps, Amos Phelps' first-born child.

The 1790 Vermont Census of Rutland County lists the Amos Phelps family:
    1 male over age 16 – Amos Phelps; 4 males under 16 – Oliver-Cromwell (age 9), Eldad (age 7), and two more – Amos Phelps Junior (b. January 1786, Rutland, VT), Luman Phelps (b. 2 December 1787, Rutland, VT); 3 females – M2 Diadama, Martha & Charlotte Phelps,

The children of Amos Senior and (m2) Diadama (Long) Phelps were:
    1. Amos B. Phelps Junior – b. January 1786, Rutland, VT; d. 19 October 1813 (War of 1812).
    2. Luman B. Phelps – b. 2 December 1787, Rutland, VT; Married (m1) Hannah Briggs/(m2) Harriet Cromwell; d. 12 December 1856, Lapeer, MI, USA.

3. <u>Jeremiah B. Phelps</u> – b. 9 June 1794, Rougemont, St. Hyacinthe, Quebec; m. Mary Margaret Collins; d. 9 May 1865, Lyle, Mower County, MI, USA.
4. <u>Selinda Phelps McRae</u> – b. 1799, Rougemont, St. Hyacinthe, Quebec; m. Christopher McRae, March 1817, All Saints, Missisquoi, Quebec; d. 1888, Waterloo, Black Hawk, Iowa, USA.
5. <u>Oliver Cromwell Phelps</u> – b. July 1803, Quebec; Married m1 Mary Josette Roi/m2 Catherine DuBois/m3 Modesto Gaudreau; d. 23 January 1890, St. Anne De Stuckeley, Sheffield, Quebec, Canada.

Amos Phelps (b. 1810 Lower Canada/ "of Stanbridge") and Elizabeth (Betsy) Phelps (b. 1812 "Spinster of Stanbridge") were the children of an Amos Phelps Senior son born Vermont given Amos Phelps III b. 1810 Iowa census states "parents born in Vermont" -

.

Not Eldad – Born 1783 in Connecticut and was age 27 in 1810/age 29 in 1812. In 1825 Quebec census his children fit age range of Amos & Elizabeth Phelps but Eldad Phelps was born in Connecticut and named his firstborn son, Amos in 1805.

Amos Jr. *– Born 1786 in Rutland Vermont, he was age 24 in 1810 at the birth of Amos Phelps III and age 26 in 1812 at the birth of Elizabeth Phelps. Left for War of 1812 and died in 1813. His Widow "H." lived alongside the Eldad Phelps (m1) family with daughter Elizabeth Phelps' age and Luman Phelps (m2).*

Not Luman – Born 1787 born in Rutland, Vermont, he was age 23 in 1810/age 25 in 1812. He did not have sons named, Amos. He left for War of 1812 during June of 1813 signing document: Luman B. Phelps.

~Amos Phelps:

<u>Born:</u>	31 March 1750, Simsbury, CT
<u>Baptism:</u>	Amos Phelps; Birth date: 31 March 1750; Birthplace: Simsbury Township, Hartford, Connecticut; Father's Name: John Phelps. *Source: Connecticut Births & Christenings, 1649-1906*
<u>Married:</u>	M1 Phebe Phelps, b/d Connecticut
<u>Married:</u>	M2 Diadama Long 1890, Franklin, Vermont

<u>1787 State Papers of Vermont VIII; General Petitions, 1778-1787:</u> Rutland, Vermont petition signer to divide Rutland into two religious societies: **Amos Phelps**. (Signed along with Eleazer Wheelock, founder of Dartmouth who married a Huntington). Listed: Timothy Phelps, Esq., Baptist; Charles Phelps Esq. Presbyterian; Solomon Phelps, Baptist.

Phelps surames in "Every Name Index:

PHELPS, Amos (p. 114), Charles (pp. 155-156), Dana (pp. 151, 154), Elnathan (pp. 3, 115), Francis (p. 148), Joel (p. 124), Lemuel (p 11), Nathaniel (p 120), Samuel (p. 130) Solomon (p. 156) & Timothy (p. 155).
Source: Vermont Religious Certificates, Picton Press, Rockport, Maine

<u>1787 Vermont, Compiled Census:</u> **Amos Phelps.** State: VT; County, Rutland County; Township: Rutland; Year: 1787; Page: 294; Database: VT Early Census Index. *Source: Vermont Census 1790-1860*

<u>State Papers of Vermont, VIII:</u> General Petitions, 1778-1787, page 293 – 294. *Source: Vermont Religious Certificates – by Alden M. Rollins, Picton Press.* "P. 293-294. A petition for the division of Rutland into two religious societies, January 25, 1787 – Signed by: **Amos Phelps** (Also signing was Eleazer Wheelock who was Dorothy Ordway Pinkham's cousin. Amos Phelps Junior's assumed daughter, Elizabeth Phelps, married Dorothy Ordway Pinkham's grandson, Comfort Carpenter Pinkham). 1786 was the year Amos Phelps Junior/"the younger" was born.

<u>1790 Census:</u> **Amos Philips** (Amos Phelps), Rutland, Rutland, VT, 4 males under age 16, 1 male over age 16, 3 females, 8 number of household members. Males under age 16: Oliver Cromwell (age (9), Eldad (age 7), Amos Junior (age 4) & Luman (age 3) Phelps. 3 Females: Diadama, Martha (age 16) & Charlotte (age 12) Phelps. *Source: 1790 Vermont Census*

<u>Rutland, Vermont Land Records:</u> 25 August 1790 to 23 February 1795 – **Amos Phelps** land grants - (7/25/1790- page 403 - Amos Phelps Grantee; Joshua Perry Grantor) (9/17/1791 – page 422 - Amos Phelps Grantor - Nathan Ongood Grantor)(9/29/1792 – page 320 - Amos Phelps Grantee to Nathan Osgood Grantor) (9/29/1792 – page 383 -Amos Phelps Grantor to Nathan Osgood Grantee) (2/19/1793 – page 420 – Amos Phelps, Grantor to Elisha Morey, Grantee – daughter Charlotte Phelps is listed as witnesses on this deed) (2/23/1793 – page 437 – Amos Phelps, Grantor to Sarah Brigham, Grantee).

<u>Land Petitions of Lower Canada 1764-1841</u> – **Amos Phelps (Senior)** Year 1791-1799 (Record #69102), Year 1795 (#1795), Year 1792-1797 (#69104) Land Petition is rejected in Quebec of 3 August 1795 by the Land Committee.

<u>1793 Immigration Records:</u> **Amos Phelps.** Born abt. 1752, age 41 Quebec, Canada. *Source: Canada National Archives of Declaration of Aliens Lower Canada, 1794-1811*

<u>Declaration of Alien status to Commissioners at Missisquoi Bay, Quebec</u> – 5 October 1794.

<u>Land Records:</u> 31 March 1802 - Sale by Caleb Tree to **Amos Phelps of Stanbridge**. Lot 11 Range 2 100 Acres. *Source: Notary Leon Lallane, Bedford District Archives, Sweetsburg, Province of Quebec*

1805 – Amos Phelps is incorrectly listed in "History of Rougemont" by Suzanne Bedard as a "squatter" "without title residing on south side of Rougemont mountain." The information is incorrect as he owned Lot 11, Range 2 – 100 Acres purchased from Caleb Tree, the father of children Amos Phelps children (Eldad Phelps to Abigail Tree/Pheba Phelps to Simon Tree) marry, and whom signs possible relation, Amos

Phelps III, son of Amos Phelps Jr, marriage record to Julia V. Johnson in 1830. While researching land grants, it is noted Amos Phelps Senior was likely a Loyalist.

Land Records: 8 July 1807 = Sale by Moses of Stanbridge to Diadama Phelps (maiden name "Long"), **wife of Amos Phelps** residing at Richelieu, Shefford Co. Lot 9, Range 2 Stanbridge, 60 acres on Pike River, west boundary the east bank of the river for 300 Spanish dollars. *Source: Notary - Leon Lalanne, Bedford District Archives, Sweetsburg, Quebec*

Land Records: 6 May 1807 – **Amos Phelps** to Eldad Phelps, his son. Lot 11 Range 2, which Amos Phelps purchased of Caleb Tree on 31 March 1802. *Source: Notary Leon Lallane, Bedford District Archives, Sweetsburg, Province of Quebec*

Land Records: 8 July 1807 - Sale by **Amos Phelps** to Moses Huckins. Lot 11 Range 2 Stanbridge, 100 acres for 300 Spanish dollars. *Source: Notary – Leon Lallanne, Bedford District Archives, Sweetsburg, Quebec*

Between 1810-1812 **Amos Phelps** purchased land on South side of Rougemont mountain by local road, Petite Caroline. The road is later changed to Phelps Road (Rue Phelps).

A Norfolk, Connecticut land record (Volume 9/p. 278) dated 6 March 1812 and recorded 14 May 1812 for Amos Phelps in Connecticut states: **Amos Phelps of Stanbridge** in the County of Worster in the Province of Lower Quebec, Canada, Kingdom of Great Britain, for $60 sells to Jedediah and Jeremiah W. Phelps (Amos Phelps' brothers), both of Norfolk…. Land which was set off to him by his father's will. The land was bounded by property owned by his two brothers (Jedediah and Jeremiah W. Phelps) and a Guiteau family. The document is signed by **Amos Phelps**, and establishes Amos Phelps of Stanbridge as the son of John Phelps, deceased of Norfolk, Connecticut.

17 November 1812 letter included within 1795 Land Grant:

> *Wilson Mill's November 17, 1812*
>
> *Sir,*
> *You are ordered to attend to -- and execute all commands which shall be received in my -- expediting the Battalion to forward all the men which will follow me by the -- you shall judge most elgible to Lt. Johns, and command you to -- with --May the -- and other friends if occasion require. Signed: -- -- Leuit. Colonel -- and Captain John Ruiter*

Notarial Records: 1 March 1820 St. Hyacinthe, Quebec, Record 1910, Sale from **Amos Phelps.** Other records for Amos Phelps sales exist.

1825 Lower Canada Census: **Amos Phelps;** Name – Amos Phelps; Number of Inhabitants – 2; Sub-District – St. Cesaire; County – Bedford; 1 Male, Married age 60 and upward; 1 Female, married, age 45 and upwards. *Source: 1825 Canada Census; Library and Archives, Ottawa, Canada*

Sons at same census location: Jeremiah Phelps and Oliver Cromwell Phelps.

1825 Lower Canada Census: Jeremiah Phelps; Name: Jeremiah Phelps; Number of Inhabitants – 6; Sub-District – Bedford; Number of family under the age of 6 – 4; 1 male, Married, age 24-40; 2 Females under the age of 14; 1 Female, Married age 14-45. *Elizabeth Phelps abt. 1811 – under age 14 in 1825.* Source: *1825 Canada Census; Library and Archives, Ottawa, Canada*

1825 Lower Canada Census: Oliver C. Phelps; Name: Oliver C. Phelps; Number of Inhabitants – 2; Sub-District – Bedford; 1 Male, married age 18-25; 1 Female, married age 14-45. Source: *1825 Canada Census; Library and Archives, Ottawa, Canada*

Listed at Bedford, Stanbridge 1825 Census, Amos Phelps Senior's sons, (m1) Eldad Phelps and (m2) "Carmen" (Luman) with families, plus, "Widow H. (or "A.") (Amos Junior) Phelps and her daughter age 14 (born abt. 1811-1812). Likely, Widow H. (A.) Phelps was Amos Phelps Junior's widow. Noted on census was misspelling of name, Luman, as "Carman Phelps." Given prior misspelling by census taker, the "A" for "Amos" was incorrectly written as, "H," a sound of "ah-sh" versus "ah" (French pronunciation for the letter, A) if the census taker had a French language background. Note Oliver Cromwell Phelps I (m1) died in VT, following Quebec immigration or prior to Oliver Cromwell II (m2) Phelps' birth.

1825 Lower Canada Census – Stanbridge, County of Bedford, Quebec:

Carman (Luman) Phelps: Number of inhabitants: 8; Subdistrict: Stanbridge. County: Bedford; Census notes in family of 6: Males: Married, age 25-40; Number in family under age 6= 3; number in family age 6-14=3. (Amos b. 1809 = 16) 2 Females under the age of 14; one female married age 14-45. (Elizabeth Phelps b. 1812=age 13).

Eldad Phelps. Number of inhabitants: 6; Subdistrict: Stanbridge. County: Bedford; Census notes in family of 6: Males: age 40-60; 1 age 25-40; 1 age 18 not 25; Number in family 14-18 = 1; number in family age 6-14=2. *(Amos b. 1809 = 16)* 2 Females under the age of 14; one female age 14-45 single; one female married age 14-45 *(Elizabeth Phelps b. 1812 = age 13)*.

Next on 1825 Census list: **Widow Mrs. H. (or A.) Phelps** with single daughter age 14-45/widow age 45 and born abt. 1780.

Family of Michael Phelps (Son of Eldad Phelps).

1831 Lower Canada Census: Thomas Phelps (**Amos Phelps**): Name: Thomas (Amos) Phelps; Occupation – Rentier (living off property investments); Number in family – 3; 1 male child between ages 5 and 14; 1 adult male married over age 60; 1 adult female married over age 45; Religion – Anglican; Sub-District – St.

Cesaire; County/District – St. Hyacinthe. *Source: 1831 Lower Canada Census, Public Archives, Ottawa, Ontario*

Individuals at same census location: Jeremiah & Oliver Phelps w/ Samuel Pinkham Jr.:

1831 Lower Canada Census: Oliver Phelps: Name: Oliver Phelps; Occupation – Cultivateur (farmer); Number in family – 8;3 children under the age of 5; 1 child between the age of 5-14; 1 male married between age 21-30; 1 male not married between age 21-30; 2 females under the age of 14; 1 female married between age 14-45; 1 female not married between age14-45; Religion – Anglican; Sub-District – St. Cesaire; County/District – St. Hyacinthe. *Source: 1831 Lower Canada Census, Public Archives, Ottawa, Ontario*

1831 Lower Canada Census: Jeremie Phelps: Name: Jeremie Phelps; Occupation – Cultivateur (farmer); Number in family – 9; 1 male married between ages 30-60; 2 females under age 14; 1 female age 14-45; 4 children age 5 and under; 2 children between ages 5-14; Religion – Anglican; Sub-District – St. Cesaire; County/District – St. Hyacinthe. *Source: 1831 Lower Canada Census, Public Archives, Ottawa, Ontario*

1831 Lower Canada Census: **Samuel Pinkham (Jr.):** Name: Samuel Pinkham; Occupation – Cultivateur (farmer); Number in family – 8; Number of people in family age 5 and below – 2; number people in family over age 5 and under age 14 – 2; males age 14-16 – 1; male married age 30-60 – 1; females under the age of 14 – 1; females between the age of 14-45 – 1 unmarried/ 1 married; Religion – Anglican; Sub-District – St. Cesaire; County/District – St. Hyacinthe. *Source: 1831 Lower Canada Census, Public Archives, Ottawa, Ontario*

Death: 1830 – **Amos Phelps**. Name: Amos Phelps; Birth date – 21 March 1750; Birth Place – Simsbury, Hartford County, Connecticut, Untied States of America; Death date – 1830; Death Place – Saint-Hyacinthe, Monteregie Region, Quebec, Canada; Burial or Cremation Place – Abbotsford, Monteregie Region, Quebec, Canada; Spouse – Diadama Phelps. *Source: FindAGrave, Canada*

~Death: 1831, Rougemont, St. Hyacinthe, Quebec, Canada. Spouse: Diadama Phelps, b. 31 March 1850 Simsbury, Hartford County, Connecticut, Death place: St. Hyacinthe, Monteregie Region, Quebec. Cemetery: St. Paul's Anglican Church Cemetery. Burial: Abbotsford, Monteregie Region, Quebec, Canada. (Parents: John Phelps and Thanks Wilcox). *Sources: Edmund West, Family Data Collection & Canada FindAGrave*

Amos Phelps Sr. death speculated by Mississquoi Archives: "After 1802-before 1818."

Children of Amos and (M1) Phebe Phelps: Baptized Connecticut:

1 Martha Phelps, baptized 18 September 1774
2 Charlotte Phelps, baptized 6 September 1778
3 Oliver Cromwell Phelps (I), baptized 29 April 1781 (died prior to 1803)

4   Eldad Phelps, baptized 1 June 1783

~Pheba Phelps: (Martha b. 1774 – age 36)/ (Charlotte b. 1778 – age 32):
   Marriage - Event date: 8 February 1810 to Simon Tree. Event Place:
   Franklin, Vermont, USA. *Source: Vermont Vital Records 1760-1954*

(Caleb Tree signed Amos Phelps III marriage record; son of Pheba Phelps Tree?)

~Charlotte Phelps - Signed deed for father in Rutland, Vermont 1790-1795.

~Oliver Cromwell Phelps: Died between 1791 Vermont and 1802 Quebec.

~Eldad Phelps: Born abt. 1783, CT. Baptized: 1 June 1783, Christ Church, CT;
   d. Quebec/USA.

   1790 Rutland Vermont Census – Age 7.

   Land Petitions of Lower Canada 1764-1841: Eldad Phelps, Year 1792-
   1805. (Record # 69116)

   Marriage (age 22): 29 January 1805; Name: Elidad Phillip; Event Type:
   Marriage; Event Place: Franklin, Vermont, US; Spouse's name: Abigail
   Tree. *Source: Vermont Vital Records, 1760-1954, State Capital Building, Montpelier, Vermont*

   Land Record: 6 May 1807 – Amos Phelps to Eldad Phelps, his son.
   Lot 11, Range 2, which Amos Phelps purchased from Caleb Tree on 31
   March 1802. *Source: Notary Leon Lalanne, Bedford District Archives, Sweetsburg, Province of Quebec*

   Birth: Olive Phelps, 9 September 1817, daughter of Eldad and Abigail
   (Tree) Phelps. Baptized 16 October 1842, *Source: Sweetsburg Archives, Quebec.*

   Land Record: 2 December 1818 – Eldad Phelps and Luman Phelps of
   Stanbridge to Simeon Wells land in township of Stanbridge Lot 4 in the 1st
   range of lots 50 acres for $200. In the presence of John Chandler and
   Joseph Winsch. Signed by Luman Phelps – same signature as in
   marriage record of Charlotte Phelps & John Chartier 1836 Abbotsford.
   Source: Notary – Leon Lalanne, Bedford District Archives, Sweetsburg, Quebec

   Land Record: 24 February 1821 – Deed of sale by Eldad Phelps to
   Lyman Tree Lot 11 Range 2 for $500 as the same was unto him
   conveyed by Amos Phelps on 6 May 1807. *Source: Notary Leon Lalanne, Bedford
   District Archives, Sweetsburg, Province of Quebec*

   1825 Lower Canada Census: Eldad Phelps. Number of inhabitants: 6;
   Subdistrict: Stanbridge. County: Bedford; Farmer/Non-real estate owner.
   Church of England. Census notes in family of 6: Males: age 40-60; 1 age
   25-40; 1 age 18 not 25; Number in family 14-18= 1; number in family age

6-14=2. (*Amos III b. 1809 = 16*) 2 Females under the age of 14; one female age 14-45 single; one female married age 14-45. (*Elizabeth Phelps b. 1812=age 13-14*). *Source: Canada, Census of Lower Canada 1825 Library & Archives, Ottawa, Ontario*

Also in 1825 County of Bedford, Stanbridge Census: Brother, Carman (Luman) Phelps, Widow Mrs. H. (Amos Jr.) (or A.) (sounded phonetically, "aye" with an accent could be "H." Phelps with single daughter age 14-45/widow age 45 and up (born abt. 1780) and family of Michael Phelps, likely the son of Eldad Phelps.

1831 Lower Canada Census: Eldad Phelps. Farmer with family of 5. Stanbridge, Missisquoi. With Joseph A. Phelps and Tree families.
Source: Canada 1831 Census, Library & Archives

Eldad Phelps did not possess "clergy reserve" lands which were tracts of land reserved for the supports of the "Protestant clergy" as noted in the "Constitutional Acts of 1791." One-seventh of surveyed Crown lands were set aside per province to fund "any parsonage or rectory that may be established by the Church of England." The reserves were lots of two-hundred acres. The "Clergy Corporation in Lower Canada" known as the "Corporation for Superintending, Managing and Conducting the Clergy Reserves within the Province of Lower-Canada," was managed by the Bishop of Quebec. (*Source: Wikipedia*). Eldad's half-brother, Luman Phelps, owned Lot Range 2 which was a clergy reserve, and the son of half-brother, Amos B. Phelps Junior, Amos Phelps III, had clergy reserve property, as well.

Eldad Phelps's children names are not all verified but Michael Phelps' is listed alongside his father and "Widow H./A." Phelps in the 1825 Quebec census, and likely a son. A son (Michael) was age twenty-five to forty (born 1800, this is prior to marriage, and incorrect) and another eighteen at the time of the 1825 census or born 1807, likely son, Amos Phelps. In addition, three daughters under age eighteen are noted: two females under age 14 (born after 1811) and one older than 14 (born before 1811). In the 1831 census, Eldad resided with the Joseph A. Phelps family leading one to assume the three sons of Eldad and Abigail (Tree) Phelps were named Amos Phelps, Michael Phelps and Joseph A. Phelps born after 1805 in Quebec. Daughter Olive Phelps was born 1817.

One son of Eldad and Abigail (Tree) Phelps was Amos Phelps, born Quebec born after the 1805 marriage. 1825 Quebec Lower Canada Census for Eldad Phelps lists, one son, age 18-20, or born 1807. This individual was likely named Amos Phelps for Eldad's father. The son of Eldad, Amos Phelps, moved to Crawford, Illinois prior to 1830 and is listed in 1830 and 1840 Crawford, Illinois, United States census records with one son age 5-10 (born 1825-1830). This Amos Phelps' son is then listed with the family name, Amos" in 1851 Canada West Oxford County census as Amos Phelps, age 26 (born 1825) with wife Elizabeth Phelps age 18 and son C. J. Phelps age two - all born Canada. The 1861 Canada West Frontenac census lists the grandson of Eldad Phelps, Amos Phelps as age 32 born 1829.

Jeremiah Phelps' son, Amos Phelps, moved to Wisconsin, USA by 1846, and Oliver C. Phelps' son, Amos Phelps is recorded in the 1851 Canada East Stuckley, Shefford County Quebec as age 33 (born 1828). Amos B. Phelps Junior/"the younger's" son, Amos Phelps III, is recorded in the 1851 Canada East Missisquoi, Quebec as Amos Phillps with family including son, Orville Phelps.

Diadama Long Phelps:

> Born: 14 January 1763, Coventry, Tolland, CT, USA
> Marriage: 1790, Franklin, VT, USA – Amos Phelps
> Died: 9 March 1837, Rougemont, Quebec, Canada
> (Parents: Samuel Long and Martha Brewster)

1837 – *"On the ninth day of March one thousand eight hundred and thirty-seven Diadama Long widow of Amos Phelps of Rougemont died in the seventy seventh year of her age and was buried on the eleventh day of the same month in the presence of witnesses…."* Abbotsford, St. Hyacinthe. *Source: Drouin*

~Before the building of St. Thomas' Anglican Church of Rougemont, the farm of Matthew Standish, Lot 552, served as the burial ground for the first inhabitants of Rougemont. The remains were later transferred to St. Thomas Cemetery, consecrated in 1848. It is likely Amos Phelps Senior is also buried at this cemetery. Many descendants of Elder William Brewster are buried in this St. Thomas Rougemont Cemetery.

Death: **Diadama Phelps**: Birth: 14 Jan 1763, Coventry, Tolland, County, Connecticut, USA. Death date: 9 March 1837, Quebec, Canada, Cemetery: Saint Paul's Anglican Church Cemetery, Abbotsford, Monterregie Region, Quebec, Canada. Spouse: Amos Phelps.
Source: FindAGrave Canada

On the same page Diadama Phelps St. Paul's record:

1837 – "*On the ninth day of March one thousand eight hundred and thirty-seven Hannah, daughter of Jeremiah Phelps of Milton (?) and Joset (Roi) his wife born on the sixth day of May last was baptized the sponsors are Diadama Chartes (?)…*" Hannah Phelps, daughter of Jeremiah and Josette Phelps - b. 6 May 1836, baptized 9 March 1837.

Diadama Long Phelps - Grandmother to Elizabeth Phelps (BREWSTER Family)

The parents of Diadama Long were Samuel Long and Martha Brewster. Brewster Family ties certify the Comfort Carpenter Pinkham-Elizabeth Phelps branch as Mayflower descendants. The line in detail as follows.

WILLIAM BREWSTER was born 1568 Scrooby, Nottinghamshire, England. He was a Pilgrim and an English teacher educated at Cambridge. His parents were William Brewster and Mary Smythe. His paternal grandparents were William Brewster (b. 1510) and Maud Mann. His paternal grandfather was William Smythe (b. 1505). He attempted to leave England for Holland in 1607 but was arrested. During 1608, a group made it to Holland where he was elected ruling elder of the congregation. After teaching English in Leiden, he left with the first group of Separatists on the *Mayflower* with his wife, Mary Brewster, and sons, Love and Wrestling Brewster. In the Plymouth Colony, William Brewster served as the religious leader of the colony.

The first-born son of William and Mary Brewster was JONATHAN BREWSTER born 12 August 1593 in Scrooby, Nottinghamshire, England. He married (m2) Lucrecia Oldham of Derby on 10 April 1624. They were the parents of eight children including BENJAMIN Brewster. Although Jonathan traveled with his father to Leiden, Holland, he did not travel on the *Mayflower* to America. Instead he stayed in Holland with his first wife and child. After they died, Jonathan traveled to Plymouth at age twenty-seven on the ship, *Fortune*, during 1621. In Plymouth, he married Lucretia Oldham, the daughter of William Oldham and Phillipa Sowter. Jonathan Brewster died on 7 August 1659 in New London, Connecticut at age 65 where he was buried in Brewster's Cemetery at Brewster's Neck, Preston, Connecticut. His children were William, Mary, Jonathan, Ruth, BENJAMIN, Elizabeth, Grace and Hannah Brewster.

BENJAMIN BREWSTER married Ann (Addis) Dart in late February of 1659-1660 *(Source: Brewster Book and Norwich, CT, T. Rec)*. Ann Dart "may have been the widow of William Addis of Cape Ann 24th." Ann Brewster, "wife of Benjamin Brewster" died 9 May 1709. Benjamin Brewster died 14 September 1710 in Norwich and was buried in Brewster's Plain. He resided at the property of his father at Brewster's Neck which he acquired from his father and brother-in-law, John Pickett. He was a man of prominence, serving as deputy to the General Court of the Colony of Connecticut (1668; 1689; 1690; 1692-1997), Lieutenant of the New London Troop in 1673 and Captain of the military company of Norwich in 1693. His children recorded in Brewster Book and Norwich, Connecticut town records include: Mary (b. 10 December 1660), Ann (b. 29 September 1662), Jonathan (b. 29 November 1664), Daniel (b. 1 March 1666) and WILLIAM (b. 22 March 1669) Brewster.

WILLIAM BREWSTER was born 22 March 1669. He married first on 8 January 1692 in Norwich, Connecticut (m1) Elizabeth Read, daughter of Josiah and Grace (Holliway) Read. She died 11 March 1692. William Brewster married (m2) Patience who died 1740. He died 11 August 1728 in Lebanon, Connecticut. The children of William and Patience Brewster were: "eldest son" William, Patience, Samuel, Ebenezer (b. 1 February 1702-3) and PETER (b. 17 February 1706-1707) Brewster born Lebanon, Connecticut.

PETER BREWSTER(WilliamBenjaminWilliamJonathanWilliam) (b. 17 February 1708-1707 Lebanon, CT) married first in Lebanon, Connecticut 18 February 1730 Mary Lee (b. 19 December 1713), the daughter of Stephen and Elizabeth Lee. Mary Lee Brewster died in Coventry, Connecticut on 17 September 1784. He married (m2) 30 November 1786 Miriam Barnard (b. 23 February 1736), daughter of Benoni and Freedom Barnard, who died in Coventry in 1818. Peter Brewster died in Coventry, Connecticut on 27 January 1802 in his 96th year. He moved from Lebanon to Coventry during 1737 where he settled on a farm. In his will dated 2 June 1800 then proved on 2 March 1802 (recorded in Hebron Probate Records, ii, p. 183), he named his eldest son, Isreal, son Jacob, and youngest son, David, the children of his son, Jesse (Ashel, Mary and Sintha Brewster), his daughter MARTHA LONG, and all the children now living of his deceased daughters, Tabitha, Mary and Patience Brewster Carpenter (b. 1738; d. 1786).

The child (of Peter Brewster's first wife) baptized in Lebanon was: MARTHA BREWSTER, baptized 6 June 1731. Martha Brewster married Lemuel Long. The children of Lemuel (b. 1727; d. 1810) and Martha (Brewster) Long were: Levi, Jesse, Diadama (b. 1762) and Ruben Long (b. 1764) The daughter of Lemuel Long and Martha Brewster was Diadama Long Phelps. Martha Brewster died in 1818 Coventry Connecticut and is buried in the Carpenter Cemetery.

That Diadama Long Phelps' mother was buried in a Carpenter Cemetery, and her granddaughter married the child of a Carpenter further connects the Brewster - Phelps- Pinkham branch. *Source: Brewster Genealogy 1566-1907 A Record of the Descendants of William Brewster of the Mayflower/Ruling Elder of the*

Children of Amos Senior and (m2) Diadama (Long) Phelps: ("…it is noted other children were born…" - Carter)

1). **Amos B. Phelps Junior/"the younger"**:

Birth: January 1786, Rutland, Vermont, USA

1790 Rutland Vermont Census: Amos Phelps: 1 male over 16 – Amos Phelps the father; 4 males under 16: Oliver-Cromwell age 9; Eldad age 7, **Amos Junior/"the younger" about 5**, Luman about 3 (2+) and 3 females: Diadama, the mother, Martha and Charlotte. *Source: 1790 Vermont Census & Carter Phelps Family*

Land Record: 7 June 1807 - Sale by George Ross to **Amos Phelps, the younger**. Lot 9 Range 2 (Stanbridge). 2 acres on the northeasterly bank of the Pike River for 100 Spanish dollars. *Source: Notary Leon Lalanne, Bedford District Archives, Sweetsburg, Province of Quebec*

Land Record: Date notation not written but prior following entry of 20 September 1808: "Bond by **Amos Phelps, senior and junior,** to George Ross for 10 pounds in an assault & battery action, Amos Phelps, senior and junior, enter a complaint against Sam Bickford & Abner Bickford. **(Signed by both Amos, Sr. & Amos Jr.).** *Source: Notary - Leon Lalanne, Bedford District Archives, Sweetsburg, Province of Quebec*

Not child of m1 Phebe Phelps because not baptized in Vermont nor Quebec.

> *Children of Amos Jr./"the younger" (b. 1786) and unknown Phelps:*
> 1) *Amos Phelps III, born 1809-1810, Stanbridge, Quebec. (Amos Jr. age 21-22).*
> 2) *Elisabeth "Betsy" Phelps, born 1812, Stanbridge Quebec. (Amos Jr. age 26).*

1812-1815 Military Service, New York Militia: **Amos B. Phelps** – Military District #9, New York and Vermont. 2 Regiment (Swift's) New York Militia. Rank: Private. "Captain Jedediah Noble's Co., 2 Regiment New York Detached Militia. Company payroll $8 for one month." *Source: United States War of 1812 Index to Service Records, 1812-1815.*

Brother, Luman B. Phelps, enlisted in War of 1812 in Vermont on 1 June 1813. Brother Jeremiah Phelps enlisted in New York Militia (as per 1866 Land Patent).

Died: 19 October 1813, **Private Amos B. Phelps**, 2 Swift's NY Militia/War of 1812. Died – October 19th after month-long illness. *Source: NARA*

Amos Phelps Jr. resided at same location (**Lot 9 Range 2 Stanbridge**) as mother, Diadama (Long) Phelps - 8 July 1807: "Sale by Moses Hunkins (Huckins) to Diadama

Phelps (maiden name, Long), wife of Amos Phelps residing at Richelieu, Shefford County, Lot 9 Range 2 Stanbridge 60 acres on Pike River, west boundry the east bank of the river for $300 Spanish dollars. *Source: Notary Leon Lallane, Bedford District Archives at Sweetsburg, Province of Quebec*

> ***Not true speculation*** -<u>Death</u>: **Amos Phelps**: Birth: January 1786, Rutland, Rutland County, Vermont, USA; Death: April 10, 1830; Inscription: Amos Phelps died April 10, 1830. Aged 48 years. Sophia wife of Amos Phelps died February 16, 1873 aged 82 years. *Source: Avon, Connecticut Free Library:*
> <u>Burial</u>: East Avon Cemetery, Avon, Harford County, Connecticut, USA; *FindAGrave Memorial.* Incorrect assumption. This Amos Phelps was born in 1782. **The son of Amos & Diadama Long Phelps was born 1786** and would be age 44 not age 48 in 1830 as listed in Farmingham, Connecticut textbook. **Fact: Amos Phelps of GRENVILLE, (Connecticut) m. Sophia Woodford of Northington, CT, on January 4, 1810.**

2). <u>Luman B. Phelps</u>:
> <u>Born</u>: 2 December 1787, Rutland, Vermont, USA
> <u>Married</u>: M1 - 11 June 1812, Franklin, Vermont to Hannah Briggs (abt.1795 Connecticut; d. 1836) by Justice of Peace: Samuel Hubbard.
> <u>Marriage</u>: 11 June 1812. Name: Luman Phelps; Event Place: Franklin, Vermont, US; Spouse's name: Hannah Briggs. *Source: Vermont Vital Records, 1760-1954*
>> Death of Hannah Phelps; Birth Date: 1795; Birth Place: Rutland County, Vermont, USA; Death date – 1830; Death place – Ontario, Canada. *Source: FindAGrave USA*
>
> <u>Married M2</u> - Harriet Cromwell (b.1802, Chazy, NY)
>
> <u>War of 1812 Military Service</u>: Luman B. Phelps, Private, Army. Event date: 1 June 1813. Event Type: Military Service, State of Vermont. *Source: United States Registers of enlistments in the U. S. Army, 1798-1914*
> Brother, Amos B. Phelps enlisted in 1812 and died 19 October 1813.

The United States issued bounty land warrants to attract enlistments during the War of 1812. Luman Phelps moved from Quebec to Ontario then settled in Michigan, USA.

> <u>Land Record</u>: 1 April 1818 – Luman Phelps, grantor in the above sale, personally appeared. Signed by Luman Phelps in Rougemont. *Source: Notary – Leon Lallane, Bedford, District Archives, Sweetsburg, Quebec*
> <u>Land Record</u>: 22 April 1820 – Addie Vincent of St. Armand, yeoman, to Luman Phelps of Stanbridge, Lot 1 Range 200 acres that was granted at the City of Quebec 2 January 1809 by His Majesty to Addie Vincent. *Source: Notary – Leon Lalanne, Bedford District Archives, Sweetsburg, Quebec*
> <u>Land Record</u>: 23 August 1820 Notary at St. Armand, County of Bedford, District Montreal, Province Lower Canada – Luman Phelps of Stanbridge to William Briggs $125 paid by William Briggs. Luman Phelps doth cede, sell, transfer and quit all the rest and remainder yet to come and unexpired of the term of 21 years commenced on 2 January 1809 – land that was transferred by Addie Vincent, 22 April 1820. Lot 1, Range 2 (a clergy

reserve) – 100 acres. Note – same signature as on 2 December 1818 sale.

1825 Lower Canada Census – Carman (Luman) Phelps. Number of inhabitants: 8; Subdistrict: Stanbridge. County: Bedford; Census notes in family of 6: Males: Married, age 25-40; Number in family under age 6= 3; number in family age 6-14=3 (Amy b. 1814 age 11, Diadama b. 1817 age 8, Charlotte b. 1819 age 6, Luana younger than age 6, Luman Jr. b. 1822 age 3, Roxana b. 1825) *Source: Canada, Census of Lower Canada 1825 Library & Archives, Ottawa, Ontario*

If is noted Hannah (Briggs) Phelps died 1830 Ontario. Since zero census records exist for Ontario, Canada until 1842, if this was the case, and Luman and Hannah Phelps moved to Ontario by 1830, then, perhaps, Elizabeth Phelps' husband, Comfort Carpenter Pinkham, followed Elizabeth's uncle to Ontario. Comfort and Elizabeth (Phelps) Pinkham are recorded in the1842 Newcastle, Ontario, Canada census.

1840 United States Pontiac, Oakland, Michigan Census: L. Phelps. *Source: United States Census, 1840*

Death: 12 December 1856, Attica Township, Lapeer, MI USA. Buried South Attica Cemetery, Attica Township, Lapeer County, Michigan, USA.

Children of M1 Luman and Hannah (Briggs) Phelps:

1) Amy Phelps – Born 26 September 1814, Stanbridge, East, Quebec. Married Welcome Chandler. *"In the district of St. Hyacinthe, during the year one thousand eight hundred and thirty-one: "On this sixteenth day of March one thousand eight hundred and thirty-one Welcome Chandler bachelor farmer of Milton of major age and Amy Phelps of Rougemont of the parish of St. Cesaire spinster of minor age were married by Banns in the presence of the subscribing witnesses by Thomas Johns, minister."* Witnesses: Oliver Warren (brother to husband, Seth Warren, of Huldah Pinkham – daughter of Sam G. Pinkham/sister of Comfort Carpenter Pinkham who married Elizabeth Phelps) and Clara A. Buzzell. Welcome Chandler refined timber potash then moved in 1854 to Burlington, Wisconsin with John Phelps, son of Jeremiah Phelps. Welcome Chandler then moved to Mower County – 10 October 1857 MN Census (Welcome Chandler age 52 born Vermont, Amy age 40, David L. age 25, John age 22, Stephen age 19, Starling age 16, Hannah age 14, George age 12, William age 9, Rosina age 5 & Celia age one all born in Canada). The census lists one record below the Abijah Pinkham family (age 30, born in Canada)- the son of Samuel Pinkham/brother to Comfort Carpenter Pinkham.

2) Diadama Phelps – Born 13 June 1817, near Abbotsford, QC. Baptized: 4 October 1834. Married Stephen Chartier; d. 1888. (*Note: Two Jeremiah B. Phelps daughter's married Chartier sons while two Samuel Junior Pinkham's sons married Chartier surname daughters - J. Samuel married Domitilde Chartier and Joseph Abijah married Rosina Chartier, all born Quebec.*)

3) Charlotte Hannah Phelps – Born 16 August 1819, Rougemont, Quebec. Married John Chartier (*or Stephan Cartier of Melton*) – 1818. Marriage certificate signed by Luman Phelps. Daughter Mary Louisa b. 9 August 1835, baptized 13 September 1835 with witnesses: Pastor Thomas Johnson, David & Esther McMillan and Diadama Phelps (Mary Louisa's grandmother). Charlotte Hannah Phelps Chartier baptismal certificate (St. Abbotsford, Quebec) reads: *"On the 20th day of August 1837, Hannah Charlotte, wife of John Chartier (nee Phelps) of Milton, born on the 16 August 1819 (an adult) baptized by me, Thomas Johnson, missionary."* Also on the same day was the baptism of Hannah and John Chartier's daughter, Ana Maria Chartier. d. 26 November 1889, Lyle, MN, USA

4) Luana Phelps

5) Lyman (Luman) J./W. Phelps, Jr. - Born abt. 1822. Michigan Deaths & Burials: L. W. Phelps. Birth date: 1822. United States Census of Union Veterans and Widows of the Civil War, 1890: Luman J. Phelps. Event date: 1890. Event Place: Hutchinson, McLeod, Minnesota. Death: Luman J. Phelps. Death date: 20 February 1903, age 81. Death place: Attica, Lapeer, Michigan. Father's name: Lyman (Luman) Phelps. Mother's name: Hanna Briggs.

6) Roxana Phelps Blinn - Birth year: 1825 Canada. Married. James Blinn on 22 Nov 1877 in Springfield, MA, USA. Spouses father: Luman Phelps.

7) Anice Phelps - m. Hiram Birch

8) Sterling Phelps - Birth abt. year: 1825. 1894 Attica, Lapeer, Michigan Census. Sterling Phelps age 69. Married to Maria L. Phalps. Son Dayton J. Phelps age 19.

Children of Luman and M2 Harriet (Cromwell) Phelps:

1) Hannah A. Phelps West - b. 1841; d. 15 Dec 1921, Lapeer, MI, USA (Luman B. Phelps died in Lapeer, MI on 12 Dec. 1856). Michigan Death Certificate: Hannah A. West. Death date: 15 December 1921. Age 83. Born abt. 1838. Event place: Imlay City, Lapeer, Michigan, USA. Marital status: Widowed. Father's name: Luman Phelps. Mother's name: Harriet Phelps.

Death: (Husband) Almond B. West. Born 19 April 1827. Died 28 February 1909 age 81. Buried: South Attica Cemetery, Attica, Lapeer County, MI, USA. *Source: FindAGrave*

Death: Hannah (Phelps) West: Born 13 April 1838. Died 15 December 1921 age 83. Buried: South Attica Cemetery, Attica, Lapeer County, Michigan, USA. *Source: FindAGrave*

2) Dorothy E. Phelps - b. 1842; d. 1912.

3) Jeremiah B. Phelps:

Born: 9 June 1794, Rougemont, St. Hyacinthe, Quebec

Birth as recorded in *Source – Edmund West*: Jeremiah Phelps – Father: Amos Phelps; Mother – Diadama Long; Birth Date – 1794; City – Rougemont; County – St. Hyct.; State – Pq; Country – Canada.

Married: Margaret Collins; Name: Jeremiah Phelps; Spouse – Margaret Collins; Event – Marriage; Marriage year – 1819-1820; Marriage Location – Chambly, Quebec; Religion – Anglican; Place of Worship – Anglican, Saint Stephen. *Source: Drouin*

Land Petitions of Lower Canada 1764-1841: Jeremiah Phelps, Year 1792-1805 (Record #69131).

1825 Lower Canada Census: Jeremiah Phelps; Name: Jeremiah Phelps; Number of Inhabitants – 6; Sub-District – Bedford; Number of family under the age of 6 – 4; 1 male, Married, age 24-40; 2 Females under the age of 14; 1 Female, Married age 14-45.

1831 Lower Canada Census: Jeremie Phelps: Name: Jeremie Phelps; Occupation – Cultivateur (farmer); Number in family – 9; 1 male married between ages 30-60; 2 females under age 14; 1 female age 14-45; 4 children age 5 and under; 2 children between ages 5-14; Religion – Anglican; Sub-District – St. Cesaire; County/District – St. Hyacinthe. *Source: 1831 Lower Canada Census, Public Archives, Ottawa, Ontaro*

(Listed at the same census location as father Amos Phelps and, brothers, Jeremiah and Oliver Phelps, plus Samuel Pinkham. All religion: Church of England/Anglican.

1831 Lower Canada Census: Thomas (Amos) Phelps. Occupation – Rentier (living off property investments); Number in family – 3; 1 male child between ages 5 and 14; 1 adult male married over age 60; 1 adult female married over age 45; Religion – Anglican; Sub-District – St. Cesaire; County/District – St. Hyacinthe. *Source: 1831 Lower Canada Census, Public Archives, Ottawa, Ontario*

<u>1831 Lower Canada Census:</u> Oliver Phelps: Name: Oliver Phelps; Occupation – Cultivateur (farmer); Number in family – 8; 3 children under the age of 5; 1 child between the age of 5-14; 1 male married between age 21-30; 1 male not married between age 21-30; 2 females under the age of 14; 1 female married between age 14-45; 1 female not married between age14-45; Religion – Anglican; Sub-District – St. Cesaire; County/District – St. Hyacinthe. *Source: 1831 Lower Canada Census, Public Archives, Ottawa, Ontario*

<u>1831 Lower Canada Census:</u> Jeremie Phelps: Name: Jeremie Phelps; Occupation – Cultivateur (farmer); Number in family – 9; 1 male married between ages 30-60; 2 females under age 14; 1 female age 14-45; 4 children age 5 and under; 2 children between ages 5-14; Religion – Anglican; Sub-District – St. Cesaire; County/District – St. Hyacinthe. *Source: 1831 Lower Canada Census, Public Archives, Ottawa, Ontario.*

<u>1831 Lower Canada Census:</u> Samuel Pinkham: Name: Samuel Pinkham; Occupation – Cultivateur (farmer); Number in family – 8; Number of people in family age 5 and below – 2; number people in family over age 5 and under age 14 – 2; males age 14-16 – 1; male married age 30-60 – 1; females under the age of 14 – 1; females between the age of 14-45 – 1 unmarried/ 1 married; Religion – Anglican; Sub-District – St. Cesaire; County/District – St. Hyacinthe. *Source: 1831 Lower Canada Census, Public Archives, Ottawa, Ontario*

<u>Baptized:</u> 23 September 1831, St. Paul Anglican Church. Same baptism day as brother, Oliver Cromwell. *Source: Drouin Collection* Listed as Protestant.

<u>Signs baptismal record 16 November 1831</u> for Oliver Warren Carpenter, as well as witness, Sam G. Pinkham, whose wife was Theodosia Carpenter and daughter Huldah Pinkham, who married Seth Warren, brother to Oliver Warren, father of Oliver Warren Carpenter, on the record preceding the baptism of Oliver Warren Carpenter. *"On this sixteenth of November one thousand eight hundred and thirty-one, Oliver Warren Carpenter, born on the twentieth day of September one thousand eight hundred and thirty-one was baptized in the presence of family and witnesses: Thomas Johnson Warren, Oliver Warren, **Sam G. Pinkham, Jeremiah Phelps**, Harriet___."* The record next to the baptism is the marriage record of Huldah Pinkham to Seth Warren in the presence of her father (Sam G. Pinkham) and his brother (Oliver Warren) and signed by: Seth Warren, Huldah Pinkham, Oliver Warren, **Betsy Phelps** and Sam G. Pinkham. *Source: Drouin Collection.*

<u>1842 Milton, Shefford County Census, Quebec:</u> (pg. 2509) Jeremie B. Phelps, non-proprietor and farmer. Number in family: 14. Natives of Ireland: 1; Natives of Canada: 13. 2 females 5 years and under; 4 males over age 5 and under age 14; 2 males single age 14-18; 1 male single age 18-21;

one male married age 30-60; 3 females married 14-45. Members of Church of England: 13. Number of acres belonging to family: 300. Number of improved acres belonging to family: 13.

1842 Lower Canada Census, Quebec: Samuel Pinkham Jr. Occupation: Farmer. Inhabitants: 7.

Landowner: Milton 1849 – Property adjacent to John Chartier (eventual son-in-law). Thomas Phelps, son of Jeremiah Phelps, bought land of Nathaniel Chartier in 1847 in Milton. Joseph Abijah Pinkham, who moved to Mower, Minnesota with Jeremiah Phelps, married Marie Rosina Chartier, sister to John Chartier. J. Samuel Pinkham married Domitilde Chartier in 1844.

1857 United States Census: Mower County, MN, USA: Jeremiah Phelps. Head of Household: Jeremiah Phelps, age 61, born in Canada, farmer; Margaret Phelps, age 61, born in Ireland; George Phelps, age 25 (born abt. 1832), born Canada, Farmer; William Phelps; age 23 (born abt. 1834), born Canada, Farmer; Diadama Phelps, age 19 (born abt. 1838), born Canada; May Phelps, age 16 born (abt.1841), born Canada. Listed on same record, son, John Phelps, age 26 (born abt. 1831) born Canada, Farmer, with his wife, Lydia Phelps, age 19, born in New York. *Source: 1857 Minnesota Census, Mower County, MN*

1860: Minnesota Census 1835-1890: Jeremiah Phelps. State: MN; County: Mower County; Township: Lyle; Year: 1860; Record: Federal Population Schedule; Page: 065: Database: MN 1860 Federal Census Index. *Source: U.S. Federal Decentenial Census*

1866 Land Patent US Department of the Interior: Jeremiah Phelps. 122 acres of MN land. Listed at land office in Chatfield; Mower County, MN; Militia: New York Militia.

United States Civil War and Later Pension: Jeremiah Phelps; Event date – 18 March 1907; Event Place – United States; File Name: 17787443. *Source: NARA*

Death: Jeremiah Phelps, 9 May 1865, Lyle, Mower County, Minnesota, USA.

Buried: 10 May 1865 in Cedar City Cemetery, Lyle, MN, USA. Cemetery records state Jeremiah Phelps was born in Canada.

Children of Jeremiah and Margaret (Collins) Phelps born Quebec:

1.) Charlotte Phelps; b. 16 August 1820; m. Thomas Bonnallie; Quebec; d. 4 Sept. 1910 Austin, Mower, MN, USA.
1860 US Mower, MN Census: Thomas (age 40 born Scotland; Charlotte age 39 born Canada; William age 8 born

Canada; Jeremiah age 6 born Wisconsin; Margaret age 5 born Wisconsin; Dama age 2 born MN.

2) Phebe Phelps; b. 3 October 1821; m. Andrew Gemmel; d. MN.

3) Amos Phelps – b. 15 June 1825, Quebec. Arrived USA 1846. Prospector for gold in Placerville, El Dorado County, CA. Died 1903, Santa Rosa, CA, USA.
Baptized: 1825; Name: Amos Phelps; Baptism Location - Chambly, Quebec; Religion – Anglican; Place of Worship – Anglican; Saint Stephen. Signed by parents: Jeremiah Phelps and Margaret Phelps. *Source: Drouin*
US Naturalized citizen: Amos Phelps born abt. 1823, age at event: 34. Court district: Illinois, Indiana, Wisconsin, Iowa. Year at arrival: 1846. Date of Action: 21 April 1857. *Source: National Archives and Records Administration NARA, DC, 1840-1950)*

Moved to Darien, Wisconsin in 1846 and to Burlington, Wisconsin as early as 1852.

Marriage: 25 February 1853, Racine, Wisconsin. To Maria Coffie Lyon (of New York). Parents: Issac and Eunice Lyon. Amos Phelps parents: Jeremiah and Margaret Phelps.
1855 Wisconsin State Census: Amos Phelps, Event Place – Burlington Town, Racine, Wisconsin, Number of White Males – 3, Number of White Females – 3. *Source: State Historical Society, Madison.*
1857 Illinois, Northern District Naturalization – Amos Phelps. Birthplace: Canada, - Phelps, Amos; Certificate 869 Vol. 1., Court Racine, Wisconsin – Country of birth – East Canada. When born for age – 34 years. Arrival in United States – June 1846, Whitehall, NY. Date: 21 April 1857.
1860 Racine, Wisconsin census: Amos Phelps age 37 born 1823 East Canada with wife Maria born New York and children Maria age 5 born Wisconsin and Jennie age two born Wisconsin.
1895 Phelps Family Newsletter of February: **Amos B. Phelps**, from "Phelps Family Papers 1851-1864 item 33, University of Michigan, William L. Clements Library, Ann Arbor, MI. 20 letters from Amos B. Phelps dated 1851-1854 describe his experience as prospector during the Gold Rush in Placerville (El Dorado County). Amos B. Phelps (1824 -) (P3682), WRONG FATHER LISTED – SHOULD BE JEREMIAH PHELPS #1569 *Alexander,* #521 Amos, #165 John, #47 Joseph, #24 Timothy, #14 William.

PROVES: Amos B. Phelps, son of Jeremiah Phelps, was named after Jeremiah Phelps brother Amos B. Phelps Junior/"the younger" who died in 1813 during the War of 1812.

In the 1842 Milton Shefford Quebec census, Jeremiah Phelps is listed as, "Jeremie B. Phelps", confirming the Amos Phelps family line repeatedly used the initial "B" as in the case of brothers, Amos B. Phelps Jr., Jeremie B. Phelps (and son, Amos B. Phelps). and Luman B. Phelps. From this line was Amos Phelps born 1709 Simsbury, CT, USA.

Death of son, Curtis A. Phelps age 22 in Santa Rosa, California with parents A. J. and M. A. Phelps of Vermont.

Voter Registration of Amos Phelps 27 July 1888 Santa Rosa, CA age 65 born Canada 1823.

Death of Amos Phelps age 79 born Canada 1824 on 24 February 1903 in Santa Rosa, California.

California Death Index: Amos Phelps. Death date: 24 February 1903. Event Place: Santa Rosa, Sonoma, California. Age 79. Married. Ethnicity: American. Occupation: Capitalist. Birth year: 1824. Birthplace: Canada.

"Amos comes from a large family, son of Jeremiah and Margaret (Collins) Phelps from Rougemont. He is a descendant of William Brewster of the Mayflower."

Birth: 15 June 1823, Quebec, Canada. Death: 24 February 1903, Santa Rosa, Sonoma, California, USA. Burial Location: Cypress Lawn Memorial Park, Colma, San Mateo, CA. *Source: FindAGrave*

Maria Coffin Lyon Phelps. Burial Place: Colma, San Mateo, California. Cemetery: Cypress Lawn Memorial Park. Death date: 1907. Birth date: 1829. Wife of Amos Phelps. *Source: FindAGrave*

California Death Index: Maria Phelps. Age: 78. Death date: 1907. Death place: California, USA. Birth year: 1829.

4) Thomas Phelps – b. 1824; m. Albina C. Runnels; d. MN.

1857 Mower County MN Census Town 101 – Range 18 (Lyle Township) – Thomas Phelps, age 32 born Canada with wife Elbina age 22 born Canada.

Daughter Edmonia T. Phelps born 1858 MN

1865 Minnesota State Census: Thomas V. Phelps. Location: Austin, Mower, Minnesota. With Anna and Anna G. Phelps.

Death: Thomas V. Phelps. 10 March 1915. Death location: Blue Earth, Minnesota. *Source: Minnesota Death Index, 1908-2002*

This individual is related to Phelps Quebec-Minnesota branch; Birth year likley incorrect.

Thomas L. Phelps. Born abt. 1838-1841 Canada. Death: 29 November 1891, California, USA.

<u>Minnesota, Grand Army of the Republic Membership Records</u>
1869-1940: Thos. L. Phipps.

<u>California Great Registers 1866-1910</u>: Thomas Lawrence
Phelps. Voter Registration. Date: 20 April 1875. Event
Place: Buena Vista, Stanislaus, California. Age 36. Birth
year: 1839. Birthplace: Canada. Wife: Martha N. Kitman
Daughter Emma Lucile Phelps born 1873; Son: Thomas L.
Phelps Jr. born MN.

Daughter Edmonia T. Phelps <u>marriage</u> to T. B. M. Mason on
30 September 1875 in Solano, California. Edmonia T.
Phelps born 1858 (MN). Spouse's father: Thomas L.
Phelps. T. B. M. Mason born 1848.

1875 Citizenship Application: Thomas Phelps. Born Canada.

<u>California Great Registers, 1866 - 1910</u>: Thomas L. Phelps. Voter
Registration. Event Date: 26 January 1879. Buena Vista
(Modesto), Stanislaus, California. Age. 39. Birth year:
1840 Canada. Occupation: Farmer (320 acres near
Oakdale). Mailing address: Knights Ferry, California, USA.

<u>California Great Registers, 1850-1920</u>: Thomas L. Phelps, age 47
born 1841 Canada. Event Date: 23 June 1888. Event
Place: Buena Vista (Modesto), Stanislaus, California.

<u>United States General Index to Pension Files 1861-1934</u>: Thomas
Phelps. Pension date: 1890. Pension place: California

California. <u>California Death Index</u>: Thomas Phelps. Age 68. Born
1841. Death date: 1909, California.

<u>Death</u> of Emma Lucille (Phelps) Cook on 6 April 1941 Los
Angeles, CA, age 68. Born 1873. Father: Thomas L.
Phelps. Mother: Martha N. Kitman. *Source: California, County Birth
and Death Records, 1800-1994.*

<u>Death</u>: 15 June 1942 Minnesota. Thomas L. Phelps. *Source: Minnesota,
Olmsted County, Cemetery Records, 1863-1998.*

5) <u>Jeremiah Phelps</u> – b. 12 March 1827, Quebec; d. 3 January
1899 Sparta, Michigan, USA.

6) <u>John Phelps -</u> b. 1831, Quebec. Marriage: Mrs Julia. H.
Chandler. Marriage year: 1853; Marriage location: St. Armand
East, Quebec. Religion: Baptist; Place of Worship – Baptist.
Source: Drouin.

1855 Militia of Stanbridge, Missisquoi, Quebec –
John Phelps, Number 12, second range; Age 26. 10 October
1857.

1857 Mower County MN Census – Town 101-Range 18 (Lyle
Township): Phelps, John (born in Canada) age 26 with wife,
Julia, age 19 born in New York.

Death: 12 November 1899, North Dakota, USA.

7) George Phelps & William Phelps – b. 21 January 1834, Quebec.

8) Hannah Phelps – b. 3 April 1836, Quebec; m. Alfred Cressey; d. 15
October 1903 in Mower, Minnesota, age 67.

9) Diadama Phelps – b. 16 October 1838, Milton, Quebec; m. John
b son. Niles; d. Minnesota, USA.

10) Edward Phelps – b. 15 May 1840; d. May 1904, Parker, South Dakota,
USA.

11) Mary Ann Phelps; b. 13 February 1842; m. Siloam Williams.

4.) Selinda Phelps MacRae:

Born: 1799, Rougemont, St. Hyacinthe, Quebec
Married: 6 March 1817 to Christopher MacRae – All Saints Church, Durham,
Quebec
Died: 1888, Waterloo, Blackhawk, Iowa, USA

Selinda married Christopher McRae whose family was born In the Monteregie
Region of Quebec (Catherine b. 1793, Philip b. 1794, Farquar b. 1795, Hurclous
b. 1796, Mary b. 1796, James b. 1798 – born Ecoste, Quebec). In 1856
Christopher McRae purchased land in Illinois (11 March 1856 – DeKalb, Illinois
Land Record/ listed alongside Duncan MdRae – son and/or brother).
Christopher McRae died in DeKalb, Illinois in May 1858. Selinda is buried in
Waterloo, Black Hawk, Iowa next to her daughter, Jane R. (McRae) Lewis.
Selinda Phelps McRae resided 113 miles from nephew, Amos Phelps III (b.
1810, son of Amos Phelp Junior) of Maquoketa, Iowa.

Children of Christopher and Selinda (Phelps) McRae:
1) Alexander   (b. 1818; d. 1895)
2) Pheba   (b. 1822)
3) Catherine   (b. 1823)
4) John   (b. 1826)
5) Margaret   (b. 1827)
6) Duncan   (b. 1828)
7) Christopher   (b. 1831)

8) Eleanor   (b. 1832)

5.) Oliver Cromwell Phelps:

Born: 17 (or 19th) July 1803, Rougemont, St. Hyacinthe, Quebec
(Named for the son of Amos and m1 Pheba Phelps, Oliver Cromwell
Phelps, who died after 1790 and before 1803).

1825 Lower Canada Census: Oliver C. Phelps; Name: Oliver C. Phelps;
Number of Inhabitants – 2; Sub-District – Bedford; 1 Male, married age
18-25; 1 Female, married age 14-45. *Source: 1825 Lower Canada Census, Public Archives,
Ottawa, Ontario.*

1831 Lower Canada Census: Olivier Phelps: Name: Olivier Phelps;
Occupation – Cultivateur (farmer); Number in family – 8;3 children under
the age of 5; 1 child between the age of 5-14; 1 male married between
age 21-30; 1 male not married between age 21-30; 2 females under the
age of 14; 1 female married between age 14-45; 1 female not married
between age 14-45; Religion – Anglican; Sub-District – St. Cesaire;
County/District – St. Hyacinthe. *Source: 1831 Lower Canada Census, Public Archives,
Ottawa, Ontario.*

Listed at the same location as Amos Sr. and Jeremiah Phelps & Samuel Pinkham, Jr.

Baptized: 23 September 1831, St. Paul's Anglican Church, Abbotsford, Quebec
*"Baptized on 23 September 1831 Cromwell Phelps of Rougemont, Farmer
born 19 July 1803 by Thomas Johnson. Baptized same day as brother,
Jeremiah Phelps. Source, Drouin* – Religion: Protestant Church.

Married: (m1) Marie-Josette Roi. Died 17 March 1849, age not given, buried by
George Slack, Anglican Church, St. Paul's of Abbotsford in presence of
Oliver C. Phelps, husband, and John Standish, friend: "Mary Josette Roi
wife of Oliver Cromwell Phelps of Rougemont farmer."

Children of Oliver Cromwell and Mary Josette (Roi) Phelps:

1) Amos Phelps – b. 1 June 1827; baptized 23 Sept. 1831. Baptism
Record: Amos Phelps; Event: Baptism; Baptism Location
Abbotsford, Quebec; Religion – Protestant. Signed by grandmother,
Diadama Phelps. Sponsors were: Jeremiah and Margaret Phelps
and Diadama Phelps. (*Source: Drouin*) M. Adelaide Metieniner, St.
Anne Catholic Church; 1861 Stuckley, Shefford, Quebec Census:
Amos Phelps age 33 (born 1828) d. 10 Jan 1893 Quebec.
2,) Diadama Phelps – b. 13 February 1829; baptized 23 September 1831.
3) Mary Phelps – b. 1 April 1831; baptized 23 September 1831. Amos,
Diadama and Mary Phelps baptized on 23 September 1831,
children of Crumwell Phelps of Rougemont farmer and Josset Roi.

Sponsors: Jeremiah Phelps, John Garden, Margaret Phelps, Diadama Phelps. By Thomas Johnson, St. Pauls' Anglican Church of Abbotsford. *Source: Drouin*

4) Hannah Phelps - b. 6 May 1836; baptized at funeral of grandmother Diadama Long Phelps on 9 March 1837. *Source: Drouin*

5.) Roxana Phelps – b. 16 April 1838; baptized on 26 August 1838; daughter of Crumwell Phelps of Rougemont (Luman Phelps written first then crossed out) and Mary King his wife. Sponsors: Silas and Harriet (Pinkham) Bachelder and Nancy Warren (Huldah Pinkham married Seth Warren 1831*). Source: Drouin*

6.) Stephen Phelps – b. 1839; baptized 22 December 1839.

7.) Starling Phelps – b. 14 October 1839; baptized 22 December 1839 Stephen and Starling Phelps baptized on 22 December 1839, sons of Cromwell and Joset Roi Phelps, Sponsors: Oliver & Nancy Warren, Daniel Bachelder. By Thomas Johnson. *Source: Drouin*

8.) Selinda Phelps – b. 13 April 1843; baptized 3 September 1843, Sponsors: Oliver Phelps, John Standish, Harriet Bachelder. Died 11 September 1847 – *"daughter of Oliver Cromwell Phelps of Rougemont."* (*Source Drouin*) Religion: Protestant Church.

1849 Married: (m2) Catherine DeBois on 29 June 1849 - *"Oliver Cromwell Phelps of the parish of St. Cesaire farmer widower to Catherine DuBois of the parish of St. Jean Baptiste widow by Frederick Robinson."* Witnesses: Joseph Drake, Antoine (his mark) Dubois, Oliver C. Phelps and Catherine (her mark) Dubois. St. Paul's Anglican Church of Abbotsford. *Source - Drouin*

1851 Rougemont, Quebec Census: Oliver Phelps, age 48 (b. 1803) & wife age 50, Children: Roxanne age 15, Sterling age 12 & Stephen age 12. Farm: "Petite Caroline." Religion: Protestant.

1858: Sold "Petite Caroline" farm

1881 Quebec Census: Oliver Phelps, age 77, birth year 1804, occupation: Rentier, ethnicity: English, Religion – Episcopalian, Stuckley, North Shefford, Quebec along with wife, Marie Phelps age 66. *Source: Census 1881*

Marriage (m3) - Modesto Gaudreau

At least 6 individuals named **Amos Phelps** lived in Quebec 1800 from same Amos Phelps Senior line:

1) **Amos Phelps,** born 1750 CT. Children: (m1) Phebe -Martha, Charlotte, Oliver Cromwell(I) and Eldad/(m2) Diadama Long - Amos Junior, Luman, Jeremiah, Oliver Cromwell (II) and Selinda Phelps. Died 1831 Quebec.

147

2) **Amos Phelps Junior/ "the younger,"** son of Amos and Diadama (Long) Phelps. Born in 1786 Rutland, Vermont. Enlisted in War of 1812. Died 19 October 1813.

3) **Amos Phelps,** son of Eldad and Abigail (Tree) Phelps. Listed in 1831 census as a male between the age of 18 and 20/ born after 1805 (marriage year of Eldad and Abigail Tree). Listed in 1830/1840/1865 United States Census Crawford, Illinois, USA. In 1830 census: Amos Phelps: 1 male between age 30 and 40 which fits 1825 Quebec, Census age. He may have moved to Ontario for work: 1851 Canada West Census: Amos Phelps, age 26 (born 1825), born Canada, Laborer with wife Elizabeth age 18 and son age 2. 1861 Ontario Canada West Census: Amos Phelps age 32 (b. 1829) Laborer but family of 1. Possibly, this Amos Phelps moved from Quebec to Illinois to Ontario then returned to Illinois.

4) **Amos Phelps III**, son of Amos Phelps Jr./"the younger" (since he stated his father was "born in Vermont"), He is the son of Amos Phelps Junior because Eldad Phelps, half-brother m1, was born in Connecticut and later in Iowa census lists parents as born in Vermont. Amos Phelps III was born in 1809/1810 Lower Canada, married Julia Johnson in 1829 with witness, Caleb Tree (relative of brother Luman Phelps' wife); died in Iowa, USA and is buried with John Phelps' (born South Hero, VT), son, Benajah Phelps. Amos Phelps and his wife, Julia V. Johnson Phelps signed his sister, Elizabeth Phelps (b. 1812) 1832 marriage license to Comfort Carpenter Pinkham. Grandson, Norris Brown, son of his daughter, Elizabeth Ann (named for sister) Phelps born 1843 Stanbridge, QC, became Nebraska Republican Senator in 1907.

5) **Amos Phelps**, son of Jeremiah and Margaret Phelps. Born 15 June 1823, Quebec. Moved to Wisconsin USA in 1846 where he resided until 1850. Phelps Family Newsletter of February 1985: **Amos B. Phelps**, from "Phelps Family Papers 1851-1864 item 33, University of Michigan, William L. Clements Library, Ann Arbor, MI. 20 letters from Amos B. Phelps dated 1851-1854 describe his experience as prospector during the Gold Rush in Placerville (El Dorado County). Amos B. Phelps (1824 -) (P3682), WRONG FATHER LISTED – SHOULD BE JEREMIAH PHELPS *#1569 Alexander, #521 Amos, #165 John, #47 Joseph, #24 Timothy, #14 William.* Died 1903 Santa Rosa, CA, USA.

6) **Amos Phelps**, son of Oliver Cromwell and Joisette (Roi) Phelps. Born 1 June 1827, Quebec, Canada. Remained in Quebec, Canada tthroughout his lifetime He was listed in the 1861 Canada East Census as a farmer age 33 who resided in Stuckley, Shefford County, Quebec, not married, no children.

~ (2)   **Amos Phelps Junior/"the younger"**(born 1786, Rutland, Vermont) - **Son of Amos Senior and Diadama (Long)Phelps**. Died October 1813 during War of 1812. Children: Amos Phelps III (b. 1809/10) and Elizabeth (Phelps) Pinkham (b. 1812) were the children of Amos Phelps Junior and Unknown (b. Vermont).

~ (3) **Amos Phelps** (born Quebec between years 1805 and 1807) - **Son of Eldad (m1) and Abigail (Tree) Phelps**. Moved to Illinois in 1830 as recorded age fits both the 1825 Stanbridge Census for Eldad Phelps, onomastics for this line (first son named Amos) and the Illinois censuses.

> 1830 United States Census: **Amos Phelps**; Name: Amos Phelps; Event Date – 1830; Event Place – Crawford, Illinois, United States. *Source: US Census 1830*
>
> 1840 United States Census: **Amos Phelps**; Name: Amos Phelps; Event Date – 1840; Event Place – Crawford, Illinois, United States; Page – 285. Amos Phelps household: 3 Males under age of 5 years; 1 male between age 5 and 10 years; 1 male between the ages of 30-40 (Amos Phelps; 1 female under the age of 5; 1 female between the age of 5 and 10 years, and 1 female between the age of 15-20 (wife of Amos Phelps). *Source: Illinois Census 1840, NARA*

> *(* Note: There is a John Lee family also listed on this census. The Ede Lee family moved from Connecticut to Stanstead, Quebec (and a Samuel & Dorothy Ordway Pinkham daughter married into the family). The household consisted of: 3 Males under the age of 5; 1 male between the age of 5 and 10; 1 male between the age of 30 and 40 (John Lee); 1 female under the age of 5 years; 1 female between the age of 5 and 10 years; and one female between the age of 15 and 20 years. That Amos Phelps and John Lee were Quebec-born friends is speculation.)*

> > *1851 Canada West Census Oxford, Ontario: Amos Phelps, age 26 (born 1825), born Canada, Laborer. With wife, Elizabeth Phelps (age 18) and son age 2.*
> >
> > *1861 Canada West Census Frontenac, Ontario: Amos Phelps age 33 (born 1829)*

This is the son of Amos Phelps who was the son of Eldad and Abigail (Tree) Phelps.

> 1865 Illinois State Census: **Amos Phelps** - Name – Amos Phelps; Event Type – Census; Event year – 1865; Event Place – Jasper, Wayne, Illinois; Number of White Males – 2; Number of White females. *Source: Illinois State Census, State Library, Springfield, Illinois*
>
> United States Civil War & Later Pension **Amos G. Phelps**: Name: Amos G. Phelps; Event Date – 2 April 1864; Event Place – Illinois, United States; Military Regiment – 38; Military Unit – Infantry; Shipping Company – D. *Source: United States Civil War and Later Pension Index, 1861-1911*

~ (4) **Amos Phelps III (**born abt. 1809/1810, Quebec) (*brother to Elizabeth Phelps Pinkham born 1812*) - **Son of Amos Phelps Junior/"the younger" and unknown.**

> **Amos Phelps**; Living in 1831 in Stanbridge, Quebec Township, *Source: Extracts from the 1831 Census of Stanbridge Township, Missisquoi County. Genealogical Research Library, Ontario, Canada; Canadian Genealogy Index, 1600s-1900s*

Amos Phelps III rented "Clergy Reserve" land in this census listing where Amos B. Phelps (III) resided with his wife, Julia V. (Victoria) (nee Johnson) Phelps, a devout Baptist. Her father, Samuel Johnson, and his family are listed at the same census page. Clergy Reserve land was set up for the "support and maintenance of the Protestant clergy." "The provincial governments were authorized to erect and financially support residences according to the establishment of the Church of England (Anglican Church). One-seventh of the public lands of Upper and Lower Canada were reserved by the 1791 Constitutional Act for the maintenance of "Protestant clergy, or the Church of England. Free land grands ended in 1820s. Bishop John Strachan decided the Church of England should sell rather than lease its lands, as it had since 1819. The Bishop sold one-quarter of the reserves in 1827.

Amos Phelps III born 1809 farmed "Clergy Reserve" land which, as the Abner B. Phelps record notes, could be given to "heirs or successors." The land owned produced: Wheat – 50; Peas – 20; Oats – 5; Barley – 20; Indian Corn – 25; Potatoes – 50; Buckwheat – 100. Whether this clergy reserve land was handed down by Amos Phelps Junior is unproven as there is only one clergy reserve document listing a Phelps surname – Abner B. Phelps, 8 June 1809. Uncle (m2) Luman Phelps also owned "clergy reserve" land whereas Luman and Amos Jr. Phelps' half-brother, (m1) Eldad Phelps, did not. If Amos Phelps Junior/"the younger" was Amos Phelps III father, then was the land inherited may have been because of (m2) Diadama (Long) Phelps.

Clergy Reserve lands were one-seventh of the public lands in Upper and Lower Canada reserved by the 1791 Constitutional Act for the maintenance of a "Protestant" clergy or the Church of England. The settlers could initially obtain other lands for free. Free lands ceased in 1819 and were sold only after 1827 which is two years after the census. Clergy Reserve land could be inherited. There are no Sweetsburg (Missisquoi district/sub-district Stanbridge) Clergy Reserve records and the Bibliotheque Nationales de Quebec only lists an Abner B. Phelps record from 1809.

> 1842 Lower Canada Census: **Amos Phelps.** Name – Amos Phelps; Occupation – Farmer; Number of Inhabitants: 6; Sub-District – Dunham; County – Missisquoi. *Source: Library and Archives Canada*

> 1851 Canada Census: **Amos Phelps.** Name: Amos Philps; Province – Canada East (Quebec); District – Missisquoi Country; District number – 16; Sub-district – Dunham; Sub-district Number – 223. This record also lists his son, Orville Phelps, who is later recorded in the Iowa census with his parents Amos and Julia V. Phelps proving the misspelling of "Philps" was actually – Phelps. *Source: Library and Archives Canada, Public Archives, Ontario*

> 1860-1890 United States Census: Maquoketa, Iowa: Amos Phelps born Quebec – father born Vermont/mother born Vermont.

> Died Maquoketa, Iowa, USA.

~ (5) **Amos Phelps (born 15 June 1825, QC) – Son of Jeremiah and Margaret (Collins) Phelps.**

150

<u>Marriage 25 February 1853</u>: **Amos Phelps son of Jeremiah and Margaret Phelps** to Maria Coffe Lyon, parents Isaac and Eunice Lyon.

<u>1855 Wisconsin State Census</u>: **Amos Phelps**, Event Place – Burlington Town, Racine, Wisconsin, Number of White Males – 3, Number of White Females – 3. *Source: State Historical Society, Madison.*

Sons of Samuel G. and Theodocia Pinkham, Caleb Pinkham and Samuel Pinkham moved to Wisconsin by 1855. Jeremiah Phelps moved to Mower, Minnesota with Samuel G. and Theodocia Pinkham's son, Joseph Abijah Pinkham. Samuel Pinkham III died in Austin, Mower, Minnesota.

<u>Department of Naturalization (Card text)</u>: **Amos Phelps**; Address: Racine, Racine county, Wisconsin; Certificate & Page: 869 – Volume 2; Place of court – Circuit Court Racine, Racine County, Wisconsin; **Country of birth – East Canada**; Age – 34 years (b. 1823). Date of entry – June 1846, Whitehall, NY; Date of naturalization: 21 April 1857. Witnesses: Charles II Jones & David Brainard, Racine, Racine County, Wisconsin.

<u>US Naturalized citizen</u>: Amos Phelps, born abt. 1823, age at event: 34, Court district: Illinois, Indiana, Wisconsin, Iowa; Year at arrival: 1846, Date of Action: 21 April 1857. *Source: National Archives and Records Administration NARA, DC, 1840-1950*

<u>1857 Illinois, Northern District Naturalization</u> – Amos Phelps. Birthplace: Canada, - Phelps, Amos; Certificate 869 Vol. 1, Court Racine, Wisconsin – Country of birth – East Canada. When born for age – 34 years. Arrival in United States – June 1846, Whitehall, NY. Document dated: 21 April 1857.

<u>1860 Racine, Wisconsin census</u>: Amos Phelps age 37 born 1823 East Canada with wife Maria born New York and children Maria age 5 born Wisconsin and Jennie age two born Wisconsin.

<u>1870 Wisconsin United States Census</u>: Amos Phelps; age 47, born Canada 1822-1823. With wife, Maria, born in New York age 41, Minnie age 15 born Wisconsin, Jennie age 12 born Wisconsin and Frankie age 9 born Wisconsin. *Source: United States 1870 Census*

<u>Died</u>: 24 February 1903, Santa Rosa, California, USA.

~ (6) **Amos Phelps** (born Quebec 1 June 1827) – **Son of Oliver-Cromwell and Josette (Roi) Phelps.** Married Quebec. Died Quebec, Canada.

> <u>1861 Canada East Census (Quebec) Stukely, Shefford County</u>: Amos Phelps, Farmer age 33 (b. 1828).

While the Pinkham & Phelps families were well acquainted the only members united in marriage from the Amos Phelps Sr. (b. 1750, CT) and Samuel Pinkham Sr. (b. 1760

Durham, NH) lines where the grandson of Samuel Pinkham Senior, Comfort Carpenter Pinkham to the granddaughter of Amos Phelps Senior, Elizabeth Phelps, in 1832, Freilighsburg, Quebec.

Samuel Pinkham (b. 5 August 1787 Louden, NH) Junior, the father of Comfort Carpenter Pinkham, was buried at the Anglican Church on 1 March 1857 at Roxton and Milton, Quebec. Samuel Pinkham's wife, Theodosia (Carpenter) Pinkham has a recorded death 9 March 1858 in Stanstead, Quebec. Amos Phelps, grandfather of Amos III and Elizabeth Phelps was buried during 1831 in Rougemont, St. Hyacinthe, Quebec. Diadama (Long) Phelps, grandmother or mother of Amos III and Elizabeth Phelps was buried in 1837 in Rougemont, Quebec.

The 1831 St. Cesaire, St. Hyacinthe Census noted Jeremie, Thomas (Amos Senior because Amos Junior died during War of 1812) & Oliver Phelps lived next to Samuel G. Pinkham Junior. All were farmers except Amos Phelps Senior, a "rentier."

In the 1832 Marriage record – Comfort Carpenter Pinkham is "of the Parish of Saint Cesaires" which fits Samuel Pinkham's 1831 residence next to Amos, Jeremiah and Oliver C. Phelps in St. Cesaire, Quebec.

"On this thirtieth day of March one thousand eight hundred and thirty-two Comfort Pinkham of the Parish of Saint Cesaire and Elizabeth Phelps Spinster of Stanbridge, both of major age, were married after publication of the Banns in presence of the subscribing witnesses by James Reid, Minister. Witnesses Amos Phelps, Julia V. Phelps. (Note: Amos Phelps married Julia V. Johnson on 30 December 1830 "with consent of parents…" In Comfort & Elizabeth (Phelps) Pinkham's marriage record, parents were not mentioned as Elizabeth's mother, "Widow A./H. Phelps," likely died)

On the Abbotsford, the St. Hyacinthe 1831 marriage record between Huldah Pinkham (daughter of Samuel & Theodosia Carpenter Pinkham/sister of Comfort Carpenter Pinkham) and Seth Warren, the couple were married in the presence of "her father" (Sam G. Pinkham) and "his brother (Oliver Warren)" which also lists the signature of "Betsy Phelps" (Elizabeth/Betsy Phelps, the future wife of Comfort Carpenter Pinkham). The record on the next page is the baptism of "Oliver Warren Carpenter, son of Oliver Warren in the "presence of …" "Sam G. Pinkham" and "Jeremiah Phelps."

Listed on the baptismal record of Oliver Cromwell's son, Starling Phelps (14 October 1839), are witnesses "Oliver & Nancy Warren." Oliver Warren was the brother to Seth Warren, the husband of Comfort Carpenter's sister Huldah Pinkham Warren. Oliver Warren signed Seth Warren & Huldah Pinkham's marriage certificate along with Betsy Phelps, Huldah's brother Comfort Carpenter's wife, and Sam G. Pinkham, Huldah Pinkham's father. Jeremiah Phelps and Sam G. Pinkham signed the baptismal record for Oliver Warren's son, Oliver Warren Carpenter, in 1831. That the Samuel Pinkham Jr. family - Samuel & Theodocia Pinkham and children, Caleb Pinkham, Comfort Carpenter Pinkham, Huldah Pinkham Warren, James O. Pinkham, J. Samuel Pinkham, Joseph Abijah Pinkham and Samuel Pinkham III - were connected to the Amos Phelps family – Amos Senior & Diadama (Long) Phelps, Amos Phelps Jr., Luman, Jeremiah, Selinda and Oliver C. Phelps, as well as the Warren family - is well documented as the families move to various states in America post 1830 together.

Recorded on the marriage record for Amy Phelps, daughter of Luman and Hannah (Briggs) Phelps to Welcome Chandler (born Vermont) is Oliver Warren, the brother to the husband of Huldah Pinkham Warren, Seth Warren. Welcome and Amy (Phelps) Chandler moved to Burlington, Wisconsin in 1854 then Austin, Mower County, Minnesota in 1857. The 10 October 1857 Mower Census listed the Welcome Chandler family next to Abijah Joseph Pinkham family. Joseph Abijah Pinkham was the son of Samuel Junior and Theodocia (Carpenter) Pinkham.

Amos Phelps (b. 1809/1810), son of Amos Phelps Junior, consistently lists his father's birthplace as, "Vermont" making his father Amos Phelps Junior (b. 1786 Rutland, VT, m2) rather than Eldad Phelps (b.1783 Connecticut, m1). The Vermont notation is key to connecting the Amos III/Elizabeth Phelps parentage to Amos Phelps Junior/ "the younger," son of Amos and Diadama (Long) Phelps who died in the War of 1812.

Betsy Sweet signed the 1829 marriage license of Amos Phelps (III) and Julia V. Johnson. Elizabeth Brown Sweet was a widow who married widower David Sweet (listed in Rutland, VT 1800 census then Stanstead, Quebec 1825). Betsy Sweet had one son, Enoch Martin Sweet in 1807. Unconfirmed is whether she was the sister of the wife of Amos Phelps Junior since she signed Amos Phelps III 1829 marriage certificate. In the 1825 Stanbridge Census it states: Widow H. Phelps or Widow A. Phelps, speculated to be Betsy Brown Sweet's sister. From the Missisquoi County Birth/Death Church records (Reel 124.8) there were two Amos Sweet-named indiividuals who died - (b. 18 July 1872; d. 2 January 1862) (b. January 1863; d. 14 July 1872) linking the "Amos" name to both the Phelps and Sweet families. During 1867, the son of Abijah and Hannah (Sleeper) Pinkham, George L. Pinkham (7) married Ella P. Sweet in Stanstead, Quebec.

Regarding the Tree Family, a connection existed between the Amos Phelps and Caleb Tree familes as they moved from Vermont to Stanstead, Quebec during the 1800s. Caleb Tree was a witness to Amos Phelps III 1829 marriage to Julia V. Johnson. Also, Amos Phelps' son, Eldad Phelps, married Abigail Tree, and the Tree siblings resided near the Phelps. Likely, the Phelps-Tree families had ties given two marriages: Eldad (m1) to Abigail Tree; Simon Tree to Pheba Phelps (m1). If brother Amos Junior/ "the younger" (m2) married a Tree surname, it is likely this Phelps-Tree line took care of brother/sister Amos III/Elizabeth Phelps after their parents died.

Amos Phelps - Tree family line Franklin, Vermont Marriages (2):
> Elidad Phillips (**Eldad Phelps**) to Abigail Tree on 29 January 1805 in Franklin, VT, USA.
> Polly Tree married Zebulon Aulger on 4 May 1809 in Franklin, VT, USA.
> Simon Tree married **Pheba Phelps** on 8 February 1810 in Franklin, VT, USA.
> Seymour Tree married Mary Adburt on 5 January 1830 in Franklin, VT, USA.

<u>31 March 1802</u> Amos Phelps purchased Lot 11, Range 2, Bedford, Quebec from Caleb Tree.

~Caleb Tree is buried on 10 June 1824 in Stanbridge, East, Monteregie Region, Quebec age 62 – born 1762. *Age close to Samuel Pinkham Junior (b. 1787 Louden, NH)/Amos Phelps Senior (b. 1750 b. CT not their children).*

<u>Marriage:</u> Amos Phelps to Julia V. Johnson 13 December 1829 – *"On this thirteenth day of December one thousand and thirty Amos Phelps, Bachelor and Farmer of major age and Julia V. P. Johnson, Spinster of minor age, both of Stanbridge, were married after publication of Banns with consent of parents in presence of the subscribing witnesses by James Reid, Minister.* Signed: Amos Phelps, Julia V. P. Johnson, Caleb N. Tree, Betsy Sweet. *Source: Anglican Church, Phillipsburg, Drouin*

<u>1831 Stanbridge, Quebec Census:</u>

Eldad Phelps – Farmer, family of 5 residing near Joseph A. Phelps, family of 10 and Seymour Tree, family of 5. In 1842 Durham, Quebec Census, Seymour Tree is listed on same page with family of 2. Abigail Tree was Eldad Phelps wife.

Caleb Tree was recorded as a farmer in the 1842 Stanbridge, Missisquoi Census with a family of 6. It is unclear whether father or son, "Caleb R. Tree," (Senior/Junior) signed the marriage certificate of Amos Phelps to Julia V.(Johnson) Phelps.

Other Tree Surname mentions in the Eastern Townships of Quebec include:

~<u>Caleb R. Tree</u> married Hannah/Maria Ayer. She is listed in the 1861 Stanbridge, Missisquoi census as born in the US in 1786 and age 75, a widow and Wesleyan Methodist (like Stanstead Pinkham/Carpenter families). Death: 23 August 1873, wife of Caleb. R. Tree who was born 1805; died 1879. Buried: Chandler Cemetery, Stanbridge East, Quebec.

~<u>Electa Tree</u>, Burial: 23 March 1872, Stanbridge, East, Monteregie Region, Stanton, Cemetery, Quebec.

~<u>Daniel Caleb Tree</u> married Dorothy Chandler (the same family Jeremiah Phelps married) on 15 October 1891 in Stanbridge, Quebec. Father: Caleb R. Tree/Mother: Hannah Ayer.

Regarding Elizabeth (Betsy) Brown Sweet who signed the marriage document alongside Caleb Tree, she was born in 1780 Vermont. A widow, she married David Sweet in Quebec and died in 1849 at St. Armand, Quebec (Methodist church). "Betsy Sweet" signed the 1829 marriage license of Amos Phelps III and Julia V. Johnson.

Proof of Elizabeth Phelps to brother, Amos Phelps III, to the Amos Phelps line:

1) Brother, **Amos Phelps,** III, born 1809/1810, Quebec, and his wife signed Elizabeth Phelps/Comfort Pinkham 1832 marriage document.
2) **Amos Phelps** married Julia V. Johnson in 1830 at the Phillipsburg, Quebec Anglican Church. Witnesses were Betsy Sweet (Elizabeth Brown Sweet) and Caleb Tree – Eldad Phelps (1/2 brother to Amos "the younger Phelps)

married Abigail Tree/Phebe Phelps married Simon Tree. Tree family bought/sold Quebec land to Amos Phelps family which proves Amos Phelps III was from this family line. *Source: Drouin*

3) 1831 Stanbridge, Missisquoi, Lower Canada Census: **Amos Phelps**, family of 2 (wife Julia V. Johnson) with land listed as "clergy above." From 23 August 1820 Luman Phelps (brother to Amos Phelps) land sale to William Briggs (Luman Phelps married Hannah Briggs) – Lot 1, Range 2 (a clergy reserve.). That the Amos Phelps family owned land listed as, "Clergy" connects this Amos Phelps to the Amos Phelps, Quebec line.

4) 1842 Lower Canada, Dunham, Missisquoi Census: **Amos Phelps**, family of 6. Resided next to father-in-law, John Johnson (wife, Julia V. Johnson).

5) Birth: **Elizabeth Ann Phelps** – 4 August 1843, Stanbridge, Quebec. Amos & Julia V. Phelps named daughter, Elizabeth, after sister, Elizabeth Phelps Pinkham. *Source: Maqueketa, Iowa Historical Society*

6) 1851 Canada East (Quebec) Census: **Amos Philps.** Province: Canada East (Quebec); District: Missisquoi County; Subdistrict: Dunham. Son, Orvile Philps, age 2 born 1849 in Bas Canada listed. *Source: Library & Archives Canada.*

7) 1855 Militia of Stanbridge, Missisquoi, Quebec: Captain John Corey's Company, 24 November 1855: **Amos Phelps, age 44 (b. 1810)** Residence: Lot 13, first Range.

8) 1860 United States Census, Iowa: **Amos Phelps.** Event place: Maquoketa, City, Maquoketa Township, Jackson, Iowa, USA. Male, age 52 born 1808 (est) in Canada West. Wife: Julia Phelps age 50 born Vermont; daughter, Sarah Phelps age 20 (Born abt. 1840) Canada West; daughter Eliza Phelps age 16 (Born abt. 1844) Canada East, Orville Phelps age 10 (Born abt. 1850). *Source: United States Census, 1860*

9) 1870 United States Census: **Amos Phelps.** Event Place: Iowa, United States. Age: 63; Birth year: 1806-1807; Born: Canada. With wife, Julia Phelps age 60 (born 1810 – Amos Phelps' birth year), Vermont, and son, Oeiralle (Orville) Phelps, age 20 (b. 1850) born Canada. *Source: United States Census, 1870* **No parents of foreign birth** (Vermont).

10) 1880 United States Census: **Amos Phelps.** Event Place: Maquoketa, Jackson, Iowa, United States. Age: 70, birth year 1810, born Canada. **Father's birthplace: Vermont, United States. Mother's birthplace: Vermont, United States.** Wife, Julia Phelps, age 69, born United States. Amos Phelps was born in 1786 Rutland, VT proving fatherhood to siblings Elizabeth Phelps Pinkham and Amos Phelps III. *Source: United States Census, 1880*

11) Death of Julia V. Phelps: 19 March 1881, Maquoketa, Jackson, Iowa. Buried in Amos Phelps owned cemetery plot at Mount Hope Cemetery. Proves Quebec-Iowa Amos Phelps III residences. *Source: FindAGrave.*

12) 1885 Iowa State Census: **Amoz Phelps** (Amos Phelps). Event Place: Maquoketa, Jackson, Iowa. Age: 78. Birth year estimated: 1807. **Amoz Phelps/Widower/born Canada/Parents born Vermont.** With son, Orvell (Orville) Phelps age 32, and Orville's wife, Bell Phelps age 21 and daughter Elna Phelps, infant. *Source: Iowa State Census, 1885*

13) Death of Amos Phelps 14 March 1891: **Amos Phelps.** Event Date: 14 March 1891. Burial: Mount Hope Cemetery. "Husband of Julia V. Phelps, aged 82 years =Birth year 1809. *Source: FindAGrave*

14) Jackson Sentinal (Newspaper Obituary), Saturday 26 March 1881: *Died: Phelps – In this city, Saturday, March 19, 1881, Mrs. Julia V. F. J. Phelps, aged 71 years. Mrs. Phelps was born in Montpelier, VT, in 1810. In 1832* (**Elizabeth Phelps and Comfort Pinkham's marriage year**: *Amos & Julia V. Phelps married 1829) she was married to the husband she leaves behind, and has lived with him 49 years. In 185-, with her family, she came to Maquoketa, and has since made this her home. She was mother of eight children, four of whom, three daughters, and one son, still survive. Mrs. Phelps has been a constant member of the Baptist Church a great many years and was a consistent Christian. She was respected by all, and in her own family was almost idolized. The good old mother has gone were troubles, cares and pains can never more afflict."*

15) Jackson Sentinal (Newspaper), 19 March 1891. *Drops Dead.* **Amos Phelps**, *an old resident of this city, was found dead Saturday in the outhouse at the residence of his son-in-law Isaac McPeak, about 4 miles north of town. He was evidently stricken down with heart disease without a moment's warning and passed away at the age of 82 years. He was for many years a resident of the first ward, but had for the past few years been living with Mr. McPeak. He was a quiet going, kind hearted old gentleman with few, if any enemies. The funeral took place from the house on Monday.*

16) Maquoketa Excelsior (Newspaper), 21 March 1891: **Amos Phelps** (Obituary). *Amos Phelps. Died suddenly of heart disease last Saturday, March 14, at the residence of his son-in-law Isaac McPeak on Sand Prairie. Deceased was 82 years old. The funeral services were held at the house Monday afternoon and the remains were brought to this city for burial.*

17) Speculation: *Amos Phelps, son of Amos Phelps Junior/"the younger" – brother of Luman, Selinda, Jeremiah and Oliver Cromwell Phelps and step-brother to Phebe, Charlotte & Eldad Phelps, moved to Maquoketa, Iowa near "Aunt" Selinda Phelps McRae. The distance between Maquoketa, Iowa and Black Hawk County, Iowa is one-hundred-and-fifteen miles.*

Amos Phelps III was the son of Amos Phelps Junior/"the younger":

Birth: Born abt. 1809-1810 – Quebec, Canada. Marriage: 30 December 1830 – Phillipsburg, Quebec, Canada. Death: 14 March 1891, Maquoketa, Iowa, USA. Buried: Mount Hope Cemetery, Maquoketa, Iowa, USA.

Parents: Father: Amos B. Phelps Junior (b. Jan. 1786, Rutland, VT). Mother: Unknown. (Birthplace – Vermont). Sister (Amos Phelps signed Elizabeth Phelps' marriage record along with wife, Julia V. Phelps) - Elizabeth (Betsy) Phelps Pinkham (b. 1812, Lower Canada). Amos Phelps named child, Elizabeth Ann, most likely for sister, Elizabeth. The listed residence on the Quebec marriage records for both Amos (1830) and Elizabeth (1832) Phelps is: Stanbridge, Quebec.

Amos Phelps was listed as owner of Lot 101 at Mount Hope Cemetery in Maquoketa, Iowa, USA. Buried at the plot is Amos Phelps (d. 14 March 1891, age 82) and his wife, Julia V. (Johnson) Phelps (d. 19 March 1881, age 71 years), Saul Phelps, a Phelps "wife" (w/o), (Elizabeth White Phelps), and Benajah Phelps (b. 3 September 1832, St. Lawrence County, New York; d. 10 February 1916 Jackson County, IA) with his wife, Ellen C. Phelps. Listed in Lot 1761 is Samuel Phelps, born 1924, the son of Benajah & Ellen Phelps.

It is assumed (few 1800-1815 Eastern Township baptisms records exist) based upon onomastics (there were no Phelps sons named "Amos" born in Vermont/Lower Canada 1790-1815 outside the family direct line) Amos Phelps (born 1809 in Lower Canada/Canada East/Quebec) was the son of Amos Phelps Jr. (born Vermont 1786), the eldest son of Diadama (Long) Phelps and Amos Phelps (born 1750, Simsbury, CT). Amos Phelps (b. 1750 Simsbury, CT) moved to Rutland Vermont by 1786 then to St. Hyacinthe, Quebec (Lower Canada/Canada East) during 1793 along with his family, wife, Diadama, daughters Martha (who may have married in VT) & Charlotte, and sons, Eldad, *Oliver Cromwell (I)*, Amos Jr. and Luman Phelps. Amos Phelps had three children born in Rougemont, St. Hyacinthe, Quebec – Jeremiah (b. 1794), Selinda (b. 1799) and Oliver Cromwell (II) (b. 1803) Phelps. Amos Phelps (b. 1750 Simsbury, CT) was the son of John Phelps (b. 20 July 1724 Simsbury, CT; d. 11 February 1812 Norfolk, Lichfield, CT) and Thanks Wilcox (born 7 March 1720, Simsbury, CT).

Why Benajah Phelps and his wife are buried in Lot 101 remains a mystery unless his father, John Phelps (born 1802 in South Hero, VT) was related to the Connecticut originated Amos-Amos (born 1786 Vermont)-Amos (born 1750 Connecticut)-John-Amos-Joseph-Joseph Phelps line. John Phelps' brother, Guy Phelps, born 1804 in South Hero, Vermont, moved to Westhampton, Iowa. Benajah Phelps, born in 1832 New York, the son of John Phelps (born 1802, South Hero, Vermont) and Sally Lucia Sawyer Phelps (born in Vermont), was buried in the lot owned by Amos Phelps, born in 1810 Lower Canada, Quebec, Canada whose parents were born in Vermont. Sarah Phelps McPeak, daughter of Amos and Julia V. Phelps, named her sons Amos and Guy Phelps. That there is a connection between these Phelps lines is probable. If one maps the Amos Phelps (b. 1750, Simsbury, CT) to son Amos Phelps Jr (b. 1786, Rutland, VT) to son Amos Phelps III (b. 1809, Stanbridge, QC; owns Iowa cemetery plot where Benajoh Phelps is buried) and Benajah Phelps (born 1770, Goshen, CT) to John Phelps (born 1802, South Hero, VT) to Benejah Phelps (born 1832, New York) it can be determined Amos Phelps III and Benjah Phelps were the same generation from grandparent to father to son. The distance between Simsbury, Connecticut and Goshen, Connecticut was twenty-five miles while the distance between Rutland, Vermont and South Hero, Vermont was eighty-five miles. In any case, Stanbridge, Quebec-born Amos Phelps III is buried in his Maquoketa, Iowa plot with his wife and children, along with Benajah Phelps born 1832, New York. *See page 238 for chart.*

The Amos Phelps III family connection:

Amos (b. 1810, Lower Canada; m. Julia Johnson 1830, Quebec; d. 1891, Maquoketa, Iowa, USA) - Amos (b. 1786, Rutland, VT; m?; d. 19 October 1813, War of 1812) -

Amos (b. 1750, Simsbury, CT; m1 Phebe at Christ Church, CT; m2 1790, Rutland, VT to Diadama Long; d. 1831, St. Hyacinthe, Quebec, Canada) - John (b. 1724, Simsbury, CT; m. Thanks Wilcox; d. 1812, Norfolk, CT USA) - Amos (b. 1708, Simsbury, CT; m. Sarah Pettibone; d. 1777, Simsbury, CT) - Joseph (b. 1667, Windham, CT; m. Mary Case; d. CT) – Joseph (b. 1628, CT; m. Hannah Nash; d. 1684, Simsbury, CT) Phelps is related to this Connecticut originated line – Benajah (b. 1832, St. Lawrence, NY; m. Eliza Barry in Iowa; d. 1916, Maquoketa, Iowa) – John (b. 1802, South Hero, VT; m. Sally Sawyer in VT; d. Brasher, NY) - Benajah (b. March 1770; Goshen, CT; m. Betsey Graham Norfolk, CT; d. South Hero, VT) Phelps.

Amos Phelps III, Brother to Elizabeth (Betsy) Phelps Pinkham:

Born abt. 1809/1810, Quebec, Canada
Marriage: 30 December 1830, Phillipsburg, Quebec, Canada
1832 Witness: Amos and Julia V. Phelps to Comfort Carpenter and Eizabeth Phelps
    "Spinster of Stanbridge" marriage, Quebec. Named daughter Eliza Ann in 1843.
Death: 14 March 1891, Maquoketa, Iowa, USA
Buried: Mount Hope Cemetery, Maquoketa, Iowa, USA

Parents: 1870 & 1880 Maquoketa, Iowa censuses note: "Parents born Vermont"
    Father: Amos Phelps Junior (Born 1786, Rutland, VT; Died 19 October 1813)
    Mother: Unknown (Birthplace - Vermont)

Marriage: 30 December 1830 Amos Phelps to spouse – Julia V.P. Johnson (b.
    Vermont). Location – Phillipsburg, Quebec, Anglican Church.

"On this thirtieth day of December on thousand eight hundred and thirty, Amos Phelps, Bachelor and Farmer of major age and Julia V. P. Johnson, Spinster of minor age, both of Stanbridge, were married after publication of Banns with consent of parents in presence of the subscribing witnesses by James Reid, Minister. Signed: Amos Phelps, Julia V. P. Johnson. Witnesses: Caleb N. Tree and Betsy Sweet.

1830 – Anglican Church at Phillipsburg - Index of Baptisms, Marriages and Burials from 14 January 1830 to 1st January 1831. *Source: Drouin*

1831 Lower Canada (Quebec) Census: **Amos Phelps**, Missisquoi district, sub-district – Stanbridge. Household of 2; Listed as farmer of wheat (50) peas (20), oats (5), barley (20), Indian corn (25), potatoes (50), buck wheat (100). Also, noted in question, under what tenure is land held by family: "Clergy lease." Religion noted: Baptist.

1831 Canadian Genealogy Index, 1600s-1900s: **Amos Phelps**

Event Living; Year 1831; Place: Stanbridge Township; Province; Quebec. Source: Extracts from the 1831 Census of Stanbridge Township, Missisquoi County

1831 Lower Canada Census Phelps surnames in Stanbridge, Missisquoi: William P. Phelps, Eldad Phelps (Brother to Jeremiah, Oliver & Luman Phelps), Joseph A. Phelps, Phil Phelps, David N. Phelps, Joel Phelps, Burk Phelps, and Amos Phelps III with father-in-law Solomon Johnson (and family). Farnham, Shefford: Elkana Phelps. St. Cesaire, St. Hyacinthe: Jeremie Phelps, Amos Phelps (Senior) and Oliver Phelps (Next listing for Samuel Pinkham Junior and family, including Comfort Pinkham, eventual husband of sister, Elizabeth Phelps 1832). *Source: Canada Archives, Lower Canada Census 1931*

Children of Amos III and Julia V. (Johnson) Phelps born Quebec (8 recorded):

1) (Unknown) <u>Zacheus A. Phelps</u> (b. 1832/abt. 1831-1836, Stanbridge, QC)
2) (Unknown) <u>Maribah A. Phelps</u> (b. 1833/abt. 1833-1836, Stanbridge, QC)
3) Unknown Phelps born 1835-1836, Stanbridge, Quebec
4) <u>R. J. (Roxana/Rosana) Phelps</u> – Born 1837, Quebec. Married (m1) Frederick Atkins (b. 1828, Vermont)/(m2) Henry Davis - R. J. Phelps Atkins, born 1837 daughter of Amos Phelps and Julia Johnson, married Henry Davis in Perry, Jackson, Iowa on 25 February 1894. *Source: Iowa County Marriages, 1838-1935*
5) <u>Joseph A. Phelps</u> – Born abt. 1839-1840, Canada East (Lower Canada/Quebec), resident of Stanbridge with parents Amos & Julia V. Phelps. *Source: Canada 1831 Lower Canada 1851 Canada East Census*
6) <u>Sarah Phelps McPeak</u> – Born abt. 1840-1841, Canada East (Lower Canada/Quebec)/Teacher *Source: 1831 Canada East Census/1860 United States Census Maquoketa City, Iowa*
7) <u>Elizabeth Ann Phelps Brown</u> – Born 4 August 1843, Stanbridge, Canada East (Lower Canada/Quebec) *Source: 1860 United States Census Maquoketa City, Iowa*
8) <u>Orville Phelps</u> – Born abt. 1849-1850, Canada East *Source: 1831 Lower Canada Census/1860 United States Census Maquoketa City, Iowa*

1842 Canada East (Quebec) Census – **Amos Phelps**, Missisquoi district, Sub-district – Durham. Amos Phelps, family of 6. *Source: Canada Archives, Canada East 1842 Census*

(Family of 8: Amos & Julia., Zacheus A., Maribah A. unknown, Roxana, Joseph A. and Sarah Phelps) (Note: Philo Phelps' daughter was Maribah Phelps)

Birth: 4 August 1843 Eliza Ann Phelps in Stanbridge, Quebec

1851 Canada East (Quebec) Census – **Amos Philps** (Phelps), Missisquoi County, District number 16, Sub-District – Dunham, Sub-District number 223, Other Phelps family members listed in census with Philps name:

Joseph A. Philps, age 11, born 1840 Canada East, District Missisquoi County, District Number 16, Sub-District – Stanbridge, Sub-district number – 224. Son of Amos and Julia V. (Johnson) Phelps.

Orville Philps, age 2, birth year 1849, birthplace Canada, Province – Canada East (Quebec), District – Missisquoi County, District number – 16, Sub-district – Dunham, Sub-district number – 223. Son of Amos and Julia V. (Johnson) Phelps.

Likely children of Amos and Julia V. Phelps:

Maribah A. Philps, Age 18, Birth year – 1833, Birthplace – Canada, Province – Canada East, District – Missisquoi County, District Number – 16, Sub-District – Stanbridge, Sub-district number 224. Page number 153/ Line number 34. *(Philo Phelps named daughter, Maribah).*

Zacheus A. Philps, Age 19, Birthplace – Canada, Province – Canada East (Quebec), District – Missisquoi County, District Number – 16, Sub-district – Stanbridge, Sub- district number – 224, Page number 153/ Line number 37. *Source: Library and Archives, Canada.*

1855 Militia of Stanbridge, Missisquoi, Quebec. Captain John Corey's Company, 24 November 1855. Roll of officers: Amos Phelps (reserve), age 44 (b. 1810), Residence: Lot No. 14, first Range. *Canadian National Defense 1855 Militia Act*

1860 United States Census: **Amos Phelps**. Name: Amos Phelps. Event date: 1860. Event Place: Maquoketa City, Maquoketa Township, Jackson, Iowa. Gender: Male. Age: 52. Race: White. Birth year: 1808. Birthplace: Canada West. Page 172. Household: Amos Phelps, M, Age 52, Birthplace – Canada West (Laborer). Julia Phelps, Female, Age 50, Birthplace – Vermont. Sarah Phelps, Female, age 20 (abt. 1840), Birthplace – Canada West (Teacher). Eliza Phelps, Female, age 16 (abt. 1844), Birthplace – Canada East. Orville Phelps, Male, Age 10 (abt. 1850), Birthplace – blank. (Note: Canada West –Ontario- was not Canada East/Quebec where the Phelps resided). *Source: U.S. Census, 186*

Marriage: 3 June 1862 – Eliza Ann Phelps, daughter of Amos & Julia V. Phelps, married William. H. H. Brown. Event place: Jackson, Iowa, US. William H. H. Brown, age 21 born 1841 to Eliza A. Phelps, age 18, born 1844. *Source: Iowa, County Marriage, 1838-1934.*
Birth of Norris Brown – 2 May 1863, Maquoketa, Jackson, Iowa. Father's name: William Henry Brown. Mother's Name: Eliza Ann Phelps. *Source: Iowa, Delayed Birth Records, 1850-1939, State Historical Society of Iowa, Des Moines.*

1870 United States Census: **Amos Phelps**. Name: Amos Phelps. Event Place: Iowa, United States. Gender: Male. Age: 63. Race: White. Birth year: 1806 - 1807. Birthplace: Canada. Value of Real Estate: $2,000. Value of Personal Estate: $200. **Father of foreign birth – no. Mother of foreign birth – no**. Page Number: 6. Household: Amos Phelps, Male, Age 63 (born abt. 1807), Birthplace – Canada (day laborer). Julia Phelps, Female, Age 60, Birthplace – Vermont (Keeper of the House). Oeirallie (Orville) Phelps, Male, Age 20 (born abt. 1850), Birthplace – Canada (day laborer). *Source: NARA United States Census 1870*

This record states Amos Phelps' father was born in the United States as was Amos B. Phelps Junior born 1787, Rutland, Vermont, USA.

1878 Owen's Jackson County, Iowa Gazetteer and Directory: **Phelps Amos**, carpenter, res Eliza, Maquoketa. Phelps, S. O. (Orville), laborer, res Olive, Maquoketa.

Birth of Leon Brown – 24 November 1879, Floyd Township, Woodbury, Iowa. Father's Name: W. O. H. Brown. Mother's Name: Eliza A. Phelps. *Source: Iowa Delayed Birth Records, 1850 – 1939. State Historical Society of Iowa, Des Moines*

1880 United States Census: **Amos Phelps**. Name: Amos Phelps. Event Place: Maquoketa, Jackson, Iowa, United States. Gender: Male. Age: 70 (Born abt. 1810). Marital status: Married. Race: White. Occupation: Carpenter. Birth year: 1810. Birthplace – Canada. **Father's birthplace – Vermont, United States. Mother's birthplace – Vermont, United States.** Household: Amos Phelps, Head of Household, Male, Age 70, Birthplace – Canada. Julia V. Phelps, Wife, Female, Age 69, Birthplace – Vermont. *Source: United States Census 1880. Maquoketa, Jackson, Iowa, United States*

Death: 19 March 1881: Julia V. Phelps. Burial – Mount Hope Cemetery, Maquoketa, Jackson, Iowa. *Source: FindAGrave*

Jackson Sentinel, Saturday, 26 March 1881: Died: Mrs. Julia V. P. J. Phelps:

PHELPS - *In this city, Saturday, March 19.1881, Mrs. Julia V. P. J. Phelps, aged 71 years. Mrs. Phelps was born in Montpelier, VT, in 1810. In 1832 she was married to the husband she leaves behind and lived with him 49 years. In 185_ with her family she came to Maquoketa and since then has made her home. She was the mother of eight children, four of whom – three daughters and a son – still survive. Mrs. Phelps has been a member of the Baptist Church a great many years and was a consistent Christian. She was respected by all, and by her family was almost idolized. The good mother has gone where troubles, cares and pains can never more afflict.*

From census and Drouin records: Amos and Julia V. Johnson's marriage took place in 1830 not 1832, the date of Elizabeth Phelps to Comfort Carpenter Pinkham where both Amos and Julia V. Phelps signed marriage record. The four surviving children of Amos and Julia V. Johnson Phelps were: Roxana/Rosana Phelps Atkins Davis (b. 1838, Stanbridge, Quebec), Sarah Phelps McPeak (b. 1841, Stanbridge, Quebec), Eliza Ann Phelps Brown (b. 4 August 1843, Stanbridge, Quebec) and Orville Phelps (b. 1849/1850, Stanbridge, Quebec). The children born Stanbridge, Quebec who died were likely: Zacheus A. Phelps (b. 1832), Maribah A. Phelps (b. 1833), unknown Phelps (born abt. 1835-1816) and Joseph A. Phelps (born abt. 1839).

Marriage: 7 July 1883 Orville Phelps to Belle Conway. Event date: 7 July 1883. Event place – Maquoketa, Jackson, Iowa, United States. Gender – Male. Age – 28. Birth year – 1855. Father's name: **Amos Phelps.** Mother's name – Julia Johnson. Spouse's name – Belle Conway. Spouse's age – 19. Spouse's birth year – 1864. Spouse's father – James Conway. Spouse's mother – Martha Van Dorn. *Source: Iowa County Marriages, 1838-1934.*

1883: Norris Brown, son of William Henry Harrison Brown and Eliza Ann Phelps Brown graduated with law degree from University of Iowa College of Law, Iowa City, IA. In 1884 admitted to bar and began law practice in Perry, Iowa. *Source: Wikipedia*

Birth: 7 February 1884 – Edna Phelps. Event place: Maquoketa, Jackson, Iowa. Gender – Female. Race – White. Father's name – Orville Phelps. Father's birthplace – Canada. Father's age – 29 (abt. 1855). Mother's name: Clarinda Bell Conway Phelps. Mother's birthplace – Iowa. Mother's age – 19. Note: birth registered in Jackson, Co., Iowa; Day Laborer; 1st child. *Source: Iowa, County Births, 1880-1935, Maquoketa, Jackson, Iowa, United States*

1885 Iowa State Census: **Amoz (Amos) Phelps.** Event year: 1885. Event Place – Maquoketa, Jackson, Iowa. Gender – Male. Age – 78. Birth year – 1807. Household: Amoz (Amos) Phelps, Widower, Male, Age 78, **Born in Canada, Parents born in Vermont**. Orvell (Orville) Phelps, Married, Male, Age 32, Place of birth: Vermont. Bell Phelps, Married, Female, age 21, born in Iowa. Elna (Edna) Phelps, Female, Age: X months. *Source: Iowa State Census, 1885*

1885 Iowa State Census: Sarah (Phelps) Mcpeak. Event year: 1885. Event Place: Andrew, Perry, Jackson, Iowa. Gender – Female. Age – 45. Birth year: 1840. Household: Isaac Mcpeak – Male, age 47; Sarah Mcpeak – Female, age 45; Charles Mcpeak – Male, age 23; Amos Mcpeak Male, age 19; Guy Mcpeak – Male; age 16; William Mcpeak – Male, age 12; Ada Mcpeak – Female, age 9 and Fred Mcpeak – Male, age 7. *Source: Iowa State Census, 1885*

1888 – Norris Brown, son of Elizabeth Phelps/grandson to Amos Phelps III & Julia V. Johnson Phelps, moved to Kearney, Buffalo County, Nebraska.

Marriage of Elwyn F. Brown, age 23, to Ethelwyn Gilchrist, age 24, on 20 June 1889 in Vinton, Benton, Iowa. Father: Wm. H. Brown. Mother: Eliza A. Phelps. *Source: Iowa, Country Marriage, 1838-1934*

Obituary – **Amos Phelps III:**

Jackson Sentinel, March 19, 1891:
Drops Dead
***Amos Phelps**, an old resident of this city, was found dead Saturday in the outhouse at the residence of his son-in-law Isaac McPeak, about 4 miles north of town. He was evidently stricken down with heart disease without a moment's warning and passed away at the age of 82 years. He was for many years a resident of the first ward, but had for the past few years been living with Mr. McPeak. He was a quiet going, kind hearted old gentleman with few, if any enemies. The funeral took place from the house on Monday.*

Maquoketa Excelsior, March 21, 1891: **Amos Phelps**.

"Obituary: ***Amos Phelps*** *died suddenly of heart disease last Saturday, March 14, at the residence of his son-in-law Isaac McPeak on Sand Prairie. Deceased was 82 years old. The funeral services were held at the house Monday afternoon and the remains were brought to this city for burial."*

<u>Burial:</u> 14 March 1891 - **Amos Phelps.** Event Place: Maquoketa, Jackson, Iowa. Cemetery: Mount Hope Cemetery. *Source: FindAGrave*

<u>Mt. Hope Cemetery, Maquoketa, Iowa, USA </u>- Burial information on the Phelps' plot

Amos Phelps was owner of Lot 101. The individuals buried in this lot:

<u>Amos</u> Phelps   82 years old; b. 1809; d. 14 March 1891 husband to Julia V.

<u>Benajah</u> Phelps   1832/1833; d. 10 February 1916
                 (Age = 83 years)   h/o-husband of Ellen C.
<u>Elizabeth</u> Phelps   (wife of ?) nee White
<u>Ellen C.</u> Phelps   b. 1829; d. 1919   w/o-wife of Benajah
<u>Julia V.</u> Phelps   71 years; d. 19 March 1881   w/o-wife of Amos Phelps
<u>Samuel B.</u> Phelps   b. 1866; d. Sept. 1924   son of Benajah Phelps
<u>Saul</u> Phelps   (son of Benajah? Joseph? Orville Phelps)

<u>25 February 1894 Marriage of R. J. Phelps</u> Atkins born 1837, daughter of Amos Phelps and Julia Johnson, in Perry, Jackson, Iowa, USA. *Source: Iowa, County Marriage, 1838-1934*

<u>Death</u> 29 December 1928 of Charles Albert McPeak, son of Sarah Phelps (daughter of Amos and Julia Phelps), born in Canada and Isaac McPeak.

Hiram H. Phelps – Event Date 1861-1949, Department of Iowa Grand Army of the Republic, Iowa, United States. Private, enlisted 26 October 1864. Related to Amos Phelps III family?

1905-1907 Elected Government Official -<u>Norris Brown</u>, grandson of Amos & Julia V. Phelps, became <u>Nebraska Attorney General</u>.

4 March 1907 – 3 March 1913 - <u>Norris Brown</u> elected Republican <u>Senator from Nebraska</u>. Chairman on Patents for the 61st/62nd Congress.

<u>Marriage:</u> Leon Brown age 47 to Zilpha Popejoy, age 32, on 16 June 1917, Des Moines, Polk, Iowa. Father's name: W. H. H. Brown. Mother's name: Eliza A. Phelps. *Source. Iowa, County Marriage, 1838 – 1934*

<u>Burial: Eliza Anne Phelps Brown</u>. Birthdate: 4 August 1843; Death date:

14 August 1919. Event Place: Des Moines, Polk, Iowa. *Source: FindAGrave* WRONG BIRTH DATE LISTED. *Named for Aunt Elizabeth Phelps Pinkham.*

Burial: Eliza Ann Phelps Brown. Born: 4 August 1843, Stanbridge, Lower Canada. Died: 7 August 1919. Buried: 12 August 1919 Glendale Abbey, Des Moines, Iowa. Parents: Amos Phelps and Julia Johnson Phelps. Married: 3 June 1862. To: W. H. H. (William Henry Harrison) Brown. Children: Sen. Norris Brown of Omaha; Leon Brown; E. F. Brown of Vinton. Sister: Sarah McPeak. *Source: Maquoketa Historical Society*

Miscellaneous: 1830 Amos Phelps and Julia V. Johnson Marriage witnesses:

~Caleb Tree – 1842 Quebec Census: Farmer/Head of family (6), Stanbridge, Missisquoi, Lower Canada (Quebec). Son of Caleb Tree – Death 10 June 1824 Stanbridge East, Monteregie Region, Quebec (Stanton Cemetery). *Source: Public Archives, Ottawa, Ontario, Canada*

~Betsey Brown Sweet – Birth: February 1780 Vermont. Death: 24 October 1846, Sutton, Monteregie Region, Quebec, Canada (Fairmount Cemetery). *Source: FindAGrave*

The wife of Amos Phelps III was Julia Victoria Johnson born 1810 in Montpelier, Washington, Vermont, USA. She was the daughter of Solomon Johnson (d. 1858 Granby, La Haute- Yamaska Regional County, Quebec, Canada) and Mary Johnson.

Solomon Johnson:

1790 United States Census: Dummerston, Windham, Vermont, US: Solomon Johnson. *Source: NARA - United States Census, 1790, Dummerston, Windham, Vermont.*

1800 United States Census: Peacham, Caledonia, Vermont, United States.: Solomon Johnson. *Source: NARA - United States Census 1800, Peacham, Caledonia, Vermont, United States.*

1810 United States Census: Moretown, Chittenden, Vermont, United States: Salman (Solomon) Johnson. *Source: NARA – United States Census –1810, Moretown, Chittenden, Vermont, United States*

1825 Lower Canada Census: Solomon Johnson; Number of Inhabitants – 6; Sub-District – Dunham; County – Bedford. *Source: Library & Archives, Canada – Bedford, Quebec, Canada.*

1831 Lower Canada Census: listed Solomon Johnson; Number in Family – 3; Sub- district – Stanbridge; County; Missisquoi.

Listed next to **Amos Phelps**, son-in- law – family of 2. (*Source: Canada, Census in Lower Canada, 1831 – Library & Archives, Canada)* Solomon Johnson died in 1858 Quebec prior to Amos and Julia V. Johnson Phelps' move to Maquoketa, Iowa,

USA.

Death: Solomon Johnson; Death date - 23 September 1858; Event Place – Granby, Monteregie Region, Quebec, Canada; Cemetery – Cowie Street Anglican Cemetery. *Source: FindAGrave*

Benajah Phelps was buried in the burial plot of Amos Phelps III in Maquoketa, Iowa. Who was the Benjah Phelps in relation to the Amos Phelps, Sr. family? Of note, in the 1790 Vermont Census, a John Phelps, likely Amos Sr.'s brother, resided in Rutland, Vermont with one head of family male, a wife, three sons and a daughter. Amos Phelps, Sr. and family resided in Rutland, VT where Amos Phelps Jr. was born in 1787.

Obituary: Benajah Phelps – 10 October 1916: *Benajah Phelps came from St. Lawrence County, New York, and settled in Bloomfield township, Clinton County, in 1856 locating on a farm 3 miles north of the present town of Delmar Junction, and went through all the privations endured by the Iowa pioneer.*

During the winter months, he taught school and devoted his attention to the farm the balance of the year. Wheat was the principal product in those days, and had to be hauled to points on the Mississippi for market. In this manner, he finally paid for the land and provided a comfortable home for his family.

Mr. Phelps was a great lover of horses and raised and owned some of the best race horses in the state, among them being, "Tim Finnigan," the most popular horse of the day.

Ben Phelps was the lady of the old boys who were famous on the turf, among who were E. G. Butcher, Wm. Welch, Wm. Arnett, Robert Thomas and Sam Williams.

About fifteen years ago Mr. and Mrs. Phelps disposed of the farm and located at Maquoketa where they spent their declining years in a snug little cottage among the hard maple trees planted by J. E. Goodenow some 60 years ago.

He possessed a wonderful mind, and was a great reader, a lover of honest recreation, and one who was always ready to go a little more than half way to meet any man on the "level."

Mr. Phelps leaves a wife, Ellen C. Phelps, and three sons – **Samuel B. (Phelps)** *of Maquoketa, George* **B.** *of Clinton and J. H. of Lost Nation.*

The funeral (died: 10 February 1916) was held at the home on Matteson Avenue Sunday afternoon and 2 o'clock, Reverend I. A. Bartholomew officiating. Burial was in Mt. Hope. Source: Maquoketa Historical Society

Burial: 1924 – Samuel Phelps (son of Benajah and Ellen Phelps). Event Place: Maquoketa, Jackson, Iowa. Cemetery: Mount Hope Cemetery. *Source: FindAGrave.*

John Phelps, father of Benajah Phelps (b. September 3, 1832, St. Lawrence County, NY; d. 1916 Maquoketa, Jackson, Iowa) was born February 1802 in South Hero, Vermont. He married twice – M1 Sally Lucia Sawyer on 18 January 1827 in South Hero, VT and in M2 in Brasher, NY. The history of Brasher, New York includes his founding of Brasher Falls: "What is known as the Quaker settlement was begun in 1824 by Peter Corbin, John Phelps and David Blowers, who were from Vermont. A company of Quakers had made purchase here prior to the above __, with the purpose of founding a colony, but the project did not succeed." *(Source: History of Brasher, New York by Gates Curtis, the Boston History Company Publishers, 1894)* John Phelps and Sally Sawyer Phelps children born in Brasher, New York were: Kate (b. August 1829; m. A. A Hawkins), Benajah (born 3 September 1832; m. Eliza Berry) and John S. (b. 6 October 1841; m. Elizabeth P. Schell) and children with M2 Mary Phelps in Brasher, NY: Elizabeth (b. 21 June 1851) and Mary Francis (b. September 1853). John Phelps is listed in both the 1840 & 1850 United States Census for Brasher, St. Lawrence, New York. The 1850 United States Census for Brasher, NY, listed the household: John Phelps, age 48 born in Vermont; wife, Mary Phelps, born in New York; children born in New York – Catherine Phelps, age 21; Benajah Phelps, age 17; John S. Phelps, age 9; Clark Hoxie, age 27 and Ellen Berry, Female, age 21 born in New York.

As a John Phelps family is listed in the 1790 Rutland, Vermont census alongside the Amos Phelps, Sr. family, this Amos Phelps Sr. - John Phelps (b. 1744) connection likely equates to brothers and sons of John Phelps born 1724 Simsbury, CT. Benajah Phelps, born 1832 New York was the son of John Phelps born 1802 South Hero, Vermont, the son of Benajah Phelps born 1770 Goshen, Connecticut.

John Phelps was the son of Benajah Phelps (b. 1770, Goshen, Connecticut; m. Betsy Graham; d. South Hero, VT). His siblings, born in South Hero, VT include: Guy Phelps, born 1804, who married Lydia Dusenbury then settled in Westhampton, Iowa. Brother Orange Phelps, born March 1806 married Maria Phelps in April of 1811 and died in South Hero, Vermont on 13 February 1882. He was a member of the State Assembly, the State Senate and an Assistant Judge in Grand Island Junction. His children (*none named Amos*) were: Graham (b. 1835), Edgar, Oscar, Jane, Albert, Edward, Frederick, Augusta, Florence and Martha (b. 1854) Phelps. John Phelps' brother, Heman Phelps, was born July 1809 and married Phoebe Childs on 22 March 1837. He was a farmer in Beekmantown, NY then later Bombay, NY. His children except the first were born in Beekmantown, NY were (*none named Amos*) Lucy (b. 1838), Eunice, Delia, Mary, James, Henry, and Mary (b. 1863). John Phelps' youngest brother, Abel Phelps was born on 15 January 1811 and married Eunice Childs on 10 June 1863. He died in South Hero, VT. Abel Phelps' children were (no children named, Amos): Ann Eliza (b 1834), Benajah (b. 9 February 1836) and Wolford N. Phelps.

From Maquoketa Historical Society files – "Benajah Phelps" biography:

Died 10 February 1916 at home age 83 years 5 month and 7 days. Funeral was at home by Bartholomew. Buried: Mt. Hope Cemetery. Married. Retired farmer. Born NY State. Parents: John Phelps, VT & Sally Lucia Sawyer, born Vermont. Cause of Death: Pneumonia." *Source: Page 279, Curson Funeral Book, Vol. 2*

From the "1886 Portrait and Biographical Album of Clinton County Iowa" by Chapman Bros. Chicago, the story of Ben Phelps reads:

"Ben Phelps. *The subject of this person sketch was an early settler in Bloomfield township, and is known throughout this section of country as a prominent farmer and man of rare educational ability. He is deeply interested in all matters concerning the advancement and progress of the day and largely is that of schools. He also pays strict attention to his agricultural pursuits and is a breeder of high-grade stock.*

Mr. Phelps was born in St. Lawrence County, N. Y., Sept. 3, 1831. His father, John Phelps, was born on the Island of South Hero, Lake Champlain (Vermont). **The grandfather of our subject, Benajah Phelps, was a native of Connecticut** *and of English and Scottish origin.* **Benajah Phelps removed from Connecticut to South Hero** *at an early day and was one of the prominent early settlers of the Island. He cleared a farm and lived upon it until his death. He was a man well known at that time, was in the battle of Plattsburgh, and his son, father of our subject, grew to manhood on his native Island where he married Sally Lucia Sawyer. The afterward removed to Saint Lawrence County, N. Y., and were early settlers of that vicinity. He bought timberland and cleared a large farm, and died in Saint Lawrence in 1876. His wife died in 1848. She (Sally Sawyer) was born on the Island of South Hero and was the daughter of Peter Sawyer, a soldier in the War of 1812, and a glorious old warrior and man. He was a pioneer of South Hero, and was the father of three children: Kate, married Alpha Hawkins; our subject is the second child; and John S. lives in St. Lawrence County, NY.*

Ben Phelps was reared on his father's farm and was educated in the public schools. He early displayed an application and industry which gave him a high place in his classes, and he was then transferred to the high school in Malone. In 1855 he made his first visit to the West. He stopped in Will County, Ill., and taught one term of school at Reed's Grove in the winter of 1855-56. In the spring of 1856, he removed to Kankakee and engaged in farming for four months. He next went North to Minneapolis, then but a small village. In the Fall he returned to New York and spent the winter, and in the spring of 1857 came to Clinton County. He had, during the fall previous, bough 120 acres of land on section 2, Bloomfield Township. There was a small frame house standing on the place and a few acres broken, which constituted the only improvements at the time. Since then he has continuously lived here, and has taught school winters in Clinton and Jackson Counties, devoting his attention to farming during the summer time. He has also brought to the place many horses of Kentucky and Illinois stock and is noted for keeping some of the finest animals in the county. The following are some of the most noted of his large stock of horses: Gipsy Queen, Tim Finnigan, Nate Doxy and Agnes Donovan.

Our subject was married on March 11, 1857, to Ellen Barry, daughter of Samuel and Rebecca (Chambers) Berry. She is a native of Ireland, but born of Scotch parents. They have three children - John, who lives at Elwood, George, who is the Superintendent of Schools of Clinton county, and Samuel, at home.

Our subject is Democratic in political sentiment and belief, and upholds the party strongly, and is well read and informed in all matters relative to private and public good. Mrs. Phelps is a member of the Methodist Episcopal Church. John married Miss Kate Taubman, and they have one child named Helen Leon Phelps.

Source: 1886 Portrait and Biographical Album Clinton County, Iowa by Chapman Bros – Chicago, Pages 457-465.

Ben Phelps as recorded in census records:

1885 Iowa State Census, Bloomfield, Clinton, Iowa – Benj Phelps age 53 with Ella Phelps age 55, Samuel Phelps age 19 and Ellen Phelps age 2. *Source: Iowa Historical Society, Des Moines,*

1895 Iowa State Census, Clinton, Iowa: Ben Phelps, age 63, Ella Phelps age 65. Samuel Phelps age 28 and George Grawl age 24. *Source: Iowa Historical Society, Des Moines.*

1900 United States Census, Bloomfield Township, Delmar Town, Clinton, Iowa – Benjami Phelps age 68 born in New York with Ellen Phelps, wife born in Ireland and son Samuel Phelps age 34 born Iowa. *Source: NARA*

1900 Maquoketa, Jackson County, Iowa Census: Benjami Phelps, Head of household, age 68 born New York with wife, Ellen Phelps age 71 born Ireland, and son Samuel Phelps, born April 1866 Iowa. *Source: Iowa Historical Society, Des Moines,*

1915 Maquoketa, Jackson, Iowa Census: Samuel Phelps, age 46 born 1869 Iowa; father born New York, mother born Ireland. *Source: Iowa Historical Society, Des Moines,*

Obituary *(Source unknown)* – George Benajah Phelps, son of Benajah Phelps:

Phelps, George Benajah of Clinton, Iowa, b. there March 12, 1861, lawyer, was city attorney 2 terms and formerly county superintendent of schools 2 terms (m. June 20, 1881 Nellie O. Dixon, daughter of Charles) and had (children) Nellie M., Ruth and Esther Phelps; son of Benajah Phelps of Delmar Iowa, b. Brasher NY on 3 Sept.1873, school teacher and farmer (m. 11 March 1857 Ellen Berry born County Cork, Ireland, daughter of Samuel Berry and Rebecca Chambers); son of John Phelps of St. Lawrence County, NY, born in South Hero, VT, 2 February 1802, died St. Lawrence County 5 March 1876 (m. 18 January 1827 Sally Lucia Sawyer, daughter of Peter Sawyer). *Source: City Clerk of Unknown Iowa County*

~Jasper County Iowa Cemeteries: Lot 87: Annie C. Phelps, d. 19 March 1874; age 23 years, 11 months and 22 days, wife of S. S. Phelps. Lillian S. Phelps, d. 18 August 1874, age 10 months, daughter of S. S. Phelps.

~Jefferson County Iowa Newspaper Death Notices: May Phelps. Died Wednesday morning, 20 April 1870 age six years and 8 months, daughter of George & Melia Phelps.

~Jefferson County, Iowa Cemeteries: Milia A. Phelps, daughter of J. & A., b. 1861, d. 24 January 1861, Smith Cemetery; Benjamin B. Phelps – 1880; Harriet E. Phelps, daughter of BB & J, b. 1849, d. 23 January 1853, Smith Cemetery; May Phelps, daughter of Geo & M, b. 1864, d. 20 April 1864.

~Benjamin R. Phelps/Benjamin R. Phelps, Jr. – Military Service – Private 44th
  Regiment, Iowa Infantry. Military Side: Union. 100 days – 1864. *Source: United States Civil War Soldiers Index, 1861-1865, NARA*

~Benjamin B. Phelps – 1889 Iowa Pension. *Source: United States General Index to Pension Files, 1861-1934*

To review, the brother of Elizabeth Phelps born 1812 Stanbridge was Amos Phelps III born 1809 Stanbridge. Siblings Elizabeth and Amos III Phelps resided in Stanbridge as children of Amos Phelps Junior/"the younger" and unknown (Widow "A." /"H." Phelps).

An 1830 Amos Phelps and Julia V. Johnson marriage record witness was from Vermont or Stanbridge Caleb Tree family. Two Amos Phelps children married Tree surnames (Eldad Phelps to Abigail Tree/Simon Tree to Pheba Phelps). Amos Phelps III moved to Maquoketa, Iowa after 1855 where he is buried with the son of a John Phelps who may have resided alongside Amos Phelps Senior in Rutland, Vermont 1790.

As it is assumed Amos Phelps, Jr. was the father of Amos Phelps III. Amos Phelps Junior/"the younger" had a sister, Selinda Phelps McRae, who also moved to Iowa.

> Mrs. **Selinda Phelps** McRae – Birth 1799, Quebec. Died 1888 Waterloo, Black Hawk County, Iowa, USA. Maquoketa, Iowa is 113 miles from Black Hawk County, Iowa.

The cousins of the Amos III and Julia V. (Johnson) Phelps' family were the children of COMFORT and Elizabeth (Phelps) PINKHAM (Generation 8):

~Cynthia Pinkham Wright: Born abt. 1832, Quebec. Married 1849 to Alfred Wright. Died 21 September 1879, Ontario, Canada.

~Electa Pinkham Eddy: Born: 15 March 1834, Quebec. Married Hiram Eddy 1854/5; Died 12 May 1916, Ontario, Canada. (*Electra*)

~Mary Pinkham Coons: Born abt. 1835, Quebec. Married Coons; Moved to Minnesota near Uncle Caleb Pinkham. Died 1875, Ashland, Dodge County, Minnesota, USA.

~Edwin A. Pinkham: Born 1840-1841, Quebec. Prior to 1867 moved to Dodge, MN. Married 12 May 1867, MN to Catherine Campbell. Moved 1900 to North Dakota then Eugene, Oregon. Died post 1905, Eugene, Oregon, USA.

~Willard Pinkham: Born 1841-1842, Quebec/Ontario. Death unknown.

~JOHN WESLEY PINKHAM: Born 20 September 1845, Clarke Township, Durham County, Ontario. Married (m1) Emma Harris/(m2) Sarah Ann Irwin/(m3) Margaret Elsworth. Died 28 October 1924, Oshawa, Durham County, Ontario, Canada.

Jane Pinkham Harris: Born 1848, Clarke Township, Durham County, Ontario. Married William Harris. Died 12 February 1919, Clarke Township, Durham County, Ontario, Canada.

~Samuel Pinkham:	Born: 6 April 1852, Ontario. Married 26 March 1872 to Margaret McLean. Died 6 July 1915, Kindersley, Saskatchewan, Canada.
~Charles W. Pinkham:	Born 11 June 1855, Manvers, Ontario. Married Lavina Corey of Quebec on 27 July 1881 in Lowell, Massachusetts, USA. Naturalized US Citizen on 21 November 1893 in Lowell MA, USA. Death undetermined post 1916.

The children of COMFORT CARPENTER and Elizabeth (Phelps) PINKHAM (Gen 8):

~Cynthia A. Pinkham Wright:

Born: 1832, Quebec

Married: Alfred Wright (son of Luther Wright and Rebekah Brown, b. 1824; d. 13 October 1908) on 6 March 1849 in Wentworth, Ontario, Canada.

Died: 21 September 1879, Clarke Township, Ontario, Canada

The children of Cynthia Pinkham and Alfred Wright born Ontario were (Generation 9):

Charles Wright (born 1849)

Lillie Jane Wright (born 1850)

George Wright (born 1851)

John Alfred Wright (born 1854)

Mary Eliza Wright (born 1859)

Albert Wright (born 1865)

> ~Married: Martha Alphretta Ogden in 1888, daughter of Jacob Ogden and Elizabeth Craigo. The children of Albert and Martha Wright (10) were: Willard Wright, (b. 1886 Manvers, Ontario, d. August 13, 1870, Manvers, Ontario), Frank Wright and Sarah Wright.

6 March 1849 – Marriage of Cynthia Pinkham: Cynthia Pinkern (Pinkham) married Alfred Wright. Marriage Place: Wentworth, Ontario, Canada. *Source: Archives of Ontario District Marriage Records*

1851 Census of Canada East, Canada West, New Brunswick and Nova Scotia – Cynthia Wright. Name: Cynthia Wright; Gender – Female; Age – 20; Estimated birth year – 1832; Birthplace – Canada; Province – Canada West (Ontario); District – Durham County; District number – 6; Sub-district – Clarke; Sub-District Number – 41; Household: Alfred Wright/Yeoman/ age 25/ birthplace – United States; Cynthia Wright/age 26/birthplace – Canada; Charles W. Wright/age

4/birthplace – Canada; Lilly J. Wright/age 2/birthplace – Canada. *Source: 1851 Canada Census, Ottawa, Canada.*

1861 Census of Canada: Cynthia Wright, Age 28, Born abt. 1833, Alfred Wright (Born: United States) age 37, Cynthia Wright age 20, Charles. W. Wright age 13, Lilly Jane Wright age 10, John A. age 11, Mary E. age 7 and Edwin A. age 2 (abt) (All ages incorrect/George Wright missing. At same location is her brother – Willard Pinkham (Willerd, Laborer, age 18), mother, Elizabeth Pinkham (age 50, widow) and brothers Samuel Pinkham (age 9) and Charles (age 6) Pinkham. *Source: Census of 1851 Canada East/West, Library of Archives, Canada*

1871 Census of Canada: Synthia Wright, age 38, Religion: Wesleyan Methodist, along with Alfred Wright (husband) age 47, Lilly Jane Wright age 21 (abt. 1850), George Wright age 19 (abt. 1852), John Alfred Wright age 18 (abt. 1853), Mary Eliza Wright age 12 (abt. 1859) and Edwin Albert Wright age 5 (abt. 1866). *Source: Library and Archives, Canada 1871 Census Place Clarke, Durham West, Ontario.*

> Marriage (Methodist) Act of Son, Albert Wright (Edwin Albert Wright), Widower, Farmer age 44 of Clarke Township, Durham, Ontario to Margaret Ann McCullough, age 38 on 25 March 1914, Pontypool, Durham, Ontario. listing parents: Father: Albert Wright / Mother: **Cynthe** (Cynthia) **Pinkham**. *Source: Archives of Ontario, Toronto, Canada, Canada Registrations of Marriages, 1869-1928*

> Children of Albert Wright (b. United States 1824) & Cynthia Pinkham (b. 1832 Quebec): Charles Wesley Wright, born 22 October 1848, Lilly Jane Wright born 1850, George Wright born 1852, John Alfred Wright born 1863, Mary Eliza Wright born 25 January 1859, Edwin Albert Wright born 1866 (& Willard Wright born 1868).

Death: Cyntha Wright, age 47, 21 September 1879; birth abt. 1832. Birthplace: Lower Canada/Quebec. Death Place: Durham, Ontario, Canada. *Source: Archives of Ontario, Toronto, Canada.*

> Burial: McCrea's Methodist Cemetery, Pontypool, Kawartha Lakes Municipality, Ontario, Canada. Spouse: Alfred Wright. Son: Willard Wright. Birth: 1832. Death date: 21 September 1879. *Source: Find A Grave Canada*

> Burial: McCrea's Cemetery, Ponlypool, Kawartha Lakes, Ontario, Canada – Son: Willard Wright. Born 2 March 1868. Died 13 August 1870 (age 2). (Named for brother, Willard Pinkham)
> Burial: McCrea's Cemetery) Pontypool, Kawartha Lakes, Death of Spouse, Alfred Wright born 1824; d.1908.

>> Death (of son): Charles Wesley Wright on 13 May 1928 in Manvers, Durham County, Ontario, Canada. Birthdate – 22 October 1840. Age 80. Father's name: Alfred Wright. Mother's name: Cynthia Pinkham. (Named for brother, Charles Pinkham)

Death (of daughter: Mary Eliza Alberta (Wright) McAllen on 25 January 1930, Toronto, Ontario, Canada. Born 20 July 1859 in Clarke, Ontario. Father's name: Alfred Wright. Mother's name: Cynthia Pinkham.

Death (of son): Albert Edwin Wright, 30 March 1930, Orono, Clarke Township, Ontario. Burial: McCrea's Cemetery, lot 23. Age: 63 (born 1876) Occupation: Farmer. Father's name: Alfred Wright born USA. Mother's Name: Cynthia Pinkham born Quebec.

~Electa Pinkham Eddy: (Name listed as both "*Electa*" and "*Electra*" in records)

Born: 12 March 1834, Quebec
Married: Hiram Eddy 1855-1856
Died: 12 May 1916, Clarke County, Ontario, Canada

The children of Electra Pinkham and Hiram Eddy born Ontario were (Generation 9):
    Charles Hiram Eddy (born abt. 1855/1856)
        Marriage Act 1877: son Charles M. Eddy marries. Parents: Father - Hiram K. Eddy; Mother – Electra Eddy. *Source: Archives of Ontario, Toronto, Canada Registrations of Marriages, 1869-1920*
    Rial Eddy (born 1858)
    Charlotte Eddy (born 1860)
    Harvey W. Eddy (born 1863)

1851 Canada West Census: Family of Pinkham Comfort, Farmer: Age 41; Elizabeth Comfort, age 42; Electra Comfort age 18; Mary Comfort age 16; Edwin Comfort age 11; Willard Comfort age 9; John Comfort age 7; Jane Comfort age 1. Last name, "Pinkham" transposed to, "Comfort." Should be Comfort Pinkham *Source: 1851 Census, Canada West, Durham County, Clarke Township*

Marriage of Electra Pinkham: to Hiram Kilburn Eddy (son of Ira Eddy and Zoa Kilburn, born in 1826 in Orono, Clark, Township, Ontario; d. 23 November 1890 in Orono, Ontario, Canada).

1861 Census: Electa Eddy (age 27, birth year - 1834, birth place - Lower Canada, religion – Methodist) with children Hiram Eddy, age 6, Rial Eddy, age 3 and Charlotte Eddy, age 1. *Source: Library and Archives 1861 Census, Ottawa, Ontario, Canada*

1871 Census: Electa Eddy, Female age 37, abt. 1834, Married, Methodist, along with Hiram Eddy (age 44), Charles Eddy (age 15), Rial Eddy (age 13), Charlotte Eddy (age 11), Harvey Eddy (Age 8). *Source: Library and Archives, Canada, Census place, Clarke, Durham West, Ontario.*

1881 Census: Electa Eddy, Female, Married, Age 47, Birth year - 1834, Birthplace - Quebec, Religion – Methodist Episcopal, Province – Ontario, District–

Durham West, Sub-district – Clarke, Household members – Hiram Eddy – age 55, Electa Eddy – age 47, Harvey W. Eddy – age 18. *Source. Library & Archives, Canada Census place Clarke, Durham West, Ontario*

1891 Census: Eleta Eddy, Female, Widow, birth year – 1834, birthplace – Quebec, Religion – Methodist, French-Canadian – No, Father's birthplace – Quebec, Mother's birthplace – Quebec. Province - Ontario, District - Durham West, Subdistrict – Clarke, Household members: Harvey W. Eddy age 28, Eleta Eddy, Age 57. *Source: Year 1891 Census, Library and Archives, Canada – Place Clarke, Durham West, Ontario*

1901 Census: Electa Eddy, Female, Widow, Age 67, Birthdate – 15 March 1834, Birthplace – Quebec, Race – English, Religion – Methodist, Occupation – Weaving, Province – Ontario, District – Durham, Sub-District – Clarke, Household members – Electa Eddy, age 67; Harvey W. Eddy, age 37. *Source: 1901 Census, Library & Archives, Canada, Census Place: Clarke, Durham, Ontario*

1911 Census: Elector Eddy, Female, Widowed, Age 77, Birthdate - March 1834, Birthplace – Quebec, Race – English, Province – Ontario, District – Durham, District Number – 64, Sub-district – 14 – Clarke. Household members – Elector Eddy, Age - 77. *Source: 1911 Census, Library and Archives, Canada, Census Place: 14 – Clarke, Durham, Ontario*

12 May 1916 Ontario Deaths – Eddy, Electa, 84 years, May 12, 1916, Clarke Township, Orono, Housewife, Widow, Father: Pinkham, Comfort. *Source: Archives of Ontario, Toronto, Canada*

12 May 1916 Death Record: Electa Eddy. Death 12 May 1916, Clarke County, Durham, Ontario, Age 84. Burial Place: Orono, Father: Comfort Pinkham. *Source: Ontario Deaths, 1869-1937, Archives of Ontario, Toronto*

Orono News (Newspaper): Death – Eddy. Date: May 1916. Orono, Durham, Ontario – Canada. Eddy –
In Orono on Friday May 12 Electa Pinkham relect of the late Hiram K. Eddy aged 84 years.

Obituary in "Victoria News": *Of the old Orono settlers, the very few now left have passed their four score years. On Friday Electra Pinkham, relect of the late Hiram K. Eddy, passed away at the grand old age of 84, after being a continuous resident here for over sixty years, coming here in 1854 and entering the house, now occupied by Mr. D. T. Allin, as a bride. The Pinkham family was of French descent and came to this township from Lower Canada.*

~Mary Pinkham Coons:

Born: 1835, Quebec

Married: *(assumed)* William Coons

1851 Canada West Census: Family of Pinkham Comfort, Farmer: Age 41; Elizabeth Comfort, age 42; Electra Comfort age 18; Mary Comfort age 16; Edwin Comfort age 11; Willard Comfort age 9; John Comfort age 7; Jane Comfort age 1. Last name, "Pinkham" transposed to, "Comfort." Should be Comfort Pinkham *Source: 1851 Census, Canada West, Durham County, Clarke Township*

Death: 9 June 1875 Ashland, Minnesota

1875 Minnesota Deaths: Mary (Pinkham) Coons, Female, Death date: 9 June 1875; Death Place – Ashland, Dodge County, Minnesota; Age- 98/Birthdate - 1777 (Actual age: 40/ born 1835); Race – White; Marital Status – Married; **Father's name: Comfort Pinkham; Father's birthplace Canada; Mother's Name- Elisabeth, Mother's birthplace – Canada).** *Source: Minnesota Deaths & Burials, 1835-1990 citing Ashland, Dodge County, Minnesota* Birth year noted is completely wrong – parent's name accurate.

Possible reference:

1865 Minnesota State Census – Mary Coon. Name – Mary Coon; Event type – Census. Event Date – 1865. Event Place – Red Rock, Mower, Minnesota, United States. Gender – Female. Volume – 6. Household – R. Coon – Female; Samuel Coon – Male; B. Coon – Female; L. Coon – Female; Mary Coon – Female. *Names son, Samuel, for grandfather Samuel Pinkham and brother, Samuel Pinkham. Moved to Mower, MN with Jeremiah Phelps family and uncle, Joseph Abijah Pinkham.*

F. A. M. Coons (son) – Minnesota Grand Army of the Republic Membership: Name – F. A. M. Coons. Event type – Military Service. Event date: 1869-1940. Event place – Winona, Minnesota, United States. Age – 20. Born in Canada.

22 January 1870 Minnesota Births and Christenings: Mary E. Coon (daughter). Name – Mary E. Coon. Gender – Female. Birthdate – 22 January 1870. Birthplace: Blue Earth, Minnesota. Father's name: William Coon. Mother's name: Mary J. Coon. *Source: Minnesota Births & Christenings, 1840-1980*

Residing in Blue Earth, Minnesota were Joseph, Charles and James Pinkham. As families moved to towns together, a family relationship is likely.

Joseph Pinkham: Born 1822
        1875 Garden City, Blue Earth, Faribault, MN Minnesota State Census: Joseph Pinkham born 1822 with wife Julie Anne Pinkham born 1835.

(James and Charles A. Pinkham, likely sons of James O. Pinkham) (Caleb's Pinkham's son, Comfort Pinkham' son: James Pinkham b. 1866 in Clayton, Wisconsin)

James Pinkham: Born 1845

> 1875 Red Wing City, Goodhue, Minnesota State Census: James Pinkham born 1845 Canada.

Charles A. Pinkham: Born 1851

> Marriage: 10 October 1873 - Charles A. Pinkham to Ella G. Palver. Location: Faribault, Minnesota, USA.
>
> 1875 Minnesota State Census Blue Earth City, Faribault, MN: C. A. (Charles A. Pinkham). Wife: Ella Pinkham born Wisconsin with G. B. Pinkham.
>
> 1876 Birth: Harriet M. Pinkham. Birth Date: 6 May 1876. Location: Blue Earth City Township, Faribault, Minnesota, USA. Father: Charles A. Pinkham. Mother: Ella G. (Palver) Pinkham.
>
> 1880 United States Census Blue Earth City, Farabault, MN: Charles A. Pinkham, Wife: Ella J. Pinkham, Hattie Pinkham born 1876 Minnesota.
>
> 1880 Minnesota State Census Blue Earth City Faribault: Chas. A. Pinkhkam. Age 29 born 1851. Married. Occupation: Hotel Keeper. Father's birthplace: *New Hampshire.* Mother's birthplace: *New Hampshire.*
>
> Children of Joseph and Julie Pinkham:
> > Alma J. Pinkham
> > Albert Pinkham
> > Alice E. Pinkham

United States Census of Union Veterans and Widows of the Civil War: 1890 – Mary J. Coons. Name – William L. Coon. Spouse's name – Mary J. Coon. Event type – Census. Event date – 1890. Event place – Mankato, Blue Earth, Minnesota, United States. *Source: United States Census of Union Veterans and Widows of the Civil War 1890*

~Edwin Pinkham:

Birth: Born abt. 1840-1841, Quebec
(Edwin Pinkham's birth year changes per census but by 1842 brother Willard Pinkham was born which means Edwin Pinkham born prior to 1841)
Married: Catherine Campbell on 12 May 1867, Dodge, Minnesota, USA
Death: Post 1905 Eugene, Oregon, USA

The Children of Edwin A. and Catherine (Campbell) Pinkham were (Generation 9):
> Elizabeth Pinkham (b. 1869, Minnesota) *(named for mother)*
> Mertie (Myrtle) J. Pinkham (b. 1871, Minnesota)
> Benjamin C. Pinkham (b. 1872, Minnesota)
> Edwin I. Pinkham (b. 1873, Minnesota)
> Martha L. Pinkham (b. 1876, Minnesota)
> Loretta (Linneta) E. Pinkham (b. 1877, Minnesota) (twin)

Orrella C. (Cynthia) Pinkham (b. 1877, Minnesota) (twin)
Catherine (Katherine) M. Pinkham (b. 1879, Kansas)
Edith M. Pinkham (b. 1882, Kansas)
Mary A. Pinkham (b.1884, Minnesota)

1851 Canada West Census: Family of Pinkham Comfort, Farmer: Age 41; Elizabeth
    Comfort, age 42; Electra Comfort age 18; Mary Comfort age 16; Edwin Comfort
    age 11; Willard Comfort age 9; John Comfort age 7; Jane Comfort age 1. Last
    name, "Pinkham" transposed to, "Comfort." Should be Comfort Pinkham *Source:*
    1851 Census, Canada West, Durham County, Clarke Township Edwin Pinkham's birth year: 1840.

Edwin Pinkham is not listed on 1861 Durham County Census with Willard Pinkham,
Elizabeth Pinkham, Samuel Pinkham and Charles Pinkham. John Wesley Pinkham
was working at a neighboring farm and listed on a separate census record so perhaps,
after the death of father Comfort Pinkham, Edwin Pinkham was a farmhand, too.

Of the Comfort Carpenter and Elizabeth (Phelps) Pinkham children, two move to
Minnesota - Mary and Edwin Pinkham. Residing in Milles Lac, Minnesota during post
1875 was their uncle, Caleb Pinkham, brother of Comfort, and sons, Comfort Pinkham
and Caleb Pinkham, Jr. families. Comfort Carpenter Pinkham's brother, Joseph Abijah
Pinkham moved to Mower, Minnesota during the 1850.

1867 Marriage of Edwin A. Pinkham to Catherine Campbell – Event Date: 12 May
    1867. Event Place – Dodge, Minnesota, United States. Source: Minnesota County
    Marriages: 1860-1949

(1868 Edw C. Pinkham – 14th Regiment, Princess of Wales" Own Rifles)

1870 United States Census - Minnesota: Edwin Pinkham: Birth year: 1843;
    Birthplace – Canada, Occupation: Farmer, Household: Edwin Pinkham (M, 27,
    born Canada), Catherine Pinkham (F, 26, born Canada), Elizabeth Pinkham (F,
    age - 1, born - Minnesota), Marty (Myrtle) Pinkham (F, age – 0; born -
    Minnesota). *Source: United States Census, 1870, Minnesota; NARA*
    (First child named for Edwin's mother – Elizabeth Phelps Pinkham)

Birth of Edwin J./E. Pinkham – 18 December 1872. Birthplace – Ashland,
Dodge, Minnesota. Father's name: Edwin A. Pinkham born Canada;
Mother's name: Catherine born Canada. *Source: Minnesota Births & Christenings, 1840-1980*

1895 Minnesota State Census: Edwin Pinkham. Event place:
Pelican Rapids Village, Otter Tail, MN. Age – 21 years. Birth year
(estimated) – 1874. Birthplace – Minnesota. With Ruby J.
Pinkham age 6 months born Minnesota. *Source; Minnesota State Census, 1895*

1900 United States Census: Edwin E. Pinkham. Event place –
Pelican Township, Pelican Rapids Village, Otter Tail, Minnesota,
US. Male, Age 28. Married 6 years (Marriage date: 1894).

Father's birthplace (Edwin Pinkham – Canada Fr) Canada France (Quebec); Mother's birthplace – Canada Eng (English). Household: Edwin E. Pinkham (head, age 28 born Minnesota), Lizzie Pinkham (wife, age 26, born Norway) & Ruby G. Pinkham (daughter age 6, born Minnesota). *Source: United States Census, 1900*

(Parents Edwin and Catherine Pinkham moved to Hillsboro Trail, North Dakota in 1900.)

1910 United States Census: Edwin E. Pinkham. Residence: Albert, Benson, North Dakota. Born 1872 Minnesota. With spouse Lizzy Pinkham. Daughter Ruby J. Pinkham.

1915 North Dakota Census: E. E. Pinkham. Event Year: 1915. Event Place: Golden Valley, North Dakota, United States. Household: E. E. Pinkham with Elizabeth (Lizzie) Pinkham. *Source: North Dakota State Census, 1915*

1940 United States Census Spokane, Washington: Edwin E. Pinkham born 1873 Minnesota. Spouse: Elsie Pinkham.

Obituary: Edwin E. Pinkham; Event Date 12 September 1957. Newspaper: *Oregonian* (Portland, Oregon). Edwin E. Pinkham, Death/Burial Place: Portland, Multnamoah Oregon. Cemetery: Rose City Cemetery. Death date: 11 September 1957. Birth date: 18 December 1872. (Son of Edwin A. and Catherine Pinkham born Minnesota)

1875 Minnesota State Census: O ("E:"). A. Pinkham, age 34 born (1841) Canada, parents born Canada with wife, Catherine, age 31, parents: father – born Ireland/mother – born Canada, with children – Lizzie (Elizabeth) age 6 born MN, Myrta J. Pinkham age 5 born MN, Benny Pinkham age 4 born MN, Edwin Pinkham age 3 born MN and Martha Pinkham born 1875 age months born MN. *Source: Minnesota State Census, 1875.* "O. A." a typo for "E. A." (wife, age 26, born Norway) & Ruby G. Pinkham (daughter age 6, born Minnesota). *Source: United States Census, 1900*

1880 United States Census – Kansas: Edwin A. Pinkham. Event Place: Courtland, Republic, Kansas, United States. Gender: Male; Marital Status – Married; Race – White; Occupation – Farmer; Head of Household; Birth year – 1843; Birthplace – Canada; Father's birthplace – Canada; Mother's birthplace – Canada. Household: Edwin A. Pinkham (head, male, age 37, birthplace – Canada); Catherine Pinkham (wife, female, age 36, birthplace – Canada); Elizabeth Pinkham (daughter, female, age 11, birthplace – Minnesota, US); Mertie J. Pinkham (daughter, female, age 9, birthplace – Minnesota, US); Benjamin C. Pinkham (son, male, age 8, birthplace – Minnesota, US); Edwin I. Pinkham (son, male, age 7, birthplace – Minnesota, US); Martha L. Pinkham (daughter, female, age 5, birthplace – Minnesota, US); Loretta E. Pinkham (daughter, female, age 3,

Minnesota, US); Orrella C. Pinkham (daughter, female, age 3, birthplace –
Minnesota, US) and Catherine M. Pinkham (daughter, female, age 1, birthplace
Kansas, US). *Source: United States Census, 1880 for Edwin A. Pinkham, Courtland, Kansas. NARA*

1885 Minnesota State Census: Edwin A. Pinkham, Head of household, Male,
Age 41, Born in Canada, Pelican Rapids, Otter Tail, Minnesota, Volume – Otter
Tail. Household of Edwin A. Pinkham (Male/41 years/Birthplace –
Canada), Catherine Pinkham (Female/ 40 years/Birthplace –Canada), Elizabeth
Pinkham (Female/17 years/Birthplace – Minnesota), Myrtle J. Pinkham
(Female/15 years/birthplace – Minnesota), B. C. Pinkham (Male/13
years/birthplace – Minnesota), Edwin J. Pinkham (Male/11 years/birthplace –
Minnesota), Martha L. Pinkham (female/9 years/birthplace – Minnesota), Linetta
E. Pinkham (female/7 years/birthplace – Minnesota), Cynthia O. Pinkham
(female/7 years/birthplace – Minnesota), Catherine M. Pinkham (female/5
years/birthplace – Kansas), Edith M. Pinkham (female/3 years/birthplace –
Kansas) and Mary A. Pinkham (female/ 1 year/ birthplace – Minnesota). *Source:*
Minnesota State Census, 1885, Otter Tail, Minnesota, State Library and Records Service, St. Paul Children
named for mother, Elizabeth and sisters – Cynthia and Mary Pinkham.

> *Minnesota Births and Christenings: Father: Edwin Pinkan. (Pinkham).*
> *Male, born 13 May 1886 in St. Paul, Ramsey, Minnesota. Father: Edwin*
> *Pinkham. Mother: Annie Pinkham. Parents born: United States.*

1895 Minnesota State Census: Edwin A. Pinkham, Pelican Rapids Village,
Otter Tail, Minnesota, age 52 years, birth year - 1843, birthplace – Canada, Race
– W, Gender – M, Household of Edwin A. Pinkham (M/52 years/birthplace –
Canada), Catherine Pinkham (F/51 years/birthplace – Canada), Myrtle J.
Pinkham (F/24 years/birthplace – Minnesota), Benjamin C. Pinkham (M/22
years/birthplace – Minnesota), Martha L. Pinkham (F/18 years/birthplace –
Minnesota), Rolla Pinkham (F/16 years/Birthplace – Minnesota), Katherine M.
Pinkham (F/14 years/birthplace – Kansas) and Charles W. Pinkham (M/2
years/Minnesota - grandson). *Source: Minnesota State Census, 1895, Otter Tail, MN, State Library &*
Records Service, St. Paul Grandson named for Edwin's brother, Charles Pinkham.

1900 US Census Hillsboro Trail, North Dakota, Edwin Pinkham, Head of
Household. Born September 1843, Canada (English), age 56. Wife, Catherine,
wife, Born July 1843, age 57. Profession – Greyline Express. Married – 1867/
33 years. US arrival: 1865. Grandson, Charles, age 7 born February 1893
Minnesota. Address: 7076 5th Street/Owned Home.

> *Daughter, Elizabeth (born 1868 Minnesota) named after mother,*
> *and Cynthia (born 1880 Kansas) after sister. Charles named after brother.*

Burial: Katherine Pinkham. Event date: 1904. Event Place: Eugene,
Lane, Oregon, USA. Cemetery: Mulkey Cemetery. Death date: 8

November 1904. *Source: FindAGrave.* Father: Edwin A. Pinkham. Katherine born 1881 Kansas (or 1879 Minnesota).

1905. From Durham County Ontario Canada, <u>Newcastle newspaper</u> - "Pinkham, Ed, formerly of Orono, returned with brother Sam of Lindsay, to his home in Eugene, Oregon." Text was dated 4 May 1905.

<u>Died:</u> Post 1905 in Eugene, Oregon, USA

> Wife (m2) of Edwin A. Pinkham – Marjorie Stafford Pinkham. Died 21 May 1994 age 84 in Portland, Oregon. Born 21 October 1909 Tarkio, Missouri. Spouse of Edwin A. Pinkham. Listed on record: David and John Pinkham.

<u>~Willard Pinkham:</u>

<u>Birth:</u> Born abt. 1841-1842, Quebec/Ontario, Canada. Death unknown (Minnesota?).

<u>1851 Canada West Census:</u> Family of Pinkham Comfort, Farmer: Age 41; Elizabeth Comfort, age 42; Electra Comfort age 18; Mary Comfort age 16; Edwin Comfort age 11; Willard Comfort age 9; John Comfort age 7; Jane Comfort age 1. Last name, "Pinkham" transposed to, "Comfort." Should be Comfort Pinkham *Source: 1851 Census, Canada West, Durham County, Clarke Township*

<u>1861 Ontario Census:</u> Willerd Pinkham: Event Place - Clarke, Durham, Ontario; Age- 18; Religion - Christan; Birthplace – Canada; Occupation - Laborer; Birth year -1843. *Source: Ontario Census 1861; Library & Archives Canada; Public Archives, Toronto*

> <u>1861 Ontario Census:</u> Elizabeth Pinkham, Female, age 50, Widow, Religion: Methodist, Home in 1861 Clarke, Durham, Canada West. Living near son, Willard Pinkham (Willerd Pinkham) (age 18, Laborer, birth year 1843, single, Christian) who was listed separately, and with sons, Samuel Pinkham, age 9, and Charles Pinkham, age 6, Pinkham. Listed nearby on same census record page is daughter Cynthia Wright with husband Alfred and two children Charles and Lilly). *Source: Library & Archives, Canada, Ottawa, Ontario Canada, Census Returns for 1861*

~Willard Pinkham was not recorded via death or marriage records after 1861. Unconfirmed is whether he died, used his middle name as his first name, or if he moved to the United States. He is last recorded in the 1861 Canada census as age 18 residing separetly from mother and younger brothers. However, if he moved to Minnesota with brother Edwin and sister Mary Pinkham Coon, as well as, cousin Joseph H. Pinkham (born abt. 1822-1831 Quebec), he may have married in Minnesota during 1889:

> <u>Marriage</u> of W. F. Pinkham to May Pashley on 16 December 1889 in Ramsey, Minnesota. *Source: Minnesota County Marriages 1860-1949*

~JOHN WESLEY PINKHAM:

Birth: 20 September 1845, Clarke, Durham County, Ontario, Canada
Marriage: M1 – Emma Harris; M2 – Sarah Ann Irwin; M3 – Margaret Elsworth
Death: 28 October 1924, Oshawa, Durham County, Ontario, Canada

Children of JOHN WESLEY and (m2) Sarah Ann (Irwin) PINKHAM (Generation 9):

Mary Estelle (Minnie) Pinkham: Born 9 Dec 1873, Ops, Ontario. Died 28 March 1917, Little Britain, Ontario, Canada.
LAWRENCE MOWBRAY PINKHAM: Born 11 August 1875, Mariposa, Ontario. Died 1945, Brock Township, Ontario, Canada.
Catherine Harriet Louise (Hattie) Pinkham Munsie: Born 3 March 1877, Brock Township, Ontario. Married James Munsie on 26 August 1906. Died August 1939, Winnipeg, Manitoba, Canada.
Lillian Elizabeth Pinkham Piper: Born 10 December 1879, Emily, Ontario. Married Dr. Charles Piper. Died 20 October 1948, Chicago, Illinois, USA.
Annie Electra Pinkham Rumney: Born 6 March 1883, Victoria County, Ontario. Married 1907 Robert Rumney. Died 11 April 1911, Little Britain, Ontario. Canada.
(Frank) Milton Ferguson Pinkham: Born 12 January 1885, Ontario. Married Mary Jane Mutchmore on 17 September 1913. Died 26 September 1957, Vancouver, British Columbia, Canada.
John Wesley Pinkham: Born 30 July 1887, Victoria County, Ontario. Died 21 May 1906, Little Britain, Victoria County, Ontario., Canada.

Records:

1851 Canada West Census: Family of Pinkham Comfort, Farmer: Age 41; Elizabeth Comfort, age 42; Electra Comfort age 18; Mary Comfort age 16; Edwin Comfort age 11; Willard Comfort age 9; JOHN COMFORT age 7; Jane Comfort age 1. Last name, "Pinkham" transposed to, "Comfort." Should be Comfort Pinkham
Source: 1851 Census, Canada West, Durham County, Clarke Township

1861 Census of Canada: JOHN PINKHAM, Event Place: Clarke, Durham, Ontario, Canada; Enumeration District – 5; Gender – Female (Male); Age – 15; Marital Status – Single; Religion – E. Church; Birthplace – Canada; Birth year – 1846/ 1845, Occupation: Servant; non-member of William Cooney family who resided District 5, Clarke Township. Lived apart from brother Willerd Pinkham (age 18, Laborer), living as non-member of District 5, Clarke Township family but same page as the Cynthia Pinkham Harris (sister, age 28, born in Lower Canada) family & mother, Elizabeth Pinkham (age 50, born in Lower Canada), whose household listed brothers Samuel (age 9, in school) and Charles age 6). *Source: Ontario Census, 1861, Library and Archives Canada, Public Archives, Toronto*

1870 - Marriage (m1): JOHN PINKHAM to Emma Harris, sister of William Harris, Cynthia Pinkham (John Wesley Pinkham's sister) Harris' husband.

Emma Harris m1: Born 1848, Clarke, Durham County, Ontario (1851 census); born 1849 Clarke, Durham County, Ontario (1861 Census). Brother William Harris born 1844 Clarke, Durham County, Ontario (1861 census). Religion: P. M.

1871 Census of Canada: J. WESLEY PINKHAM; Gender – Male; Birth year -1846 (1845); Birthplace – Ontario; Marital Status – Married; Nationality – English; Religion – W. Meth; Event place – Ops, South Victoria, Ontario; Household members: J. Wesley Pinkham, Age 25; Emma (Harris) Pinkham, Age 22. *Source: 1871 Canada Census – Ops, Victoria, South, Library and Archives, Canada*

Marriage (m2) on 20 November 1872; From the Victoria News: Vol. 23, Page. 399 – JOHN PINKHAM, 27, widower, farmer, Clark, Ops, s/o Comfort & Elizabeth, married Sarah Ann IRWIN, 19, Mariposa, same, d/o Robert and Mary J. Witness Eretus Smith and William Galbraith, both of Mariposa, November 20, 1872, Mariposa.

Marriage (m2) on 20 November 1872: From Ontario County Marriage Register, 1858-1869. JOHN PINKHAM; Marriage; Date: 20 Nov 1872; Event Place: Victoria, Ontario, Canada; Age – 27; Birth year – 1875; Birthplace – Clarke; Father's Name – Comfort Pinkham; Mother's Name – Elizabeth Pinkham; Spouse's name – Sarah Ann Irwin; Spouse's Age – 19, Spouse's birth year – 1853; Spouse's birthplace – Mariposa; Spouse's Father's Name – Robert Irwin; Spouse's Mother's Name – Mary J. Irwin. *Source: Ontario County Marriage Registers, 1858-1869. Victoria, Ontario, Canada; Archives of Ontario, Toronto*

(The Robert Irwin Family Tree - page 285)

1881 Census of Canada: JOHN PINKAM. Male; Married status – Married; Age: 40; Birth year: abt 1841; Birthplace: Ontario; Occupation: Farmer. Wife: Mary (not Sarah Ann); Age 37 years born 1832 Ontario; Married; Children: Minnie Age 7 born 1874 Ontario/Occupation: "Going to school," Lorence age 7 born 1876 Ontario/Occupation – "Going to school," Hattie Age 3 born 1878 and Lillie age one born 1880. Pinkam (Pinkham) family listed as "Irish" (Sarah Anne Irwin - Irish) and Wesleyan Methodists. *Source: Canada 1881 Census*

1891 Census of Canada: JOHN PINKHAM; Gender – Male; Marital status – Married; Age – 45; Birth Year – abt. 1846; Birthplace – Ontario; Relation to Head of Household – Head; Religion – Methodist; French-Canadian – No; Spouse's name – Sarah A. Pinkham; **Father's birthplace – Quebec; Mother's birthplace – Quebec;** Province – Ontario; District – Ontario North; Sub-district – Brock; Household Members: John Pinkham (Age 45), Sarah A. Pinkham (Age 37), Minnie Pinkham (Age 17), Lawrence Pinkham (Age 15), Harriet Pinkham (Age 13), Elizabeth Pinkham (Age 11), Annie Pinkham (Age 9), Milton Pinkham (Age 6), John W. Pinkham (Age 4). *Source: 1891 Canada Census Brock, Ontario North, Library and Archives Canada, Ottawa, Ontario*

1901 Census of Canada: JOHN PINKHAM; Gender – Male; Age – 55; Birth Day & Month – 20 September; Birth Year – 1845; Birthplace – Ontario; Relation to Head of Household – Head; Racial or Tribal Origin – English; Nationality – Canadian; Religion – Methodist; Occupation – Farmer; Province – Ontario; District – Victoria South; District Number – 120; Sub-district – Mariposa; Household Members: John W. Pinkham (Age 55): Sarah A. Pinkham (Age 48); Mary E. Pinkham (Age 27); Harriet L. Pinkham (Age 23); Annie E. Pinkham (Age 18); Milton F. Pinkham (Age 16); John W. Pinkham (Age 13).

1901 Victoria South, Ontairo 31 March 1901 Census:

Mary Estelle	b. 1874	dau. John Wesley and Sarah A. Irwin
Harriet L.	b. 1878	dau. John Wesley and Sarah A. Irwin
Annie E.	b. 1883	dau. John Wesley and Sarah A. Irwin
Milten F.	b. 1885	son, John Wesley and Sarah A. Irwin
John W.	b 1888	son John Wesley and Sarah A. Irwin

Children of John Wesley and Sarah (Irwin) Pinkham by 1901:

Mary Astilla	b. 19 December 1873, Ops, Victoria, Ontario
Harriet Louisa	b. 3 March 1877, Mariposa, Victoria, Ontario
Annie Electa	b. 6 March 1882, Mariposa, Victoria, Ontario
Milton Ferguson	b. 12 January 1885, Mariposa, Victoria, Ontario
John Wesley	b. 29 July 1887, Brock, Ontario

1911 Census of Canada: JOHN W. PINKHAM; Gender – Male; Marital Status – Married; Age – 65; Birth date – September 1845; Birthplace –Ontario; Relation to Head of House – Head; Race or Tribe – English; Province – Ontario; District – Victoria; Sub-district – -Mariposa. Place of Habitation – Mariposa 21; Household Members: John W. Pinkham (Age 65), Sarah Ann Pinkham (Age 57), Mary Estella Pinkham (Age 36).

Marriage (m3) on 5 July 1917: JOHN WESLEY PINKHAM; age – 71; birth year – abt. 1846; birthplace – Ontario, Canada; Marriage date – 5 July 1917;   Marriage place – Ontario, Canada; Father – Carpenter Pinkham; Mother – Betsey Phelp; Spouse – Margaret Elsworth. *Source: Archives of Ontario, Toronto, Ontario, Canada, Registrations of Marriages, 1869-1928*

1921 Census of Canada: JOHN PINKHAM; Gender: Male; Marital Status – Married; Age – 75; Relation to Head of Household – Head; Spouse's Name: Margaret Pinkham; Province – Ontario; District – Victoria; Sub-district – Mariposa Township; City, Town or Village – Mariposa; Street or Township – Mariposa. Household Members: John Pinkham (Age 75), Margaret Pinkham (Age 60). *Source: Library and Archives, Canada, Census Place Mariposa Township; Victoria; Ontario*

Death: JOHN W. PINKHAM; Gender: Male; Birth date: abt. 1845; Birth place: Clark; Death date: 28 October 1924; Death Place: Ontario, Canada. *Source: Archives of Canada, Toronto, Ontario, Canada*

Burial: Little Britain United Church Cemetery, Little Britain, Kawartha Lakes, Ontario.
Headstone: JOHN WESLEY PINKHAM (1844-1924); Sarah Ann Irwin
Pinkham (1852-1914); Annie E. Pinkham Rumney (1885-1911); John
Wesley Pinkham (1889-1906) JOHN WESLEY PINKHAM (son of Comfort
Carpenter and Elizabeth Phelps Pinkham)

Marriages recorded for children of John Wesley and Sarah (Irwin Pinkham:
Hattie Piinkham birth 1881; marriage 22 August 1927; father John
Pinkham/Mother: Annie Irwin
Annie Electra Pinkham birth 1882; marriage 20 December 1907;
father John Wesley Pinkham, mother Sarah Ann Irwin.
Spouse: Robert John Rumney.

JOHN WESLEY PINKHAM Analysis:
Born: 20 September 1845, Clarke, Durham County, Ontario, Canada.
Died: 28 October 1924, Oshawa, Durham County, Ontario, Canada.

Marriage (M1) to Emma Harris (b. 1849; d. 1872)
Marriage (M2) on 20 November 1872; "Victoria News: Vol. 23," JOHN WESLEY
PINKHAM. Page. 399 – John PINKHAM, 27, widower, farmer, Clark, Ops, s/o
Comfort & Elizabeth, married Sarah Ann IRWIN, 19, Mariposa, same, d/o Robert
and Mary J. Witness Eretus Smith and William Galbraith, both of Mariposa,
November 20, 1872, Mariposa. *Source: Victoria News, 1872*
Marriage (M3) to Margaret Elsworth

Note Informant (son, Lawrence "Lorne" Mowbray Pinkham) was incorrect regarding he
stated John Wesley Pinkham's "Father" was "born in England." John Wesley Pinkham's
father was Comfort Carpenter Pinkham born 1811 in Quebec, the son of Samuel and
Theodosia (Carpenter) Pinkham of Stanstead, Quebec. His mother was Eiizabeth
Phelps, the daughter of Amos Phelps, the younger, and unknown. The 1891 census
confirms John Wesley Pinkham's parents were: "born Quebec."

Comfort Carpenter Pinkham died likely during 1855 when John Wesley Pinkham was 10
years old. That Lorne Pinkham did not know his grandfather's name was likely.

Proof Comfort Carpenter Pinkham was not born in England, which some census state:

1851 Census, Canada West, Durham County, Clarke Township: Family of Pinkham
Comfort (Last name is transposed): Farmer, Age 41; Elizabeth Comfort
(Pinkham), Age 42, Electra Comfort (Pinkham), Age 18; Mary Comfort
(Pinkham), Age 16; Edwin Comfort (Pinkham), Age 11; Willard Comfort
(Pinkham), Age 9; JOHN COMFORT (PINKHAM), Age 7; Jane Comfort
(Pinkham), Age 1.

<u>1861 Census, Canada West, Durham County, Clarke Township</u>: JOHN PINKHAM.
Event place: Clarke, Durham, Ontario; Enumeration District – 5; Gender –
Female (Male); Age – 15; Marital Status – Single; Religion – E. Church;
Birthplace – Canada; Birth year – 1846; Occupation – Servant; non-member to
William Cooney family who resided in District 5, Clark Township. Lived apart
from brother, Willerd Pinkham, (Age 18, Laborer, living as non-member of a
different District 5, Clarke Township family) but on same census page as rest of
the Comfort Pinkham family: Cynthia (Pinkham) Harris (sister, age 28, *born in
Lower Canada* – Quebec) family, mother, Elizabeth Pinkham (Age 50; *born
Lower Canada*) whose household include brothers, Samuel (Age 9, in school)
and Charles (Age 6) Pinkham. *Source: Ontario Census, 1861, Library and Archives Canada*

<u>Victoria News</u>, Victoria County, 1872 (Ontario, Canada): Vol. 23 Pg. 399- JOHN
PINKHAM, 27, widower, farmer, Clark, Ops, **s/o Comfort & Elizabeth,** married
Sarah Ann IRWIN, 19, Mariposa, same, d/o Robert and Mary J. Witness Eretus
Smith and William Galbraith, both of Mariposa, November 20, 1872, Mariposa.

<u>Marriage Record(M2)</u>: JOHN PINKHAM to Sarah Ann Irwin. Name: John Pinkham;
Event: Marriage; Event Date: 20 Nov 1872; Event Place: Mariposa, Victoria,
Ontario, Canada; Gender: M; Age – 27; Birth year – 1845; **Father's Name:
Comfort Pinkham**; Mother's Name: Elizabeth Pinkham.

<u>Marriage Record</u>: Samuel Pinkham (brother) to Margaret McLean. Name: Samuel
Prickham (Pinkham); Age: 20; Birth year: abt. 1852; Birth place: Clark, Ontario;
Marriage Date: 26 March 1872; Marriage Place: Victoria, Ontario, Canada;
Father: Comfort Prickham (Pinkham); Mother: Elizabeth Prickham (Pinkham).

<u>Baptismal Record</u>: Charles Pinkham (youngest brother to John Wesley Pinkham).
Event: Baptism. Baptism Year: 1877. Baptism Location: Frelighsburg, Quebec.
Place of Worship: Methodist Church.

*"Charles **son of Comfort Pinkham** and **Elizabeth Phelps** his wife was born in
township of Manvers Province of Ontario on the eleventh day of June one thousand
eight hundred and fifty-five and was baptized on the eleventh day of November one
thousand eight hundred and seventy-seven in the presence of outstanding witnesses by
me. H. Cairnes, M(Methodist) Minister. Witness: W. Caivers (sp?), R. Holder.*

<u>Marriage record</u>: Charles Pinkham (brother of John Wesley Pinkham). Name: Charles
W. Pinkham; Event type: Marriage; Birth Date: abt. 1855: Marriage date – 27
July 1881; Marriage Place: Lowell, Massachusetts; Marriage age: 26; **Father's
name: Comfort**; Mother's name: Elisabeth. *Source: Massachusetts Town and Vital Records,
1620-1988*

References:
<u>Recorded Ontario Births</u>:
Name: Mary Astilla Pinkham; Event – Birth; Event date – 19 December
1873; Event Place – Ontario; Registration date – 1874; Gender – Female;

Father's Name – **John W. Pinkham**; Mother's Name – Sarah Ann Irvin; Certificate number – 019689. *Source: Ontario Births, 1869-1912, Archives of Ontario, Toronto*

Name: Lawrence Mowbray Pinkham; Event type – birth; Event Date - 10 August 1875; Event place – Mariposa, Victoria, Ontario, Canada; Gender –Male; Father's name – **John Pinkham**; Mother's Name – Sarah Ann Irwin; Certificate Number 20928. *Source: Ontario Births, 1869-1912, Archives of Ontario, Toronto*

Name: Harriet Louisa Pinkham; Event – Birth; Event date – 3 March 1877; Event Place – Mariposa, Victoria, Ontario, Canada; Gender – Female; Father's name – **John Pinkham**; Mother's name – Sarah Ann Irwin; Certificate number – 29944. *Source: Ontario births, 1869-1912; Archives of Ontario, Toronto*

Name: Annie Electra Pinkham; Event – Birth; Event date – 6 March 1882; Event place – Emily, Victoria, Ontario, Canada; Gender – Female; Father's Name – **John Pinkham;** Mother's Name – Sarah Ann Irwin; *Source: Ontario birth's, 1869-1912; Archives of Ontario, Toronto*

Name: Milton Ferguson Pinkham; Birth Date: 12 January 1885; Birthplace – Mariposa, Victoria, Ontario; Father's Name: **John Wesley Pinkham**; Mother's Name: Sarah Annie Irwin. *Source: Archives of Canada*

Name: John Wesley Pinkham; Gender – Male; Birthdate – 29 July 1887; Birthplace – Brock Township, Ontario; Father's name – **John Wesley Pinkham**; Mother's Name – Sarah Ann Irion (Irwin). *Source: Archives of Canada*

Ontario Marriages:
Name: Lorne Pinkham; Birth date – 1875; Age 26; Spouse – Annie Gordon; Spouse's birth date – 1879; Spouse's age – 22; Event date – 4 September 1901; Event place – Toronto, York, Ontario, Canada; Father's Name – **John Pinkham**; Mother's Name – Sarah Ann Irwin; Spouse's Father's Name – John Gordon; Spouse's Mother's Name – Mary McDonald. *Source: Canada Marriages 1661-1949.*

Name: Hattie Pinkham – Spouse: James Munsie; Event type – marriage; Event date – 22 August 1906; Event Place – Mariposa, Victoria, Ontario, Canada; Gender – Male; Age – 29; Birth year – 1877; Father's name – Alexander Munsie; Mother's name – Mary Williamson; Spouse's name – Hattie Pinkham; Spouse's gender – Female; Spouse's Age – 25; Spouse's birth year – 1881; Spouse's father's name – **John Pinkham**; Spouse's mother's name – Annie Irwin. *Source: Ontario Marriage, 1869-1927, Archives of Ontario, Toront.*

Ontario Deaths:
Name: John Wesley Pinkham: Death – 21 May 1906; Event Place – Mariposa, Victoria, Ontario, Canada; Gender – Male; Age – 17 (17 years,

10 months); Birthplace – Canada (Farmer/Single/Appendicitis for 7 days); Father's Name: **John Pinkham**. *Source: Ontario Deaths, 1869 – 1937, Archives of Ontario, Toronto*

Name: Mary Estilla Pinkham; Death – 25 March 1917; Event Place – Victoria, Little Britain, Mariposa, Ontario, Canada; Gender – Female; Age – 43; Birthplace – Ops; Birth year – 1874 (Single/Teacher/Appendicitis); Burial place – Victoria, Division of Mariposa; Father's Name – **John Pinkham**; Mother's name – Sarah Ann Irwin; *Source: Ontario Deaths, 1869-1937; Archives of Ontario, Toronto*

Death Record:
Electa Eddy (sister of John Wesley Pinkham): Name: Eddy, Electa; Female, Age 84 years, Clarke Township, Orono. **Father's name: Pinkham, Comfort.**

Marriage Record (M3): JOHN WESLEY PINKHAM: Age – 71; Birth Year: 1846; Birth place: Ontario, Canada; Marriage Date: 5 July 1917; Marriage Place: Ontario, Canada; **Father: Carpenter Pinkham;** Mother: Betsey Phelps; Spouse: Margaret Elsworth. *Source: Archives of Ontario, Toronto, Ontario, Registration of Marriage, 1809-1928*

~Jane (Phebe) Pinkham Harris:

Birth: February 1848, Clarke Township, Durham Country Ontario

Married: William Harris (b. 1845) 1871

Death: 12 February 1919, Clarke Township, Ontario

The children of Jane (Pinkham) and William Harris (Generation 9) born in Clarke Township, Durham County, Ontario were:

Ida May Harris: (b. 3 August 1871)

~Birth of Ida May Harris on 3 August 1871 to Father – William Harris/Mother – Jane Pinkham; Event Place – Clarke Township, Northumberland, Ontario, Canada. *Source: Canada Births & Baptisms, 1868-1912, Archives of Ontario, Toronto*

Lucy J, Harris: (b. 15 November 1872)

~Birth of Lucy J. Harris on 15 November 1872 to Father – William Harris/Mother – Jane Pinkham; Event place – Clarke Township, Northumberland & Durham, Ontario, Canada. *Source: Canada Births and Baptisms, 1661-1950*

~Marriage of Lucy Harris age 19 (Father's name – William Harris/Mother's name – Jane Pinkham) to George W. Taylor age 24 on 23 March 1892, Clarke, Durham, Ontario, Canada. *Source: Ontario Marriage, 1869-1927, Archives of Ontario, Toronto*

<u>Olive Electra Harris:</u> (b. 30 July 1874)
>   ~<u>Birth</u> of Olive Electra Harris on 30 July 1874 to Father – William
>   Harris/Mother – Jane Pinkham; Event Place – Clarke,
>   Northumberland, Durham, Ontario. *Source: Canada Births and Baptisms, 1661-1959* Died prior to 1881 census; speculated death year 1876.

<u>Olivia Elizabeth Harris:</u> (b. 1876)
>   ~<u>Birth</u> of Olivia Elizabeth Harris in 1876 to Father – William Harris/Mother -
>   Jane Pinkham; Event Place – Clarke, Durham, Ontario, Canada.
>   *Source: Ontario Births, 1869-1912, Archives of Ontario, Toronto.* Listed as Elizabeth O.
>   on 1881 Census).

<u>William Albert Harris:</u> (b. 21 February 1878)
>   ~<u>Birth</u> of William Albert Harris on 21 February 1878 to Father – William
>   Harris/Mother – Jane Pinkham/ Event Place – Clarke, Durham,
>   Ontario, Canada. *Source: Ontario Births, 1869 – 1912, Archives of Ontario, Toronto*
>
>   ~<u>Marriage</u> of William Albert Harris age 38 (Father's name – William Harris/
>   Mother's name – Jane Pinkham) to Caroline Boulding age 25 on
>   14 April 1917 in Bowmanville, Durham, Ontario, Canada. *Source: Ontario marriages, 1869-1927, Archives of Ontario, Toronto*

<u>Charles Thomas Harris:</u> (b. 12 July 1882)
>   ~<u>Birth</u> of Charles Thomas Harris on 12 July 1882 to Father – William
>   Harris/Mother – Jane Pinkham/ Event Place – Clarke, Durham,
>   Ontario. *Source: Canada Births and Baptisms, 1661-1959*

<u>Lavina (Louisa) Jane Pinkham:</u> (b. 11 August 1885)
>   ~<u>Birth</u> of Lavina (Louisa) Jane Pinkham on 11 August 1885 to Father –
>   William Harris/Mother – Jane Pinkham. Event place – Clarke,
>   Durham, Ontario, Canada. *Source: Ontario births, 1869-1912, Archives of Ontario, Toronto*
>   ~<u>Marriage</u> of Louisa Jane Harris age 21 (Father's name – William Harris/
>   Mother's name – Jane Pinkham) to Robert B. McGahey age 28 on
>   20 June 1906 in Clarke, Durham, Ontario, Canada. *Source: Archives of Ontario, Toronto*

<u>Hattie Grace Harris:</u> (b. 1887)
>   ~<u>Marriage</u> of Hattie Grace Harris, age 26 born 1887 (Father's name-
>   William Harris. Mother's name - Jane Peckham.) to William John
>   Malley age 28 born 1885 (Father Samuel Malley. Mother - Sarah
>   Mountain) on 2 June 1913 in Clarke, Durham, Ontario, Canada.

<u>1881 Ontario Census:</u> Jane Harris – Female/33 years/Birthplace – Ontario.
Household of William Harris; age 36 years; birthplace – Ontario; Marital status –
Married; Occupation – Farmer; Ethnicity – English; Religion – C. Methodist; Head
of household name – William Harris; Event place – Clarke, Durham West,
Ontario, Canada; Household: William Harris (Male/36 years old/Birthplace –

Ontario), Jane Harris (Female;/33 years old/Birthplace – Ontario), Lucy J. Harris (Female/9 years old/Birthplace – Ontario), Elisabeth O. Harris (Female/5 years old/Birthplace – Ontario), William A. Harris (Male/3 years old/Birthplace – Ontario), Elisabeth Pincombe (Female/68 years old/Birthplace – Quebec.) Source: Canada Census 1881, Library & Archives Canada, Ottawa, Ontario

Note: Elizabeth (Phelps) Pinkham resided with her daughter, Jane (Pinkham) Harris and family until her death. Last name spelled *Pincombe*. Birth Location: 1813 Quebec.

1911 Canada Census: Pheba Jane Harris – Female/age 71/ Birthplace – Ontario. Birthdate – February 1840 (not correct – 1848/age 63). Household of William Harris (Head, Male, age 68, born in Ontario – should be age 71 with February 1840 birthdate), Pheba Jane Harris (Wife, Female, age 71, birthplace Ontario – should be age 68), William Albert Harris (Son, Male, age 32, birthplace Ontario), Hattie Grace Harris (Daughter, Female, age 13, birthplace – Ontario) and boarder. Source: Canada Census 1911, Library and Archives of Canada, Ottawa, Ontario

~Samuel A. Pinkham:

Birth: 6 April 1852, Ontario

Married: 26 March 1872 to Margaret McLean

Death: 6 July 1915, Kindersley, Saskatchewan

Born on 6 April 1852, Ontario. Married on 26 March 1872 to Margaret McLean (b. 1853, Traver, Ireland, father Matthew McLean, mother Selina McLean d. Fenelon Falls, Ontario). Died on 6 July 1915 in Kindersley, Saskachewan. The Canada marriage license lists a Samuel "Prickham" as marrying Margaret McLean. The parents, Comfort and Elizabeth, are listed as, Comfort "Prickham" and Elizabeth "Prickham."

The children of Samuel and Margaret (McLean) Pinkham (Generation 9) born Clarke Township, Ontario were:

Selina (Selena) Pinkham: (b. 23 December 1872)

~Birth of Selena Pinkham on 23 December 1872 to Father – Samuel Pinkham and Mother – Margaret McLean at Clarke Township, Northumberland & Durham, Ontario, Canada. Source: Ontario births, 1869 – 1912; Archives of Ontario, Toronto

~Married: James Shaw, 1893 Lindsay, Ontario.

The children of Selena Pinkham and James Shaw (10) were:

Albert James Shaw
Eva Maud Shaw
John Gordon Shaw
Wilfred Roy Shaw

~Death: 13 January 1909 Death of Selina Elizabeth (Pinkham) Shaw (born 23 December 1873 in Clark Township, Ontario) in Lindsay, Victoria, Ontario, Canada. Father's name – Samuel Pinkham/Mother's name – Margaret McLean. *Source: Ontario Deaths, 1869-1937, Archives of Toronto.*

Albert James Pinkham: (b. 23 November 1874 Ontario, d. prior to July 1876)

~Birth of Albert James Pinkham on 23 November 1874 to Father - Samuel Pinkham and Mother – Margaret McLean at Mariposa, Victoria, Ontario, Canada. *Source: Ontario Births, 1869 – 1912, Archives of Ontario, Toronto*

Albert (Ernest) James Pinkham: (b. 1 July 1876)

~Birth of Alfred Ernest Eddie Pinkham on 1 July 1876 at Mariposa, Victoria, Ontario, Canada to Father –Samuel Pinkham/ Mother – Margaret McLean in Mariposa, Victoria, Ontario, Canada. *Source: Ontario Births – 1869 – 1912, Archives of Ontario*

~Married: Margaret Martin on 31 January 1900.

~Death: Ernest Pinkham, 27 June 1913 Age 36 (born Fenelon Falls, Ontario in 1877), in Midland, Simcoe, Ontario. Father's name: Samuel Pinkham. *Source: Ontario deaths, 1869 – 1937. Archives of Ontario, Toronto*

Ida Estella Pinkham: (b. 25 July 1878)

~Birth of Ida Estella Pinkham on 25 July 1878 to Father – Samuel Pinkham/Mother – Margaret McLean at Mariposa, Victoria, Ontario, Canada. *Source: Ontario Births 1869-1912, Archives of Ontario, Toronto.*

Susan Maud Pinkham: (b. 1882) Married Charles Henry Wissler.

~Birth of Susan Maud Pinkham on 28 August 1881 to Father – Samuel Pinkham/ Mother – Margaret McLean at Emily, Victoria, Ontario, Canada. *Source: Archives of Ontario, Toronto*

~Marriage: 16 October 1907 Marriage of Susan Maud Pinkham (Father's name – Samuel Pinkham/Mother's name – Margaret McLean) age 26, in Toronto, Ontario, Canada to Charles Henry Wissler, Age 26. *Source: Ontario Marriages, 1869-1927; Archives of Ontario, Toronto*

Fannie C. Pinkham: (b. 25 July 1884)

Charles Pinkham: (b. 21 April 1886)

~Birth of Charles Pinkham on 21 April 1886 to Father – Samuel Pinkham/Mother – Margaret McLean at Verulam, Victoria, Ontario, Canada. *Source: Ontario births, 1869-1912. Archives of Ontario, Toronto*

Wilfred Eddy Pinkham: (b. 28 May 1888)

~<u>Birth</u> of Wilfred Eddy Pinkham on 28 May 1888 to Father – Samuel
Pinkham/Mother – Margaret McLean at Verulam, Victoria, Ontario,
Canada. *Source: Ontario Births, 1869-1912, Archives of Ontario, Toronto*

Samuel Pinkham (8) was most likely named for Comfort Pinkham's father, Samuel
Pinkham Junior (6) and grandfather, Samuel Pinkham Senior (5).

<u>26 March 1872 Marriage of Samuel Pinkham</u>: Samuel Pinkham, born abt. 1852 Clarke,
Ontario married Margaret McLean (born Ireland) on 26 March 1872 in Victoria,
Ontario, Canada. Last name spelled: Prickham. Samuel Prickham of Clark,
Farmer. Names of parents; Comfort Prickham and Elizabeth Prickham. *Source:
Ontario, Toronto, Canada "Registrations of Marriage, 1869-1928*

<u>Marriage 23 March 1872</u> from the <u>Victoria News</u>: Vol.23, Pg. 419. Samuel
Prickham, 20, farmer, Clark, Ontario, same, s/o Comfort & Elizabeth, married
Margaret McLean, 19, Travers, Ireland, Clark, d/o Matthew and Selina. Witness
Florence Uylott and L.E.G.G. Smithett both of Lindsay, March 23, 1872, Lindsay.
Source: Victoria News, 1872

<u>1881 Census</u>: Samuel Pinkham, Married, age - 28, Birth year – 1853, Birthplace
– Ontario, Religion – Methodist Church, Nationality – English, Occupation –
Farmer, Province, Ontario, District Number – 129, District – Victoria South, Sub-
district – D/Emily, Division – 2, Household Members: Samuel Pinkham age 28,
Margaret Pinkham (born Ireland) age 26, Seneca Pinkham age 8, Albert Jas.
Pinkham age 6, Alfred Pinkham age 4, Ida Estelle Pinkham age 3. *Source:
1881 Census, Library and Archives, Canada, Census Place: Emily, Victoria – South, Ontario*

<u>1891 Census</u>: Samuel Pinkham, Married, Age 36, Birth year – 1855, Ontario,
Head of Household, Religion – Methodist, French-Canadian – No, Spouse's
Name: Margaret Pinkham, Father's birthplace – England (?), Mother's birthplace
– Quebec, Province – Ontario, District – 121/Victoria South, Sub-district –
Verulam, Household members: Samuel Pinkham age 36, Margaret Pinkham age
35, Albert Pinkham age 17, Earnest Pinkham age 14, Ida Pinkham age 13, Maud
Pinkham age 9, Fanny Pinkham age 7, Charles Pinkham age 5. *Source: 1891 Census,
Library and Archives Canada, Census Place – Verulam, Victoria South, Ontario*

<u>1901 Census</u>: Samuel Pinkham, Married, Age 48, Birth 6 April, Birth year –
1852, Birthplace – Ontario, Head of Household, Race – English, Nationality –
Canadian, Religion – Methodist, Occupation – Farmer, Province – Ontario,
District – Victoria South, District Number – 120, Sub-District – Verulam/G-3,
Household members: Samuel Pinkham age 48, Margaret Pinkham age 46,
Fannie C. Pinkham age 16, Charles Pinkham age 14, Wilfred E. Pinkham age
12. *Source: Library and Archives, Canada, 1901 Census Place, Verulam, Victoria South*

<u>1911 Canada Census</u>: Samuel Pinkham, Male, Married, Brother to Head of
Household – Charles Pinkham, Birth date: April 1852, Birth place: Canada, Head
of household, Race – English, Province – Saskatchewan, District – Moosejaw,
District number – 211, Sub-district – 115, Household Members: Charles

190

Pinkham, age 56; Samuel Pinkham, Age 59. *Source: Library and Archives Canada, 1911 Census Place, Moosejaw, Saskatchewan*

Samuel A. Pinkham founded the town of Pinkham, Sakachewan in 1911 along with his realtor brother, Charles Pinkham. The town of Pinkham had both a post office and a Canadian National Railway station. Pinkham, SK remains a town in Saskatchewan located twenty-four kilometers (15 miles) from Kindersley, Saskatchewan on highway Route 7 which connects Saskatoon to Calgary, Alberta. Pinkham, SK is located at Latitude 51.4334 and Longitude -109.4515. In the book, People Places: Saskatchewan and Its Names by Bill Barry, text states of the town of Pinkham, SK: "Former CN (Canadian National railroad) siding (PO 1911-70), southeast of Flaxcombe, named for pioneer realtor, Charles Pinkham." Charles Pinkham worked for the railroad, and was also listed as a real estate agent in both Stanbridge, Quebec and Lowell, Massachusetts. Upon the death of his Stanbridge-born wife, Lavina Corey Pinkham Charles Pinkham returned to Canada where he is recorded with his brother, Samuel Pinkham, in Moose Jaw, Saskatchewan by 1911.

Brother Samuel and Charles Pinkham are listed as residing in Moose Jaw, Saskatchewan in 1911 where it is noted Charles Pinkham, "real estate investor" immigrated (from Lowell, Massachusetts, USA) to Canada in 1909. Moose Jaw was founded in 1881 as a division for the Canadian Pacific Railway. Charles, a former conductor for the Canadian Pacific Railway, and Samuel, an Ontario farmer, would find this location ideal as it became a junction for shipping agricultural products. The town of Pinkham, SK was located near Flaxcombe, SK, towns situated southeast of the "rural municipality of Kindersley (No. 290). Both Flaxcombe, SK, which currently has a population of one-hundred-and-twenty residents, and Pinkham, SK, were on Route 7. Flaxcombe, SK is located 27 kilometers from the Alberta - Saskatchewan border. There is a Pinkham Cemetery near rural town of Kindersley (#2910) which is located at SW34-28-25-W3 or SW34 (section)-28 (township) - 25 (range) - W3 (meridian). Neither Samuel A. Pinkham nor Charles Pinkham are buried at Pinkham Cemetery.

Death: Samuel A. Pinkham in Pinkham, Sakachewan in 6 July 1915. Samuel A. Pinkham's estate bequeathed one-third of his assets, which included 3,200 acres in Pinkham, Saskatchewan, to his wife Maggie Pinkham in Fenelon Falls, Ontario with brother, Charles Pinkham, executor of the will. The death record noted Samuel A. Pinkham of post office in Pinkham, SK who died in Kindersley, SK on 6 July 1915. The 1916 probate took place in Kindersley, Saskatchewan.

The will bequeathed one-third of Samuel A. Pinkham's assets to Maggie Pinkham (wife) of Fenelon Falls, Ontario and one-twenty-oneth to children and grandchildren states as - Daughter: Susie Maud (Pinkham) Wessler of Sundridge, Ontario. Daughter: Fannie Pinkham of Toronto, Ontario. Daughter: Ida (Pinkham) Murdoch of Rochester, NY, USA. Son: Willfred Eddy Pinkham, address unknown. Son: Charles Pinkham, address unknown. Grandchildren (age at date of will establishment: William Leslie Shaw, active service, listed with adult children of Samuel A. Pinkham; Charles Victor Shaw, active service, age 19; Albert James Shaw of Lindsay, Ontario age 17; John Gordon Shaw of Lindsay, Ontario age 15, Eve Maud Helena Shaw of Lindsay, Ontario age 12, Jennie Addela Pinkham of Midland, Ontario age 12; Harvey Victor Pinkham of Midland, Ontario age 9; Ida Velma Pinkham of Midland, Ontario age 6; Ernest Leslie Pinkham of Midland, Ontario age 4.

The text reads: "In the surrogate court of the Judicial District of Kindersley in the Estate of Samuel A. Pinkham, deceased, the petition of Charles W. Pinkham, of the post office of Pinkham, in the Province of Saskatchewan, humbly shows that Samuel A. Pinkham, late of the post office of Pinkham, aforesaid, deceased, died at the town of Kindersley on or about the sixth day of July A.D. 1915, and at the time of his death, had fixed his place of abode on the North East quarter of Section Thirty (30) in Township Twenty-eight (28) in Range Twenty-five (25) West of the Third Meridian in the Judicial District of Kindersley. That this aid deceased in his life time duly made his last will and testament bearing date the second of July 1915.... The value of his property does not exceed Four thousand and Thirteen ($4,013.00): Household Goods $9, farming equipment (plow, mill seeder_ $190, horse ($100), Securities and Money ($480), Cash in Hand ($34) and Real Estate ($3,200).

Scheule A is referred in the affidavit and relationship of: Charles W. Pinkham and sworn to on the 29th day of June 1916 in Pinkham, Saskatchewan.

~Charles W. Pinkham:

Birth: 11 June 1855, Ontario, Canada

Married: 27 July 1881 to Lavina Corey, Lowell, MA, USA

Death: Unknown post 1916 (*not SK-ON-QC or BC, Canada; MA, NY, ME, CA, USA*)

Charles Pinkham was the youngest of Comfort and Elizabeth's children. At age twenty-two he was baptized in the Frelighsburg, Quebec, Anglican Church of his Quebec ancestors. He then left Quebec and married a Quebec-native, Lavina A. Corey, in Lowell, MA on 27 July 1881. Charles W. Pinkham became a naturalized American citizen on 21 November 1893. His wife, Lavina (Corey) Pinkham, was buried in the Monteregie Quebec Cemetery and a descendant of the Quebec Corey family. Her tombstone reads, "wife of C W Pinkham, b. 16 November 1853, d. 28 February 1911." After his wife's death, he moved to Saskatchewan with brother, Samuel where they were both listed in the 1911 Saskatchewan census as residing in Pinkham, SK.

11 November 1877 Baptism of Charles Pinkham, Freilighsburg, Quebec, *Methodist* Church. *"Charles son of Comfort Pinkham and Elizabeth Phelps his wife was born in the Township of Mares Province of Ontario on eleventh day of June one thousand-eight-hundred and fifty-five was baptized on the eleventh day of November one thousand eight-hundred and seventy-seven in the presence of subscribing witnesses by H. Cairns, Minister."* Source: Drouin

Certificate to Charles Pinkham of Competency as Second Mate by Lords of
        Board of Trade 5 April 1878. Office of the Registrar General of Shipping and
        Seamen.

~US Immigration year – 1877. Arrival to Lowell, Massachusetts on 14 November 1879.

1880 United State Census: Charles Pinkham, age 24, birth year – Abt. 1856
(1855), birthplace: Ontario, Canada, Home in 1880: Lowell, Middlesex,
Massachusetts, Race – White, Marital Status – Single, *Father's Birthplace –
Ontario, Canada, Mother's Birthplace – Ontario, Canada,* Occupation:
Carpenter, Boarder. *Source: 1880 Census, Tenth Census of the United States (NARA). Census Place:
Lowell, Middlesex, Massachusetts.*

27 July 1881 Marriage of Charles W. Pinkham: Charles Pinkham born 11 June
1855 in Ontario, Canada, railroad conductor, married Lavina A. Corey
(born 1852, Quebec to parents Luther and Huldah A. Corey) in Lowell,
Massachusetts. Parents: Father – Comfort; Mother – Elizabeth). *Source:
Massachusetts Vital Records 1840-1915 New England Historic Genealogical Society, Boston, Massachusetts.*

Letter from Charles W. Pinkham Real Estate Agent, dated Lowell, MA.
May,1892 – *"My friend Linnie, Your letter has just arrived and I will say
that your potatoes are worth from 45-50 cents for a bushel, and I will give you that for
them if you ship it right away. About horses, I have go to buy one soon. The one I have
is with foal and I will have to return it out to pasture soon. What is your horse worth
now? If I do not trade my land for one, I will send for him soon. All the folks are well as
usual. Write soon. From your friend, Charles. W. Pinkham*, 35 Merrimack Street
(Lowell, MA, USA)." *Source: Missisquoi Museum, Stanbridge, Quebec*

United States Naturalization Records 21 November 1893: Petition Charles W.
Pinkham, age 38, birthdate – 11 June 1855 in Manvers, Ontario, Canada.
Arrival: 14 November 1879; Arrival Place: Lowell, Massachusetts. Petition date:
21 November 1879. Petition Place: Lowell, Massachusetts, USA. Petition
Number 1154. *Source: National Archives at Boston, Waltham, Massachusetts, ARC Title: copies of Petitions and
Records of Naturalization in New England Courts; Records of the immigration and Naturalization Service, 1787-2004*

1900 United States Census: Charles W. Pinkham. Age 44. Born June 1855. Real
Estate Agent. Married 21 years. Born Canada (English). Parents born Canada
(English). Owned home and house. Resided 21 years in USA; arrived 1879.
Wife: Lavina Pinkham age 47 born March 1853. Born Canada (English).
Parents born Canada (English). Zero children born; zero children died. 19 years
married.

1910 United States Census: Charles W. Pinkham, Age in 1910 – 55,
Birthplace – Canada, Home in 1910 – Lowell Ward 1, Middlesex,
Massachusetts, Street – Anne, House number – 29, Race – White,
Immigration year – 1877, Head of Household, Married, Spouse's name –
Lavina Pinkham, Father's Birthplace – Canada, Mother's Birthplace –
Canada, Native Tongue – English, Occupation – Agent, Industry – Real
Estate, Employer – Own Account, Home – Rent, Naturalization Status –
Naturalized, Able to Read - Yes, Able to Write – Yes, Years Married – 29,

Household Members – Lavina Pinkham, age 56; Charles W. Pinkham, Age 55. *Source: NARA, Department of Commerce and Labor, Bureau of Census, Thirteenth Census of the United States 1910*

<u>27 February 1911 Commonwealth of Massachusetts Certificate of Death</u>: Lavina A. Pinkham (nee Corey) (Charles W. Pinkham). Residence Street: 29 Anne Street, Lowell, MA. Occupation: Boarding Housekeeper. Married. Born 16 March 1852 Stanbridge, Canada East (Quebec). Died: 58 years, 11 months and 12 days. Father: Luther Corey born Stanbridge, Canada East. Mother: Aurilla Martindale born Stanbridge, Canada East. Cause of death: Cardiac asthma between 3 February 1911 to 27 February 1911. Buried Stanbridge, Canada East on 4 March 1911.

> ~Lavina Pinkham – death date – 16 March 1853 – Lavina A. Pinkham, birth date: 16 March 1853, death date 28 February 1911, Cemetery – Ridge Cemetery, Burial – Monteregie Region, Quebec, Canada, Bio: Lavina A. Corey, wife of C. W. Pinkham (Married 27 July 1881 in Lowell, Massachusetts, USA). Parents: Luther Corey (1825 – 1887) & Aurilla Martindale Corey (1824-1861), Sibling – Julia A. Corey *Akerly*. *Source: FindAGrave Canada*

<u>1911 Canada Census:</u> Charles Pinkham, Male, Single, Birth date: June 1855, Birth place: United States of America (*wrong*), Head of household. Immigration year – 1909, Race – English, Province – Saskatchewan, District – Moosejaw, District number – 211, Sub-district – 115, Household Members: Charles Pinkham, age 56; Samuel Pinkham, Age 59. *Source: Library and Archives Canada, 1911 Census Place, Moosejaw, Saskatchewan*

<u>Charles W. Pinkham:</u> Death: post 1916 unknown (*Not in CA, MA, ME, NY USA or SK, ON, QC or BC, Canada*)

As noted from Samuel A. Pinkham's history, "pioneer realtor" Charles W. Pinkham is credited for founding Pinkham, Saskatchewan, a town with a post office and station along the Canadian National railroad route from Saskatoon to Calgary, Alberta. When his brother, farmer Samuel Pinkham died in 1915, Charles W. Pinkham became executor of the will which noted Samuel A. Pinkham owned 3,200 acres of land in this town near Kindersley, SK. Where Charles W. Pinkham moved next is unconfirmed. Although many "Charles (W.) Pinkham" named individuals existed in the United States and Canada, the son of Comfort and Elizabeth Pinkham's death date was searched for post 1916 and not found in SK, ON, QC or BC, Canada nor MA, ME, NY or CA, USA.

The problem of ancestry and rumor is confirmed from text my grandfather, Robert Earlby Pinkham, who wrote: "John (Wesley Pinkham) had two brothers and a sister Cynthia who married a Wright in the Lindsay area. Brother Charles headed west...brother Sam went back to New York..." "Sam" did not head to New York but instead died in Pinkham, Saskatchewan where he owned 3,200 acres of farmland and had moved with his brother, Charles who initially moved to Quebec then Lowell, Massachusetts – or East - after getting baptized at age twenty-two in the exact

Frelighsburg, Quebec church where his parents were married. After his Stanbridge-Quebec-born wife died, Charles went "West" (Saskatchewan) with his brother, Samuel (who did not go to New York). Again, the children of Comfort and Elizabeth Pinkham (Generation 8) were Cynthia, Electra, Mary and, likely, Edwin, born in Quebec with Willard, John Wesley, Jane, Samuel and Charles W. Pinkham born in Ontario.

JOHN WESLEY PINKHAM (Generation 8) was Comfort and Elizabeth Pinkham child born in Ontario, Canada. Elizabeth Phelps was buried in the same cemetery as John Wesley and his wife in Little Britain, Victoria Country, Ontario so it can be assumed the widow Elizabeth Pinkham lived near son, John Wesley. John Wesley was born on 20 September 1845. When his father died, he was listed in the 1861 census as working on a farm. He married (m1) Emma Harris (born abt. 1849) prior to the 1871 Census where the couple was recorded as "Wesleyan Methodists" living in the sub-district of Ops in Brock County, Ontario with Emma Harris Pinkham age twenty-two and John Pinkham age twenty-five. Emma Harris was likely the sister of William Harris, husband of John Wesley's sister, Jane. After Emma Harris Pinkham died (The Orono Cemetery headstone reads: In memory, wife of John Pinkham, died 19 January 1872 age 22 and 11 months), John Pinkham married (m2) Sarah Ann Irwin on 20 November 1872. The text from the "*1872 Victoria News*, Vol. 23, Page 399" reads: "John Pinkham, 27, widower, farmer, Clark, Ops, son of Comfort and Elizabeth, married Sarah Ann Irwin, 19, Mariposa, daughter of Robert and Mary J., Witness Eretus Smith and William Galbraith, both of Mariposa, November 20, 1872, Mariposa." John Wesley and Sarah Ann Pinkham are buried in an Anglican Church cemetery in Little Britain with Elizabeth Phelps Pinkham.

John Wesley Pinkham (8) was described by his grandson Robert Earlby Pinkham (10) as being a mild-mannered man, gentile of character and short of stature but robust and energetic. He operated a farm in the area surrounding Little Britain until, after three barns burned down, two a result of lightening, he moved the family of seven into town (Sunderland, Ontario) during 1915. When his horse grew too old to haul the buggy and mail, a job acquired late in his life, John Wesley Pinkham bought a Model T Ford. His grandson, Robert Earlby Pinkham, had "the distinction and pleasure" of teaching him how to drive when John Wesley Pinkham was seventy-four years old and Robert Earlby Pinkham was fifteen. For a while, when Robert Earlby Pinkham had problems with the brake, his grandfather, John Wesley Pinkham, would holler, "Whoa-o-a."

Sarah Ann Irwin was born on 8 February 1855 in Ontario and died 3 September 1994 in Little Britain, Victoria County, Ontario, Canada. The Irwin family were Wesley Methodists from Ireland. Sarah's father, Robert Irwin has lineage tracing back to 1761 in County of Monaghan, Ireland (Sarah's mother was Mary Jane Taylor of Cavan County, Ireland). A book written about Robert Irwin (b. 1813, d. 1876) was printed in 1921. According to my grandfather Robert Earlby (10), "Sarah Anne was a fairly large woman of regal bearing and seemed to be in command of all situations. I was always careful as to what I said or did in her presence. Following a visit to my grandparents as a small boy, I had to write and thank them for having a real nice visit. For the lack of something additional to say, I mentioned the only exception was, I didn't get quite enough to eat. For this false observation, I was, in due course, properly chastised." (*Irwin*

Family Tree located on page 286)

The children of JOHN WESLEY and Sarah (Irwin) PINKHAM (Generation 9) were:

~Mary Estelle (Minnie) Pinkham: Born 19 December 1873, Ops Township, Ontario. Died 28 March 1917, Little Britain, Victoria County, Ontario. According to Robert Earlby Pinkham, "Minnie was the first child and a replica of her mother Sarah Anne. She taught at the Royal Oak School four miles from the family home. Her means of transportation was her own pony and rig. One of her trials was she had as one of her pupils her brother Lorne (Robert Earlby's father) in his High School entrance year. On at least one occasion she had to expel him from the classroom. To get even, Lorne drove the pony and buggy home. This action backfired as his father (John Wesley Pinkham) sent Lorne Pinkham back with the buggy and pony for his sister and ordered Lorne to walk home. Minnie never married. She taught school for half of her short life dying at age thirty-nine of appendicitis."

~LAWRENCE MOWBRAY (LORNE) PINKHAM: Born 11 August 1875, Mariposa, Ontario. Died 1945, Brock Township, Ontario, Married Annie Loretta Gordon (b. 1878, Toronto; d. 27 April 1960, daughter of John Gordon and Mary McDonald) on 4 September 1901 in Brock Township.

According to his son, Robert Earlby Pinkham (10), Lorne (9) was an equal blend of his mother and father and a happy lad and full of mischief. He stayed with his parents on the farm until he met Annie Gordon, a comely Scottish lass who played the organ in the church near Cannington. Because Annie was a Presbyterian and Lorne Anglican, a simple compromise was in order. They joined the Methodist Church in Sunderland. During 1914, they sold the farm and purchased a Furniture and Funeral business (L. M. Pinkham & Sons) in Sunderland, Ontario. Lorne did not completely leave farm ownership behind as he rented a small parcel of land close to town with a barn where he kept show horses and several cows. The farm was more for his personal amusement and diversion to keep his sons busy before and after school. Lorne loved the farm and especially good horses.

Lorne Pinkham established L. M. Pinkham & Son Funeral Home after purchasing the business from Robert Charter, the founder. The L. M. Pinkham & Son Funeral Home was sold by his son, Ralph Pinkham, and became the Thorne Funeral Home, a hundred-plus year old continuous business with only three owners and a "Pinkham Chapel" still in existence today.

Annie Gordon was the daughter of John and Mary (McDonald) Gordon born Scotland. John Gordon was born 1841 and Mary McDonald born 1842. Their children, all born Eldon, Victoria North, Ontario, Canada were: Dugal Gordon born 1863; Elsie Jane Gordon born 1865, John Gordon born 1869, Mary Ellen Gordon born 1870, James Alexander Gordon born 1874, William Gordon born 1875, Ann G. Gordon born 1879 and Margaret Gordon born abt. 1880 -1881. The family was listed as C. Presbyterian.

The Gordon Family Bible notes the mother's name was Mary McDonald. "Father" (John Gordon) was born 11 January 1841. Children births were: Dougal Gordon born 11

January 1863, Elsie Jane Gordon born 16 December 1864, John Gordon born 23 June 1868, Mary Ellen Gordon born 21 December 1869, James Gordon born 10 July 1873, Willie (William) born 20 April 1875, Annie (Loretta) born 23 November 1878 and Maggie (Margaret) born 28 September 1880. The Bible is inscribed to son, "James A. Gordon of Vroomanton, Ontario on 25 December 1904 from "Mother and Father." The 1891 Brock, Ontario North census noted both John and Mary Gordon as born in Scotland and members of the "Free Church." The 1901 Ontario census recorded the family as Presbyterian with Annie Gordon age 22, her parents, John and Mary (McDonald) Gordon age 60, brother James Gordon age 27 and brother William Gordon age 22. John Gordon's brother, Andrew Gordon, age 51 born Scotland 1836 was also listed, along with Annie B. Gordon, a Gordon grandchild born 18 March 1898 age 2. The 1901 census noted John and Andrew Gordon arrived in Ontario, Canada during 1846. The census record incorrectly listed a last name of, "Gorders," rather than, "Gordon.'

As Lorne's granddaughter, Barbara Anne Pinkham (11) recalls, the girls (she and her sister, Bette) would love to ride in the buggy while a show horse pulled it. Once, Barbara Pinkham, who was not quite five years old, was told to stay with a show horse, but she was scared so she ran inside leaving the horse alone. Barbara recalls her grandfather was cross because as he stated, his granddaughter didn't stay put but the show horse did. Along with the show horses, Barbara remembers cows behind the barn. The furniture and funeral business was located behind the house and where both Barbara and Bette Pinkham (11) played on visits, running among the caskets and furniture then typing letters to pretend customers in the office. On one occasion, the young sisters bravely touched the hand of a deceased person. The library in the Lorne Pinkham house had a player piano which both girls loved to listen to when visiting their grandparents. Their grandparents and parents were usually found in the library playing weekend bridge games. However, once while the grandparents and parents were playing bridge on Sunday, "Doc" Oliver, the Methodist minister, stopped by and Barbara and Bette watched while the Pinkham elders hid their cards to removed the bridge game from sight.

Lorne Pinkham (9) was elected member of township councils and became the Deputy Warden of the County (Reeve of the County, an executive county Canadian position). He was also a Mason chosen as Master for the Sunderland lodge. Lorne Pinkham was an active and personable person who loved people and life. In the fall of 1947 he was diagnosed with a brain tumor. His granddaughter Barbara Pinkham (11) remembers him lying in his bed and him asking, "aren't you going to kiss me goodbye?" She did, and that was the last time she saw him as she left for a weekend at a friend's lake cottage. Lawrence Mowbray Pinkham died six days before his seventy-third birthday. Lorne Pinkham's funeral was under Masonic auspicies.

The Uxbrodge Times-Journal: Thursday 12 August 1948 -

Lorne M. Pinkham Passes to His Reward

In the death on Thursday, last week of Mr. L. M. Pinkham, "Lorne" as he was so well known for so many years throughout this district, the community loses one of its most popular and highly respected residents.

He was suddenly stricken with paralysis a little over a year ago and for a short time improved and was able to get around a little, but a few months ago took a turn for the worse and despite the very best of care and attention gradually weakened until the end came early Thursday evening.

The funeral, one of the largest ever held in the community, took place at the Sunderland cemetery on Sunday, August 8th, 1948, services being conducted in the United Church by Rev. Mr. Pelley assisted by Rev. Mr. Corscadden. The pall-bearers were his four sons, Ted Johnson and Rupert Harrison.

The late Lorne M. Pinkham was born near Enniskillen, Ontario, a son of the late John Pinkham and Sarah Ann Irwin, and came with his parents to Brock Township when a very young lad. For many years they farmed in Brock. In 1902 Lorne married Miss Annie Gordon and in 1915 he took over the late Robert Charter undertaking and furniture business which he continued until a short time ago when he took his son Ralph into the business with him, who continues to carry on.

All of his life he was a most honorable and high-principled man, industrious and hard-working, and took a great interest in everything in the community, where he will be greatly missed.

He served the township as Councillor, Deputy-Reeve and Reeve for many years, was a member, director and president of the Brock Agricultural Society; the Library Board, Cemetery Board, and for many years on the School Boards. It was in Masonry that he took perhaps his greatest interest and was very active member of the King Edward Lodge No. 64, A.F. & A. M. passing through all the offices and continued to devote a great deal of his time and energy to the welfare of the lodge. This was particularly noticeable as the funeral services were held under Masonic auspices and one of the largest attendance of officers and members of outside lodges were present at the funeral from all parts of the district showing the high esteem in which he was held by members of the craft. He was also member of the Beaverton Lodge of the Eastern Star and in his younger days of the Orange and Black Knights.

His one particular hobby was horses. He surely loved a good horse and always had one or two particularly good stepping drivers that he took the greatest delight in attending practically all the Fall Fairs in the district with, and won a great many prizes.

Left to mourn his passing are his sorrowing wife, and four sons, Earlby of Leaside; Gordon, Sunderland; Wesley of Bowmanville and Ralph at home. A brother Milton F. of Leipzig, Saskatchewan and sister, Mrs. (Dr.) Piper, Chicago, Illinois, to whom the deepest sympathy is extended in their sad loss of a kind and loving husband and father.

~ Catherine Harriet (Hattie) Louise Pinkham Munsie: Born in 1881, Mariposa, Victoria County, Ontario, Canada. Died abt. 12 October 1935 age 55 in Winnipeg, Manitoba, Canada. Married James Munsie on 22 August 1906, Mariposa Township, Victoria, Ontario. James A. Munsie was born 3 March 1877 Ontario and died on 12 August 1839 in Winnipeg, Manitoba, Canada. The marriage license records Hattie Pinkham as age 25 born 1881 in Mariposa, Victoria, Ontario, a "farmer's daughter" whose parents were

John and Annie Pinkham. James Munsie was age 29 born 1877, the son of Alexander and Mary (Williamson) Munsie. Hattie was the aunt Robert Earlby Pinkham did not remember well except she had pretty, reddish-brown hair. She settled in Minnedosa, Manitoba after marrying James Munsie moving later to Winnipeg where her husband worked in the grain exchange. The children (10) of Harriet and James Munsie were Lillian Jean Munsie (b. 7 June 1907, Minnedosa, Manitoba; Married Len Greer a mining engineer and moved to Thunder Bay, Ontario), Mary Beryl Munsie (b. 21 March 1909, Minnedosa, Manitoba; Married Perry. Bower and resided in Winnipeg), James Irwin Munsie (b. 9 September 1914, Minnedosa, Manitoba) and Alexandria (Lexie) Munsie (b. 27 May 1912, Minnedosa, Manitoba). Roberta Munsie was born in 1916, Minnedosa, Manitoba as recorded in the Canada Prairie Province Census of 1916 of which James A. and Hattie L. Munsie, both born Ontario, were listed with ethnicity of Scotch.

The 1926 Canada Prairie Province Census of Winnipeg, Manitoba, Canada recorded James Munsie age 48 born Ontario 1878 and Hattie Munsie age 44 born Ontario 1882 as Scotch with Munsie children born Manitoba: Lillian Munsie age 18 born 1908, Mary Munsie age 17 born 1909, Alexandra Munsie age 13 born 1913, James Munsie age 11 born 1915, Roberta Munsie age 10 born 1916 and Robert Munsie age 8 born 1918.

The obituary for Harriet Pinkham Munsie reads: *Mrs. J. A. Munsie - Harriet Munsie, 55, wife of James A. Munsie, died Tuesday at the home of her daughter, Mrs. Perry S. Bower, 418 Kingston Crescent. Burial will take place Thursday in Elmwood cemetery following funeral services in the A. B. Gardiner Chapel at 2:45 pm. A native of Lindsay, Ontario, Mrs. Munsie came to reside in Winnipeg 30 years ago. Four daughters and three sons survive her besides her husband: Mrs. Perry S. Bower, Lillian, Lexie, Roberta, James, Robert and Wesley, all of Winnipeg.* The article was printed on 14 October 1935.

The obituary for James A. Munsie reads: *James A. Munsie - James Alexander Munsie, grain inspector for the Ogilvie Flour Mill Company since 1916, died Saturday at his home, 39 Lipton Street. He was 65 years of age. Born in Bolton County, Ontario, he came West in 1902 as a young man. He had been employed by Ogilvie's for 38 years, and for a number of years was grain buyer for the company in Minnedosa, Manitoba before he became a grain inspector. He was a member of Chalmers United Church. Surviving him are four daughters, Lillian, Mary, Lexie and Roberta and three sons, Robert, Wesley and James. Mrs. Munsie died three years ago. Funeral services will be held at 2:45 pm in Gardner's Funeral Home. Burial will be at the Elmwood Cemetery.* The article was printed on 14 August 1939.

Both James A. and Harriet (Louise) (Pinkham) Munsie were buried in Winnipeg, Manitoba, Canada at the Elmwood Cemetery.

Son Wesley Pinkham Munsie, born 15 November 1921 Manitoba, moved to Vancouver where he attended University of British Columbia during the early 1940s where met his wife, Florence Mercer. He enlisted in the Canadian navy and became the youngest ever training officer for the Navy and commanded a Fairmile in Halifax. He retired 1945 after the war and returned to Vancouver and UBC, then attended Univeristy of Oregon's dental program because it allowed for both a BA and dental degree which he achieved by communting between Vancouver and University of Oregon. Wesley Pinkham Munsie became president of the Canadian Dental Association, the BC College of Dental Surgeons and British Columbia Lions. Three children from his marriage are: Cindy Munsie Grauer (b. 21 May 1950 Vancouver, BC; Pinkham family genealogist), James Mercer Munsie (b. 27 October 1951 Vancouver, BC; UBC BA & Queens Law School Kingston, Ontario graduate), Wesley Ward Munsie (b. 3 August 1957 Vancouver, BC; USC BA and MBA Thunderbird School at Arizona State)

~Lillian Elizabeth Pinkham Piper: Born 10 December 1879 in Emily, Ontario. Married Lake, Indiana on 15 April 1924 to Dr. Charles Wiliam Piper. Died 20 October 1948 in Chicago, three months after her brother Lorne Pinkham passed away. Lilly was a beautiful blonde, according her nephew, Robert Earlby Pinkham (10) who described Lilly as his favorite aunt who called him, "Robbie," while he called her, "Aunt Lil." On her several visits to his house she came loaded with tricycles, mechanical trains and other toys for her nephews. Lilly was a nurse in Los Angeles, California, where she met then married Dr. Charles Piper who was born in Illinois and whose parents were from New York and Canada. Dr. and Mrs. Charles Piper moved to Chicago and had a daughter named Mary Alice Piper (10). Mary Alice married T.L. Davis and had two daughters, (11) Mary Lou Davis (b. 7 January 1949) and Kathy Jo Davis (b. 24 August 1952). Kathy Jo married unknown Pauts. Dr. Charles Piper was a Mayflower descendant.

As per recorded documents, Indiana Marriage records of 1811-2019 note Charles William Piper married Lillian Pinkham on 15 April 1924 in Lake, Indiana. Illinois Cook County birth certificates confirm their daughter, Mary Alice Piper, was born in Chicago, Illinois on 31 October 1925 to Charles William Piper age 60 born 1865 Chicago and Lillian Pinkham age 43 born Lindsay, Ontario, Canada. Dr. Charles W. Piper died on 11 July 1934 at age 69 (birthdate 11 June 1865, Chicago, Illinois). His parents were Thomas Piper and Alice McGorry. He died in Chicago and was buried at Mount Hope Cemetery. The address of Dr. and Mrs. Charles Piper in 1934 was 6748 South Union Avenue (Highland Park), Chicago, Illinois. A daughter named Jean Minette Rupany was born 1 February 1941 (parents: Mary Alice Piper and Henry Louis Rupany) to Mary Alice Piper. Mary Alice Piper born 1926 married in Saline, Arkansas on 20 April 1947 to Thomas L. Davis, born 10 May 1927 Arkansas. Thomas L. Davis died at age 58 on 30 October 1985 when he was buried at Mount Hope Cemetery, the son of Thomas Luther and Dorothy (Binns) Davis. Mary Alice Piper Davis, daughter of Lillian Pinkham Piper, resided at 9417 Country Club Drive in Evergreen Park, Cook County, Illinois.

~Annie Electra Pinkham Rumney: Born 6 March 1883, Victoria County, Ontario. Died 11 April 1911, Little Britain, Mariposa, Victoria County, Ontario. She married Robert John Rumney (b. 24 December 1870, Somerville, Victoria County) in 1907 in Mariposa Township, Victoria County. Annie Electra was a teacher who died at age 29. Annie and Robert Rumney's child (10) was: (Mary) Lillian Rumney (b. 18 December 1907, Mariposa, Ontario). Lillian (10) married Charles Aubrey Bowins and their children were (11): Lois Isabel Bowins (b. 13 November 1920; d. 6 January 1993), Robert (Bob) Bowins (b. 11 April 1930; d. December 1979, Ottawa), William Lorne Bowins (b. 8 January 1934; d. 11 July 1942) and Elizabeth Anne Bowins (b.1 June 1938; d. January 1993) who had a daughter Anne (12) who resided in Ottawa, Ontario, Canada.

~(Frank) Milton Ferguson Pinkham: Born 12 January 1885, Ontario. Married Mary Jane Mutchmore (b. 25 November 1884, Providence Bay, Manitoulin Island, Ontario) on 17 September 1913. Died 26 September 1957 in New Westminster, British Columbia.

The 1921 Canadian census records M. F. (Milton "Frank" Feguson) Pinkham as living in Saskatoon, Saskatchewan, which is near Pinkham, Saskatchewan, a town founded by his uncles, Samuel and Charles Pinkham. "M. F." Pinkham and Mary Jane (Mutchmore) Pinkham's children (Generation 10) born Saskatoon, Saskatchewan were Altamyra (b. 1914), Donald McKechnie (b. 1916), Neil Wesley (b. 1918) and John M. (b. 1925) Pinkham. Milton Pinkham, a CPR railroad station agent, was later stationed at Hardisty, Alberta prior to moving to Kelfield then Handel, Saskatchewan by 1944. He married Mary Jane Mutchmore born 1883 in Ontario, Canada to parents John and Christina (Mckechnie) Mutchmore. The 31 March 1901 Ontario Canada census recorded Mary Jane Mutchmore with parents, John and Christina Mutchmore, and siblings, Wesley, Annie and Grace Mutchmore. Also present was (Mary Jane McKenchie's parents or siblings), Annie McKenchie and Neil McKechnie, plus Merthie McIntyre. John and Christina Mutchmore moved to Saskatchewan in 1916 with children.

It is assumed Altamyra Pinkham was born on 5 May 1914 in Wilkie, Saskatchewan. Wilkie is a station on the Canadian Pacific Railway line from Portage la Prairie from Saskatoon to Edmonton, 160 kilometers west of Saskatoon. Wilkie was established with post office on 2 February 1907 and named for Daniel Robert Wilkie who was president of the Imperial Bank of Canada and packer of the Canadian Pacific Railway. As Milton Frank Pinkham worked for CPR, it is likely he moved stations along the line. Altamyra Pinkham married Victor Booth. A child (11) of Altamyra Pinkham Booth was named Anne Christine Booth who married Jan Vuurens. (Altamyra Pinkham - Mother. Spouse: Victor Booth. Child: Anne Christine Vuurens. Other: Jan Vuurens. *Source: Canada, British Columbia Death Registrations, 1872-1986*). Altamyra Mutchmore Pinkham Booth, and her husband and family moved with her father, Milton (Frank) Pinkham, and mother, Mary Jane (Mutchmore) Pinkham and brothers, Donald Pinkham and Neil Pinkham, to Vancouver and New Westminster, British Columbia while brother, John Pinkham and wife Dorothy, remained in Saskatoon, Saskatchewan.

> Altamyra Muchmor Pinkham: Spouse: Victor Cecil Booth. Other: John Booth, Rosina Quick. *Source: Canada, British Columbia Death Registrations, 1872-1986*
>
> > Victor Cecil Booth; Sex: Male; Death date: 26 July 1979; Death Place: New Westminster, British Columbia, Canada; Birth Date: 24 May 1916. Birthplace: New Westminster, British Columbia. Marital Status: Married. Father's name: John Booth. Mother's name: Rosina Quick. Spouse's name: Altamyra Muchmor Pinkham.

Donald McKechnie Pinkham was born on 5 May 1916 in Wilkie, Buffalo No. 409, Saskatchewan, Canada. His father was M. F. Pinkham, mother was Mary Pinkham and siblings were Altamyra, Neil and John Pinkham. Donald was also possibly born Scott, Saskatchewan. He was a CPR Railway station agent like his father in towns which included Kelfield during 1940-1941 then Handel, the next CPR station north. When he returned as a private in the army, given injuries he was released from service then, according to the Edmonton Journal, returned to "Hardisty." Two months prior to this article, the <u>Star Phoenix</u> reported him residing with his parents at Handel which is twenty miles south of Wilkie, SK. Donald Pinkham married Helen Lydia Tadsen (b. 1926 Saskatchewan, dau. of Richard and Martha Tadsen; Swift's Current #137, Saskatchewan *1926 Canada Prairie Provinces Census*: Helen Tadsen born 1926 SK with siblings, Esther, Ella, Hilda and Walter Tadsen). A child of Donald Mckenchie and Helen (Tadsen) Pinkham was Helen Lydia Pinkham (*Source: British Columbia Death Registrations 1872-1986*). Donald Pinkham moved to New Westminster, British Columbia with his father, mother, sister, the Altamyra Booth family and brother, Neil Pinkham. He died in Vancouver, BC (Donald Mckechnie Pinkham. Birth: 5 May 1916. Death: 12 May 1981 Vancouver, British Columbia, Canada. Father: Frank Melville Pinkham. Mother: Mary Jane Muchmor. Spouse: Helen Tadson.) *Source: Canada, British Columbia death Registrations, 1872-1986*

Donald Mckechnie Pinkham's Spouse died 1977. Spouse: Helen Lydia Pinkham. Other: Tadsen. *Source: Canada, British Columbia Death Registrations, 1872-1986*
Helen Lydia Pinkham. Sex: Female. Age: 52. Death Date: 23 Nov. 1977. Death Place: New Westminster, British Columbia, Canada. Birthdate: 27 March 1926. Birth Year: 1925. Birthplace: Saskatchewan. Marital Status: Married. Father's Name: Tadsen. Spouse's Name: Donald Mckechnie Pinkham

Neil Wesley Pinkham born 4 July 1918 in Scott, SK where it was recorded his father was M. F. Pinkham, mother was Mary Pinkham and siblings were Donald and John Pinkham. *Source: Canada, Prairie Provinces Census, 1926.*   Neil Pinkham married Myra Elizabeth Tweten (b. 31 Dec 1921) and died in Strathmore, Alberta, Canada: Neil Wesley Pinkham. Born: 1918. Death: 1995. Burial: Strathmore, Alberta, Canada. Cemetery: Strathmore Cemetery. *Source: FindAGrave* Neil Pinkham's obituary reads: "*On March 1, 1995, Mr. Neil Wesley Pinkham of Strathmore passed away at the age of 75 years. Survived by his loving wife Norma, his four children, Wesley (Jean), Sharon (Ray) Goulet, Marilyn Pinkham and Don, one brother, John (Dorothy), four granddaughters and two grandsons, two great-granddaughters and two great-grandsons… Predeceased by his parents, his brother Don and sister Myra, Neil was a Northern Alberta Railway station master for thirty-six years…*"

The youngest child of Milton Francis and Mary Jane (Mutchmore) Pinkham, named for Milton's father, was John M. Pinkham. John Pinkham's gravestone notes he died at age 81 in 2007 and was born in 1925. He is buried with his wife, Dorothy M. Pinkham (1922-2004) at Hillcrest Memorial Gardens in Saskatoon, SK, Canada. *Source: FiindAGrave*

Milton Francis Pinkham died in 1957 in Vancouver (Child: Milton Francis Pinkham. Father: John Pinkham. Spouse: Irwin. Other: Mary Jane Mutchmor). *Source: Canada, British Columbia Death Registrations, 1872-1986*) (Milton Francis Pinkham. Birth: 12 January 1885. Death: 26 September 1957. Burial: Greater Vancouver, British Columbia, Canada. *Source: FindAGrave* (Brother Lorne Pinkham's obituary noted in 1948 Milton resided 16 miles from Wilke in Leipzig, SK.) Milton Francis Pinkham's wife died in 1981:
Mary Jane Pinkham. Sex: Female. Age: 96. Death Date: 19 March 1981. Death Place: New Westminster, British Columbia, Canada. Birth Date: 25 November 1884. Birth Year: 1885. Birthplace: Providence Bay, Ontario. Marital Status: Widowed. Father's name: John Mutchmar. Mother's name: Christine Mckeehnie. Spouse's name: Francis Melville Pinkham.

The sons (Donald, Neil and John Pinkham - Generation 10) of Milton Ferguson Pinkham were the only male heirs of this branch's Pinkham surname, and their male descendants the only source of Pinkham surnames to continue the John Wesley Pinkham (Generation8 from Richard Pinkham1) line.

~John Wesley Pinkham: Born 30 July 1887, Victoria County, Ontario, d. 21 May 1906, Little Britain, Victoria Country, Ontario. John Wesley (9) died of appendicitis at age nineteen.

The children (10) of LAWRENCE MOWBRAY and Annie (Gordon) PINKHAM were:

~ROBERT EARLBY PINKHAM: (b. 4 March 1904, Ontario; d. 9 March 1979, Sarasota, FL, USA) Co-author of text and story to follow.

~Gordon Franklin (Gerald) Pinkham: (b. 17 May 1905, Ontario; d. 13 November 1975, Ontario) Married Jessie C. Harris (b. 1914; d. 1992) in 26 May 1934. Gordon was a teacher who became a principal of elementary schools at Sunderland, Milford Bay and the Muskoka Lakes District. Gordon was most like his mother Annie Gordon, whose Scottish ancestry reflected a somewhat serious approach to life. He had a dry sense of humor that was always ready to be used. He served as Master of his father's Mason Lodge in Sunderland and later became Deputy Grand Master of the Victoria, Ontario district. He died of cancer at his home in Bracebridge, Ontario.

~John Wesley Pinkham: (b. 7 September 1907, Ontario; d. 11 February 1969, Ontario) After completing high school "Wes" joined the Bank of Commerce in his hometown in Sunderland. He married Dorothy Ruth Babcock (b. 4 May 1910; d. 28 August 1983) in July of 1938. He served in numerous roles at the bank from accounting to management. He eventually was moved to the head office in Toronto where he worked in the Properties department until retiring in 1967. He fell ill to pneumonia in 1971 and died at his Lindsay, Ontario home. John Wesley and Dorothy Pinkham's children (11) were Lorna Grace (b. 22 June 1930 Belleville, Ontario; d. 27 July 2011, Ontario) and *PRIVATE* (b. 5 March 1953, Lindsay, Ontario; resides Ontario). The daughters of Robert Earlby Pinkham called this John Wesley Pinkham, "Uncle Wes."

~Ralph Lawrence Pinkham: (b. 22 July 1909, Ontario; d. 30 May 1983, Sunderland, Ontario) Married Iva M. Bresaur (b. 1911; d. 1979) on 24 September 1936. Ralph, according to his oldest brother, "Earl," took "considerable flack and buffeting from his three older brothers. He was equal to it and came on strong when he assumed the management of the funeral and furniture business while Dad (Lorne Pinkham) bowled or played with his horses at the local fall fairs."

In partnership, Lorne Pinkham (9) and Ralph Pinkham (10) got along well. Following Lorne Pinkham's death, Ralph expanded the furniture and funeral business into the neighboring town of Beaverton. He also bought a business in Cannington, another neighboring town. During 1970, he sold the business completely and retired. While vacationing in Florida he suffered a heart failure and stroke that left his right side severely crippled. He learned to live with his physical disability and remained at his home in Sunderland, Ontario. Ralph was also a Mason at the Sunderland Mason lodge.

~Anna Beryl Pinkham: (b. 1 October 1913, Ontario; d. 1 September 1916, Ontario) The only girl in the Lorne and Annie (Gordon) Pinkham family, Anna died of the measles at age three. Her rocking chair, which has a depiction of Dutch children running in front of a windmill, was given to the oldest granddaughter placing ownership in the hand of Barbara Anne Pinkham (11) and Anne Louise Manrique (12).

~ROBERT EARLBY PINKHAM: Robert Earlby "Earl" Pinkham was, as he describes, "born on March 4, 1904 on a farm 3 ½ miles from Sunderland, Ontario." When Robert Earlby was ten years old Lorne Pinkham (9) moved the family into Sunderland as he purchased the Furniture and Funeral Business. After graduating from high school Lorne Pinkham thought Robert should be a teacher so he sent his son to Peterborough Normal School (Teachers College). However, because most of his future students would be taller than him, something he felt would lead to a lack of respect, Robert Earlby went back to Lindsay Collegiate to complete his senior matriculation (first year of university). His university study was statistics. During the Spring of 1929, Robert Earlby moved to Toronto to work at Imperial Oil Limited. After two years in Toronto in 1931, he was transferred to assist in opening an Imperial Oil office in Hamilton, Ontario where he met, Margaret Webster Milne (b. 30 June 1912 Hamilton; d. 2 February 1998, Toronto) whom he married on 21 July 1935. Margaret was the daughter of James Guthrie and Christina (Breckin) Milne from Aberdeen, Scotland. She was also the youngest student in her business school studies (secretarial school) and first in her class. During 1939, the family moved back to Toronto, settled in the suburb of Leaside and purchased a home on Airdrie Road. The children (11), Barbara, Bette and Louise Pinkham graduated from Leaside High school then attended University of Toronto where Barbara and Bette graduated from Victoria College. Like his father and brothers and father, Robert Earlby was a Mason at the Sunderland Lodge. Imperial Oil was purchased by Esso (Exxon) before Robert Earlby retired. Robert Earlby, at one point, owned a motorcycle and his daughter, Barbara, remembers he enjoyed driving his cars very fast (sometimes ninety miles per hour) on country roads. Robert Earlby died of a heart attack in Sarasota, Florida where he and his wife, Margaret, resided during the winter months annually. The death certificate states Robert Earlby was a retired "Standard Oil Human Resources Executive."

Margaret Milne born on 30 June 1912 in Hamilton, Wentworth, Ontario, Canada, the eldest child of James Guthrie Milne and Christina (Brechin), both born Aberdeen, Scotland. The birth record of Margaret Webster Milne notes she was the daughter of James Milne, machinist and Christina Brechin who married 29 July 1911 in Hamilton, Ontario, Canada. The Milne-Brechin marriage record states James Guthrie Milne was age 24 and born Scotland; machinist; resident of Hamilton; Presbyterian. Christina Brechin was age 25 born Scotland, Presbyterian and the daughter of William Brechin and Elizabeth Harris. Family history noted Christina Brechin was adopted. *Source: Hamiton MacNab Presbyterian Church*

The home of James Guthrie and Christina (Brechin) Milne was 45 William Street in Hamilton, Ontario where their children, Margaret Milne (age 8), Gertrude Milne (age 6) and Douglas Milne (age 2) are recorded during the 1921 census. The youngest child was Roy Milne born post 1921. James Milne eventually became the Borden Milk delivery person for Hamilton. Grandchild Barbara Pinkham remembers Scottish bagpipers playing at her grandparent's home on New Years eve. Doug Milne married in Hamilton where he was employed as Eaton's store manager. Roy Milne married and had one child. Gertrude Milne married Harry Sisler; sons named Bob & Ken Sisler.

The marriage between Robert Earlby Pinkham and Margaret Webster Milne took place in Hamilton, Wentworth County, Ontario on 21 July 1936 when Robert Earlby Pinkham was age 32, a clerk for Esso. His religion was listed as United (Methodist), and he resided at 83 Grant Avenue in Sunderland, Ontario. His parents were recorded as: Lawrence Mowbray Pinkham and Annie Pinkham. Margaret Webster Milne was recorded as a Bookkeeper and twenty-four years old. A Spinster and Presbyterian, she resided at 45 Williams Street, Hamilton, Ontario, Canada.

The children of ROBERT and Margaret PINKHAM (11): BARBARA ANNE PINKHAM (b. 19 January 1937, Hamilton, Ontario; m. J. Manrique of California on 20 July 1963 in Toronto, Ontario, Canada; resides California, USA), Bette Margaret Pinkham (b. 7 June 1938, Hamilton; m. J. Robinson of Ontario on 1 July 1961 in Burlington, Ontario; d. 27 March 2013, Windswept Club, Nassau, Bahamas) and Louise Christine (b. 7 June 1945, m1 F. Allen/m2 B. Tiffen; resides Ontario, Canada) Pinkham.

Robert and Margaret had seven grandchildren (Generation 12 from Richard Pinkham). Bette and J. Robinson had three boys: James Robert (b. 19 January 1964, Burlington, Ontario), Jeffery Wade (b. 7 January 1967, Burlington, Ontario) and Scott Alfred (b. 6 May 1969, Burlington, Ontario) Robinson. Barbara and J. Manrique had two girls: Anne Louise (b. 31 October 1965, California, USA) and Private Manrique (b. 1967, California, USA). Louise and F. Allen had two boys: Lee Frederick (b. 27 September 1970, Ontario) and Jeremy Jay Allen (b. 26 February 1972, Ontario).

My recollection of my grandfather, ROBERT EARLBY PINKHAM (10) is he had many activities going on and did them all with a sense of humor. In 1965, the year I was born, my grandparents purchased a cottage at the end of Long Point (110 Maple Lane) that overlooked Angel Island and was located on Balsam Lake, the highest of the Kawartha Lakes on the Trent-Severn waterway lock system. Besides winterizing the property, my grandfather made wine in the basement and crafted my doll high chair and cradle in a workshop on the property. Memories with my grandfather were often boating related and include him letting me drive his boat (no matter if it was in circles), traveling through the locks to Fenelon Falls to get ice cream and accompanying him to fill the boat with gas, an errand I enjoyed because red or black licorice twine was wrapped around my wrist while we waited dockside. My grandfather also taught me how to ride my bicycle, a moment I specifically remember because I had been chatting with him, but, then upon realizing he was not alongside given I was riding my bike, I turned around to find him at the other end of the court and promptly fell off. Having read his ancestry text, I now realize my grandfather taught his seventy-four-year old grandfather to drive a Model T Ford and his young granddaughter to bike during his lifetime, moments that must have been meaningful to him.

ROBERT EARLBY PINKHAM (10) and I were not good at sitting so I accompanied him on his many outings, one of which included gardening at his Long Point plot by the tennis courts. After the gardening tool hit something, we carefully unearthed the object.

My grandfather and I were amazed to find an Indian arrowhead. We were both entranced by the find - imagining the history of the implement and how or why it ended up in the soil of a Kawartha Lake garden. We speculated about the history of the arrowhead many times after the find. The arrowhead would have been something Richard Pinkham (1) might have seen in 1634 Dover but we (Generations 10 & 12) saw it together at the Kawartha Lakes, Ontario, Canada during the 1970s.

<u>BARBARA ANNE PINKHAM</u> is Generation 11 from Richard Pinkham and my mother. She was taught piano at the University of Toronto Conservatory of Music from grades seven through eleven. Barbara studied French and German throughout high school while in honors classes (including Latin) and graduated from Leaside High at the top of her class, the only person from her high school to earn entrance to the Honors program at University of Toronto, Victoria College where she majored in Modern Languages (French, German) and Literature. The honors program meant she earned both a Canadian Bachelor's and Master's degree (MA in French and Literature) (she earned another MA in English while a US citizen). During her fifth-year she went to the U of T Ontario Secondary School (Level) Teacher Federation (OSSTF) to complete a graduate teaching certificate to teach at university, a degree she used to teach British Literature and Shakespeare courses at Stanislaus State University in Turlock, California, USA.

<u>Bette Margaret Pinkham</u> worked during high school summers at Onondaga Camp in New York, perhaps inspired by childhood summers at the First United Methodist camp with her sister, Barbara, and many Leaside neighborhood classmates. Bette graduated from University of Toronto the same year as her sister, Barbara, and earned a teaching credential, using the degree as an elementary school teacher. She was active with sports as a life-long golfer and curler, and enjoyed frequent trips to Nassau, Bahamas for years. The family owns a business which once employed three generations. The children of Bette Pinkham and J. Robinson born Burlington, Ontario are James, Jeffery and Scott Robinson.

<u>Louise Christine Pinkham</u> attended University of Toronto then resided in both Barrie, Ontario and Sarasota, Florida. Her sons born Ontario are Lee and Jeremy Allen.

If my grandfather Robert Earlby Pinkham were alive today, I would tell him our English ancestors were early settlers of both the United States of America and Canada. As he began genealogical text for his grandchildren, it was most meaningful to learn in detail the history of our family.

Anne Manrique

Generation 12 from Richard Pinkham of Dover, New Hampshire, 1633.

~ Daughters of American Revolution Patriot: Abijah Pinkham

~Mayflower Descendant: William Brewster (Pending Review. Application submitted 10/2021)

Like the mystery surrounding the "Samuel Pinkham" born in New Hampshire, there are alternative Pinkham Generation 2-4 Theories which hypothesize Richard (1) and Julia Pinkham MAY NOT HAVE had just three sons:

~Richard (b. 1640) m. Elizabeth Leighton
~John (b. 1644) m. Rose Otis
~Thomas (b. 1650)

but also:

~Elizabeth Pinkham Long (b. 1647). Married Samuel Long. Child -Deacon Robert Long
~Matthew Pinkham (b. 1648; d. 1671)
~Nathaniel Pinkham (b. 1660; d. 1689)

Also, the "Thomas Pinkham-Sarah Bunker" line is speculated to also have possibly begun from John Pinkham's (2) sons - Richard (John 2, Generation 3 from Richard Pinkham) or from Thomas (John 2, Generation 3 from Richard Pinkham).

John Pinkham (2), brother to Richard (2), is buried at Settler's Graveyard at Dover Point. He had children Richard, Thomas, Amos, Rose (Tuttle), James, Solomon, Elizabeth (Nute), Sarah and Otis Pinkham.

One alternative ancestry line has John Pinkham's son, Richard (b. 1675) and his wife (?) had children John, Richard, Ann, Elizabeth and THOMAS (Generation 4). It was this Thomas (b. 1708, Oyster River, NH; d. 1742, Dover, NH) from whom the Pinkham Quebec/Ontario line enters Canada and would change the generation arrived in Quebec from Generation 6 to Generation 7. Another assumption is that John's son Thomas (3) (b. 1678), who married Mercy Elizabeth and had children Sarah (Austin), Ebenezer, Benjamin Sr., Joseph, Mary, Richard and Martha Pinkham, also had a child named, Thomas Pinkham.

However, there is no proof in historical text to these alternative scenarios therefore the Pinkham ancestral line remains as previously stated:

Richard1Richard2Thomas3Abijah4Samuel5Samuel6Comfort7John8Lawrence9 Robert10Barbara11PinkhamAnneManrique12 (daughter of Barbara11Pinkham)

The Pinkham family moved from Canada to the United States together post 1830s.

Minnesota: Pinkham Surnames from Quebec to Minnesota

<u>Joseph Abijah and Rosina (Chartier) Pinkham</u> to Mower, MN after 1849-1858 WI.
>   Son of Samuel Junior and Theodocia (Carpenter) Pinkham.
>   <u>1860 United States Census Austin, Mower, MN:</u> Abijah Pinkham
>   >   Born 1830 Quebec (son of Samuel and Theodocia Pinkham). Wife:
>   >   Rosina (Chartier) born 1832 Canada (Quebec)
>   <u>Children of Joseph Abijah and Rosina (Chartier) Pinkham:</u>
>   >   Mary Pinkham (b. 1849, Wisconsin)
>   >   Rosina Pinkham (b. 1851, Wisconsin)
>   >   Sarah A. Pinkham (b. 1853, Wisconsin)
>   >   Samuel Pinkham (b. 1855, Wisconsin)
>   >   Theodocia Pinkham (b. 1858, Wisconsin)
>   >   John Pinkham (b. 1865, Mower, MN)
>   <u>1865 Minnesota State Census Lyle, Mower, Minnesota</u>: Joseph A. &
>   >   Rosina Pinkham with children Mary, Rosina Sarah Ann
>   >   Samuel & John Pinkham. *Moved with Jeremiah Phelps.*
<u>Caleb Pinkham</u>: Son of Samuel Junior and Theodocia (Carpenter) Pinkham.
>   Born 1810 Quebec: brother to Joseph Abijah Pinkham; Samuel III
>   <u>1880 Census Princeton, Mille Lac, MN:</u> M2 - Deborah Pinkham with
>   >   daughter Minnie.
<u>Samuel Pinkham III:</u> Son of Samuel Junior and Theodocia (Carpenter) Pinkham
>   to Mower, MN post 1860.
<u>Comfort Pinkham:</u> Son of Caleb Pinkham. Born 1831 Quebec.
>   <u>1870 United States Census Milo Township, Mills Lac, MN:</u> Comfort
>   >   Pinkham with wife Altha, born New York.
>   >   <u>Children of Comfort and Altha</u>:
>   >   >   Orrin Pinkham (b. 1858, Wisconsin)
>   >   >   James Pinkham (b. 1865, Wisconsin)
>   >   >   Theodosia Pinkham (b 1860, Wisconsin)
>   <u>1875 Minnesota State Census Milo, Mille Lacs, MN:</u> Comfort Pinkham
>   >   with wife Ammerica Pinkham, born New York.
>   >   <u>Children of Comfort and Ammerica Pinkham</u>:
>   >   >   Orrin Pinkham, (b. 1858, WI)
>   >   >   James Pinkham
>   >   >   Theodosia Pinkham
>   <u>1880 United States Census Milo, Mille Lac, Minnesota</u>: Comfort Pinkham
>   >   born 1831 Canada (Quebec); wife Aurilia born 1840 New York.
>   >   <u>Children of Comfort and Aurilla Pinkham</u>:
>   >   >   Ovrin Pinkham (b. 1858, Wisconsin)
>   >   >   James Pinkham (b. 1866, Wisconsin)
<u>Caleb Pinkham, Jr.</u>: Son of Caleb Pinkham, brother Comfort; Josephus.
>   <u>1875 Minnesota State Census Princeton, Mille Lac, MN:</u> Caleb Pinkham
>   >   Jr. with wife: Elvira Pinkham, born New York.

Children of Caleb Jr. and Elvira Pinkham:
>> Melinda Pinkham (b. 1872, MN)
>> Hattie Pinkham (b. 1868, MN)
>> 1880 Census Princeton, Mille Lacs, MN: Caleb Pinkham, Jr. with wife
>> Elvira Pinkham born 1833 New York.
>> Children of Caleb Pinkham, Jr. and Elvira:
>> Melinda Pinkham (b. 1867, Minnesota)
>> Jessie Pinkham (b. 1876, Minnesota)
>> Hattie Pinkham (b. 1878, Minnesota)

Edwin Pinkham: Son of Comfort Carpenter & Elizabeth (Phelps) Pinkham.
>> Born: 1840-1841, Quebec or Ontario.
>> 1870 United States Census Ashland Township, Dodge, MN
>> wife Catherine born 1844 Canada.
>> Children of Edwin and Catherine Pinkham:
>> Elizabeth Pinkham (b. 1869, MN)
>> Marty Pinkham (b.1879, MN)
>> 1875 Ashland, Dodge Minnesota State Census: Edwin Pinkham born
>> 1872 MN (*son of Edwin Pinkham*), Lizzie Pinkham (b 1869 MN)
>> and Mysta J. (born 1870, MN).

Mary Pinkham Coons: Daughter of Comfort Carpenter & Elizabeth (Phelps)
>> Pinkham. Born: 1835 Quebec. Death: 9 June 1875 Ashland, MN.
>> 1875 Minnesota Deaths: Mary (Pinkham) Coons, Female, Death date: 9
>> June 1875; Death Place – Ashland, Dodge County, Minnesota;
>> Age- 98/Birthdate - 1777 (Actual age: 40/ born 1835); Race –
>> White; Marital Status – Married; Father's name: Comfort
>> Pinkham; Father's birthplace Canada; Mother's Name-
>> Elisabeth, Mother's birthplace – Canada). *Source: Minnesota Deaths &
>> Burials, 1835-1990 citing Ashland, Dodge County, Minnesota;* Birth year noted is wrong
>> – parent's name accurate.

Willard Pinkham: Marriage of W. F. Pinkham to May Pashley on 16
>> December 1889 in Ramsey, Minnesota. *Source: Minnesota County
>> Marriages 1860-1949.* Son of Comfort and Elizabeth (Phelps) Pinkham.

Wisconsin: (*1855 Amos B. Phelps, son of Jeremiah Phelps and Amos Phelps, son of
>> Eldad Phelps moved to Wisconsin with Amos Phelps, son of Eldad, half-
>> brother to Amos B. Phelps, Jr, to 1830 Crawford, WI.*)

J. Samuel Pinkham- Son of Samuel Junior and Theodocia (Carpenter) Pinkham.
>> 1855 United States Union, Rock County, Wisconsin Census
>> 1879 death - Union, Rock, Wisconsin

Caleb Pinkham: Son of Samuel Junior and Theodocia (Carpenter) Pinkham.
>> 1855 United States Clayton, Crawford County, Wisconsin Census
>> 1860 United States Clayton, Crawford County, Wisconsin Census

Calvin W. Pinkham: Son of Abijah and Hannah (Sleeper) Pinkham.
>> Baptism:1838 Stanstead, Quebec

Naturalization: Charles W. Pinkham: 5 April 1859, Fond Du Lac, WI
Wisconsin, County Naturalization records - 1807-1992.
1870 United States Fond du Lac, Wisconsin Census: C. W. Susan,
James B. Pinkham and Sarah Jane Pinkham, born 1864 WI.
1880 United States Census: Fond Du Lac, Wisconsin, w/ Calvin C, Susan
D. & Burton.
1880 United States Census: Fond du Lac, WI w/ Calvin C, Susan D. &
Susie Jane Pinkham and Burton.
Wisconsin Death Index, 1820-1907: Susan D. Pinkham, 12
February 1896 Fond Du Lac, WI. Death Record for Susan Davis
(Sleeper) Pinkham: Born 23 January 1826 Stanstead, QC. Father:
Ira D. Sleeper. Mother: Polly Sleeper.
Samuel K. Pinkham: Father's name: (Joseph) Abijah Pinkham. Mother's name:
Rosina (Chartier) Pinkham. Spouse: Susan Frilda Copas. Father's
Name: John Copas. Mother's Name: Eva Copas.
1900 Clayton, Crawford, Wisconsin Census: Samuel Pinkham. Birth
April 1857 Minnesota. Parents: Father born: Canada (Joseph
Abijah Pinkham). Mother born: Canada (Rosina Chartier).
Children of Samuel and Susan Pinkham: (surname: Dinkham)
Adam Pinkham (age 14 born 1886, Wisconsin)
Eve Pinkham (age 14 born 1886, Wisconsin)
Varney Pinkham (age 10 born 1890, Wisconsin)
Mary Pinkham (age 3 born 1897, Wisconsin)
Elizabeth Pinkham (age 1 born 1899, Wisconsin)
1920 Crawford, Wisconsin Census. Susan (married) Pinkham. Father:
born Ohio. Mother: born Ohio. Age 57; born 1863, Wisconsin.
Married to Samuel Pinkham. Age 62, born 1858, Minnesota.
Children of Samuel and Susan Pinkham:
Erving Pinkham (age 26 born 1894 Wisconsin)
Elizabeth Pinkham (age 20 born 1900 Wisconsin)
Son-in-law Delbert Orick (age 25 born Wisconsin)
Mary (Pinkham) Orick (age 23 born 1897, Wisconsin)
Susan Pinkham:1900 Clayton, Crawford, Wisconsin Census:
Susan Pinkham. Born June 1860, Wisconsin; age 40 in
1900; married. Father born Virginia; Mother born: Ohio -
Eve. A. Copas age 79. Married: 1879.
Joseph Abijah Pinkham: Son of Samuel Junior and Theodocia (Carpenter)
Pinkham, brother to Caleb Pinkham. Wisconsin 1849-1858 as per
birth of children.
1860 United States Census Austin, Mower Minnesota. Born 1830
Quebec Wife: Rosina (Chartier) born 1832 Canada (Quebec).
Children of Joseph Abijah and Rosina Pinkham born Wisconsin:
Mary Pinkham (b.1849, Wisconsin)
Rosina Pinkham (b. 1851, Wisconsin)
Sarah A. Pinkham (b. 1853, Wisconsin)
Samuel Pinkham (b.1855, Wisconsin)

Theodocia Pinkham (b. 1858, Wisconsin)
John Pinkham (b. 1865, Mower, MN)
<u>1875 United States Census Clayton, Crawford, Wisconsin</u>: A. Pinkham
Number of females: 4; Number of Males: 3.
<u>1895 United States Census Clayton Town, Crawford, Wisconsin</u>: J. A.
Pinkham. Number of males: 1. Number of females: 1.
<u>Comfort Pinkham</u>: Son of Caleb Pinkham, brother to Josephus and Caleb, Jr.
Pinkham. Uncle Joseph Abijah Pinkham. Wisconsin 1858-1866.
<u>1853 Wiota, Wisconsin marriage</u>
<u>1860 Wiota Wisconsin census</u>
<u>Children of Comfort and Altha Pinkham</u>:
Orrin Pinkham (born 1858, Wisconsin)
Theodocia Pinkham (born 1860, Wisconsin)
James Pinkham (born 1865-6, Wisconsin)
<u>Caleb Pinkham, Jr.</u>: Son of Caleb Pinkham, brother to Josephus and Comfort.
1855 Wiota, Wisconsin
<u>Huldah Pinkham Pickett</u>: Daughter of Caleb Pinkham, sister to Josephus,
Comfort and Caleb Jr. Pinkham.
1850-1910 - Wiota, Lafayette, Wisconsin
<u>Josephus Pinkham</u>: Son of Caleb Pinkham, brother to Comfort and Caleb, Jr.
1855 - 1910 Wiota, Wisconsin census
1885 marriage (m2) Wisconsin
Death: 1927 Wisconsin
<u>Joseph Pinkham</u>: Son of Samuel Senior and Dorothy (Ordway) Pinkham. 1855-
1859 WI. Daughter Laura Pinkham born 1858 Wisconsin (m3).

Massachusetts:
<u>Joseph Pinkham</u>: Son of Samuel Senior and Dorothy (Ordway) Pinkham. 1840
Grafton, MA 1855-1859 Wisconsin. 1860-1878 Grafton, MA.
<u>James O. Pinkham</u>: Son of Samuel Junior and Theodocia (Carpenter) Pinkham.
<u>Charles W. Pinkham</u>: Son of Comfort Carpenter and Elizabeth (Phelps)
Pinkham; grandson of Samuel Pinkham Jr. Lowell, MA.

California:
<u>Loelah Pinkham Lee</u>: Daughter of Abijah and Hannah (Sleeper) Pinkham,
Moved 1890 to Los Angeles, California. Died 1905, Los Angeles, CA.
<u>Joseph Abijah Pinkham</u>: Son of Samuel Pinkham Junior. Moved 1904 to
(Central Valley) Madera, CA. Died 1909, Madera, California.
<u>Michael Pinkham</u>: Son of Joseph Abijah Pinkham. Moved 1900 to Madera,
California. Died Wisconsin.
<u>Theodocia Pinkham Copas</u>: Daughter of Joseph Abijah Pinkham. Moved 1900
to Madera, CA; Died Madera, CA.
<u>Mary Pinkham Townsend</u>: Daughter of Joseph Abijah Pinkham. Moved 1910 to
Madera, CA. Died Madera, CA.

<u>Amos B. Phelps</u>: Son of Jeremiah Phelps. Moved to1880 Sierras in California. Died 1903 Santa
Rosa, California. (*Named for Elizabeth Phelps' father, Amos B. Phelps Jr. & Amos Sr.*)
<u>*Thomas L. Phelps, Jr.*</u>: *Born 1839 Canada. Possible grandson of Jeremiah Phelps, son of
Thomas L. Phelps.1879 Central Valley (Modesto); d. 1909 CA.*

Pinkham surnames in Minnesota likely related to Eastern Township Pinkham family:

James Pinkham: *Son of James O. Pinkham, son of Samuel Pinkham Junior?*
    1853 Quebec, QC marriage of James Pinkham to Marianne Faulkner
    <u>1870 United States Princeton Mille, Lac, MN census</u>: Jas. Pinkham. Born
      1847 Canada.
    <u>1875 Red Wing City, Goodhue, Minnesota State Census</u>: James
      Pinkham born 1845 Canada.

John Pinkham: *Son of Joseph and Sarah (Moulton) Born abt. 1836.*
    <u>1880 United States Mower, MN Census</u>: Born *1836* Canada. Son of
      Joseph & Rosina Pinkham, John Pinkham b.1865 Mower, MN.

Joseph Pinkham**:** *Not son of Joseph, Samuel or Abijah Pinkham, sons of*
    Samuel Senior. Possible son of James and Marie-Matilda Pinkham.
    <u>1875 Garden City, Blue Earth, Faribault, MN Minnesota State Census</u>:
      Joseph Pinkham born 1822, wife Julie Anne Pinkham born 1835.
      <u>Children of Joseph and Julie Pinkham</u>:
        Alma J Pinkham
        Albert Pinkham
        Alice E. Pinkham

Charles W. Pinkham: Possible son of James & Marie-Matilda Pinkham.
    Baptized: 1850 St. Cecile de Milton, QC

Charles A. Pinkham: *Possible son of James O. Pinkham*
    <u>1873 Marriage</u>: Charles A. Pinkham to Ella Palver. Date: 10 December
      1873. Location: Farilbault, Minnesota, USA.
    <u>1875 Blue Earth City, Faribault, MN Minnesota States Census</u>: C. A.
      (Charles A. Pinkham). Wife: Ella Pinkham born Wisconsin, G. B.
      Pinkham.
      <u>Birth</u>: Harriet A. Pinkham born 6 May 1876 Blue Earth City,
      Faribault, MN. Father: Charles A. Pinkham. Mother: Ella G.
      Pinkham.
    <u>1880 United States Census Blue Earth City, Farabault, MN</u>: Charles
      Pinkham, Wife: Ella J. Pinkham. Daughter Hattie Pinkham born
      1876 Minnesota.
    <u>1880 Census Blue Earth City, Faribault, Minnesota</u>. Chas. A Pinkham.
      Age 29 born 1851 New Hampshire. Occupation: Hotel Keeper.
      Father's birthplace: New Hampshire. (Father born Quebec).

Why did Comfort Carpenter Pinkham move to Ontario when family members moved to USA? Uncle Joseph Pinkham married Sarah Moulton whose father resided Stanstead.

MOULTON Quebec: <u>1790 Rutland, Vermont Census:</u> Moulton surname: John Moulton

<u>1825 Quebec Census:</u> MOULTON surnames
    <u>Avery Moulton</u> (family of 11) Richelieu, Stanstead, QC
    <u>Abiel Moulton</u> (family of 6), Richelieu, Stanstead, QC
    <u>Harris Moulton</u>, Richelieu, Stanstead, Quebec - *Sarah Moulton's brother*
    <u>William Moulton</u>, Richelieu, Stanstead, Quebec - *Sarah Moulton's father*
        1881 Stanstead Plain, Stanstead, Quebec Census with wife Sarah/Sally
        and daughter, Adeline Moulton
    <u>Calvin Moulton</u>, Buckinghamshire, Ascott, Quebec. Married to Polly Moulton
        Son: Hiram Moulton - born 1798 Vermont, USA
    <u>Oren Moulton,</u> Buckinghamshire, Ascott, Quebec
Misc. Moulton surnames Quebec:
    Lydia Moulton b. 1798 US; 1871 Stanstead Plain, Stanstead, Quebec census
    Helen Moulton; 1871 Stanstead Plain, Stanstead, Quebec census
    Abiel Moulton (b. 1798 USA) with Fanny Moulton born 1798 Stanstead Plain, QC
<u>1842 Clarke, Newcastle, Durham, Ontario Census</u> MOULTON surnames
    <u>Joseph Moulton</u> - Farmer (Family of 6)
    <u>Jno Moulton</u> - Farmer (Family of 13)
    <u>Anson Moulton</u> - Marriage m1: Hester Ann Draper Moulton; Children: Sophrina
        J. Moulton, Annie Moulton, Joel Draper Moulton
                Marriage son Anson Moulton m1: Bessie Henderson. Child William
                H. Moulton (death Michigan); Daniel J. Moulton m. Ann Jane Coyle;
                M2: Elizabeth Chalice. Child: Isabelle Harper Moulton.
    <u>Hiram Moulton</u> (born 1798 Vermont). Marriage m1: 26 March 1846 Newcastle,
        Durham, Canada West to Lois Hopkins; 1851 Darlington, Durham,
        Canada West Census, born 1798 USA.
    <u>Calvin Moulton</u>: Newcastle, Durham, Ontario (father of Hiram Moulton)
<u>1851 Clarke, Durham, Ontario (Canada West) Census:</u>
    <u>Hiram Moulton</u>; age 53 born 1798 Vermont USA) (son of Calvin Moulton).
    Marriage m2:   11 February 1860 Durham, Ontario, Canada to Sophia Lord.
    Parents: Calvin Moulton/ Polly Moulton
Misc Moulton deaths Orono, Durham, Ontario
    Wealthy Moulton Hall - b. 1808; d. 8 January 1894
    Vesta Moulton Smith - b. 20 May 1810; d. 20 February 1862
    Mary Moulton Gamsby - b. 1806; d. 26 April 1882

<u>1842 Clarke, Newcastle, Durham, Ontario Census CARPENTER</u>
    <u>John Carpenter</u> - Farmer, born Vermont
<u>1852 Tax Assessment Canada West British Colonial America:</u> John B. Carpenter
<u>1861 Ontario, Canada census: Durham, Ontario, Canada:</u> John Carpenter, born
    Vermont

Quebec Pinkham families were not listed in birth-death-marriage records until 1818

Pinkham Surnames in Quebec 1818-1900 Eastern Townships

Marriages: Pinkham

1818	Hatley, QC	Nathaniel Bartlett	Martha Pinkham
1824	Hatley, QC	Elijah (Abijah) Pinkham	Hannah Sleeper
1829	Hatley, QC	Manda T. Cushing	Dorothy Pinkham
1832	Freilighsburg,	Comfort Pinkham	Elizabeth Phelps
1833	Stanstead, QC	Thomas Pinkham Jenkins	Miranda Ruiter
1836	Stanstead, QC	Samuel Pinkham Bacheldor	Mary Ann Hunt
1842	St. Pie, QC	James Pinkham	Mathilde Tetreau-Duchame
1844	St. Pie, QC	J. Samuel Pinkham	Domitilde Chartier
1847	Stanstead, QC	Samuel Pinkham	Mary M. Ball
1849	St. Cecile de Milton	Joseph Pinkham	Rosalie Chartier
1850	Stanstead, QC	John Parker Lee	Loelah Pinkham
1853	Quebec, QC	James Pinkham	Marianne Faulkner
1867	Stanstead, QC	Charles Tisdal-Day	Mary Florence Pinkham
1867	Stanstead, QC	George L. Pinkham	Ella P. Sweet
1872	Valcourt, QC	Joseph Levesque	Rosalie Pinkham
1876	Bury, QC	James Pinkham	Mary Coates
1890	Stornoway, QC	W. H. Pinkham	Dolly Meads
1895	Bury, QC	Charles, Eley Mayhew	Emma Maud Pinkham
1895	Bury, QC	John Boyle	Susie Mytie Pinkham

Baptisms: Pinkham

1835	Stanstead, QC	Abijah Pinkham
1835	Stanstead, QC	Aurilla-Susanna Pinkham
1835	Stanstead, QC	Julia-Ann Pinkham
1835	Stanstead, QC	Ursula Pinkham
1838	Stanstead, QC	Calvin Pinkham
1845	Stanstead, QC	Georgiana Pinkham
1849	St. Cecile de Milton	Joseph Pinkham
1849	St. Cecile de Milton	Marie-Matilda Pinkham
1850	St. Cecile de Milton	Charles Pinkham
1853	Stanstead, QC	Loelah Pinkham
1862	Stanstead, QC	Abijah Pinkham
1862	Stanstead, QC	Albert-Knight Pinkham
1852	Stanstead, QC	Edward-Renfrew Pinkham
1862	Stanstead, QC	Loelah Pinkham
1862	Stanstead, QC	Mary Florence Pinkham
1862	Stanstead, QC	Samuel Clarence Pinkham
1862	Stanstead, QC	Samuel Sleeper Pinkham

Deceased:

1845	Stanstead, QC	Georgiana Pinkham
1847	Stanstead, QC	Louis-Abijah Pinkham
1850	Stanstead, QC	Dorothy Ordway Pinkham
1852	Stanstead, QC	Sarah Pinkham
1861	Stanstead, QC	Betsy Pinkham
1871	Stanstead, QC	Deborah Pinkham
1872	Bury, QC	Isaac William Pinkham
1884	Bury, QC	Isaac William Pinkham
1896	Scotstown, QC	Wilfred Harrison Pinkham
1896	Eaton, QC	William Cleveland Pinkham
1896	Eaton, QC	Ida May Pinkham
1897	Cookshire, QC	Elyah (Abijah?) Pinkham
1900	Scotstown, QC	Edwin-Dewey Pinkham
1902	Scotstown, QC	Bertha Marie Pinkham
1920	Eaton, QC	Wright-Hale Pinkham
1922	Bury, QC	Susan Pinkham
1938	Bury, QC	Warren William Pinkham
1943	Scotstown, QC	Addie Mary Pinkham

Separated by town to learn of family groups:

Hatley: *Children of Samuel and Dorothy (Ordway) Pinkham*: Abijah, Martha, Dorothy

1818	Hatley, QC	m.	Nathaniel Bartlett	Martha Pinkham
1824	Hatley, QC	m.	Elijah (*Abijah*) Pinkham	Hannah Sleeper
1829	Hatley, QC	m.	Manda T. Cushing	Dorothy Pinkham

Stanstead:

1833	Stanstead, QC	m.	Thomas Pinkham Jenkins/ Miranda Ruiter	
1835	Stanstead, QC	bap.	Abijah Pinkham	
1835	Stanstead, QC	bap.	Aurilla-Susanna Pinkham	
1835	Stanstead, QC	bap	Julia-Ann Pinkham	
1835	Stanstead, QC	bap.	Ursula Pinkham	
1836	Stanstead, QC	m.	Samuel Pinkham Bacheldor/Mary Ann Hunt	
1838	Stanstead, QC	bap.	Calvin Pinkham	
1845	Stanstead, QC	d.	Georgiana Pinkham	
1847	Stanstead, QC	d.	Louis-Abijah Pinkham	
1847	Stanstead, QC	m.	Samuel Pinkham	Mary M. Ball
1850	Stanstead, QC	m.	John Parker Lee	Loelah Pinkham
1850	Stanstead, QC	d.	Dorothy Ordway Pinkham	
1853	Stanstead, QC	bap.	Loelah Pinkham	
1862	Stanstead, QC	bap.	Abijah Pinkham	
1862	Stanstead, QC	bap.	Albert-Knight Pinkham	
1852	Stanstead, QC	bap.	Edward-Renfrew Pinkham	

215

1852	Stanstead, QC	d.	Sarah Pinkham		
1861	Stanstead, QC	d.	Betsy Pinkham		
1862	Stanstead, QC	bap.	Loelah Pinkham		
1862	Stanstead, QC	bap.	Mary Florence Pinkham		
1862	Stanstead, QC	bap.	Samuel Clarence Pinkham		
1862	Stanstead, QC	bap.	Samuel Sleeper Pinkham		
1867	Stanstead, QC	m.	Charles Tisdal-Day/ Mary Florence Pinkham		
1867	Stanstead, QC	m.	George L. Pinkham/ Ella P. Sweet		
1871	Stanstead, QC	d.	Deborah Pinkham		

St. Pie, QC:

1842	St. Pie, QC	m.	James Pinkham	Mathilde Tetreau-Duchame
1844	St. Pie, QC	m.	J. Samuel Pinkham	Domitilde Chartier

St. Cecile de Milton, QC:

1849	St. Cecile de Milton	m.	Joseph Pinkham	Rosalie Chartier
1849	St. Cecile de Milton	bap.	Joseph Pinkham	
1849	St. Cecile de Milton	bap.	Marie-Matilda Pinkham	
1850	St. Cecile de Milton	bap.	Charles Pinkham	

Quebec City, QC:

1853	Quebec, QC	m.	James Pinkham	Marianne Faulkner

Bury, QC:

1872	Bury, QC	d.	Isaac William Pinkham	
1884	Bury, QC	d.	Isaac William Pinkham	
1876	Bury, QC	m.	James Pinkham	Mary Coates
1895	Bury, QC	m.	Charles, Eley Mayhew	Emma Maud Pinkham
1895	Bury, QC	m.	John Boyle	Susie Mytie Pinkham
1922	Bury, QC	d.	Susan Pinkham	
1938	Bury, QC	d.	Warren William Pinkham	

Misc, QC:

1872	Valcourt, QC	m.	Joseph Levesque	Rosalie Pinkham
1890	Stornoway, QC	m.	W. H. (Wilfred Harrison) Pinkham/ Dolly Meads	
1896	Scotstown, QC	d.	Wilfred Harrison Pinkham	
1896	Eaton, QC	d.	William Cleveland Pinkham	
1896	Eaton, QC	d.	Ida May Pinkham	
1897	Cookshire, QC	d.	Elyah (Abijah?) Pinkham	
1900	Scotstown, QC	d	Edwin-Dewey Pinkham	
1902	Scotstown, QC	d.	Bertha Marie Pinkham	
1920	Eaton, QC	d.	Wright-Hale Pinkham	
1943	Scotstown, QC	d.	Addie Mary Pinkham	

Listed Pinkham surnames from Canada census record:

(Not in line: *Thomas Pinkham of Bonaventure, QC 1831*)

1825-1842: 6 **Pinkham** surnames listed in Quebec census records.

Abijah Pinkham	1825	Stanstead, Quebec	son of Samuel & Dorothy
Samuel Pinkham	1825	Stanstead, Quebec	Samuel & Dorothy Ordway
Joseph Pinkham	1825	Stanstead, Quebec	son of Samuel & Dorothy
Samuel Pinkham	1825	St. Cesaire, QC	son of Samuel & Dorothy
Samuel Pinkham	1842	Milton, Shefford, QC	son of Samuel Jr. or Joseph
Samuel Pinkham	1831	St. Cesaire, QC	son of Samuel & Dorothy

Listed Pinkham surnames in St. Cesaire, Bedford, QC with Phelps surnames:

Samuel Pinkham,7	1825	St. Cesaire, Bedford, QC	son of Samuel & Dorothy
Amos Phelps Sr., 2	1825	St. Cesaire, Bedford, QC	with wife Diadama Long
Jeremiah Phelps, 6	1825	St. Cesaire, Bedford, QC	son of Amos Phelps, Sr.
Oliver C. Phelps, 2	1825	St. Cesaire, Bedford, QC	son of Amos Phelps, Sr.

And Surnames;

Jacques Roi, 4	1825	St. Cesaire, Bedford, QC	dau. married Jeremiah Phelps
Jacques Roi, 6	1825	St. Cesaire, Bedford, QC	dau. married Jeremiah Phelps.
Cyrus Bachelder, 6	1825	St. Cesaire, Bedford, QC	Bachelder married Pinkhams
David Bachelder, 4	1825	St. Cesaire, Bedford, QC	Bachelder married Pinkhams
Amos Chandler, 4	1825	St. Cesaire, Bedford, QC	Chandler married PhelpsPinkham

Land Records 1795 Land Grant for Amos Phelps in Milton, QC

1831 St. Cesaire, Bedford, QC Census: (listed consecutively):

Samuel Pinkham, 8	1831	St. Cesaire, St. Hycinthe	Cultivateur
Jeremie Phelps, 9	1831	St. Cesaire, St. Hycinthe	Cultivateur
Thomas (Amos) Phelps, 3,	1831	St. Cesaire, St. Hycinthe	Rentier
Oliver Phelps, 8	1831	St. Cesaire, St. Hycinthe	Cultivateur

And Phelps surnames listed in 1831 Lower Canada Census:

Charles G. Phelps	1831	Stanbridge, Missisquoi, QC	
William P. Phelps	1831	Stanbridge, Missisquoi, QC	son of Eldad Phelps
Eldad Phelps, M1	*1831*	*Stanbridge, Missisquoi, QC, son of Amos Phelps, Sr*	
Joseph A. Phelps	1831	Stanbridge, Missisquoi, QC	son of Eldad Phelps
Philo Phelps	1831	Stanbridge, Missisquoi, QC	
Elkana Phelps	1831	Stanbridge, Missiqsuoi, QC	
David N. Phelps	1831	Stanbridge, Missisquoi, QC	
Joel Phelps	1831	Stanbridge, Missisquoi, QC, son moved to Ontario	
Burk Phelps	1831	Stanbridge, Missisquoi, QC	
Amos Phelps III	*1831*	*Stanbridge, Missisquoi, QC, son of Amos Phelps, Jr.*	
Elkhana Phelps	1831	Farnham, Shefford, QC,	

Tracking individuals named, Samuel Pinkham, from Samuel m. Dorothy Pinkham line
revealed the middle initial in records was often wrong and inconsistent.

Note: Abijah and Rachel (Huckins) Pinkham did not name sons, "Samuel.". The children, born New Hampshire included Thomas Pinkham, who did not have sons named, Samuel; Samuel Pinkham, who named his son, Samuel G. Pinkham (Junior); Abijah Pinkham Junior, born 1763 New Hampshire, had two sons born New Hampshire - Augustus born 1791 New Hampshire and John S. born 1793 New Hampshire. Unconfirmed is whether the sons of Abijah Pinkham Junior had (grand)sons born New Hampshire named Samuel. The son of Abijah and Rachel Pinkham, Paul Pinkham born 1776 who married in New Hampshire in 1789, could also be the father or grandfather of the "mystery" Samuels.

Not related to the Samuel Pinkham Quebec line was the son of Joseph Tuttle Pinkham born 1786 New Hampshire - Samuel W. Pinkham born 1825. Joseph T. Pinkham married Jennie Woods on 3 April 1810 in Adams, Cheshire County, New Hampshire. The family, including Samuel W. Pinkham, resided in 1850 and 1860 United States Census in Jefferson, Coos, New Hampshire. Perhaps distantly related, John Pinkham (Generation 3) had a daughter, Rose Pinkham (Generation 3, born March 1725) who married, in Dover, New Hampshire, James Tuttle on 7 April 1788. Samuel W. Pinkham born 1809 in Milton, New Hampshire (1850 Census) was also not part of the Comfort Carpenter Pinkham line. Instead, these "Samuel W. Pinkham" named individuals were sons of Augustus, John S. or Paul Pinkham, the sons of Abijah and Rachel (Huckins) Pinkham. Likely related, was Samuel K. Pinkham born 1883 noted in a Massachusetts census. As James O. Pinkham, the son of Samuel Junior and Theodocia (Carpenter) Pinkham died in Massachusetts, and it is noted the individual was born "in Canada" this Samuel might have descended from the Quebec Samuel Pinkham Senior branch.

Three Pinkham sons of Samuel Senior and Dorothy (Ordway) Pinkham:

<u>Joseph Pinkham</u>: Married Sarah Moulton, QC.

Samuel G. Pinkham, Jr. Married Theodocia Carpenter, QC.

Sons Caleb, J. Samuel, James O., Samuel III and Joseph Abijah Pinkham moved USA.

Caleb Pinkham, 1855, Wiota, WI/Mille Lac, MN, USA.
Son: <u>Josephus</u> Pinkham
Son: ***Samuel Issac*** Pinkham-b. 1857 WI
Comfort Pinkham listed with: *Samuel Pinkham born 1844 NY*
Comfort Carpenter Pinkham, 1851, Clarke, Ontario.
Son: ***Samuel Pinkham*** born 1847 Ontario. Died 1906 Pinkham, SK, Canada.

218

J. **_Samuel_ Pinkham:** Born abt. 1817. Moved to Union, Rock, WI by 1855. Sons born Quebec - Joseph 1845 & Cephus 1847 Married 1844 Domitilde Chartier: Is this son Samuel W. w/ Comfort Pinkham: **_Samuel Pinkham (age 16) b. 1844 NY_**?

James O.: d. Massachusetts, USA.
        Son: unknown Samuel
Samuel W. Pinkham signs Minnesota land grants w/ Cephas Pinkham...

Joseph Abijah Pinkham: MN; WI; CA, USA.
        Son: **Samuel K. Pinkham** b. 1855 WI; died 5 July 1935 WI

Samuel Pinkham III: d. Mower, Minnesota, USA.

Abijah Pinkham: Married: Hannah Sleeper QC.
        Son: **_Samuel_ Sleeper Pinkham**, b./d. Quebec

1825 New Hampshire-born <u>Samuel Pinkham</u>: Likely descendant of NH-VT-QC branch:

<u>Minnesota Surviving Soldiers, Sailors, and Marines and Widows:</u> **Samuel Pinkham.** Rank: Private. Name of Regiment: 9 New Hampshire Infantry. _Enlist date: 12 April 1847_. Discharge date: March 1848. Length of service: 11 months.

<u>United States Census of Union Veterans and Widows of the Civil War, 1890</u> – **Samuel Pinkham,** Braed, Crow Wing, Minnesota, United States.
Source: NARA; "United States Census of Union Veterans and Widows of the Civil War, 18903.

1895 Minnesota State Census: **_Samuel Pinkham_**_; Name –Samuel Pinkham; Event Place – Crow Wing township, Crow Wing, Minnesota;_ **_Age - 70 (b. 1825); Birthplace – New Hampshire_**_; Race – W; Gender – Male; Page number – 2: Household of Joel Smith (age 52 – NY); Lovie Smith (F-32y-NH); Gar Smith (M-5y-MN); ? (F-1y-Minnesota); Samuel Pinkham (M-70y-NH); Arthur Smith (M-26Y-NY); Edor Ramberg (M-18Y-MN); Edward Steel (M-37Y-Iowa)._ Source: Minnesota 1895 Census, State and Library Records Service; St. Paul.

The household was a mix of New York, New Hampshire, Minnesota and Iowa-born individuals. Whether they were related is unknown. The below record connects this line given location:

    Death of Clara Jane Maxin, age 65, on 9 January 1923, Brainerd, Crow Wing, Minnesota. Birth date: 1858. Married to Winslow Maxin. Father's name: **_Samuel Pinkham_**.

The only Samuel Pinkham III would be the son of Samuel Pinkham Junior. That Jeremiah Phelps and Joseph Abijah Pinkham families moved to Austin, MN makes this likely the youngest son of Samuel Pinkham Junior: Samuel III Pinkham.

<u>1869 – 1940 Minnesota, Grand Army of the Republic Membership</u>- **Samuel Pinkham:** Event place – Austin, Minnesota, US – Age: 53 (b. 1816). Born New Hampshire. Source: Minnesota Historical Society, St. Paul "Minnesota, Grand Army of the Republic Membership Records, 1869-1940."

Mower, Minnesota was the city Joseph Pinkham's brother, Samuel G. Pinkham, Junior's son, Joseph Abijah Pinkham resided post 1850 with the Jeramiah Phelps' family. Samuel Pinkham III, son of Samuel, Jr. and Theodocia (Carpenter) Pinkham, was born in Quebec not New Hampshire which makes the below records not connect to this Pinkham line, but of interest given the use of "Samuel" as the first name.

<u>"Old Soldiers Buried in Austin, MN Cemeteries"</u> – 30 May 1913 – **Samuel Pinkham, III**
    Calvary

The sons of Abijah and Rachel (Huckins) Pinkham were born in New Hampshire. Son Thomas Pinkham's children were accounted for with zero Samuel Pinkhams. A possible father to a Samuel Pinkham born New Hampshire might be from Abijah Junior Pinkham's sons (Augustus and John S. Pinkham) or his brother, Paul Pinkham. Samuel Pinkham Senior named son, Samuel G. Pinkham Junior. Samuel Pinkham Junior and his wife, Theodocia (Carpenter) Pinkham's named their son, Samuel Pinkham III who was born in Quebec and died in Union, Rock, Wisconsin during 1879.

Pinkham surnames resided near Braed, Crow Wing, MN including, *SAMUEL PINKHAM.* Joseph, Charles and James Pinkham were likely brothers and sons of James O. Pinkham. James O. Pinkham was son of Samuel and Theodocia Pinkham Junior.

    <u>James Pinkham:</u> <u>1875 Red Wing City, Goodhue, Minnesota State Census:</u>
        James Pinkham born 1845 Canada.
    <u>Joseph Pinkham:</u><u>1875 Garden City, Blue Earth, Faribault, MN Minnesota State</u>
        <u>Census:</u> Joseph Pinkham born 1822 with wife Julie Anne Pinkham born
        1835. <u>Children of Joseph and Julie Pinkham:</u> Alma J Pinkham, Albert
        Pinkham and Alice E. Pinkham.
  Charles A. Pinkham: *A Charles Pinkham was baptized in 1850 Quebec.*
        <u>1873 Marriage:</u> Charles A. Pinkham to Ella Palver. Date: 10 October 1873.
        Location: Faribault, Minnesota, USA.
        <u>1875 Blue Earth City, Faribault, MN Minnesota States Census:</u> C. A. (Charles A.
        Pinkham). Wife: Ella Pinkham born Wisconsin, G. B. Pinkham.
        <u>1880 United States Census Blue Earth City, Farabault, MN:</u> Charles Pinkham,
        Wife: Ella J. Pinkham, Hattie Pinkham born 1876 Minnesota.
        <u>1880 Blue Earth City, Faribault, Minnesota Census:</u> Chas A. Pinkham. Age 29.
        Born 1851. Birthplace: New Hampshire. Married. Occupation: Hotel
        Keeper. Father's birthplace: New Hampshire. Mother's birthplace: New
        Hampshire.

Miscellaneous Forename **Phelps Quebec 1800-1840** Records

(Amos Phelps, Sr. born 1750 CT descendants**) = (AMOS SENIOR)**

(Amos III-Elizabeth Phelps; children of Amos Phelps, Jr. b. 1786 descendants) = **(AMOS JUNIOR)**
(Note: The AMOS JUNIOR line also fits within the AMOS SENIOR line)

Abner B.   Clergy Reserve land purchase on 8 June 1809, Eastern Townships, Quebec. 5th Range in the town of Stanstead on 20th day of September 1809. From text: Had term of 21 years for 200 acres for amount of 25 shillings or 8 bushels. Land could have been passed down to "heirs or successors" for 50 shillings or 16 bushels.

Adelia: Born 1806. Died 1 June 1869 at age 63. Buried Mystic Cemetery. Wife of Benjamin Robinson (d. 22 November 1864; age 48).

Almira: Born 1833. Died 7 January 1913, age 80. Wife of Asa Russell. Buried Stone Cemetery.

Amos, Sr: Born 31 March 1750, Hartford, CT, USA. Died 1830, Rougemont, St. Hyacinthe, Quebec. Amos Phelps married (m1) Phebe & (m2) Diadama Long. Children from M1 born Connecticut: Martha Phelps (baptized 18 September 1774), Charlotte Phelps (baptized 6 September 1778), Oliver Cromwell Phelps (baptized 29 April 1781) & Eldad Phelps (baptized 1 June 1783). M2 children: Amos Phelps Jr. (the younger) (born January 1786, Rutland, VT), Luman Phelps (born 2 December 1787, Rutland, VT), Jeremiah Phelps (b. 9 June 1794, Rougemont, Quebec), Selinda Phelps McRae (b. 1799, Rougemont, Quebec) & Oliver Cromwell Phelps (b. July 1803 Rougemont, Quebec). <u>1825 & 1831 St. Cesaire, Bedford Census.</u>
                                          (AMOS SENIOR)

Amos B. Jr.:   Born January 1786, Rutland, Vermont, USA. Died 19 October 1813. Parents: Amos and Diadama (Long) Phelps. Father of Amos III and Elisabeth Phelps. Enlisted War of 1812, NY Militia – Private Amos B. Phelps. Recorded as Amos Phelps "the younger:" Land Record: 7 June 1807 – Sale by George Ross to Amos Phelps "the younger" Lot 9 Range 2 (Stanbridge). 2 acres on the northeasterly bank of the Pike River for 100 Spanish dollars *Source: Notary Leon LaLanne, Bedford District Archives* Prior to September 1808 – "Bond by Amos Phelps, senior and junior, to George Ross for 10 pounds in an assault & battery action. Amos Phelps, senior and junior, enter a complaint against Sam Bickford & Abner Bickford (signed by both Amos, Sr. and Amos, Jr." *Source: Bedford District Archives/ Leon Lallanne.* Children born Stanbridge: Amos III (born abt. 1809-1810/m. 1829) & Elizabeth (born 1812/ m. 1832) Phelps.   **(AMOS JUNIOR)**

    <u>Widow H. (A.). Phelps:</u> <u>1825 Stanbridge, Bedford, Quebec census.</u> Family
         – 2 Inhabitants. I female age 14-40 single; 1 female 45 and

upwards single (widow). Listed nearby – Michael (son of Eldad?) Phelps and with ½ brother Eldad Phelps and brother Carmen (Luman), on same record. Likely Widow "H./A." wife of Amos Junior Phelps (Died War of 1812 on October 1813) with daughter Elizabeth Phelps of Stanbridge.

Amos III: Born 1809-1810 Stanbridge, Bedford, QC. Died 14 March 1891, Maquoketa, Iowa, USA. Marriage to Julia V. P. Johnson, 1830, Phillipsburg, Quebec, Anglican Church – *"On this thirteenth day of December one thousand eight hundred and thirty Amos Phelps Bachelor and Farmer of major age and Julia V. P. Johnson, Spinster of major age were married after publication of Banns, with the consent of parents in presence of the subscribing witnesses."* Minister: James Reid. Witnesses: Caleb N. Tree* & Betsey Sweet. 1831 Stanbridge Census (family of 2) "Clergy Reserve" owned land/Baptist. Wife, Julia V. Johnson's father, Samuel Johnson, is listed as next entry in 1831 Stanbridge Census record with uncle, Eldad Phelps, Church of England. 24 November 1855 – Militia of Stanbridge, Missisquoi, Quebec – Captain John Corey's Company. Compulsive force of all able-bodied males aged 18 – 60 organized along county lines. Amos Phelps – Age 44, Lot Number 13, First Range. 1860/1870/1885 United States Census – Maquoketa, Iowa, USA – Born Quebec; Father's birthplace: Vermont; Mother's birthplace: Vermont. Children born Quebec: *Unconfirmed*: *Zacheaus* b. 1831, *Maribah* b. 1833 and Joseph A. born abt. 1839/1840 Phelps. Verified children: Roxana (b. 1837; d. Iowa), Sarah Phelps (b. 1841 (m. Issac McPeak; d. Iowa), Elizabeth Ann Phelps (b. 4 August 1843; m. W.H. H.-William Henry Harrison Brown; d. 7 August 1919, Des Moines, Iowa) and Orville Phelps (born abt. 1849/1850 Quebec; m. Clarinda Belle Conway 1883 Maquoketa, Iowa). Some children not accounted for. Son of Amos Phelps Junior/"the younger" and Unknown Phelps.
(AMOS SENIOR)   **(AMOS JUNIOR)**

Amos: Born abt. 1805-1806, Quebec. Son of Eldad and Abigail (Tree) Phelps. Moved to Crawford, Illinois, USA. Listed in 1830 United States Census and 1840 United States Census, Crawford, Illinois. Likely named his son born 1825-1830 (1840 census - son age 5-10), Amos Phelps. This Amos Phelps is the grandson of Amos Phelps Senior and listed in the 1851 Canada West Oxford County, Ontario, census as Amos Phelps, age 26 (born 1825) with wife Elizabeth Phelps age 18 and son C. J. Phelps age two. The 1861 Canada West Frontenac, Ontario census lists the grandson of Eldad Phelps, Amos Phelps, as age 32 born 1829.
(AMOS SENIOR)

Amos: Born 15 June 1823, Rougemont, Rouville, Quebec. Baptism 1825 – Chambly, Quebec, Anglican Church/St. Stephen. Parents: Jeremiah and Margaret (Collins) Phelps. Moved to Darien, Wisconsin in 1846 then

Racine, Wisconsin in 1857. Naturalized American Citizen 21 April 1857 Illinois/Indiana/Wisconsin. Michigan Civil War service 21st regiment. Prospector in Placerville, CA gold rush. Children – Amos B. Phelps (b. 1824), Alexander, John, Joseph, Timothy & William Phelps. *Source: Phelps Family Newsletter dated January 1985*. Died 24 February 1903, Santa Rosa, CA, USA. **(AMOS SENIOR)**

Amos: Born 1 June 1827. Baptized 23 September 1831 (record signed by grandmother Diadama Phelps). Parents: Oliver Cromwell & Mary Josette (Roi) Phelps. Sponsors Jeremiah & Margaret Phelps. Married Adelaide Metienier. 1816 Canada East Stukley, Shefford County census lists Amos Phelps age 33 (born 1828). Died 10 January 1893, Quebec. **(AMOS SENIOR)**

Amy: Born 26 September 1814, Stanbridge, Quebec. Parents: Luman & (m1) Hannah (Briggs) Phelps. Married Welcome Chandler in 1831 in Abbotsford at a Protestant Church. Moved 1854 to Burlington, Wisconsin with John Phelps, son of Jeremiah Phelps (her cousin) then to Mover, MN with Jeremiah Phelps family (and Abijah Joseph Pinkham, brother of Comfort Carpenter Pinkham). Hannah Phelps Chandler's mother was Amy Phelps, daughter of Luman and Hannah (Briggs) Phelps & Welcome Chandler. **(AMOS SENIOR)**

Anice: Born 1825-1830, Quebec. Parents: Luman and Hannah (Briggs) Phelps. Married Hiram Birch. **(AMOS SENIOR)**

Betsey Ganza: Born 29 October 1800, Stanbridge, Quebec. *Parents: Philo & Urana Phelps.* Baptized – Steward's Book.

Burk   1831 Stanbridge, Quebec Census

Charlotte: Born 16 August 1820, Rougemont, Rouville, Quebec; d. 18 August 1865, Austin, Mower, MN, USA. Parents: Jeremiah and Margaret (Collins) Phelps. Married Thomas Bonnallie (Died September 1910, Austin, Mower, MN). (1860 United States Census: Thomas (age 40 born Scotland), Charlotte (age 38 born Canada) children: William (age 8 born 1852 Canada), Jeremiah (age 6 born Wisconsin 1854), Margaret (age 5 born Wisconsin 1855) and Dama (Diadama?) (age 2 born Minnesota 1858). **(AMOS SENIOR)**

Charles A: Born 1799. Farmer. Marriage 20 February 1822 to Esther Sweet (1804-1879) (Perhaps related to Betsy Sweet who signed Amos Phelps 1829 marriage). Witnesses Hiram W. Pratt and Mary Phelps of Stanbridge. Signed Stanbridge Temperance no alcohol pact – 20 January 1831. 1831 Stanbridge, QC Census: Charles G. Phelps. Perhaps, Charles Alanson (1808)? Charles "A." Phelps buried Mystic Cemetery 8 Sept

1862 – Charles, Phelps, son of A P. and Mary L. Ball Phelps died in Stanstead - *Source: Sherbrooke Gazette*

Charles J: 1822 Marriage – Freilighsburg, Anglican Church, Holy Trinity. 1825 Stanbridge, Bedford, Quebec Census – Charles J. Phelps; Family of 4. *Listed alongside Elkanah Phelps.* 1831 Stanbridge, QC Census: Charles G. Phelps. Signed son, Hiram Phelps' 1840 marriage record. 1851 Stanbridge Canada East Census ("C. J. Phelps" – signed marriage document for *son Hiram Phelps with wife, Cynthia Phelps; dau. Cynthia.*

Cynthia: Signed 20 January 1831 Stanbridge Temperance Society "no alcohol" pact. Died 1847 Stanbridge, Quebec, Anglican Church. *Source: Drouin.* Wife of Charles J. Phelps. Son, Hiram named daughter Cynthia for mother.

Charles W. Pinkham: Born 11 June 1855, Manvers, Ontario, Canada. Parents: Elizabeth Phelps & Comfort Carpenter Pinkham. Baptized 11 November 1877 in Freilighsburg, Quebec. Text: "...*Charles, the son of Comfort Pinkham and Elizabeth Phelps his wife* ..." Married 27 July 1881 in Lowell, MA, US to Lavina Corey of Stanbridge, Quebec. US citizen naturalization - 21 November 1893, Lowell, MA, USA. Founded Pinkham, Saskatchewan as "pioneer realtor" with brother, Samuel Pinkham in 1911.
  (AMOS JUNIOR)

Charlotte Hannah: Born 16 August 1819, Rougemont, Quebec. Parents: Luman & Hannah (Briggs) Phelps. Married John Chartier. Died 26 November 1889, Minnesota. Known as: *Hannah Charlotte.* **(AMOS SENIOR)**

Cordelia: Born abt. 1808. Marriage 1828 to Matthew Sax, Farmer, at Freilighsburg, Anglican Church, Holy Trinity. Witnesses: James Scagel & Peter Sax. All residents of Stanbridge.

Cynthia: Married 1837 William Henry Gordon, Esq., Montreal Presbyterian St. Gabriel. From *Misskoui Standard*: Married in Montreal on the 17th of July 1837 by the Rev. H. Esson, William H. Gordon, Esq. merchant of Stanbridge, Lower Canada to Miss Cynthia Phelps, of the same place. Father: Hiram Phelps, son of Charles J. & Cynthia Phelps; Mother: Isabella Phelps; d. Mystic Cemetery, Quebec.

Cynthia Pinkham: Born 1832, Quebec. Parents: Elizabeth Phelps and Comfort Carpenter Pinkham. Married 1849 in Ontario to Alfred Wright (born USA). Died 21 September 1879, Pontypool, Kawartha Lakes, Ontario.
  (AMOS JUNIOR)

David Nash: Born 4 October 1796, New Haven, VT. Died 15 April 1884, Stanbridge, Missisquoi, Quebec. Married 29 April 1821, Saint-Armand West, QC to

Elizabeth Hungerford Phelps (b. 1797 USA, d. Bedford, Quebec, Methodist 1878), Phillipsburg, Quebec, Anglican Church. 1825 Census Stanbridge, Bedford, Quebec – Family of 6; David N. Phelps. 1831 Census Stanbridge, Missisquoi – January 1831.; 1851 Canada East, Missisquoi County, Stanbridge – David N. Phelps, age 56, born 1795 in Vermont. 1861 Quebec Census – D. N. Phelps, Age 65, born in Vermont 1796, Married, Wesleyan Methodist. 1871 Stanbridge, Missisquoi, Canada Census: Nash D. age 74, Wesleyan Methodist with wife Elizabeth Phelps age 74. 1881 Canada Census - Stanbridge, Age 84 (abt. 1797); Widower, Born in United States - VT. Son (child 7) of Phineas Phelps and M2 Lydia Lawrence (F37833).

From Elizabeth Hungerford Phelps biography: Elizabeth Hungerford born 7 February 1787 married: Nash David Phelps born New Haven, VT on 4 October 1796; died Quebec 15 April 1884. The children of David Nash and Elizabeth Hungerford Phelps, all born in Stanbridge, Quebec were: Lydia (b. 2 December 1825; m. Henry H. Bucklin; d. 12 February 1826), Esther (m. Alexander Douglas – both d. Stanbridge), David Alfred (m. Victoria Sawyer), Edgar Joshia (b. 20 November 1831; d. 29 June 1932), Almira Eudora (b. 18 September 1832; m. Asa Russell; d. 7 January 1913, North Stanbridge), Mary Elizabeth (b. 20 September 1830; m. 20 April 1853 Horacio Nelson), Helen Ann (b. 21 December 1837; m1 Heman Mitchell; m2 Samuel Fairfield; d. 21 October 1914), Caroline Alexandra (b. 3 July 1840; m. 8 September 1863 Horace Brayton Leach; d. 29 March 1921) and Alvira Jane (b. 30 September 1845; m. 13 December 1864 Arvide Martin; d. Clarenceville, Quebec) Phelps. *Source: "Three Hundred Colonial Ancestors…" by Mrs. Elizabeth M. Leach Rixford.* (David Nash Phelps Bacheldor: Married 1822 Phillipsburg, Anglican Church.)

(Marriage 7 November 1877 Nelson, Buffalo, Wisconsin, United States: Frederich Augustus Phelps born Vermont. Father: D. N. Phelps; Mother: Sarah L. Phelps. Marriage to Mary B. M. Read, daughter of Abbot R. Read and Permia Read.)

D. W. - Daniel Walter: Married 1849 to H. R. Goddard, Shefford, Quebec, Methodist Church. *Source: Drouin*

Diadama Long: Daughter of Samuel and Martha (Brewster) Long. Born 14 January 1763, Coventry, Tolland Country, Connecticut. *Source: Edmund West* Married: 1790 to Amos Phelps, Franklin, VT, USA. Children: Amos Junior, Luman, Jeremiah, Oliver Cromwell and Selinda Phelps. Died 9 March 1837, Abbotsford, Monteregie Region, Quebec, Canada. Buried: Saint Paul's Anglican Church Cemetery. **(AMOS SENIOR)**

Diadama: Born 13 June 1817 near Abbotsford, Quebec. Baptized 4 October 1834. Parents: Luman and Hannah (Briggs) Phelps. Married: Stephen Chartier. Died 1888 Minnesota, USA. **(AMOS SENIOR)**

Diadama: Born 13 February 1829, Quebec. Baptized 23 September 1831. Parents: Oliver C. & Mary Josette (Roi) Phelps. **(AMOS SENIOR)**

Diadama: Marriage 30 May 1839, Abbotsford, St. Hyacinthe, Protestant. Parents: Jeremiah Phelps (farmer of Milton) and his wife, Margaret. *"Born 16 October 1830, spouses are Stephen Chartier and Diadama Chartier and Charlotte Hannah Cartier. Signed by Stephen Chartier, Diadama Phelps, Hannah Chartier."* **(AMOS SENIOR)**

Born 16 October 1838, Milton, Quebec. Parents: Jeremiah and Margaret (Collins) Phelps. Married John B. Niles of Minnesota. Died Minnesota, USA.

Dorcus: Born 1814. Died 25 January 1873 age 59. Buried Stanton Cemetery. (Possible parents: Cynthia & Ebenezer Phelps/Cynthia Phelps & Charles A. Phelps, Cynthia Phelps b. 1811.).

Dorothy E.: Born 1842. Died 1912. Parents: Luman and (m2) Harriet (Cromwell) Phelps. **(AMOS SENIOR)**

D. W. -Daniel Walter: Married 1849 to H. R. Goddard, Shefford, Quebec, Methodist Church. *Source: Drouin*

Ebenezer: 1825 Stanbridge, Bedford, Quebec Census. Wife Cynthia B. Soule (b. 1775/d. 1849). Child: Joseph Albro Phelps d. 21 May 1832. Inscription: *Son of Ebenezer & Cynthia Phelps in the 28th year of his age.* Buried: Stanton Cemetery, Stanbridge, East, Monterregie-Region, Quebec. Possible siblings: Charles Jay Phelps (b. 1799; d. 1873) & Orcelia Phelps (b. 1815; d. 1841).

Edward: Born 15 May 1829, Rougemont, Rouville, Quebec.

Edward: Born 15 May 1840, Quebec. Parents: Jeremiah and Margaret (Collins) Phelps. Died May 1904, Parker, SD, USA. **(AMOS SENIOR)**

Edwin A. Pinkham: Born abt. 1840-1841, Quebec. Parents: Comfort Carpenter and Elizabeth (Phelps) Pinkham. Moved to Dodge, Minnesota. Married MN 12 May 1867 to Catherine Campbell. 1900 Hillsboro, North Dakota Census with wife, Catherine, Farmer/owned home age 56 with grandson, Charles, age 7 born Minnesota. Died Eugene, Oregon, USA post 1905. **(AMOS JUNIOR)**

Eldad: Baptized 1 June 1783, Connecticut, USA. Parents: Amos & M1 Phebe Phelps. ½ brother to Amos Jr., Luman, Jeremiah, Selinda & Oliver Cromwell Phelps. Married Abigail Tree 29 January 1805, Franklin, VT. 1825 Bedford County, Stanbridge Quebec census listed alongside family members - sons, unnamed (Joseph) Phelps and Michael Phelps, half-brother Carman (Luman) Phelps and brother Amos Phelps, Jr.'s Widow H/A Phelps. 1831 Stanbridge, Missisquoi Quebec census noted a listing with deceased brother Amos Phelps Jr.'s son, Amos Phelps III. Child name confirmed: Olive Phelps born 9 September 1817/Baptized 16 October 1842, Stanbridge, Quebec. 1825 census listed a family of three sons: Michael, Joseph and Amos Phelps. Three daughters were not recorded, except for Olive Phelps. Children of Eldad and Abigail (Tree) Phelps were Michael, Joseph, Amos, Olive and two female children (unknown first names) Phelps.   **(AMOS SENIOR)**

Electa Pinkham: Born 15 March 1834, Quebec. Parents: Comfort Carpenter and Elizabeth (Phelps) Pinkham. Married 1854/1855 Ontario to Hiram Eddy. Died 12 May 1916, Durham, Ontario, Canada. (*Electra*) **(AMOS JUNIOR)**

Elkannah: Born 1779 in Norfolk, CT then moved to New Haven, VT then Stanbridge – Full name: Elkannah Wilcox Phelps. <u>1825 Stanbridge, Bedford Census</u> – Elkanah Phelps – Family of 11. Married Anna C. Phelps (d. 20 August 1823 Coventry, Vermont age 44; b. 1779). Sons include: Joel, Philo, Burt and Elnathan. Listed with Charles J. Phelps, Stanbridge Family of 4. Married (son? - Elkannah). 1826 to Emily Chappel, Freilighsburg, Quebec, Anglican Church, Holy Trinity. *Source: Drouin.* <u>1831 Stanbridge Missisquoi Census</u> – Ekana Phelps & Elkana Phelps – <u>1831 Farnham, Shefford, Quebec Census.</u> Therefore – father Elkannah & son Elkannah, as well as, Elnathan. Father – Elkannah Phelps of MA, USA. From War of 1812 Death or Deceased files: Elkannah Phelps – served Captain Kellogg's Company New York Militia. *Source: NARA*

Elkanah*:* Born 1794, Connecticu/Stanbridge QC/Son (child 5) of Phineas Phelps and Lydia Lawrence. Married to Emily Chappel. (*Source unproven*). <u>1831 Farnham Shefford, Quebec Census.</u>

Elnathan: Born 1795, Orwell, VT (#1763). Son of Elkannah Phelps (#1031 – MA, USA). Married Phoebe (Bridge?) Tuttle (b. 1778; d. 20 January 1865 – age 87, Orwell, VT, USA; listed on 1850 Orwell, Vermont census with son, Alonzo Phelps b. 1819 age 31). War of 1812 – Elnathan Phelps – Private in United States Infantry with Captain Farrington *Source: NARA.* "Donation – 3 September: Elkena Phelps to Elnathan Phelps." Married January 1823 - Elnathan Phelps to Phebe Blakely. <u>1825 Stanbridge, Bedford Census</u> – family of 4. Listed (1 male under age 6; I male unmarried 18-25; 1 male married age 25-40; 1 female age 14-45). David N. (David Nash) Phelps listed nearby. Death of son - "Zachius Blakely Phelps, son of Elnathan Phelps, yeoman of the township of Stanbridge, and his wife, Phoebe, born 6 March 1831, and died 2 January 1833; buried 3 January 1833." <u>1842 Stanbridge Census</u> (occupation - carpenter) family of 9. <u>1851 Canada East (Quebec) Census</u>; District – Missisquoi County; Sub-district – Stanbridge; Age 57, abt. 1794. *Son Elnathan Philips –* <u>1861 Quebec census</u> *– Age 37, Birth year 1824, Event Place – St. Jacques le Mineur, Laprairie, Quebec; Married, Wesleyan Methodist.*

(Elnathan Phelps Bacheldor – Marriage 1822 Phillipsburg, Anglican Church.)

Elizabeth   Born 1812, Stanbridge, Bedford, Quebec. 1832 marriage to Comfort Carpenter Pinkham Frelighsburg, Quebec, Anglican Church, Holy Trinity. *"On this thirteenth day of March one thousand eight hundred and thirty-two Comfort Pinkham of the Parish of Saint Cesaires, and Elizabeth Phelps Spinster of Stanbridge, both of major age, were married after publication of Banns in the presence of subscribing witnesses. Minister: James Reid. Witnesses: Amos Phelps, Julia V. Phelps."* Source: Drouin. 1851/1861/1872 Ontario Durham County Census as Elizabeth Pinkham. Child of Amos Phelps Jr./"the younger" and unknown. Signed Huldah Pinkham, sister of Comfort Pinkham, marriage certificate: Betsy Phelps, same name as listed on Ontario-born son, John Wesley Pinkham's M3 marriage record - parents: Comfort Carpenter/Betsy Phelps. Children born Quebec: Cynthia, Elect(r))a, Mary, Edwin and *Willard* Pinkham. Ontario born children: John Wesley (b. 1845), Jane (b. 1850), Samuel (b. 1852) and Charles W. (b. 1855) Pinkham who returned to Stanbridge then was baptized in the same Frelighsburg, Quebec church as parents were married; married Lavina Corey of Stanbridge, Quebec. Died 1883 Ontario. **(AMOS SENIOR)**   **(AMOS JUNIOR)**

Eliza A.   Born 1834. Death: 1867. Buried South Stukely Cemetery.

Elizabeth Ann: Born 4 August 1843, Stanbridge, Quebec. Parents: Amos III and Julia V. (Johnson) Phelps. Named likely for aunt Elizabeth Phelps Pinkham. Married 3 June 1862 to W. H. H. (William Henry Harrison) Brown. Son – Senator/AG Norris Brown of Omaha, Nebraska. Died: 14 August 1919, Des Moines, Iowa, USA.   **(AMOS JUNIOR)**

Esther: Born 1825. Death 1905. Buried: Mystic Cemetery. Married: Alexander Douglas (1816-1871). Children: Bertha Douglas (1852-1869) and John Leslie Douglas (1867-1901).

George: Born 21 January 1834, Quebec. Twin to William Phelps. Parents: Jeremiah and Margaret (Collins) Phelps. Moved to 1850 Mower, MN, USA.   **(AMOS SENIOR)**

Hannah A.: Born 1841 Stanbridge, Quebec. Daughter of Luman and (m2) Harriet (Cromwell) Phelps. Married Almond B. West. Died 15 December 1921, Lapeer, Michigan, USA.   **(AMOS SENIOR)**

Hannah Charlotte* Born 16 August 1819, Rougemont, Quebec. Daughter of Luman and (m1) Hannah (Briggs) Phelps. Married John Chartier. Baptism record on 20 August 1837: *"Hannah Charlotte, wife of John Chartier nee Phelps of Milton born 16 August 1819 is baptized. Signed by Diadama Phelps,* *grandmother."* Baptized with daughter, Ana Maria Charter. Died 26 November 1889, Lyle, MN, USA.   **(AMOS SENIOR)**

Hannah: Born 3 April 1836, Rougemont, Rouville, Quebec. Baptized 9 March 1837 at funeral of grandmother, Diadama Long Phelps. Parents: Jeremiah and Margaret (Collins) Phelps. Married: Alfred Cressey. Died 15 October 1903, Austin, Mower, MN, USA.   **(AMOS SENIOR)**

Hannah Wife of Joel Phelps/Mother of Joel Phelps born 1813. (Re)married Ontario 1879.

Henel A. Born 1837. Died 1920. Buried Mystic Cemetery. Wife of Samuel Fairchild (1841-1914).

Henrietta: Baptism:16 September 1832. *"Henrietta Phelps, an adult person of the Township of Stanbridge was baptized on the 16th day of September 1832 by me, D. Robertson, Missionary. In the presence of Stephen Chandler and Nancy Chandler."*

Hiram: Born 28 August 1800. M1/M2(?) Isabelle Tylor 1840, Frelighsburg, Quebec Anglican Church, Holy Trinity. "C. J. & Cynthia Phelps," signed marriage license. Quebec. *Source: Drouin* 1851 Stanbridge, Canada East, Quebec Census. Named daughter, "Cynthia…" Cynthia Phelps mother. Children listed: Hiram, John, Cynthia, Lucinda & Orville Phelps. Only son of David Phelps of Waitsfield, Vermont, USA.

Horatius Nelson: Married 1849 to Louisa Dyomthia Briggs, Dunham, Quebec at Methodist Church. *Source: Drouin*

Isaac Lawrence: Marriage 1831, St. Armand, Methodist Church (same location as Samuel Nash Phelps). *Possibly related to David Nash Phelps and Elizabeth Hungerfield family.*

James: James Turner Phelps (4206) born Fairfield, Vermont. Moved to Stanbridge, Canada East with father unknown. Married Lucy Jane Mitchel. Moved to Chelsea, MA, USA.

James: Born 13 October 1807, Stanbridge, Quebec. Parents: Philo & Urana Phelps. Baptized – Steward's Book.

Jane Phebe Pinkham: Born 1848, Clarke Township, Durham County Ontario, Canada. Parents: Elizabeth Phelps & Comfort Carpenter Pinkham. Married William Harris. Died 12 February 1919, Clarke Township, Durham County Ontario, Canada.   **(AMOS JUNIOR)**

Jeremiah: Born 9 June 1794, Rougemont, St. Hyacinthe, Quebec. Parents: Amos & Diadama (Long) Phelps. Marriage: 1819-20 to Margaret Collins at Chambly, Quebec, Anglican Church/St. Stephen. Listed with Samuel Pinkham family & father Amos/brother Oliver Cromwell in 1825 & brothers Amos/Oliver C. Phelps (and Samuel Pinkham family) in 1831 St. Cesaire, St. Hyacinthe Quebec censuses. Died: May 1865, Lyle, Mower County, MN. Children: Charlotte, Phebe, Amos, Thomas, Jeremiah, John, George, William, Hannah, Diadama, Edward and Mary Ann Phelps.
(AMOS SENIOR)

Jeremiah: Born 12 March 1827, Rougemont, Rouville, Quebec. Parents: Jeremiah and Margaret (Collins) Phelps. Died 3 January 1899, Sparta, MI, USA.
(AMOS SENIOR)

Jerusha Lucrecia: Born 8 April 1812, Stanbridge, Quebec. Parents: Philo & Urana Phelps. Baptized – Steward's Book.

Jerusha Allusha: Born 21 July 1819, Stanbridge, Quebec. Parents: Philo & Urana Phelps. Baptized – Steward's Book.

Joel: Born 1813, Quebec. 1830 Episcopal Missisquoi Bay marriage- St. Armand 25 February 1830. Joel Phelps and Charlotte Turner of Stanbridge married. Witness: Nancy Phelps. 1831 Stansbridge, Quebec Census. 1851 Canada East Census (Quebec), Missisquoi County, Stanbridge. Related to Philo (and Sarah) Phelps. Father of Philo is Joel Phelps. This entry – Perhaps grandson (From Drouin – Joel Phelps married 1830 Frelighsburg, Anglican Church, Holy Trinity.). (Remarried 1 September 1879 marriage of Joel Phelps age 66 born 1813 in Walkerton, Bruce, Ontario. Father of Joel Phelps (Jr.) was Joel Phelps. Mother of Joel Phelps is Hannah Phelps. Spouse Annie Maria Thorton age 30 born 1849 (parents Robert & Jennett Thorton).

John B: John Burk – born 5 June 1805, Stanbridge, Quebec. Parents: Philo & Urana Phelps. Baptized – Steward's Book. Episcopal Congregation St. Paul marriage – 12 March 1829, John B. Phelps and Rachel Blakely of Stanbridge. Witness: Mary H. Phelps. (1829 Marriage - Philipsburg Anglican Church). 1831 Census - Stanbridge, Mississquoi, Quebec – listed as "Burk." 1851 Canada East (Quebec) Census; District – Missisquoi County; Subdistrict – Stanbridge; Quebec.

John H.: Buried Harris/Hillsdale Cemetery. Birth: 3 Dec. 1821. Death: 9 Feb. 1892.

John W: Born 3 April 1831, Rougemont, PQ, Canada. Son of Jeremiah and Margaret (Collins) Phelps. 1853 Marriage to Mrs. H. Chandler, St. Armandest Quebec, Baptist Church. *Source: Drouin* 1855 Militia of

Stanbridge, Missisquoi, Quebec – Captain John Corey's Company; John Phelps, Number 12, second range, Age 26. <u>1857 Mower County</u>, MN USA census with wife, Julia; d. 12 November 1899, Enderlin, ND, USA.

(AMOS SENIOR)

<u>John Wesley Pinkham</u>: Born 1845 Ontario, Canada. Parents: Elizabeth Phelps & Comfort Carpenter Pinkham. Married/Died 1924, Ontario, Canada.

(AMOS JUNIOR)

Joseph Albro: Marriage 1829, Freighsburg, Quebec, Anglican Church, Holy Trinity to Harriet Chandler – signed by Sally Phelps. Signed 20 January 1831 Stanbridge Temperance Society "no alcohol" pact. 1831 Stanbridge, Missisquoi Census. Burial: 21 May 1832, Stanbridge East, Monteregie Region, Quebec. Stanton. Cemetery: *Inscription: "Son of Ebenezer & Cynthia Phelps in the 28th year of his age."* Possible Siblings: Charles Jay Phelps b. 1799/d 1873, Sally and Orcelia Phelps b. 1815/d.1841.

Joseph A: Born 1833 (Son of Joseph Albro). Married Emily Horskin (b. 1837-1910). Died 1899. Buried Mystic Cemetery.

Joseph: Son of Eldad and Abigail (Tree) Phelps. Listed without forename in 1825 Quebec census with father Eldad Phelps and brother Michael Phelps.

(AMOS SENIOR)

Joseph A.: Born 1839/1840, Quebec. Parents: Amos III and Julia V. (Johnson) Phelps.

(AMOS JUNIOR)

Luman B.: Born 2 December 1790, Rutland, VT. Married 11 June 1812, Franklin, VT to (m1)Hannah Briggs/(m2) Harriet Cromwell. <u>1825 Stanbridge, Bedford Quebec Census.</u> (Family of 8). Listed alongside ½ brother, Eldad, with Widow H. (Possibly Widow "A." for Amos Jr.) & Michael Phelps. Died 12 December 1858, Lapeer, MI, USA. Son of Amos & Diadama Phelps, brother to Amos Phelps Junior, Jeremiah, Oliver Cromwell and Selinda Phelps. Children: Amy, Diadama, Charlotte Hannah, Luana, Roxana, Anice, Sterling, Hannah (died Lapeer, MI, USA) & Dorothy Phelps.

(AMOS SENIOR)

> <u>Hannah</u> Briggs: Born 1795, Rutland, VT; d. 1830, Ontario - M1 Hannah (Briggs) Phelps to Luman Phelps b. 1790 Rutland, VA. *Source: FindAGrave*

Luman J/W: Born 1822. Father: Luman Phelps. Mother: Hannah Briggs. <u>1890 United States Census of Union Veterans and Widows of the Civil War</u>: Luman J. Phelps. Event location: Hutchinson, McLeod, Minnesota. <u>Michigan Deaths</u>: L. W. Phelps. 20 February 1903. Age: 81. Death Place: Attica, Lapeer, Michigan, USA.

(AMOS SENIOR)

Luana: Born abt. 1820, Stanbridge, QC. Parents: Luman and Hannah (Briggs) Phelps.   **(AMOS SENIOR)**

Lydia: Died 1826, 1 year 3 months, 10 days. Buried Mystic Cemetery. Possible *Phineas Phelps family member.*

Lydia: Born 1826. Died 19--. Buried Mystic Cemetery. Wife of Henry Buckland. *Possible Phineas Phelps family member.*

Mary: Born 1 April 1831. Baptized 23 September 1831 – "Amos, Diadama, and Mary Phelps baptized on 23 September 1831" – *children of (Oliver) Crumwell Phelps and Joset Roi.* Sponsors: Jeremiah & Margaret Phelps/Diadama Phelps.   **(AMOS SENIOR)**

Mary Ann Pinkham: Born 1835, Quebec. Parents: Elizabeth Phelps and Comfort Carpenter Pinkham. Married Ontario. Died Minnesota, USA.   **(AMOS JUNIOR)**

Mary Ann: Born 13 February 1842, Quebec. Parents: Jeremiah and Margaret (Collins) Phelps. Married Siloam Williams.   **(AMOS SENIOR)**

Mary Miranda: Born 6 January 1810, Stanbridge, Quebec. Parents: Phil & Urana Phelps. Baptized – Steward's Book. Married 1832 Stanbridge Anglican Church.

Michael: 1825 Stanbridge, Bedford, Quebec Census. Listed alongside brother forename unlisted (Joseph) Phelps, uncle Luman (Carmen) Phelps and father Eldad Phelps. Listed near Widow H. Phelps and daughter likely Elizabeth Phelps and widow of Amos B. Phelps, Jr., the half-brother of Eldad Phelps. Son of Eldad and Abigail (Tree) Phelps. **(AMOS SENIOR)**

Miranda M. (Mary): Born 1820 Stanbridge (siblings: Charles Alanson, Mary Elizabeth, James Turner, Edward-Liberty/twins, Lucy Jane); m. 1832 to Harrison Jewell, Stanbridge, Quebec, Anglican Church. *Source: Drouin* Died Michigan City, Indiana, USA.

Oliver Cromwell (I): Born 1781, Connecticut. Parents: Amos and M1 Phebe Phelps. Brother to Martha, Charlotte and Eldad Phelps; ½ brother to Amos, Luman, Jeremiah, Selinda & Oliver Cromwell (2) Phelps of Quebec. Died prior to 1803.   **(AMOS SENIOR)**

Oliver Cromwell: Born 19 July 1803, Rougemont, St. Hyacinthe, Quebec. Parents: Amos and (m2) Diadama (Long) Phelps. Married (m1) 1825 at Chambly, Anglican church – Saint Stephen to Josette Roi (d. 17 March 1849)/(m2) Catherine DeBois (on 29 June 1849)/(m3) Modesto Gaudreau. Died: 23 January 1890, Ste. Anne De Stuckeley, Sheffield, Quebec, Canada.

Listed 1825 (with father Amos/brother Jeremiah) & 1831 (with brothers Amos & Jeremiah) St. Cesaire, St. Hyacinthe, Quebec census. Children with (m1) Joisette Roi: Amos, Diadama, Mary, Hannah, Roxana, Stephen, Starling & Selinda Phelps. **(AMOS SENIOR)**

Orill (Orville?): Born: 29 May 1813, Stanbridge, Quebec. Parents: Philo & Urana Phelps. Baptized – Steward's Book.

Orville: Born abt. 1825, Quebec, Canada. Parents: Amos III & Julia V. (Johnson) Phelps. Naturalized citizen of USA 27 October 1886. Married Clarinda Bell Conway in Maquoketa, Iowa. Died Maquoketa, Iowa, USA. **(AMOS JUNIOR)**

Philo: Born 1770, Norfolk, CT then New Haven, VT then with father, Elkannah. Son: Elnathan m. Blakeley, Orville d. Stanbridge - not married, James Phelps – m. Lucy Mc__, Betsey Ganza, John Burk, Mary Miranda and Jerusha (Allusha) Phelps. 1825 Stanbridge, Bedford, Quebec Census: Family of 9. 1831 Stanbridge, Missisquoi Quebec Census. 1842 Lower Canada Census – Family of 3; Occupation – Shoe Maker; Shefford, Lower Canada. Daughter: Maribah Phelps – married Samuel Hungerford, younger brother of Elizabeth Hungerford who married David Nash Phelps. Mirabah Phelps died 6 May 1850, "daughter of Philo and Sarah (Gilbert) Phelps, and granddaughter of Joel Phelps." *Source: "300 Colonial Ancestors" by Rixford – see David Nash Phelps.* Son - Philo Phelps born 1807 – 1851 Canada East Census: Phila Philo) Phelps. Age 44 birth year 1807. Birthplace – Stanbridge, St. Hyacinthe, Canada East. 1861 Quebec Census – Philo Phelps. Event Place – Stanstead, Quebec. Age 53; Birth year – 1808, Lower Canada. Married; Wesleyan Methodist.

Phineas: Born 10 April 1767, Norwalk, CT. Parents: Joel Phelps/Jerusha Nash. Married 1795 to Lydia (Larnce) Lawrence abt. 1767, New Haven, Addison, Vermont, USA. Died 20 April 1813, Mystic, Quebec, Canada. Lydia Lawrence (b. 1761, Canaan, Litchfield, Connecticut, USA; d. September 1813, NY, USA); (m1) David Roberts in 1781, Groton, MA, USA. Daughter of Isaac Lawrence Jr. and Mary Brown. Children of Phineas and Lydia Phelps – Child 1 – Polly Phelps (m. J. Wright); Child 2 – Caroline Phelps (m. William Norton); Child 3 – Pamelia Phelps; Child 4 – Teresa Phelps; Child 5 – Daniel Phelps; Child 6 – Elkanah Phelps born 1794 Stanbridge, CT; m. M. Chappell; Child 7 – David Nash Phelps born 4 October 1796 New Haven, VT; m. Elizabeth Hungerford 29 April 1821, St. Armand West, Quebec; d. 15 April 1884, Stanbridge, Missisquoi, Quebec; Child 8 – Lawrence Phelps born 1810; (m1) Ursula Steward/(m2) Mary Fessenden; died 6 April 1888; child of Lawrence Phelps -Elphord Phelps.
Lydia Phelps: Born 1767. Died 20 September 1813. *Wife of Phineas Phelps – Lydia (Larnce) Lawrence m. Phineas Phelps.*

Died Cowensville, Monteregie Region, Quebec; Burial – Mystic Cemetery, Monteregie Region, Quebec.

Phebe: Born 5 October 1821, Rougemont, Quebec. Parents: Jeremiah and Margaret (Collins) Phelps. Married: Andrew Gemmel. Died: 4 September 1909, Austin, Mower, MN, USA.   **(AMOS SENIOR)**

Roxana: Born 1822. Parents: Luman and Hannah (Briggs) Phelps. Married James Blinn 22 November 1877, Springfield, MA, USA.   **(AMOS SENIOR)**

Roxana: Born 1837, Stanbridge, Quebec. Also, known as Rosiana – R. J. Phelps. Parents: Amos III and Julia V. (Johnson) Phelps. Married Iowa. Died Iowa, USA.   **(AMOS JUNIOR)**

Roxana: Born 16 April 1838.   Baptized 26 August 1838. *"Daughter of (Oliver) Crumwell Phelps (Luman Phelps written and then crossed out) and Mary King, his wife"* (signed by Harriet *Pinkham* Bachelder and Nancy Warren, wife of Oliver Warren. Huldah Pinkham married Seth Warren, Oliver's brother. Samuel Pinkham, father of Huldah/Comfort Pinkham and Jeremiah Phelps signed baptism record of Nancy/Oliver Warren's son).   **(AMOS SENIOR)**

Sally: Marriage 1829, Freilighsburg Anglican Church, Holy Trinity. Brother: John B. Phelps. Parents: Ebenezer and Cynthia Phelps.

Samuel Nash: Marriage 1831, St. Armand, Methodist Church. Same as Isaac Lawrence Phelps. *David Nash Phelps m. Elizabeth Hungerfield family.* Signed Stanbridge Temperance Society 20 January 1831 "no alcohol pact." – S. N. Phelps.
        Abigail Phelps: Signed 20 January 1831 Stanbridge Temperance Society "no alcohol" pact. *Wife of S. N. Phelps.*

Samuel Pinkham: Born 6 April 1852, Ontario. Parents: Elizabeth Phelps & Comfort Carpenter Pinkham. Named for Comfort Carpenter Pinkham's father, Samuel Pinkham Junior, who was named for Samuel Pinkham, Senior. Married 26 March 1872 Margaret McLean. Died 6 July 1915, Kindersley, Saskatchewan.   **(AMOS JUNIOR)**

Sarah: Born 1841, Quebec. Parents: Amos III and Julia V. (Johnson) Phelps. Teacher, Maquoketa, Iowa 1860. Married Issac McPeak. Son, Amos McPeak, born 1866 Iowa. Died Iowa, USA.   **(AMOS JUNIOR)**

Selinda: Born 1799, Rougemont, St. Hyacinthe, Quebec. Parents: Amos and (m2) Diadama (Long) Phelps. Married Christopher McRae on 6 March 1817 at All Saints Church, Durham, Quebec. Died 1888, Waterloo, Black Hawk, IA, USA. (Nephew Amos Phelps III also resided Iowa)   **(AMOS SENIOR)**

Selinda: Born 13 April 1843. Baptized 3 September 1843. Parents: Oliver Cromwell and Josette (Roi) Phelps. Sponsor at baptism: Harriet (Pinkham) Bachelder, sister of Samuel Pinkham Senior. Died 11 September 1847, Quebec.   **(AMOS SENIOR)**

Starling: Born 14 October 1839. Twin to Stephen. Baptized: 22 December 1839.
Sterling: Parents: Oliver Cromwell & Mary Joisette (Roi) Phelps. Sponsors: Oliver & Nancy Warren (Huldah Pinkham married Oliver Warren's brother/Jeremiah Phelps & Samuel Pinkham, father of Huldah/Comfort Pinkham, signed baptism record of Oliver & Nancy Warren's son). Name spelled either Starling or Sterling.   **(AMOS SENIOR)**

Sterling: Born 1825, Quebec. Parents: Luman and Hannah (Briggs) Phelps. 1894 Michigan State Census: Sterling Phelps. Birth year: 1825. Age: 69. Husband to Maria L. Phelps age 64. Son: Dayton J. Phelps age 19. Event location: Attica, Lapeer, Michigan, USA.   **(AMOS SENIOR)**

Stephen: Born 14 October 1839. Twin to Starling/Sterling. Baptized: 22 December 1839. Parents: Oliver Cromwell & Mary Joisette (Roi) Phelps. Sponsors: Oliver & Nancy Warren (Huldah Pinkham married Oliver Warren's brother/Jeremiah Phelps & Samuel Pinkham, father of Huldah/Comfort Pinkham, signed baptism record of Oliver & Nancy Warren's son).   **(AMOS SENIOR)**

Thomas: Born 13 June 1825, Rougemont, Rouville, Quebec. Parents: Jeremiah & Margaret Collins Phelps. Married Albina Runnels; 1857 Mower County Minnesota Census – Age 32 with wife Elbina age 22 Born in Canada. Died 10 October 1857 MN. Minnesota Olmsted County, Oakwood Cemetery Records: Thomas L. Phelps. Death - 15 June 1942 Minnesota. Son: Thomas Phelps' son: Thomas Lawrence Phelps: California Great Registers 1866-1910: Son: Thomas Lawrence Phelps Jr. Voter Registration. Date: 20 April 1875. Event Place: (Modesto) Buena Vista, Stanislaus, California. Age 36. Birth year: 1839. Birthplace: Canada. California Great Registers, 1866 - 1910: Thomas L. Phelps. Voter Registration. Event Date: 26 January 1879. (Modesto) Buena Vista, Stanislaus, California. Age. 39. Birth year: 1840 Canada. Occupation: Farmer. California Great Registers, 1850-1920: Thomas L. Phelps, age 47 born 1841 Canada. Event date: 22 June 1888 (Modesto) Buena Vista, Stanislaus, California. United States General Pension Files, 1861-1934: Thomas Phelps 1890 California. California Death Index: Thomas Phelps age 68 born 1841 Canada. Death: 1909 California.   **(AMOS SENIOR)**

Willard Pinkham: Born abt. 1841-1842, Quebec or Ontario. Death unknown. Parents: Comfort Carpenter and Elizabeth (Phelps) Pinkham.   **(AMOS JUNIOR)**

William: Born 21 January 1834, Quebec. Twin to George. Parents: Jeremiah & Margaret (Collins) Phelps. Moved to Austin, Mower, MN, USA in 1850.

(AMOS SENIOR)

William J.:   Born 1802. <u>1855 Militia of Stanbridge, Missisquoi, Quebec</u>. Captain John Corey's Company – 24 November 1855. William J. Phelps – Age 53; Lot Number 11, Third Range.

William Pitt: Married 1827 Freilighsburg, Anglican Church, Holy Trinity, Quebec.

Miscellaneous Notes:

From this list, missing names include:

~2 Quebec-born children names unknown born to Amos III & Julia Johnson
    Phelps 1829-1855 which were likely Zacheus A. Phelps born 1832 and
    Maribah Phelps born 1833.   **(AMOS JUNIOR)**
~Unknown names of Eldad Phelps' (2 daughters) children born 1805-1830. Sons:
    Michael, Joseph and Amos Phelps. Daughter Olive Phelps. **(AMOS SENIOR)**

~Four to five Quebec-born children of Comfort Carpenter and Elizabeth (Phelps)
    Pinkham - Cynthia (b. 1832), Elect(r)a (b. 1834), Mary (b. 1835), Edwin A. (born
    abt. 1835-1840) and maybe Willard (born abt. 1841-1842) - Pinkham birth
    records for city and date are unknown as were parent's 1811 and 1812 Eastern
    Township birth records.

In 1812 listing below: Elizabeth Phelps (Betsey Phelps) is NOT the daughter of Philo &
Urana Phelps given their eldest child was named, Betsey (b. 1800) and their other
daughter, Jerusha Lucrecia was born in 1812.

1812 Steward's Book for Dunham Circuit. Vital records translated by Missisquoi
Historical Society: "*N. B. Whereas Fletcher Circuit has been divided the former records
may be found on the Stewards book for that Circuit. Enoch Pomeroy Circuit Steward
Elected Oct 3, 1812.*"

Phelps   Sequence N. 203, Sequence No. 260
203: Phelps, Betsey Ganza was born on Oct. 29, 1800 and was baptized on Sept. 29,
      1813, d/o Philo & Uran Phelps. Baptized at Stanbridge by John T. Addonis.

204   Phelps, Orril was bron on May 29, 1813 and was baptized on Sept. 29, 1813, s/o
      Phil & Urana Phelps. Baptized at Stanbridge by John T. Addonis.

205   Phelps, John Burk was born on June 5, 1805 and was baptized on Sept. 29,
      1813, s/o Philo & Urana Phelps. Baptized at Stanbridge by John T. Addonis.

206   Phelps, James Turner was born on Oct. 13, 1807 and was baptized on Sept. 29,
      1813, s/o Philo & Urana Phelps. Baptized at Stanbridge by John T. Addonis.

207   Phelps, Mary Maranda was born on Jan. 6, 1810 and was baptized on Sept. 29,
      1813, d/o Philo & Uran Phelps. Baptized at Stanbridge by John T. Addonis.

208   Phelps, Jerusha Lucrecia was born on Apr. 8, 1812 and was baptized on Sept.
      29, 1813, d/o Phio & Urana Phelps. Baptized at Stanbridge by John T. Addons.

260: Phelps, Jerusha Allusha was born on July 21, 1819 and was baptized on Sept. 9,
      1819, d/o Philo & Sally Phelps. Baptized at Stanbridge by Fitch Reed.

Vermont Phelps (a few investigated with "A" or "E" initials…) - results include:

Amos M.   Marriage 24 April 1861 to Mary Dyer in Manchester, VT. Father John
            Phelps.
E. Phelps: Death Addison, VT 28 April 1864. "Age 84 years, six months and 26
            days." Born New Haven (Addison County, VT). Eldad Phelps born 1783
            Christ Church, CT.
Martha: Born 1790. Attached to Martha Brewster *Family Search* file. 1860
            Norwich, Windsor, Vermont Census: Martha Phelps age 70 (b. 1790
            Vermont) with Tabitha J. Brewster age 73 (b. 1793 Vermont), Patience
            Phelps age 37 (b. 1823 Vermont) and Samuel Phelps age 28 (b. 1832
            Vermont). With Cyrus A. Williams age 7 and Obediah Hosford age 75, b.
            Vermont.

~~~~~~~~~~~~~

Map of Amos Phelps to Benajah Phelps line:

Amos Phelps III   (buried Makoqueta, Iowa plot together) Benejah Phelps

Amos Phelps III (b.1809, Quebec)   Benejah Phelps (b. 1832, NY)

Amos Phelps Jr. (b 1786, Rutland, VT)   John Phelps (b. 1802, South Hero, VT)

Amos Phelps Sr. (b. 1750, Simsbury, CT)   Benajah Phelps (b. 1770, Goshen, CT)

    ~Moved to Rutland, VT by 1790   ~Moved to South Hero, VT by 1790

John Phelps (b. 1724, Simsbury, CT)   Lt. Abel Phelps (b. 1750, Goshen, CT)

Amos Phelps (b. 1708, Simsbury, CT)   Litchfield, CT; Father unknown)

Note: Amos Phelps Sr (b. 1750 Simsbury, CT) = Lt. Abel Phelps (b. 1750 Goshen, CT)

The Bachelder Family

Compiled by B. F. Hubbard:

Forest and Clearings, the History of Stanstead County, Province of Quebec

Text abridged from B. F. Hubbard book and Jacqueline Russell compelation, The Bachelder Families of Stanstead County, Quebec by B. F. Hubbard (August 2020)

Information about the Bachelder family follows because several Pinkham members from this Samuel and Dorothy Pinkham line married into the Bachelder family

Samuel and Dorothy (Ordway) Pinkham descendants are underlined

Descendants of REV. STEPHEN BACHELDER

REV. STEPHEN (Generation 1) BACHELDER was born abt. 1561 in England and died 1660 in England. He married (m1) MARY BAILEY, (m2) HELENA, (m3) ANN BATE, (m4) CHRISTIAN WEARE on 2 March of either 1623 or 1624.

Children of STEPHEN BACHELDER and ANN BATE (Generation 2):

i.   NATHANIEL (2) BACHELDER, born abt. 1590, England; d. 1645, England.
ii.   ANNE (2) BACHELDER, born abt. 1601; d. Wherwell, Hampshire, England.
iii.   THEODATE (2) BACHELDER, born abt. 1603; d. 20 October 1649, Hampton, Rockingham County, New Hampshire.
iv.   DEBORAH (2) BACHELDER, m. JOHN WING.

Generation No. 2:

NATHANIEL (2) BACHELDER (STEPHEN1 BACHELDER) was born abt. 1590 in England; d. 1645 in England. Married HESTER MERCER (daughter of JAN LE MERCIER and JEANNE LE CLERE, MERCER born abt. 1594 in Southhampton, England.).

Child of NATHANIEL (2) BACHELDER and HESTER MERCER was:
i.   NATHANIEL (3) BACHELDER, JR., born abt. 1630; d. 17 January 1709/10, Hampton, Rockingham, Rockingham, New Hampshire.

The child of ANNE (2) BACHELDER (STEPHEN1) was born abt. 1601; died in Wherwell, Hampshire, England. She married (m2) UNKNOWN SANBORN. The child of ANNE BACHELDER and UNKNOWN SANBORN was: JOHN (3) SANBORN, born abt. 1620, England; d. 20 October 1692, Hampton, Rockingham County, New Hampshire.

THEODATE (2) BACHELDER (STEPHEN1BACHELDER) was born abt. 1603; d. 20 October 1649 in Hampton, Rockingham County, New Hampshire. Married to CHRISTOPHER HUSSEY (b. 1598; d.1685). The children of THEODATE BACHELDER and CHRISTOPHER HUSSEY were (Generation 3):

i.   HULDAH (3) HUSSEY, born abt. 1643, Hampton, Rockingham County, New Hampshire.
ii.   JOHN (3) HUSSEY, b. 1634; d. 1706.

NATHANIEL (Generation 3) BACHELDER, JR. (NATHANIEL2, STEPHEN1 BACHELDER) born abt. 1630; d. 17 January 1709/10 in Hampton, Rockingham, Rockingham, New Hampshire. Married (m1) MARY CARTER and (m2) DEBORAH SMITH (b. 10 December 1656, daughter of JOHN SMITH and DEBORAH PARKHURST. SMITH born abt. 1645 and d. 8 March 1675/76 in Hampton, Rockingham County, New Hampshire.).

The child of NATHANIEL BACHELDER and MARY CARTER was:
i.   SAMUEL (4) BACHELDER, b. 10 January 1679/80, Hampton, Rockingham County, New Hampshire.

The children of NATHANIEL BACHELDER and DEBORAH SMITH were:
i.   DEBORAH (4) BACHELDER, b. 12 October 1657.
ii.   DEACON NATHANIEL (4) BACHELDER, b. 24 December 1659, Hampton, Rockingham County, New Hampshire; d. 1745, Hampton, Rockingham County, New Hampshire.
iii.   RUTH (4) BACHELDER, b. 9 May 1662.
iv.   ESTHER (4) BACHELDER, b. 22 February 1664/65.
v.   ABIGAIL (4) BACHELDER, b. 28 December 1667.
vi.   JANE (4) BACHELDER, b. 8 January 1669/70.
vii.   STEPHEN (4) BACHELDER, b. 31 July 1672; d. 7 December 1672, Hampton, Rockingham County, New Hampshire.
viii. BENJAMIN (4) BACHELDER, b. 19 September 1673, Hampton, Rockingham County, New Hampshire.
ix.   STEPHEN (4) BACHELDER, b. 8 March 1675/76.

JOHN (3) SANBORN (ANNE2 BACHELDER, STEPHEN1 BACHELDER) born abt. 1620 in England; d. 20 October 1692 in Hampton, Rockingham County, New Hampshire. Married (m1) MARY TUCK, daughter of ROBERT TUCK and JOANNA UNKNOWN. TUCK born abt. 1624 in Gorlston, Suffolk, England; d. 30 December 1668 in Hampton, Rockingham County, New Hampshire. Married (m2) MARGARET PAGE, daughter of ROBERT PAGE. Married (m3) MARGARET PAGE on 2 August 1671 in Hampden, Rockingham County, New Hampshire. PAGE born abt. 1630 in England; d. 13 July 1699 in Hampton, Rockingham County, New Hampshire.

Children of JOHN SANBORN and MARY TUCK were:
i.   DEACON BENJAMIN (4) SANBORN, b. 20 December 1668, Hampton, Rockingham County, New Hampshire; d. 15 December 1740.
ii.   JOHN (4) SANBORN, born abt. 1649.
       Child of JOHN SANBORN and MARGARET PAGE was:

i   JONATHAN (4) SANBORN, b. 25 May 1672, Hampton, Rockingham County, New Hampshire; d. 20 June 1741, Kingston, Rockingham County, New Hampshire.

HULDAH (3) HUSSEY (THEODATE2 BACHELDER, STEPHEN1 BACHELDER) born abt. 1643 in Hampton, Rockingham County, New Hampshire. Married JOHN 'THE COOPER' SMITH, son of JOHN SMITH and DEBORAH PARKHURST. SMITH d. 2 December 1708 in Hampton, Rockingham County, New Hampshire.

The children of HULDAH HUSSEY and JOHN SMITH were:
    i.   THEODATE (4) SMITH, b. 16 December 1667.
    ii.   JOHN (4) SMITH, b. 21 August 1669.
    iii. DEBORAH (4) SMITH, b. 7 April 1671.
    iv.   SAMUEL (4) SMITH, b. 31 October 1672.
    v.   STEPHEN (4) SMITH, b. 23 April 1674.
    vi.   HULDAH (4) SMITH, b. 6 July 1676.
    vii. CHRISTOPHER (4) SMITH, b. 12 December 1677.
    viii. DEBORAH (4) SMITH, b. 12 April 1679.
    ix.   PHILIP (4) SMITH, born abt. 1683.
    x.   ELISHA (4) SMITH, born abt. 1685.
    xi.   ABIGAIL (4) SMITH, b. 24 February 1685/86.
    xii. MARY (4) SMITH, born abt. 1690.

JOHN (3) HUSSEY (THEODATE2 BACHELDER, STEPHEN1 BACHELDER) was born 1634 and died 1706. Married REBECCA PERKINS.

Child of JOHN HUSSEY and REBECCA PERKINS was:

    i.   JOHN (4) HUSSEY, b. 18 January 1675/76, Hampton, Rockingham County, New Hampshire; d. 1733, New Castle County, Delaware.

SAMUEL (4) BACHELDER (NATHANIEL3, NATHANIEL2, STEPHEN1 BACHELDER) born 10 January 1679/80 in Hampton, Rockingham County, New Hampshire. Married ELIZABETH DAVIS.

Child of SAMUEL BACHELDER and ELIZABETH DAVIS was:
    i.   NATHANIEL (5) BACHELDER, b. 2 March 1729/30, Hampton, Rockingham County, New Hampshire.

DEACON NATHANIEL (4) BACHELDER (NATHANIEL3, NATHANIEL2, STEPHEN1 BACHELDER) born 24 December 1659 in Hampton, Rockingham County, New Hampshire: d 1745 in Hampton, Rockingham County, New Hampshire. Married ELIZABETH FOSS, daughter of JOHN FOSS and MARY BERRY. FOSS b. 1666; d. 18 August 1746 in Hampton Falls, Rockingham County, New Hampshire.

The children of NATHANIEL BACHELDER and ELIZABETH FOSS were:

i.	DEBORAH (5) BACHELDER, b. 9 April 1686, Hampton, Rockingham County, New Hampshire.
ii.	NATHANIEL (5) BACHELDER, b. 19 February 1689/90, Hampton, Rockingham County, New Hampshire.
iii.	JOHN (5) BACHELDER, b. 28 July 1692, Hampton, Rockingham County, New Hampshire.
iv.	JOSIAH (5) BACHELDER, b. 1 July 1695, Hampton, Rockingham County, New Hampshire; d. 9 October 1759; m. SARAH PAGE; b. 18 October 1698; d. May 1781.
v.	JETHRO (5) BACHELDER, b. 2 January 1697/98, Hampton, Rockingham, Rockingham, New Hampshire; d. 1723.
vi.	NATHAN (5) BACHELDER, b. 2 July 1700, Hampton, Rockingham County, New Hampshire.
vii.	PHINEAS (5) BACHELDER, b. 1 November 1701, Hampton, Rockingham County, New Hampshire.
viii.	EBENEZER (5) BACHELDER, b. 10 December 1710, Hampton, Rockingham County, New Hampshire.

BENJAMIN (4) BACHELDER (NATHANIEL3, NATHANIEL2, STEPHEN1 BACHELDER) born 19 September 1673 in Hampton, Rockingham County, New Hampshire. Married (m2) SUSANNA PAGE on 25 December 1696 in Rockingham County, New Hampshire, daughter of DEACON FRANCIS PAGE.

The child of BENJAMIN BACHELDER and UNKNOWN was:
i.	THEOPHILUS (5) BATCHELDER, b. 10 August 1715, Hampton, Rockingham County, New Hampshire.

Child of BENJAMIN BACHELDER and SUSANNA PAGE was:
ii.	SUSANNAH (5) BACHELDER.

DEACON BENJAMIN (4) SANBORN (JOHN3, ANNE2 BACHELDER, STEPHEN1 BACHELDER) born 20 December 1668 in Hampton, Rockingham County, New Hampshire; d. 15 December 1740. Married SARAH WORCESTER, daughter of TIMOTHY WORCESTER and SUSANNAH UNKNOWN. WORCESTER b. 15 August 1667 in Salisbury, Essex County, Massachusetts; d. 29 January 1719/20 in Hampton, Rockingham County, New Hampshire.

The children of BENJAMIN SANBORN and SARAH WORCESTER were:
i.	MARY (5) SANBORN, b. 27 October 1690; m. WILLIAM HEALEY on 12 January 1715/16.
ii.	JOANNA (5) SANBORN, b.1 December 1692; d. 1717, Kingston, Rockingham County, New Hampshire; m. CORNELIUS CLOUGH, 13 January 1713/14, Kingston, Rockingham County, New Hampshire.
iii.	SARAH (5) SANBORN, b. 30 September 1694; m. REUBEN SANBORN on 28 December 1714.

•

iv.   THEODATE (5) SANBORN, b. 1696; d. 10 October 1756, Kingston, Rockingham County, New Hampshire; m. JONATHAN SANBORN, JR. on 31 December 1719, Kingston, Rockingham County, New Hampshire; b.28 April 1700, Kingston, Rockingham County, New Hampshire.

v.   DOROTHY (5) SANBORN, b. 27 October 1698, Hampton, Rockingham County, New Hampshire; d. 10 September 1757, Kensington, Rockingham County, New Hampshire.

vi.   ABIAL (5) SANBORN, b. 22 July 1700; m. ENOCH COLBY, 16 December 1725, Hampton Falls, Rockingham County, New Hampshire.

vii.   JEMIMA (5) SANBORN, b. 17 May 1702.

viii.   SUSANNA (5) SANBORN, b. 20 September 1704; d. 21 July 1776, Hampton Falls, Rockingham County, New Hampshire; m. JOSHUA BLAKE on 19 July 1750.

ix.   BENJAMIN (5) SANBORN, b. 1 June 1706.

x.   BENJAMIN (5) SANBORN, b. 7 November 1712, Hampton, Rockingham County, New Hampshire; m. (1) HANNAH TILTON on 23 December 1733; TILTON b. 3 July 1714; m. (2) DOROTHY (PRESCOTT on 1 October 1737, Hampton Falls, Rockingham County, New Hampshire.

xi.   JUDITH (5) SANBORN, b. 26 October 1808.

JOHN (4) SANBORN (JOHN3, ANNE2 BACHELDER, STEPHEN1 BACHELDER) was born Abt. 1649. Married JUDITH COFFIN.
     The child of JOHN SANBORN and JUDITH COFFIN was:
     i.   JUDITH (5) SANBORN, b. 8 August 1675.

JONATHAN (4) SANBORN (JOHN3, ANNE2 BACHELDER, STEPHEN1 BACHELDER) born 25 May 1672 in Hampton, Rockingham County, New Hampshire; d. 20 June 1741 in Kingston, Rockingham County, New Hampshire. Married ELIZABETH SHERBURNE, b. 5 February 1671/72 in North Hampton, Rockingham County, New Hampshire.

The child of JONATHAN SANBORN and ELIZABETH SHERBURNE was:
     i.   JONATHAN (5) SANBORN, JR., b. 28 April 1700, Kingston, Rockingham County, New Hampshire; m. THEODATE SANBORN on 31 December 1719, Kingston, Rockingham County, New Hampshire; SANBORN b. 1696; d. 10 October 1756, Kingston, Rockingham County, New Hampshire.

JOHN (4) HUSSEY (JOHN3, THEODATE2 BACHELDER, STEPHEN1) born 18 January 1675/76 in Hampton, Rockingham County, New Hampshire; d. 1733 in New Castle County, Delaware. Married ANN INSKEEP.

The children of JOHN HUSSEY and ANN INSKEEP were:
     i.   JOHN (5) HUSSEY, b. 1703; d. 1770.
     ii.   CHRISTOPHER (5) HUSSEY.

NATHANIEL (5) BACHELDER (SAMUEL4, NATHANIEL3, NATHANIEL2, STEPHEN1 BACHELDER) born 2 March 1729/30 in Hampton, Rockingham County, New Hampshire. Married RUTH SANBORN, daughter of JEREMIAH SANBORN and LYDIA DEARBORN. SANBORN b. 7 May 1744 in Hampton, Rockingham County, New Hampshire.

The child of NATHANIEL BACHELDER and RUTH SANBORN was:
    i.   MOLLY (6) BACHELDER, b. 7 July 1775, Hampton, Rockingham County, New Hampshire.

JETHRO (5) BACHELDER (NATHANIEL4, NATHANIEL3, NATHANIEL2, STEPHEN1 BACHELDER) born 2 January 1697/98 in Hampton, Rockingham, Rockingham, New Hampshire; d. 1723. Married DOROTHY SANBORN on 15 May 1721, daughter of BENJAMIN SANBORN and SARAH WORCESTER. SANBORN b. 27 October 1698 in Hampton, Rockingham County, New Hampshire; d. 10 September 1757 in Kensington, Rockingham County, New Hampshire.

The children of JETHRO BACHELDER and DOROTHY SANBORN were:
    i.   ABRAHAM (6) BACHELDER, b. 4 September 1721, Hampton Falls, Rockingham County, New Hampshire; d. Abt. 1805, New Hampshire.
    ii.   JETHRO (6) BACHELDER, JR., b. 1723, Hampton Falls, Rockingham County, New Hampshire; d. 17 October 1803, Loudon, Merrimack County, New Hampshire.

THEOPHILUS (5) BATCHELDER (BENJAMIN4 BACHELDER, NATHANIEL3, NATHANIEL2, STEPHEN1 BACHELDER) born 10 August 1715 in Hampton, Rockingham County, New Hampshire.
The child of THEOPHILUS BATCHELDER was:
    i.   DEACON TIMOTHY (6) BATCHELDER.

SUSANNAH (5) BACHELDER (BENJAMIN4, NATHANIEL3, NATHANIEL2, STEPHEN1 BACHELDER) married EBENEZER WEBSTER on 20 July 1738. Ebenezer was the son of EBENEZER WEBSTER and HANNAH JUDKINS, b. 10 October 1714.
The children of SUSANNAH BACHELDER and EBENEZER WEBSTER were:
    i.   COL. EBENEZER (6) WEBSTER.
    ii.   SUSANNAH (6) WEBSTER, b. 31 January 1740/41, East Kingston, Rockingham County, New Hampshire; d. 27 April 1783, Salisbury, Merrimack County, New Hampshire; m. ANDREW BOHONON on August 25, 1762; BOHONON b. 11 August 1737, Boscawen, Merrimack County, New Hampshire.

DOROTHY (5) SANBORN (BENJAMIN4, JOHN3, ANNE2 BACHELDER, STEPHEN1 BACHELDER), born 27 October 1698 in Hampton, Rockingham County, New Hampshire; d 10 September 1757 in Kensington, Rockingham County, New Hampshire. Married (m1) JETHRO BACHELDER on 15 May 1721, son of NATHANIEL

BACHELDER and LIZABETH FOSS. BACHELDER, b. 2 January 1697/98 in Hampton, Rockingham, Rockingham, New Hampshire: d. 1723. Married (m2) ABRAHAM MOULTON on 13 October 1736. Children are listed above under JETHRO BACHELDER.

JUDITH (5) SANBORN (JOHN4, JOHN3, ANNE2 BACHELDER, STEPHEN1 BACHELDER), b. 8 August 1675; m. to EBENEZER GOVE.

The child of JUDITH SANBORN and EBENEZER GOVE was:
    i.   EDWARD (6) GOVE, b. 1696.

JOHN (5) HUSSEY (JOHN4, JOHN3, THEODATE2 BACHELDER, STEPHEN1 BACHELDER) born 1703; d. 1770; Married. to MARGARET RECORD.
The child of JOHN HUSSEY and MARGARET RECORD:
    i.   RECORD (6) HUSSEY, d. 1784.

CHRISTOPHER (5) HUSSEY (JOHN4, JOHN3, THEODATE2 BACHELDER, STEPHEN1 BACHELDER) married to ANN GARRETSON.
The child of CHRISTOPHER HUSSEY and ANN GARRETSON was:
    i.   STEPHEN (6) HUSSEY, b. 10 July 1739, York County, Pennsylvania.

MOLLY (6) BACHELDER (NATHANIEL5, SAMUEL4, NATHANIEL3, NATHANIEL2, STEPHEN1 BACHELDER) born 7 July 1775 in Hampton, Rockingham County, New Hampshire; married. to SAMUEL GARLAND.
The child of MOLLY BACHELDER and SAMUEL GARLAND was:
    i.   JOSEPH (7) GARLAND, b. 12 August 1811, Parsonfield, York County, Maine; m. CLARISSA LORING on 10 December 1844, Winslow, Kennebec County, Maine; LORING b. 2 February 1811, Norridgewock, Somerset County, Maine.

ABRAHAM (6) BACHELDER (JETHRO5, NATHANIEL4, NATHANIEL3, NATHANIEL2, STEPHEN1 BACHELDER) born 4 September 1721 in Hampton Falls, Rockingham County, New Hampshire; d. 1805 in New Hampshire; married. SARAH UNKNOWN.

The children of ABRAHAM BACHELDER and SARAH were:
    i.   ISAAC (7) BACHELDER.
    ii.   JACOB (7) BACHELDER.
    iii.   ABRAHAM (7) BACHELDER, JR., b. 14 March 1743/44.
    iv.   DOROTHY (7) BACHELDER, b. 12 December 1744.
    v.   SARAH (7) BACHELDER, b. 12 July 1750.
    vi.   ABIGAIL (7) BACHELDER, b. 5 October 1751.
    vii.   MARY (7) BACHELDER, born abt. 1756.
    viii.   JETHRO (7) BACHELDER, born abt. 1761.
    ix.   THOMAS (7) BACHELDER, born abt. 1766.

JETHRO (6) BACHELDER, JR. (JETHRO5, NATHANIEL4, NATHANIEL3, NATHANIEL2, STEPHEN1 BACHELDER) born 1723 in Hampton Falls, Rockingham County, New Hampshire; d. 17 October 1803 in Loudon, Merrimack County, New Hampshire. Married to ABIGAIL LOVERING, daughter of DANIEL LOVERING and MARY CILLEY. LOVERING, b. 15 December 1725 in Exeter, Rockingham County, New Hampshire; d. 15 December 1813 in Loudon, Merrimack County, New Hampshire. The children of JETHRO BACHELDER and ABIGAIL LOVERING were:

    i.   JETHRO (7) BACHELDER, b. 11 November 1745, Chester, Rockingham County, New Hampshire; d. 10 January 1825, Loudon, Merrimack County, New Hampshire; m. LYDIA WALCOTT; b. 1743; d. 27 February 1830, Loudon, Merrimack County, New Hampshire.

    ii.   MARY (7) BACHELDER, b.25 May 1747, Chester, Rockingham County, New Hampshire.

    iii.   DOROTHY (DORITY) (7) BACHELDER, b. Chester, Rockingham County, New Hampshire.

    iv.   DANIEL (7) BACHELDER, b. 15 August 1750, Chester Twp., Rockingham County, New Hampshire; d. 17 January 1832, Stanstead, Stanstead County, Quebec, Canada.

    v.   NATHANIEL (7) BACHELDER, b. 9 July 1752, Chester, Rockingham County, New Hampshire; married (m1) DOROTHY PAGE on 16 September 1781, Deerfield, Rockingham County, New Hampshire; married (m2) ANNA HOOK, 9 February 1794, Chichester, Merrimack County, New Hampshire.

    vi.   LIBBE (7) BACHELDER, b. Chester, Rockingham County, New Hampshire; d. 27 August 1839, Loudon, Merrimack County, New Hampshire.

    vii.   WILLIAM (7) BACHELDER, b. 1766, Chester, Rockingham County, New Hampshire; d. 15 February 1805, Loudon, Merrimack County, New Hampshire.

    viii.   ABRAHAM (7) BACHELDER, b. 1762, Chester, Rockingham County, New Hampshire; d. 20 March 1834, Loudon, Merrimack County, New Hampshire.

DEACON TIMOTHY (6) BACHELDER (THEOPHILUS5, BENJAMIN4 BACHELDER, NATHANIEL3, NATHANIEL2, STEPHEN1 BACHELDER) married MARY C. HINCKLEY. The child of TIMOTHY BACHELDER and MARY HINCKLEY is:

    i.   EMERSON (7) BACHELDER, b. 11 July 1779, Phippsburg, Sagadahoc County, Maine; d. 20 May 1838.

COL. EBENEZER (6) WEBSTER (SUSANNAH5 BACHELDER, BENJAMIN4, NATHANIEL3, NATHANIEL2, STEPHEN1 BACHELDER) married ABIGAIL EASTMAN 13 October 1774, daughter of ROGER EASTMAN and JERUSHA FITTS. EASTMAN b. 27 September,1739 in Salisbury, Essex County, Massachusetts; d. 14 April 1816 in Salisbury, Essex County, Massachusetts. The child of EBENEZER WEBSTER and ABIGAIL EASTMAN was:

i.   DANIEL (7) WEBSTER, b. 18 January 1782, Salisbury, Merrimack County, New Hampshire; d. 24 October 1852, Marshfield, Plymouth County, Massachusetts.

EDWARD (6) GOVE (JUDITH5 SANBORN, JOHN4, JOHN3, ANNE2 BACHELDER, STEPHEN1 BACHELDER) born 1696. Married BETHIA CLARK.
The child of EDWARD GOVE and BETHIA CLARK was:
i.   NATHANIEL (7) GOVE, b. 20 June 1721.

RECORD (6) HUSSEY (JOHN5, JOHN4, JOHN3, THEODATE2 BACHELDER, STEPHEN1 BACHELDER) died 1784. Married MIRIAM HARRY, d. 1809.
The child of RECORD HUSSEY and MIRIAM HARRY was:
i.   LYDIA (7) HUSSEY, b. 1757; d. 1843.

STEPHEN (6) HUSSEY (CHRISTOPHER5, JOHN4, JOHN3, THEODATE2 BACHELDER, STEPHEN1 BACHELDER) born 10 July 1739 in York County, Pennsylvania. Married MARTHA CHAMNESS, b. 1746 in Frederick County, Maryland.
The child of STEPHEN HUSSEY and MARTHA CHAMNESS was:
i.   CHRISTOPHER (7) HUSSEY, b. 19 November 1770, Chatham County, North Carolina.

ABRAHAM (7) BACHELDER, JR. (ABRAHAM6, JETHRO5, NATHANIEL4, NATHANIEL3, NATHANIEL2, STEPHEN1 BACHELDER) born 14 March 1743/44. Married ANNE JUDKINS on 7 May 1772. JUDKINS daughter of JOSIAH JUDKINS and HANNAH HUNTOON b. 19 February 1750/51 in Kingston, Rockingham County, New Hampshire; d. in Kingston, Rockingham County, New Hampshire. The child (Generation 8) of ABRAHAM BACHELDER and ANNE JUDKINS was:
i.   JONATHAN BACHELDER, b. 26 April 1790, Loudon, Merrimack County, New Hampshire.

DANIEL7 BACHELDER (JETHRO6, JETHRO5, NATHANIEL4, NATHANIEL3, NATHANIEL2, STEPHEN1 BACHELDER) born 15 August 1750 in Chester Twp., Rockingham County, New Hampshire; d. 17 January 1832 in Stanstead, Stanstead County, Quebec, Canada. Married (1) JUDITH "JUDAH" JUDKINS 22 September 1774 in South Hampton, Rockingham County, New Hampshire. JUDKINS daughter of JOSIAH JUDKINS and HANNAH HUNTOON, b. 17 March 1756 in Kingston, Rockingham County, New Hampshire; d.1796 in Danville, Caledonia County, Vermont. Married (m2) ZEURIAH MORRILL 1798 in Danville, Caledonia County, Vermont. MORRILL born abt. 1779; d. 24 August 1854 in Stanstead County, Quebec, Canada.
The children of DANIEL BACHELDER and JUDITH JUDKINS were:
i.   ABIGAIL (8) BACHELDER.
ii.   MARY "POLLY"(8) BACHELDER.
iii.   DOROTHY (8) BACHELDER, b. 1774, New Hampshire.
iv.   JONATHAN (8) BACHELDER, b. 9 October 1776, Danville, Caledonia County, Vermont; d. 20 February 1842.

v. HANNAH (8) BACHELDER, born abt. 1778, Vermont; d. 23 July 1871, Coaticook, Stanstead County, Quebec, Canada.

vi. ANNA (8) BACHELDER, born abt. 1780, Danville, Caledonia County, Vermont.

vii. JUDITH (8) BACHELDER, b. 4 February 1782, New Hampshire; d. February 1833, Stanstead County, Quebec, Canada.

viii. JETHRO (8) BACHELDER, b. 20 December 1784, Vermont; d. 1866, Stanstead County, Quebec.

ix. SAMUEL (8) LOCKE BACHELDER, b. 1786; m. NANCY STEARNS.

x. NATHANIEL BACHELDER, b. 12 February 1792, Danville, Caledonia County, Vermont; d. 14 August 1865, Stanstead, Stanstead County, Quebec, Canada.

xi. SIAS (8) BACHELDER, b. 21 July 1796, Danville, Caledonia County Vermont; d. 15 August 1875, Rougemont, Quebec, Canada; m. HARRIET HYDE; b. 14 September 1797, United States; d. 1877. Child of DANIEL BACHELDER and ZEURIAH MORRILL is: UNKNOWN.

xii. DANIEL (8) BACHELDER, JR., b. 18 February 1798, Danville, Caledonia County, Vermont; d. 2 May 1882.

LIBBE (7) BACHELDER (JETHRO6, JETHRO5, NATHANIEL4, NATHANIEL3, NATHANIEL2, STEPHEN1 BACHELDER) born in Chester, Rockingham County, New Hampshire; d. 27 August 1839 in Loudon, Merrimack County, New Hampshire. Married LOVE BLAISDELL. The children of LIBBE BACHELDER and LOVE BLAISDELL were:

i. NABBY (8) BACHELDER.

ii. PETER (8) BACHELDER.

iii. DOLLY (8) BACHELDER.

iv. POLLY (8) BACHELDER.

v. SUSAN (8) BACHELDER, b. 8 March 1790, Loudon, Merrimack County, New Hampshire; d. 20 November 1876, Concord, Merrimack County, New Hampshire; m. ISAAC VIRGIN; b. 14 July 1789, Penacook, Merrimack County, New Hampshire. VIRGIN d. 12 January 1870, Concord, Merrimack County, New Hampshire.

vi. MANLEY (8) BACHELDER.

vii. BETSEY (8) BACHELDER.

viii. SALLY (8) BACHELDER.

ix. HARRIET (8) BACHELDER.

WILLIAM (7) BACHELDER (JETHRO6, JETHRO5, NATHANIEL4, NATHANIEL3, NATHANIEL2, STEPHEN1 BACHELDER) born 1766 in Chester, Rockingham County, New Hampshire; d. 15 February 1805 in Loudon, Merrimack County, New Hampshire. Married ABIAH INGALLS on 13 November 1783 in Pembroke, Merrimack County, New Hampshire. The child of WILLIAM BACHELDER and ABIJAH INGALLS was:

i. WILLIAM (8) BACHELDER, JR., b. 28 March 1791, Loudon, Merrimack County, New Hampshire.

ABRAHAM (7) BACHELDER (JETHRO6, JETHRO5, NATHANIEL4, NATHANIEL3, NATHANIEL2, STEPHEN1 BACHELDER) born 1762 in Chester, Rockingham County, New Hampshire, and died 20 March 1834 in Loudon, Merrimack County, New Hampshire. Married BETSEY SMITH. SMITH b. 11 June 1758; d. 15 December 1844. The child of ABRAHAM BACHELDER and BETSEY SMITH was:

    i.   ENOCH (8) WOOD BACHELDER, b. 1798.

EMERSON (7) BATCHELDER (TIMOTHY6, THEOPHILUS5, BENJAMIN4 BACHELDER, NATHANIEL3, NATHANIEL2, STEPHEN1 BACHELDER) born 11 July 1779 in Phippsburg, Sagadahoc County, Maine; d. 20 May 1838. Married LUCY BATCHELDER on 1 October 1812 in Georgetown, Sagadahoc County, Maine. The child of EMERSON BATCHELDER and LUCY BATCHELDER was:
    i.   EMERSON (8) BATCHELDER, JR., b. 5 April 1813, Bath, Sagadahoc County, Maine; d. 14 December 1851.

DANIEL (7) WEBSTER (EBENEZER6, SUSANNAH5 BACHELDER, BENJAMIN4, NATHANIEL3, NATHANIEL2, STEPHEN1 BACHELDER) born 18 January 1782 in Salisbury, Merrimack County, New Hampshire; d. 24 October 1852 in Marshfield, Plymouth County, Massachusetts. Married (m1) UNKNOWN. Married (m2) GRACE FLETCHER on 10 June 1808, daughter of ELIJAH FLETCHER. FLETCHER d. 1828. Married (m3) CAROLINE LE ROY in 1829. LE ROY daughter of JACOB LE ROY. The children of DANIEL WEBSTER and GRACE FLETCHER were:
    i.   JULIA (8) WEBSTER, b. 16 January 1818; d. 28 April 1848, Marshfield, Plymouth County, Massachusetts.
    ii.   FLETCHER (8) WEBSTER, b. 23 July 1813, Portsmouth, Rockingham County, New Hampshire; m. CAROLINE STORY WHITE, 1836.

NATHANIEL (7) GOVE (EDWARD6, JUDITH5 SANBORN, JOHN4, JOHN3, ANNE2 BACHELDER, STEPHEN1 BACHELDER) born 20 June 1721. Married SUSANNA STICKNEY, daughter of MOSES STICKNEY and SARAH WARDWELL. STICKNEY b. 10 April 1724 in Newbury, Essex County, Massachusetts; d. in Kensington, Rockingham County, New Hampshire. The child of NATHANIEL GOVE and SUSANNA STICKNEY was:
    i.   ABIGAIL (8) GOVE, b. 23 September 1761.

LYDIA (7) HUSSEY (RECORD6, JOHN5, JOHN4, JOHN3, THEODATE2 BACHELDER, STEPHEN1) born 1757; d. 1843. Married JACOB GRIFFITH. GRIFFITH b. 1757; d. 1841. The child of LYDIA HUSSEY and JACOB GRIFFITH was:
    i.   AMOS (8) GRIFFITH, born abt. 1798; d. 1871.

CHRISTOPHER (7) HUSSEY (STEPHEN6, CHRISTOPHER5, JOHN4, JOHN3, THEODATE2 BACHELDER, STEPHEN1 BACHELDER) born 19 November 1770 in Chatham County, North Carolina. Married SARAH BROWN. The child of CHRISTOPHER HUSSEY and SARAH BROWN was:

i.   SARAH (8) HUSSEY, b. 19 February 1795, Chatham County, North Carolina; d. 1 October 1834, Wayne County, Indiana.

JONATHAN (8) BACHELDER (ABRAHAM7, ABRAHAM6, JETHRO5, NATHANIEL4, NATHANIEL3, NATHANIEL2, STEPHEN1 BACHELDER) born 26 April 1790 in Loudon, Merrimack County, New Hampshire. Married LOIS WELLS, b. 18 February 1795. The children of JONATHAN BACHELDER and LOIS WELLS were:

i.   STEPHEN (9) W. BACHELDER, b. 1820, Loudon, Merrimack County, New Hampshire; d.17 November 1862.

ii.   WILLIAM (9) T. BACHELDER, b. 25 September 1823, Loudon, Merrimack County, New Hampshire; (m1) MEHITABLE BERRY; (m2) HANNAH C. DANIELSON

iii.   NATHAN (9) BACHELDER, b. 15 May 1825, Loudon, Merrimack County, New Hampshire; m. SUSAN A. MOULTON on 12 November 1857; MOULTON b. September 1839, Loudon, Merrimack County, New Hampshire.

iv.

MARY "POLLY" (8) BACHELDER (DANIEL7, JETHRO6, JETHRO5, NATHANIEL4, NATHANIEL3, NATHANIEL2, STEPHEN1 BACHELDER) married JOSEPH D. MEARS 16 January 1803 in Danville, Caledonia County, Vermont. MEARS born abt. 1780 in Massachusetts. The children of MARY BACHELDER and JOSEPH MEARS were:

i.   ROXANNA (9) T. MEARS, b. 22 September 1803, Danville, Caledonia County, Vermont; m. AHIRA GREEN on 13 January 1829, Danville, Caledonia County, VT; GREEN b. 1808, VT.

ii.   SALLY (9) K. MEARS, b. 16 March 1808, Danville, Caledonia County, Vermont.

iii.   MARY (9) MEARS, b. 9 April 1810, Danville, Caledonia County, Vermont.

iv.   ARABELLA (9) R. MEARS, b. 2 May 1812, Danville, Caledonia County, Vermont.

v.   JUDITH (9) J. MEARS, b. 26 November 1818, Danville, Caledonia County, Vermont.

vi.   JOSEPH (9) WARREN MEARS, b. 10 May 1817, Danville, Caledonia County, Vermont.

vii.   DOROTHY (9) EMELINE MEARS, b. 9 August 1822, Danville, Caledonia County, Vermont.

viii.   ABIGAIL (9) B. MEARS, b. 24 January 1805, Danville, Caledonia County, Vermont.

DOROTHY (8) BACHELDER (DANIEL7, JETHRO6, JETHRO5, NATHANIEL4, NATHANIEL3, NATHANIEL2, STEPHEN1 BACHELDER) born 1774 in New Hampshire. She married DUDLEY DAVIS. DAVIS b. 20 May 1770 in Barrington, Strafford County, New Hampshire; d. 8 October 1852 in Stanstead County, Quebec, Canada. The children of DOROTHY BACHELDER and DUDLEY DAVIS were:

i.   MARY (9) DAVIS, b. 5 December 1794; m. JOSEPH MOONEY.

ii.   DANIEL (9) DAVIS, b. 8 July 1796; m. HANNAH BLOUNT.

iii.   SARAH (9) DAVIS, b. 4 March 1797.

iv.   DUDLEY (9) DAVIS, JR., b. 5 December 1799, USA; d. September 2, 1884, Stanstead County, Quebec, Canada.

v.   LOIS (9) DAVIS, b. 4 March 1802, Stanstead County, Quebec, Canada; d. December 21, 1846; m. CAPT. IRA STEVENS.

JONATHAN (8) BACHELDER (DANIEL7, JETHRO6, JETHRO5, NATHANIEL4, NATHANIEL3, NATHANIEL2, STEPHEN1 BACHELDER) born 9 October 1776 in Danville, Caledonia County, Vermont; d. 20 February 1842. He married BETSEY PINKHAM, daughter of SAMUEL PINKHAM and DOROTHY ORDWAY. BETSEY PINKHAM was born 22 May 1784 in Rockingham County, New Hampshire, and died 2 October 1861. The children of JONATHAN BACHELDER and BETSEY PINKHAM were (*cousins to children of Samuel Junior and Theodocia Pinkham (Gen 7)*):

i.   JUDITH (9) J. BACHELDER, b. 30 December 1801, Stanstead County, Quebec, Canada; m. Robert Kelsey; d. 8 April 1843, Danville, Caledonia County, Vermont.

ii.   DANIEL (9) B. BACHELDER, b. 29 May 1804, Stanstead County, Quebec, Canada; m. Sally Chadwick; d. February 1874, Danville, Caledonia County, Vermont.

iii.   DAVID (9) BACHELDER, b. 12 June 1806, Stanstead County, Quebec, Canada; d. 17 May 1884, Palo, Linn County, Iowa.

iv.   ABIGAIL (9) BACHELDER, b. 11 April 1808, Stanstead County, Quebec; d. 1810, Stanstead County, Quebec.

v.   ELECTA (9) BACHELDER, b. 8 April 1810, Stanstead County, Quebec, Canada; m. ISRAEL EZRA HOITT; b. 3 July 1807, Stanstead County, Quebec, Canada.

vi.   SAMUEL (9) PINKHAM BACHELDER, b. 23 May 1812, Stanstead County, Quebec, Canada; m. Mary Ann Hunt; d. 26 September 1885.

vii.   JAMES (9) WRIGHT BATCHELDER, b. 18 February 1814, Stanstead, Stanstead County, Quebec, Canada.

viii.   MAHALA (9) BACHELDER, b. 27 March 1816, Stanstead County, Quebec, Canada; m. Stephen Smith; d. 19 September 1851.

ix.   MARTHA (9) BACHELDER, b. 28 January 1818, Stanstead County, Quebec; m. HOLLIS PHIPPS.

x.   LASURA (9) BACHELDER, b. 28 September 1819, Stanstead County, Quebec, Canada; m. David Houghton

xi.   ELIZA (9) JANE BACHELDER, b. 2 November 1821, Stanstead County, Quebec; m. Joshua Little; d. 30 April 1857, Stanstead, Stanstead County, Quebec, Canada.

xii.   SOPHRONIA (9) BACHELDER, b. 22 March 1822, Stanstead County, Quebec, Canada; m. DAVID W. HILL, on 9 November 1841, Stanstead County, Quebec, Canada.

xiii.   EMILY (9) BACHELDER, b. 10 February 1824, Stanstead County, Quebec; m. JONAS KENT, on 12 December 1844, Stanstead County, Quebec, Canada.

HANNAH (8) BACHELDER (DANIEL7, JETHRO6, JETHRO5, NATHANIEL4, NATHANIEL3, NATHANIEL2, STEPHEN1 BACHELDER) born abt. 1778 in Vermont; d. 23 July 1871 in Coaticook, Stanstead County, Quebec, Canada. Married CAPT. HEZEKIAH SLEEPER, JR. on 7 May 1797 in Danville, Vermont. SLEEPER son of HEZEKIAH SLEEPER and MARTHA WOOD, b. 7 May 1770 in Kingston, Rockingham County, New Hampshire; d. 23 September 1849 in Compton, Sherbrooke County, Quebec, Canada. The children of HANNAH BACHELDER and HEZEKIAH SLEEPER were:

    i.   MARTHA (9) SLEEPER, b. 17 August 1797, Danville, Caledonia County, Vermont; d. 1842, Hatley, Stanstead County, Quebec, Canada.

    ii.   IRA (9) SLEEPER, b. 1801, Danville, Caledonia County, Vermont; d. 13 October 1885, Rochester, Monroe County, New York.

    iii.   HIRAM (9) SLEEPER, b. 1802, Stanstead County, Quebec, Canada; d. 14 December 1879, Green, Lake County, Wisconsin.

    iv.   MARY ANN (9) SLEEPER, born abt. 1798, Danville, Caledonia County, Vermont; d. 27 November 1859, Ripon, Fond du Lac County, Wisconsin.

    v.   <u>HANNAH (9) SLEEPER</u>, b. 18 June 1805, Stanstead, Stanstead County, Quebec; d. 14 October 1884, Stanstead, Stanstead County, Quebec, Canada. <u>HANNAH SLEEPER MARRIED ABIJAH PINKHAM, SON OF SAMUEL SENIOR AND DOROTHY (ORDWAY) PINKHAM.</u>

    vi.   ESQ. LEWIS (9) L. SLEEPER, b. 31 October 1807, Coaticook, Barnsford Twp., Quebec, Canada; d. 23 August 1885, Coaticook, Barnsford Twp., Quebec, Canada.

    vii.   HARRIET (9) SLEEPER, born abt. 1810, Stanstead County, Quebec, Canada; d. Missouri; m. EBENEZER DAVIS, on 19 March 1832, Stanstead County, Quebec, Canada. DAVIS b. 3 May 1808, New Hampshire; d. Missouri.

    viii.   JUDITH (9) ADELINE SLEEPER, b. 19 March 1818, Stanstead County, Quebec, Canada; d. 2 November 1904, Coaticook, Barnsford Twp., Quebec, Canada; married (m1) JACOB SMITH on 12 November 1836. SMITH born Quincy, Adams, Illinois; d. 1859, Galveston, Galveston County, Texas. Married (m2) REV. WILLIAM C. SOMERVILLE, on 11 November 1868 in Texas. SOMERVILLE b. 1816, Ireland; d. 1899, Coaticook, Stanstead County, Quebec, Canada.

    ix.   WRIGHT (9) SLEEPER, b. 2 March 1820, Smith's Mills, Stanstead County, Quebec; d. 5 November 1894, Coaticook, Barnston Twp, Stanstead County, Canada.

    x.   JOSEPH (9) SLEEPER, b. 24 July 1824, Stanstead County, Quebec, Canada; d. 1880.

ANNA (8) BACHELDER (DANIEL7, JETHRO6, JETHRO5, NATHANIEL4, NATHANIEL3, NATHANIEL2, STEPHEN1 BACHELDER) born abt. 1780 in Danville,

Caledonia County, Vermont. Married THOMAS RANDALL, son of ISRAEL RANDALL and SARAH CHESLEY. RANDALL b.19 March 1780. The children of ANNA BACHELDER and THOMAS RANDALL were:

i.   JUDKINS (9) RANDALL, b. 4 November 1799, Danville, Caledonia County, Vermont; m. PLUMA PILLSBURY; born abt. 1800, New Hampshire.

ii.   JAMES (9) H. RANDALL, b. 29 December 1814, Danville, Caledonia County, Vermont; m. BETSEY; born abt. 1820, Vermont.

iii.   ANAHILLIA (9) RANDALL, b. 1 February 1802, Danville, Caledonia County, Vermont.

iv.   JOB (9) RANDALL, b. 20 October 1803, Danville, Caledonia County, Vermont.

v.   THOMAS (9) RANDALL, b. 14 November 1805, Danville, Caledonia County, Vermont.

vi.   NABBY (9) B. RANDALL, b. 16 July 1807, Danville, Caledonia County, Vermont.

vii.   NATHANIEL (9) BACHELDER RANDALL, b. 23 July 1809. Danville, Caledonia County, Vermont; d. 18 January 1895.

viii.   SAMUEL (9) B. RANDALL, b. 31 October 1811, Danville, Caledonia County, Vermont.

ix.   NOAH (9) RANDALL, b. 29 November 1813, Danville, Caledonia County, Vermont.

x.   ASA (9) RANDALL, b. 22 June 1817, Danville, Caledonia County, Vermont.

JUDITH (8) BACHELDER (DANIEL7, JETHRO6, JETHRO5, NATHANIEL4, NATHANIEL3, NATHANIEL2, STEPHEN1 BACHELDER) born 4 February 1782 in New Hampshire; d. February 1833 in Stanstead County, Quebec, Canada. Married JOSEPH ROGERS. RODGERS b. 12 April 1777 in Chichester, New Hampshire. The children of JUDITH BACHELDER and JOSEPH ROGERS were:

i.   PHILIP (9) ROGERS, b. 10 November 1801.

ii.   BETSEY (9) ROGERS, b. 29 March 1813, Stanstead County, Quebec, Canada.

iii.   ZERUIAH (9) ROGERS, b. 26 April 1816, Stanstead County, Quebec, Canada.

iv.   GEORGE (9) ROGERS, b. 1817, Stanstead County, Quebec, Canada; d. February 07, 1887, Stanstead, Stanstead County, Quebec, Canada; married (m1) MARIA E. FOX; d. 12 October 1855, Stanstead County, Quebec, Canada; married (m2) ELIZA M. HANEY on 14 May 1857, Stanstead County, Quebec, Canada.

v.   DEAN ROGERS, b. 1819, Stanstead County, Quebec, Canada.

vi.   JOSEPH ROGERS, JR., b. 1821, Stanstead County, Quebec, Canada; d. October 20, 1853, Manchester, Hillsborough County, New Hampshire.

JETHRO (8) BACHELDER (DANIEL7, JETHRO6, JETHRO5, NATHANIEL4, NATHANIEL3, NATHANIEL2, STEPHEN1 BACHELDER) born 20 December 1784 in Vermont; d. 1866 in Stanstead County, Quebec. Married (m1) ESTHER SMITH. SMITH died 23 June 1844 in Stanstead County, Quebec. Married (m2) BETSEY MOORE. MOORE died 1813 in Stanstead County, Quebec. Married (m3) MARY SLOANE. Married (m4) CHARLOTTE AYER on 14 October 1845. AYER died 1 August 1848 in Hatley, Stanstead County, Quebec, Canada. The children of JETHRO BACHELDER and m1 ESTHER SMITH were:

i.   SMITH (9) E. BACHELDER, b. 19 February 1815, Stanstead County, Quebec; d. 20 April 1883, Barnston, Stanstead County, Quebec, Canada.

ii.   HANNAH (9) SMITH BACHELDER, b. 9 July 1817, Stanstead County, Quebec, Canada; married (m1) BENJAMIN HEATH; married (m2) JAMES WALKER on 19 December 1838.

iii. BETSEY (9) BACHELDER, b. 9 October 1821, Stanstead County, Quebec, Canada; d. 27 October 1909, Coaticook, Stanstead County, Quebec, Canada.

iv.   MILTON (9) JETHRO BACHELDER, b. 8 September 1824, Stanstead County, Quebec, Canada; d. 1913, Stanstead County, Quebec, Canada.

The children of JETHRO BACHELDER and m2 BETSEY MOORE were:

v.   JANE (9) BACHELDER, b. 25 February 1807; m. WILLIAM HENRY, October 24, 1831, Stanstead County, Quebec, Canada.

vi.   NARCISSA (9) BACHELDER, b. 10 October 1810; d. 3 July, 1840, Stanstead County, Quebec, Canada.

vii. SIAS (9) BACHELDER, b. 5 May 1813, Stanstead County, Quebec, Canada; d. 26 February 1842, Stanstead County, Quebec, Canada.

NATHANIEL (8) BACHELDER (DANIEL7, JETHRO6, JETHRO5, NATHANIEL4, NATHANIEL3, NATHANIEL2, STEPHEN1 BACHELDER) born 12 February 1792 in Danville, Caledonia County, Vermont; d. 14 August 1865 in Stanstead, Stanstead County, Quebec, Canada. Married MARY WADLEIGH on 12 March 1815 in Danville, Vermont, daughter of EPHRAIM WADLEIGH and ALICE LITTLE. WADLEIGH b. 20 December 1797 in Sutton, New Hampshire; d. 4 February 1873 in Stanstead, Stanstead County, Quebec, Canada. The children of NATHANIEL BACHELDER and MARY WADLEIGH were.

i.   GEORGE (9) BACHELDER, b. 1810; d. 1825.

ii.   SALLY (9) BACHELDER, b. 28 February 1816, Stanstead County, Quebec, Canada; d. 6 February 1893, Beebe Plain, Stanstead County, Quebec, Canada; m. (1) CHARLES SPRAGUE KNIGHT on 15 November 1837, Stanstead County, Quebec, Canada. KNIGHT b. 23 September 1813; m (2) ISAAC LIBBEE on 5 June 1860. LIBBEE; b. 5 June 1802.

iii. LAURA (9) BACHELDER, b. 30 May 1817, Stanstead County, Quebec, Canada; d. 8 March 1869, Barnston, Stanstead County, Quebec, Canada.

iv.   MARY (9) BACHELDER, b. 17 August 1822, Stanstead County, Quebec, Canada; d. 10 April 1894, Stanstead, Stanstead County, Quebec, Canada.

v.   GEORGE (9) BACHELDER, b. 11 June 1825, Stanstead County, Quebec, Canada; d. 3 November 1910, San Francisco, San Francisco County, California.

vi.   ALICE (9) BACHELDER, b. 27 November 1839.

DANIEL (8) BACHELDER, JR. (DANIEL7, JETHRO6, JETHRO5, NATHANIEL4, NATHANIEL3, NATHANIEL2, STEPHEN1 BACHELDER born 18 February 1798 in Danville, Caledonia County, Vermont; d. 2 May 1882. He married (m1) PHEBE HYDE 1823 in Franklin, Franklin County, Vermont. HYDE b. in Vermont. He married (m2) ELECTA KELLAM on 31 March 1832. KELLAM b. 28 April 1808; d. June 1845. He married (m3) CAROLINE REYNOLDS in 1853. The children of DANIEL BACHELDER and m1 PHEBE HYDE were:

i.   LUTHER (9) P. BACHELDER, b. Quebec, Canada; d. 1855, Vermont; m. HELEN SLOGGETT.

ii.   PHEBE (9) BACHELDER, b. 1822, Quebec, Canada.

iii.   HARRIET (9) BACHELDER, b. 1826, Rougemont, Quebec.

iv.   HARLOW (9) HYDE BACHELDER, b. 1828, Quebec, Canada; d. 24 March 1899, Magog, Stanstead County, Quebec, Canada.

v.   JUDITH (9) ANN BACHELDER, b. 1832, Quebec, Canada; d. 1878, Quebec, Canada; m. JAMES CODE.

The children of DANIEL BACHELDER and m2 ELECTA KELLAM were:

vi.   SIAS (9) BENJAMIN BACHELDER, b. 8 January 1835, Quebec, Canada; d. 1903, Nebraska.

vii.   MARIETTA (9) BACHELDER, b. 24 December 1836, Quebec, Canada; d. 1909.

viii.   JETHRO (9) BACHELDER, b. 27 July 1840, Rougemont, Quebec, Canada; d. 1933.

WILLIAM (8) BACHELDER, JR. (WILLIAM7, JETHRO6, JETHRO5, NATHANIEL4, NATHANIEL3, NATHANIEL2, STEPHEN1 BACHELDER) born 28 March 1791 in Loudon, Merrimack County, New Hampshire. Married MARY BAILEY. The child of WILLIAM BACHELDER and MARY BAILEY was:

i.   JOHN (9) BACHELDER, b. 7 March 1817, Weare, Hillsborough County, New Hampshire; d.1906, Michigan.

ENOCH WOOD (8) BACHELDER (ABRAHAM7, JETHRO6, JETHRO5, NATHANIEL4, NATHANIEL3, NATHANIEL2, STEPHEN1 BACHELDER) born 1798. Married DOROTHY DUMMER COLMAN on 1 November 1825 in New Hampshire. The child (Generation 9) of ENOCH BACHELDER and DOROTHY COLMAN was:

i.   ELLEN (9) "NELLIE" RELIEF BACHELDER, born abt. 1840, Holderness, Grafton County, New Hampshire.

EMERSON (8) BATCHELDER, JR. (EMERSON7, TIMOTHY6, THEOPHILUS5, BENJAMIN4 BACHELDER, NATHANIEL3, NATHANIEL2, STEPHEN1 BACHELDER) born 5 April 1813 in Bath, Sagadahoc County, Maine; 14 December 1851. Married SUSAN CROSBY RUSSELL on 25 September1838 in Bath, Sagadahoc County, Maine. RUSSELL daughter of JESSE RUSSELL and ELIZABETH BROWN b. 9 January 1814 in Bath, Sagadahoc County, Maine. The children of EMERSON BATCHELDER and SUSAN RUSSELL were:

    i.   WINFIELD (9) SCOTT BATCHELDER, b. 29 March 1841, Phippsburg, Sagadahoc County, Maine.

    ii.   EMERSON (9) CROSBY BATCHELDER, b. 10 April 1845, Phippsburg, Sagadahoc County, Maine.

JULIA (8) WEBSTER (DANIEL7, EBENEZER6, SUSANNAH5 BACHELDER, BENJAMIN4, NATHANIEL3, NATHANIEL2, STEPHEN1 BACHELDER) born 16 January 1818; d. 28 April 1848 in Marshfield, Plymouth County, MA. Married SAMUEL APPLETON 24 September 1839 in London, England, son of EBEN APPLETON and SARAH PATTERSON. APPLETON died 4 June 1861 in Boston, Suffolk County, Massachusetts.   The children of JULIA WEBSTER and SAMUEL APPLETON were:

    i.   COL. SAMUEL (9) APPLETON, JR., b. 25 November 1841, Boston, Suffolk County, Massachusetts; d. 21 May 1925, St. Paul, Ramsey County, Minnesota.

    ii.   CAROLINE (9) LEROY APPLETON, b. 4 October 1841, Boston, Suffolk County, Massachusetts; d. November 1911.

ABIGAIL (8) GOVE (NATHANIEL7, EDWARD6, JUDITH5 SANBORN, JOHN4, JOHN3, ANNE2 BACHELDER, STEPHEN1 BACHELDER) born 23 September 1761. Married WILLIAM CHASE. The child of ABIGAIL GOVE and WILLIAM CHASE was:

    i.   POLLY (9) CHASE, b. 15 August 1784, Haverhill, Essex County, Massachusetts.

AMOS (8) GRIFFITH (LYDIA7 HUSSEY, RECORD6, JOHN5, JOHN4, JOHN3, THEODATE2 BACHELDER, STEPHEN1) born abt. 1798; d. 1871. He married EDITH PRICE. PRICE b. 1801; d. 1873. The child of AMOS GRIFFITH and EDITH PRICE was:

    i.   ELIZABETH (9) PRICE GRIFFITH, b. 28 April 1827, Washington County, Pennsylvania; d. 3 May 1923, Whittier, Los Angeles County, California.

SARAH (8) HUSSEY (CHRISTOPHER7, STEPHEN6, CHRISTOPHER5, JOHN4, JOHN3, THEODATE2 BACHELDER, STEPHEN1 BACHELDER) born 19 February 1795 in Chatham County, North Carolina; d. 1 October 1834 in Wayne County, Indiana. She married ISAAC WILLIAMS. WILLIAMS b. 27 November 1784 in Chatham County, North Carolina. The child of SARAH HUSSEY and ISAAC WILLIAMS was:

    i.   BETTY (9) WILLIAMS, b. 23 February 1813, Highland County, Ohio; d. 6 March 1895, Fairmont, Grant County, Indiana.

ABIGAIL B. (9) MEARS (MARY "POLLY"8 BACHELDER, DANIEL7, JETHRO6, JETHRO5, NATHANIEL4, NATHANIEL3, NATHANIEL2, STEPHEN1 BACHELDER) was born 24 January 1805 in Danville, Caledonia County, Vermont. Married SAMUEL FARLEY SHATTUCK on 6 December 1825 in Danville, Caledonia County, Vermont. The child of ABIGAIL MEARS and SAMUEL SHATTUCK was:

    i.   ABBIE (10) AUGUSTA SHATTUCK, b. 8 May 1847, Wheelock, Caledonia County, Vermont; m. DR. ORVILLE R. KELSEY on 11 March 1868; KELSEY b. 17 November 1841, Danville, Caledonia County, Vermont.

SARAH (9) DAVIS (DOROTHY8 BACHELDER, DANIEL7, JETHRO6, JETHRO5, NATHANIEL4, NATHANIEL3, NATHANIEL2, STEPHEN1 BACHELDER) born 4 March 1797. Married HARRIS MOULTON, son of WILLIAM MOULTON and JUDITH LADD. <u>BROTHER TO SARAH MOULTON WHO MARRIED JOSEPH PINKHAM, BROTHER TO SAMUEL JUNIOR AND ABIJAH PINKHAM, SONS OF SAMUEL SENIOR AND DOROTHY PINKHAM.</u> MOULTON b/ 2 October 1793; d. 5 October 1847 in Stanstead, Stanstead County, Quebec, Canada. The children of SARAH DAVIS and HARRIS MOULTON were:

    i.   LUCIUS (10) MOULTON, born abt. 1831, Stanstead County, Quebec, Canada; d. 22 February 1851, Stanstead, Stanstead County, Quebec, Canada.

    ii.   JOHN (10) MOULTON, born abt. 1836; d.29 March 1860, Stanstead, Stanstead County, Quebec, Canada.

DUDLEY (9) DAVIS, JR. (DOROTHY8 BACHELDER, DANIEL7, JETHRO6, JETHRO5, NATHANIEL4, NATHANIEL3, NATHANIEL2, STEPHEN1 BACHELDER) born 5 December 1799 in USA; d. 2 September 1884 in Stanstead County, Quebec, Canada. Married EMILY BLISS on 2 September 1827 in Stanstead County, Quebec, Canada. BLISS b. 26 April 1809 in USA; d. 24 September 1897. The children of DUDLEY DAVIS and EMILY BLISS were:

    i.   DUDLEY (10) DAVIS, b. 14 March 1828, Quebec, Canada; d. 15 February 1916; m. CLARA A. BALDWIN on 18 September 1855, Stanstead County, Quebec, Canada; BALDWIN b.10 March 1835, Quebec, Canada; d. 12 February 1903, Coaticook, Stanstead County, Quebec, Canada.

    ii.   CARLOS (10) DAVIS.

JUDITH J. (9) BACHELDER (JONATHAN8, DANIEL7, JETHRO6, JETHRO5, NATHANIEL4, NATHANIEL3, NATHANIEL2, STEPHEN1 BACHELDER) born 30 December 1801 in Stanstead County, Quebec, Canada; d. 8 April 1843 in Danville, Caledonia County, Vermont. Married ROBERT KELSEY on 9 March 1824 in Derby, Orleans County, Vermont. KELSEY born abt. 1801 in Vermont; d. 10 June,1879. The children of JUDITH BACHELDER and ROBERT KELSEY were:

    i.   DR. ORVILLE (10) R. KELSEY, b. 17 November 1841, Danville, Caledonia County, Vermont; m. ABBIE AUGUSTA SHATTUCK on 11

March 1868; SHATTUCK b. 8 May 1847, Wheelock, Caledonia County, Vermont.

ii. WILBUR (10) F. KELSEY, b. 17 November 1835, Danville, Caledonia County, Vermont; d. 28 February 1842, Danville, Caledonia County, Vermont.

iii. BETSEY (10) DOROTHY KELSEY, b. 12 August 1837, Danville, Caledonia County, Vermont.

iv. HIRAM (10) ALBERT KELSEY, b. 16 July 1830, Danville, Caledonia County, Vermont; m. DIANTHA CALISTA NICHOLS on 2 January 1866, Danville, Caledonia County, Vermont; NICHOLS b. 15 June 1837, Danville, Caledonia County, Vermont.

v. JONATHAN (10) BACHELDER KELSEY, b. 1 December 1828, Danville, Caledonia County, Vermont; d. 8 April 1903, Burlington County, New Jersey; married (m1) UNKNOWN; married (m2) LAURA VIRGINIA HAMILTON, on 3 September 1863, Randolph County, Arkansas; b. September 1841, Ohio; d. 14 April 1923, Pemberton, Burlington County, New Jersey.

DANIEL B. (9) BACHELDER (JONATHAN8, DANIEL7, JETHRO6, JETHRO5, NATHANIEL4, NATHANIEL3, NATHANIEL2, STEPHEN1 BACHELDER) born 29 May 1804 in Stanstead County, Quebec, Canada; d. February 1874 in Danville, Caledonia County, Vermont. Married (m1) SALLY SHATTUCK on 4 July 1826 in Danville, Caledonia County, Vermont, daughter of SIMEON SHATTUCK and LUCY CHANDLER. SHATTUCK b. 7 November 1804 in Wheelock, Caledonia County, Vermont; d. 31 December 1843 in Danville, Caledonia County, Vermont. Married (2) HANNAH EMERSON on 15 January 1845 in Danville, Caledonia County, Vermont. EMERSON was born abt. 1800 in Vermont. The children of DANIEL BACHELDER and SALLY SHATTUCK were:

i. JUDKINS (10) R. BATCHELDER, b. 13 December 1826, Danville, Caledonia County, Vermont; m. MARTHA WASHINGTON ROOT on 10 June 1848, Vermont. ROOT born abt. 1826, Vermont.

ii. LUCY (10) C. BACHELDER, b. 6 June 1828, Danville, Caledonia County, Vermont.

iii. SIMEON (10) M. BACHELDER, b. 20 March 1830, Danville, Caledonia County, Vermont.

iv. SAMUEL (10) S. BACHELDER, b. 10 December 1831, Danville, Caledonia County, Vermont; d. 9 April 1911, Oakland, Alameda County, California; m. DORCAS JENNIE HEATH, on 17 March 1858, Danville, Caledonia County, Vermont; HEATH b. November 1839, Vermont.

v. DANIEL (10) W. BACHELDER, b. 20 August 1836, Danville, Caledonia County, Vermont; m. MARY J.; born abt. 1842, Canada.

vi. JONATHAN (10) WILLARD BACHELDER, b. 13 April 1839, Danville, Caledonia County, Vermont; d. 25 July 1854, Danville, Caledonia County, Vermont.

vii. JUDITH (10) D. BACHELDER, b. 30 December 1843, Danville, Caledonia County, Vermont.

DAVID (9) BACHELDER (JONATHAN8, DANIEL7, JETHRO6, JETHRO5, NATHANIEL4, NATHANIEL3, NATHANIEL2, STEPHEN1 BACHELDER) born 12 June 1806 in Stanstead County, Quebec, Canada; d. 17 May 1884 in Palo, Linn County, Iowa. Married (m1) ROSETTA G. KIMBALL, daughter of TRUEWORTHY KIMBALL and MARY SLEEPER. KIMBALL b. 1828 in Quebec, Canada; d. 1909. Married (2) AMANDA KELLAM on 20 June 1826 in Derby, Orleans County, Vermont. KELLAM b. 5 January 1806 in Derby, Orleans County, Vermont; d. 9 December 1872 in Stanstead County, Quebec, Canada. The children of DAVID BACHELDER and AMANDA KELLAM were:

i. HANNAH (10) MARIA BACHELDER, m. ALBERT BACHELDER on 7 September 1864, Stanstead County, Quebec, Canada.
ii. MARY (10) ANN BACHELDER, b. 7 October 1843, Stanstead County, Quebec, Canada; d. 4 February 1884; married (m1) DANIEL JAMES COVEY, on 7 September 1864, Stanstead County, Quebec, Canada; COVEY b. 30 January 1842, Caldwell's Manor, Missisquoi County, Quebec, Canada; d. 9 October 1869, Dehli, Ingham County, Michigan; married (m2) WILLIAM WALLACE HUCKINS on 29 December 1872, Barnston, Stanstead County, Quebec, Canada.
iii. ELECTA (10) BACHELDER, born abt. 1827; d. 25 July 1849, Lowell, Middlesex County, Massachusetts.
iv. DAVID (10) BACHELDER, JR., born abt. 1835, Stanstead County, Quebec, Canada; d. 1 July 1860, California.
v. ROBERT (10) R. BACHELDER, born abt. 1848; d. 18 August 1852.
vi. PRESTON (10) A. BACHELDER, born abt. 1853, Quebec, Canada; m. BETSEY ELVINA (10) AURINGER; born abt. 1849, Quebec, Canada.

SAMUEL PINKHAM (9) BACHELDER (JONATHAN8, DANIEL7, JETHRO6, JETHRO5, NATHANIEL4, NATHANIEL3, NATHANIEL2, STEPHEN1 BACHELDER) born 23 May 1812 in Stanstead County, Quebec, Canada; d. 26 September 1885. Married MARY ANN HUNT on 23 October 1836, daughter of ZEBULON HUNT and HANNAH GLINES. HUNT born abt. 1819 in Quebec, Canada; d. 25 November 1885 in Fitch Bay, Stanstead County, Quebec, Canada. The children of SAMUEL PINKHAM BACHELDER and MARY HUNT were (Pinkham Generation 8) (Cousins to Comfort Carpenter and Elizabeth Phelps Pinkham's children):

i. SAMUEL (10) G. BACHELDER, b. 1 November 1842, Stanstead County, Quebec, Canada; d. 8 November 1907; m. (m1) ORA A. MERRILL on 8 October 1863, Georgeville, Stanstead County, Quebec, Canada; MERRILL b. 23 January 1845, Stanstead, Stanstead County, Quebec, Canada; d. 15 July 1870, Stanstead, Stanstead County, Quebec, Canada; m. (m2) ORELIA L. WILSON on

27 March 1871, Fitch Bay, Stanstead County, Quebec, Canada; WILSON b. 18 October 1846, Quebec, Canada.

ii. ALMIRA (10) JUDITH BACHELDER, born abt. 1843, Stanstead County, Quebec, Canada; d. 30 December 1864; m. LOINS H. LEWIS on 13 January 1863, Georgeville, Stanstead County, Quebec, Canada.

iii. ZEBULON (10) GEORGE BACHELDER, born abt. 1846, Stanstead County, Quebec, Canada; d. 23 March 1863.

iv. HANNAH (10) S. BACHELDER, b. 26 February 1847, Stanstead County, Quebec, Canada; d. 21 June 1935; m. LAWSON B. CLEFFORD on 14 November 1865, Stanstead, Stanstead County, Quebec, Canada; CLEFFORD b. 14 November 1838, Quebec, Canada; d. 25 July 1922.

JAMES WRIGHT (9) BATCHELDER (JONATHAN8 BACHELDER, DANIEL7, JETHRO6, JETHRO5, NATHANIEL4, NATHANIEL3, NATHANIEL2, STEPHEN1 BACHIELDER) born 18 February 1814 in Stanstead, Stanstead County, Quebec, Canada. Married MARY ANN INGALLS on 10 July 1839 in Danville, Caledonia County, Vermont, daughter of SAMUEL INGALLS and MARION RANKIN. INGALLS b. 29 August 1817 in Danville, Caledonia County, Vermont; d. 28 January 1892. The children of JAMES BATCHELDER and MARY INGALLS were:

i. CALISTA (10) E. BATCHELDER, born abt. 1845, Danville, Caledonia County, Vermont; m. JOHN COOK on 27 February 1868, Boston, Suffolk County, Massachusetts; COOK born abt. 1838, New York City, New York.

ii. ISAAC (10) WATTS BATCHELDER, born abt. 1847, Charlestown, Suffolk County, Massachusetts.

iii. HARRIET (10) LOWELLAH BATCHELDER, b. 31 August 1849, Charlestown, Suffolk County, Massachusetts.

iv. GEORGE (10) W. BATCHELDER, born abt. 1870, Vermont; m. DORA G. HOOKER; HOOKER, b. February 1873, Vermont.

MAHALA (9) BACHELDER (JONATHAN8, DANIEL7, JETHRO6, JETHRO5, NATHANIEL4, NATHANIEL3, NATHANIEL2, STEPHEN1 BACHELDER) born 27 March 1816 in Stanstead County, Quebec, Canada; d. 19 September 1851. Married STEPHEN H. SMITH on 16 September 1841 in Stanstead County, Quebec, Canada. The children of MAHALA BACHELDER and STEPHEN SMITH were:

i. MARY (10) M. SMITH, d. 21 August 1848.

ii. MARTHA (10) M. SMITH, born abt. 1851; d. 10 August 1857, Ruiter's Corner Cemetery, Ruiter's Corner, Stanstead County, Quebec, Canada.

LASURA (9) BACHELDER (JONATHAN8, DANIEL7, JETHRO6, JETHRO5, NATHANIEL4, NATHANIEL3, NATHANIEL2, STEPHEN1 BACHELDER) born 28 September 1819 in Stanstead County, Quebec, Canada. Married DAVID GOSS HOUGHTON. The children of LASURA BACHELDER and DAVID HOUGHTON were:

i. EMMA (10) HOUGHTON, b. 1843.

ii.   CORNELIUS (10) J. HOUGHTON, b. December 1845, Vermont; d. 15 May 1908, Caledonia County, Vermont; m. MARY EMERY; EMERY b. 25 June 1844, New Hampshire.

iii.   PLUMA (10) HOUGHTON, b. 1846.

iv.   LOISA (10) G. HOUGHTON, b. 1848; d. 1851.

v.   ESTELLA (10) HOUGHTON, b. 13 April 1851; d. 3 January 1864.

vi.   MARIA (10) L. HOUGHTON, b. August 1853; d. 27 December 1863.

vii.   CHARLES (10) M. HOUGHTON, b. 3 August 1859; d. 5 July 1863.

ELIZA JANE (9) BACHELDER (JONATHAN8, DANIEL7, JETHRO6, JETHRO5, NATHANIEL4, NATHANIEL3, NATHANIEL2, STEPHEN1 BACHELDER) born 2 November 1821 in Stanstead County, Quebec; d. 30 April 1857 in Stanstead, Stanstead County, Quebec, Canada. Married JOSHUA LITTLE on 16 March 1841 in Stanstead, Stanstead County, Quebec, Canada. LITTLE b. 15 September 1821 in Quebec, Canada; d. 1 August 1901 in Way's Mills, Stanstead County, Quebec, Canada. The child of ELIZA BACHELDER and JOSHUA LITTLE was:

i.   SARAH (10) L. LITTLE, born abt. 1841, Stanstead County, Quebec, Canada; d. 12 September 1864, Stanstead, Stanstead County, Quebec, Canada.

MARTHA (9) SLEEPER (HANNAH8 BACHELDER, DANIEL7, JETHRO6, JETHRO5, NATHANIEL4, NATHANIEL3, NATHANIEL2, STEPHEN1 BACHELDER) born 17 August 1797 in Danville, Caledonia County, Vermont; d. 1842 in Hatley, Stanstead County, Quebec, Canada. Married HARLEY IVES on 24 March 1818, son of JOSEPH IVES and CLARISSA HALL. IVES was b. 20 August 1792 in Magog, Stanstead County, Quebec, Canada; d. 1868 in Hatley, Stanstead County, Quebec, Canada. The children of MARTHA SLEEPER and HARLEY IVES were:

i.   JOSEPH (10) IVES.

ii.   OZRO (10) IVES.

iii.   MARY (10) IVES.

iv.   ALFRED (10) IVES, b. 3 October 1822, Stanstead County, Quebec, Canada; d. 26 July 1903, Hatley, Stanstead County, Quebec; m. AMANDA MELVINA PARKER on 23 October 1869, Temple, Hillsborough County, New Hampshire; PARKER b. 23 June 1836, Stanstead County, Quebec, Canada; d. 16 November 1911, Hatley, Stanstead County, Quebec, Canada.

v.   RILEY (10) IVES, b. 31 March 1829, Hatley, Stanstead County, Quebec, Canada; d. 2 September 1866, Hatley, Stanstead County, Quebec, Canada; m. MARIA SUSAN LITTLE during 1856, Lancaster, Erie County, New York; LITTLE born abt. 1831, Canada.

vi.   EMILY (10) C. IVES, b. 1832, Stanstead County, Quebec, Canada; d. 1859.

IRA (9) SLEEPER (HANNAH8 BACHELDER, DANIEL7, JETHRO6, JETHRO5, NATHANIEL4, NATHANIEL3, NATHANIEL2, STEPHEN1 BACHELDER) born 1801 in Danville, Caledonia County, Vermont; d. 13 October 1885 in Rochester, Monroe County,

New York. Married POLLY DAVIS in 1827, daughter of UNKNOWN DAVIS and UNKNOWN. DAVIS b.1 March 1805 in Meredith, Belknap County, New Hampshire; d. 14 May 1881 in Lancaster, Lancaster, Erie County, New York. The children of IRA SLEEPER and POLLY DAVIS were:

- i. MARY (10) ANN SLEEPER, b. 24 April 1824, Stanstead County, Quebec, Canada; m. ALBERT DUTTON WILBOR on 13 August 1846, Elma, Erie County, New York; WILBOR b. 14 January 1821, Alexander, Genesee County, New York; d. 28 January 1903, Rochester, Monroe County, New York.
- ii. SUSAN (10) SLEEPER, b. 1827, Quebec, Canada; m. CALVIN PINKHAM; born abt. 1825, Quebec, Canada. CALVIN PINKHAM WAS SON OF ABIJAH AND HANNAH (SLEEPER) PINKHAM.
- iii. JANE (10) A. SLEEPER, b. 31 May 1828, Stanstead County, Quebec, Canada; d. 11 September 1912, Elma, Erie County, New York; m. ALONZO CLINTON BANCROFT on 2 September 1849; BANCROFT b. 27 November 1826, Vermont; d. 1904, Elma, Erie County, New York.
- iv. MARTHA (10) SLEEPER, b. 1831, Stanstead County, Quebec, Canada.
- v. CHARLES (10) SLEEPER, born abt. 1833.
- vi. IRA (10) SLEEPER, JR., b. 25 August 1837, Lancaster, Erie County, New York; d. 16 March 1921, Omaha, Nebraska; m. HELEN ELIZABETH 'NELLIE' DELBRIDGE on 11 June 1858, Beloit, Rock County, Wisconsin; DELBRIDGE b. 6 February 1841, New York; d. 7 October 1924, Omaha, Nebraska.
- vii. HENRY (10) SLEEPER, b. 1840; d. 1891, Elma, Erie County, New York.
- viii. EMMA (10) SLEEPER, b. 1846, New York.

HIRAM (9) SLEEPER (HANNAH8 BACHELDER, DANIEL7, JETHRO6, JETHRO5, NATHANIEL4, NATHANIEL3, NATHANIEL2, STEPHEN1 BACHELDER) born 1802 in Stanstead County, Quebec, Canada; d.14 December 1879 in Green Lake County, Wisconsin. Married NANCY CAROLINE DAVIS on 4 February 1824 in Stanstead County, Quebec, daughter of UNKNOWN DAVIS and UNKNOWN. DAVIS b. 23 October 1811 in Barnstead Twp., Belknap County, New Hampshire; d. 23 March 1879 in Green Lake County, Wisconsin. The children of HIRAM SLEEPER and NANCY DAVIS were:

- i. SARAH (10) SLEEPER, b. 1826, Canada.
- ii. NANCY (10) E. SLEEPER, b. 1832, Canada.
- iii. MARY (10) SLEEPER, b. 1835, Lancaster, Erie County, New York.
- iv. HIRAM (10) H. SLEEPER, b. 1838, Lancaster, Erie County, New York; d. December 28, 1864, Florence County, South Carolina; m. ROSABELLA A.
- v. CHARLES (10) ALBERT SLEEPER, b. April 1840, New York; married (m1) UNKNOWN; married (m2) MARY E.; born abt. 1856, New York.
- vi. EVA (10) MAY SLEEPER, born abt. 1863.

MARY ANN (9) SLEEPER (HANNAH8 BACHELDER, DANIEL7, JETHRO6, JETHRO5, NATHANIEL4, NATHANIEL3, NATHANIEL2, STEPHEN1 BACHRELDER) born abt. 1798 in Danville, Caledonia County, Vermont; d. 27 November 1859 in Ripon, Fond du Lac County, Wisconsin. Married TRUEWORTHY KIMBALL on 14 January 1825 in Hatley, Stanstead County, Quebec, son of TRUEWORTHY KIMBALL and UNKNOWN TRUE. KIMBALL b. 18 January 1799 in Gilmanton, Belknap, New Hampshire; d. in Wisconsin. The children of MARY SLEEPER and TRUEWORTHY KIMBALL were:

i. JOHN (10) TRUE KIMBALL, b. 1825, New Hampshire; d. 1856, Quebec, Canada; m. EMILY ANN EMERSON on 13 June 1849, Danville, Richmond County, Quebec, Canada; EMERSON born abt. 1831, Canada.

ii. GEORGE (10) KIMBALL, b. 1831.

iii. ADELINE (10) HARRIET KIMBALL, b. March 1831, Quebec, Canada; m. LUCIUS NORMAN EMERSON on 25 March 1851, Quebec; b. March 1827, Quebec, Canada.

iv. HIRAM (10) SLEEPER KIMBALL, b. 12 September 1835, Compton, Compton County, Quebec, Canada; d. 1899; m. ELLEN 'NELL' ELIZA BARTO during 1882; BARTO b. 10 June 1854, Winooski Falls, Chittenden County, Vermont; d. 29 November 1922, Sherman, Grayson County, Texas.

v. DARIUS (10) LOUGEE KIMBALL, b. 1839, Canada.

vi. CHARLES (10) WILLIAM KIMBALL, b. 4 September 1842, Compton, Compton County, Quebec, Canada; d. 4 October 1914, Sherman, Grayson County, Texas; m. HARRIET 'HATTIE' BARTOW; b. 26 July 1845, Vermont; d. 7 February1936, Sherman, Grayson County, Texas.

vii. EMMA (10) GEORGIA KIMBALL, b. November 1845, Canada; m. GEORGE L. REMINGTON; REMINGTON b. August 1843, New Hampshire.

viii. ROSETTA (10) G. KIMBALL, b. 1828, Quebec, Canada; d. 1909; m. DAVID BACHELDER; BACHELDER b. 12 June 1806, Stanstead County, Quebec, Canada; d. 17 May 1884, Palo, Linn County, Iowa.

HANNAH (9) SLEEPER (HANNAH8 BACHELDER, DANIEL7, JETHRO6, JETHRO5, NATHANIEL4, NATHANIEL3, NATHANIEL2, STEPHEN1 BACHELDER) born 18 June 1805 in Stanstead, Stanstead County, Quebec, d. 14 October 1884 in Stanstead, Stanstead County, Quebec, Canada. Married ABIJAH PINKHAM (Samuel5, Abijah4, Thomas3, Richard2, Richard1) on 4 February 1824 in Stanstead County, Quebec, Canada, son of SAMUEL SENIOR AND DOROTHY (ORDWAY) PINKHAM. PINKHAM born 5 March 1802 in Stanstead County, Quebec; died 26 September 1886 in Stanstead, Stanstead County, Quebec, Canada. Abijah (6) Pinkham was the son of SAMUEL (5) PINKHAM (Abijah4, Thomas3, Richard2, Richard1) and brother to Samuel (6) Pinkham (Samuel5, Abijah4, Thomas3, Richard2, Richard1) whose children included Comfort (Generation 7) Carpenter Pinkham,

The children of HANNAH SLEEPER and ABIJAH PINKHAM and Pinkham Generation 8 – Cousins to COMFORT CARPENTER PINKHAM, PINKHAM GENERATION 7 are:

i.　　　SAMUEL (10) SLEEPER PINKHAM, b. 10 January 1825, Stanstead County, Quebec, Canada; d. 4 January 1892; m. MARY MACK BALL on 8 March 1847, Stanstead, Stanstead County, Quebec, Canada; BALL b. 26 April 1829, Quebec, Canada; d. 13 January 1897, Peacham, Caledonia County, Vermont. PINKHAM GENERATION 7

ii.　　　LOELAH PINKHAM, b. 9 November 1830, Stanstead County, Quebec, Canada; d.18 February 1905, Los Angeles, Los Angeles County, California; m. JOHN PARKER LEE on 19 September 1850, Stanstead County, Quebec, Canada; LEE b. 15 January 1821, Stanstead County, Quebec, Canada. Died 18 February, Los Angeles, California, USA 1905, PINKHAM GENERATION 7

iii.　　GEORGIANNA PINKHAM, b. 30 November 1844, Stanstead County, Quebec, Canada; d. 1 April 1845, Stanstead County, Quebec, Canada. PINKHAM GENERATION 7

iv.　　LEWIS ABIJAH PINKHAM, b. February 1846, Stanstead County, Quebec, Canada; d. 1 March 1847, Stanstead County, Quebec, Canada. PINKHAM GENERATION 7

(incomplete B. F. Hubbard list for the children of Hannah Sleeper and Abijah Pinkham).

THE DOVER COMBINATION

The "Combination of the People of Dover to Establish a Form of Government" was entered into in 1640.

The original was in existence upon the Town Records about 1665, when it was quoted by Hubbard, but it could not be found when Dr. Belknap wrote his History. A copy made by Governor Cranfield in 1682 has since been found in the Public Record Office in London, of which the following is a transcript:

Whereas sundry Mischeifes and inconveniences have befaln us, and more and greater may in regard of want of Civill Government, his Gratious Matie haveing hitherto setled no Order for us to our Knowledge:

Wee whose names are underwritten being Inhabitants upon the River Piscataquack have voluntarily agreed to combine our Selves into a Body Politique that wee may the more comfortably enjoy the benefit of his Maties Lawes. And do hereby actually ingage our Selves to Submit to his Royal Maties Lawes together with all such Orders as shalbee concluded by a Major part of the Freemen of our Society , in case they bee not repugnant to the Lawes of England and administred in the behalfe of his Majesty.

And this wee have Mutually promised and concluded to do and so to continue till his Excellent Matie shall give other Order concerning us.

In Witness wee have hereto Set our hands the two & twentieth day of October in the Sixteenth yeare of the Reign of our Sovereign Lord Charles by the grace of God King of Great Brittain France & Ireland Defender of the Faith &c Annoq Domi: 1640.

John Follett	Samuel Haines	Robert Nanney
John Underhill	William Jones	Peter Garland
Philip Swaddow	William Jones	Richard Pinckhame
Steven Teddar	Bartholmew Hunt	John Upgroufe
William Bowden	Thomas Canning	John Wastill
John Phillips	John Heard	Tho: Dunstar
John Hall	Fran: Champernoon	Abel Camond
Hansed Knowles	Henry Beck	Edward Colcord
Robert Huggins	Henry Lahorn	Thom. Larkin
Edward Starr	Richard Waldern	James Nute
William Waldern	Anthony Emery	William Storer
Richard Laham	William Furber	William Pomfret
Tho: Layton	John Crosse	Tho: Roberts
George Webb	Bartholmew Smith	James Rawlins

This is a True Copy compared with ye Originall by me Edw Cranfield (Endorsed)
New England N. Hampshire:The Combination for Government by ye people at Pascataq. 1640

Robert Huggins=Robert Huckins: Tho: Layton=Thomas Leighton

From *Notable Events in the History of Dover*, N. H. by George Wadleigh, c. 1913.

Dover Combination: Signed by Richard Pinkham (Generation 1)

Abijah Pinkham, Revolutionary War Patriot (Generation 4):

PINKHAM, ABIJAH

Ancestor #: A089162

Service: NEW HAMPSHIRE   Rank: SERGEANT

Birth: 2-9-1734   DOVER NEW HAMPSHIRE

Death: 3-3-1779   DURHAM STRAFFORD CO NEW HAMPSHIRE

Service Source:

HAMMOND, ROLLS OF THE SOLS IN THE REV WAR, NH STATE PAPERS, VOL 14, PP 233, 234; NARA, M881, COMP MIL SERV RECS, ROLL #560

Service Description: **1)** ALSO PVT; CAPT SMITH EMERSON'S CO

RESIDENCE

1) **City:** DURHAM - **County:** STRAFFORD CO - **State:** NEW HAMPSHIRE

SPOUSE

Number	Name
1)	RACHEL HUCKINS

1780 West Point by Samuel Pinkham Senior (Generation 5):

Name					To my time & expense making up the Roll 3 days at 22.10 per d⁞
Paul Burnham	do	12	do	3.15	do
Sam¹ Pinkham	do	12	do	3.15	do
Nichº Carpenter	do	3	do	3.24	do
John Tibbets	do	3	do	3.24	do
Paul Wentworth	do	3	do	3.24	do
Paul Yetton	do	3	do	3.24	do
Tobias Cole	do	3	do	3.24	do
Joseph Tate	do	3	do	3.24	do
Thomas Picker	do	21	do	3. 6	do
John Spencer	do	22	do	3. 5	do
Simeon Hains	do	10	do	3.17	do
Pike Burnham	do	11	do	3.16	do
Lemuel Nutter	do	10	do	3.17	do
James Thomas	do	5	do	3.22	do
Aaron Hays	do	9	do	3.18	do
Stephen Tibbits	do	9	do	3.18	do
Joseph Clark	do	9	do	3.18	do
Benaiah Dore	do	9	do	3.18	do
James Emery	do	9	do	3.18	do
Joseph Wingate	do	9	do	3.18	do
Jonathan Hurd	do	9	do	3.18	do
Amariah Goodwin	do	9	do	3.18	do
Tristram Richards	do	9	do	3.18	do
Thomas Pinkham	do	9	do	3.18	do
Amos Spencer	do	9	do	3.18	do
Jonª Wallingford	do	9	do	3.18	do
Amariah Wentworth	do	3	do	3.24	do

(1) Including £472 for Rations.

(2) Including £236 for

This is a true roll —Timothy Emerson Capt :—

Rockingham ss. Exeter Jany 26, 1781 — The truth & justice of the within Roll sworn to before John Calfe Jus Peace

In Committee of Claims Exeter 26 Jany 1781 — The Ballance of this Roll amounts to Eight hundred forty three pounds 14s. 6½, Bills of the New Emission —— Ex^d Jos. Gilman

Jany 26, 1781. Received an order on the Treasury for the Ballance of the within Roll, being eight hundred forty three pounds fourteen shillings & six pence half penny

[No signature.]

[Captain Timothy]

Pay Roll for Capt Timothy Emerson's Company
which Reg^t was raised by the State of New Hampsh
of West Point — 1780. —

[NAMES.]	Rank	Time of engagement 1780	Time of discharge 1780	Time in Service mo. dys	Rate per month £
Timothy Emerson	Capt	June 29	Oct 26	3.28	804.
Joseph Pinkham	Lieut	do	do	3.28	536.
James Burnham	Ens^n	do	do	3.28	402.
John Dame	Serg^t	July 18	do	3. 9	201.
Joseph Applebee	do	21	do	3. 6	201.
David Wingate	do	9	do	3.18	201.
Saml Rendall	Corp^t	3	do	3.24	147.8
Robert Hard	do	13	do	3.14	147.8
John Allen	do	9	do	3.18	147.8
Jonathan Dore	Priv^t	9	do	3.18	134.
Thomas Applebee	do	10	do	3.17	do
Timothy Davis	do	13	do	3.14	do
John Smith	do	13	do	3.14	do
Benj^a Leathers	do	13	do	3.14	do
Enoch Leathers	do	13	do	3.14	do
Samuel Yetton	do	13	do	3.14	do
Isaac Small	do	12	do	3.15	do
Edward Leathers	do	12	do	3.15	do
Jonathan Dowe	do	12	do	3.15	do
Timothy Gleason	do	12	do	3.15	do

Abner Morrill — 1800
David Morrill — 1809
Isaac Morrill — 1806
Paul Morrill — 1803
William Morrill — 1800
Rev. Avery Moulton — 1800
William Moulton — 1798
Oliver Nash — 1805
Adam Noyes — 1812
Israel Parsons — 1815
Andrew Patton — 1804
James Paul — 1800
Jedediah Peasley — 1803
Wilder Pierce — 1816
Samuel Pinkham — 1800
Selah Pomeroy — 1798
John Quimby — 1808
Nathaniel Rix — 1799
John Roberts — [   ]
Isaac Rogers — 1801
Joseph Rogers — 1802
Philip Rogers — 1802
William Rogers — 1798
Edward Rose — 1800
Timothy Rose — 1800
Capt. John Ruiter — 1800
Capt. H. Sleeper — 1801
Ichabod Smith — 1810
Joel Smith — 1803
Nathaniel Stearns — 1804
Johnson Taplin — 1796
Jacob Taylor — 1800
Silas Taylor — 1805
Joseph H. Terrill — 1800
Nathaniel Tilton — [   ]
David Wallingford — 1806
Peter Weare — 1803
Dr. Isaac Whitcher — 1799
Calvin Wilcox — 1817
Capt. Israel Wood — 1797
Edward Worth — 1800
Joseph Worth — 1800

Settler's Monument Stanstead, Quebec: Samuel Pinkham 1800 (Generation 5)

Comfort Carpenter — 1800
Francis Cass — 1800
John Cass — 1800
Theophilas Cass — 1798
Seth Caswell — 1820
Col. Wright Chamberlain — 1809
Marcus Child, M. P. — 1809
Dr. Samuel Clark — 1797
William Clark — 1979
Moses French Colby, M.D. — 1814
Daniel Curtis — 1800
Capt. Dudley Davis — 1800
Silas Dickerson — 1813
Jesse Farley — 1803
Johnathan Field — 1808
Silas Fox — 1800
Uriah Fox — 1803
George T. Gates — 1823
Rev. Joseph Gibb — 1829
Jacob Goodwin — 1798
Johnathan Gordon — 1800
Oliver Hartwell — [   ]
Daniel Heath — 1804
Peter Heath — 1804
Pliny Hibbard — [   ]
Daniel Holmes — [   ]
Rev. Austin Hubbard — 1807
Phineas Hubbard — 1805
Francis Judd — [   ]
Col. Charles Kilborne — 1804
Capt. Joseph Kilborn — 1792
Capt. Samuel Knight — 1823
Nathaniel Ladd — 1800
John Langmayde — 1798
Major Daniel Lee — 1797
Rev. Jason Lee — 1803
Jeremiah/Jedediah Lee - [   ]
Abraham Libby — 1798
Ebenezer Lincoln — 1807
James Locke — 1800
James Lyford — 1802
Daniel Mansur — 1802
Abraham Martin — [   ]
Asa May — 1805
Hezikiah May — 1806
Charles McClary — [   ]
William McClary — 1798

Settler's Monument Stanstead, Quebec: Comfort Carpenter 1800

Quebec, Richelieu Census, settled 1797 – Samuel Pinkham, Sr., Abijah Pinkham (son), Joseph Pinkham (son), Widow Thankful Carpenter (wife of Comfort Carpenter, patriot; parents of Theodosia Carpenter married to Samuel Pinkham, Jr.), Amos Carpenter (brother of Comfort Carpenter, patriot), Thomas Ruiter (husband of Samuel Pinkham Senior's daughter).

Samuel Pinkham Senior with sons, Abijah Pinkham and Joseph Pinkham, Stanstead, Quebec

1900 Pinkham, Saskatchewan founded by Charles (pioneer realtor) and Samuel (farmer) Pinkham (Generation 9).

Lorne (Lawrence Mowbray) Pinkham (Generation 9) with wife Annie Gordon and sons (left to right) Ralph, Wesley, Gordon and Robert Earlby Pinkham (Generation 10). 1936, Sunderland, Ontarion Canada.

Lorne Pinkham (Generation 9) with granddaughters (Generation 11) seated on lap - Bette, daughter of Robert Earlby Pinkham and Lorna, daughter of Wesley Pinkham. Standing, daughter of Robert Earlby Pinkham, Barbara Pinkham. 1940 Sunderland, Ontario, Canada

Lorne and Annie (Gordon) Pinkham (Generation 9)

Lorne Pinkham (Generation 9), Sunderland, Ontario, Canada

The Pinkham Family
By Robert Earlby Pinkham (Generation 10)

Perhaps the one valid reason for recording the living and dying of any family would accrue from outstanding achievement in some form of human endeavour. The number who fit into this category, however, is relatively small and, for this reason, there may be some excuse for setting out in brief detail the lives of an average family, if only to satisfy the historical interest of the progeny.

Unfortunately, the recorded information on the Pinkham family starts late and the name appears to be ending all too soon due to the lack of male heirs. This brief outline may be of some interest to our grandchildren and to those who follow.

Actual recorded detail starts with the old family Bible of John and Sarah Anne Pinkham in 1845. If there were any records prior to that, they have long since been lost or forgotten in someone's attic. Therein, however, legendary information which has been passed down through the family and to which relative fact and circumstances lend credence to its authenticity. As a boy, I recall my father, Aunt Lilly and my grandfather discussing family history.

The name "Pinkham" originated in Wales. One regent of the family emigrated from England in the mid-seventeen-hundreds and, probably landed in Massachusetts. It is believed they first settled in New Hampshire. Today there are numerous families of the name living in the state. The "Pinkham Notch" is a well-known ski and winter resort in the White Mountains. As of recent years, Pinkham's Ladies Gloves has been a well-known brand name in England.

John Pinkham's grandfather or great-grandfather (this point is not clear) married a Pennsylvania Dutch girl and they moved from the States into Canada with the United States Loyalists and settle somewhere in the Prince Edward County area west of Belleville, Ontario. It is presumed they crossed Lake Ontario in small boats with the U.E.L. settlers. History records the Loyalists entering Canada and numerous points all the way from Ontario east to New Brunswick and Nova Scotia.

A check of the U.E.L. records at the Association Headquarters in Toronto failed to reveal the Pinkham name on the registration. This could very well be because they failed to take the time or trouble to register with the Association years ago. Many Loyalists were issued grants of land from the British Crown, but I have not researched this aspect.

While dealing with the legendary phase of the Pinkham story, it may be appropriate to relate here the part played by Bishop Pinkham of Calgary. When I was a lad, my father and his family, talked a good deal about the Bishop and I had the impression that he and grandfather John were close blood relatives. Before I started this write-up, Mary Alice Davis (Chicago) was kind enough to send me a newspaper clipping regarding the Bishop that had been kept by her mother (my Aunt Lilly). The article was not dated, but from this information it contained, the printing year would be 191(4). The picture accompanying the article bore a striking resemblance to Grandpa John right down to full beard which they both wore. The Bishop also had a prominent place in a three-part story published in Chatelaine Magazine in 1967 (Canada's Centennial year) which dealt with four families having important roles in the development of the Canadian West around the turn of the century - 1875 to 1925. The article was titled, "The Crosses of the West." The family names included were:
1) Drever - Hudson's Bay Company factor and fur-trader.
2) McLeod - Head of Royal Canadian North West Mounted Police.
3) Pinkham - Bishop of Calgary - his wife and daughter.
4) Cross - Prominent in the development of the West.
Here briefly is the story of the Bishop:

William Cyprian Pinkham
> Born - Nov. 11, 1844 - St. John, Newfoundland.
> Married - Dec. 29, 1868 - Jean Drever in Fort Garry (now
> > Winnipeg).
> Died - July 18, 1928 - Calgary, Alberta.

After his elementary education in Newfoundland, his father, an Anglican priest, sent him to England to prepare for the clergy. He attended St. Augustine College in Canterbury. It was intended that he go to India as a missionary. His church superiors, however, claimed there was insufficient funds to send him to India. He returned home and was then persuaded to prepare to minister in the newly developing Canadian West.

He was consequently ordained in the Anglican Church in London, Ontario on July 16, 1868 and he promptly proceeded by overland route to Manitoba. There he married Jean Anne, the daughter of William Drever, a successful fur trader with the Hudson's Bay Company.

In 1888, he was appointed Bishop of Calgary and Saskatchewan. In 1890, he became chairman of the Board of Education. The Bishop and Jean Anne had seven children - Lila, Augustine, James, McLeod, Mary, Madeline, Margaret (Peggy) and Ernest born in Calgary in 1890. Jean Anne, besides raising a large family, was a tireless worker in public service. She was the principal founder of the Calgary General Hospital for which she was awarded the Order of the British Empire. She was born 1850 and died in 1939. Her daughter, Mary, was also awarded the O.B.E. for a life devoted to Red Cross work. She was born in 1878 and died in 1964.

There is a village of Pinkham just off the Highway running west from Saskatoon new the Alberta border.

When you look in the mirror you get a reflected image of yourself. If you hold it right, you may get a view of what is behind you or where you came from. Let's turn the mirror on some of those people in your past who had, from a genetic standpoint some degree of influence or who and what you are. For the cast of characters and their relative positions in the line, see the accompanying Family Tree Chart. A thumbnail sketch of each follows in chronological order of his or her appearance on the scene.

JOHN PINKHAM - Born in Clarke Township, Victoria County of Ontario in 1845. He was a mild-mannered man, gentle of character and short of stature but robust and energetic. He married Sarah Anne Irwin in Oakwood, Ontario. They raised a family of seven while he operated a farm in the area called, Little Britain. They suffered considerable adversity, having had three barns burned down, two of them because of lightning. He gave up the farm in 1915, moved to town and took on a rural mail contract. When his horse grew too old to haul the buggy and the mail, he acquired a model T Ford car. I had the distinction and pleasure of teaching him to drive. He was 74 and I was 15. For a while when I had problems if the brake wouldn't respond, Grandpa hollered, "Whoa-o-a." He eventually mastered driving.

John had two brothers and a sister Cynthia who married a Wright in the Lindsay area. Brother Charles headed West a hundred years ago with other pioneering souls. Brother Sam went back to New York whence the family came two-hundred years ago. William Cyprian, the Bishop, I am sure was not a brother, but could very well have been from a first-cousin, but records are too few and vague to explain how.

Sarah Anne predeceased John by ten years. They are buried in the Anglican Church cemetery on the western outskirts of Little Britain.

SARAH PINKHAM - Born in 1852. Her parents, Robert Irwin and Mary Jane Taylor, came to Canada from Ireland. Sarah Anne was a woman of regal bearing and seemed to be in command of all situations. I was always very careful as to what I said or did in her presence. Following a visit to my grandparents as a small boy, I had to write and thank them for having a real nice visit. For the lack of something additional to say, I mentioned the only exception was, I didn't get quite enough to eat. For this false observation, I was, in due course, properly chastised.

MINNIE ESTELLE - The first child was a replica of her mother Sarah Anne - born 1879. She taught at the Royal Oak School four miles from the family home. Her means of transportation was her own pony and rig. One of her trials was that she had as one of her pupils her brother Lorne in his High School entrance year. On at least one occasion she had to expel him from the classroom. To get even, he drove the pony and buggy home. However, that back-fired when his father sent him promptly back with definite orders to walk home. Minnie never married. She taught school for half of her short life, dying at age thirty-nine of appendicitis.

ROBERT LAWRENCE MOWBRAY - Known simply as, Lorne. Born August 11, 1875. He seems to have been an equal blend of his father and mother - was a happy lad and full of mischief. He stayed with his parents on the farm until he met Annie Gordon, a comely Scottish lass who played the organ in the church near Cannington. They were married and rented a farm 3 ½ miles north of Sunderland on what is now Highway 12. Because Annie was Presbyterian and Lorne Anglican, a simple compromise was in order. They joined the Methodist Church in Sunderland.

In 1914, they sold out the farm and bought the Furniture and Funeral Business in town. He didn't completely leave the farm because, a short distance from Sunderland, he rented a small parcel of land and a barn where he kept show horses and several cows. This was more for his own personal amusement and diversion and to keep his sons busy before and after school because he loved the farm and especially good horses.

HATTIE - Born 1877. Do not remember her well except she had pretty, reddish-brown hair. She married James Munsie and they settled in Minedosa, Manitoba, moving several years later to Winnipeg where he had a position on the grain exchange. The Munsies raised a large family. The eldest, Lillian, married Len Greer, a mining engineer, and as of this fate, they lived in Thunder Bay, Ontario. The second, Mary, is Mrs. Bower and still lives in Winnipeg, as does James, the first son. See chart for names only of other children. The youngest, Wesley, is a dentist in Vancouver, BC.

LILLIAN - Born 1879. A beautiful blonde and certainly my favorite aunt. On her several visits to our home, she came loaded with tricycles, mechanical trains and other toys for my brothers and me. Lilly was a nurse in Los Angeles where she met and married Dr. Charles Piper. They later moved to Chicago where their daughter Mary Alice Davis now lives. I recall the shock I felt when I learned of her death in Chicago just about three months after my father Lorne died.

ANNIE - Born 1882. Did not know Aunt Annie other than that she married Robert Rumney and they lived somewhere between Lindsay and Coboconk. They had one daughter, Lillian. Annie died at the age of 29.

FRANK MILTON: Born 1885. Milt, as he was called, was the swashbuckling member of the family. He seems to be all over and either coming or going. I remember distinctly one of his last visits to our home on the farm near Sunderland. Uncle Milt would pick my brother Gordon and me up by our blouse fronts and hoist us up and down at arms-length like a pair of dumbbells. I will also not forget the look on my mother's face when he pulled out his revolver and, snapping open the cartridge chamber, spewed bullets all over the kitchen floor.

Milt when West and got a job with the railway. Nothing was heard from him for many years until his son, Neil, came to Ontario and lived with Margaret and me for several months. Neil's employment here didn't last and he returned to Alberta. The last we heard of Uncle Milt was about 1952 when he was preparing for retirement from the railway and appealing to my brother, Ralph, to provide proof of age for him. I do not know where or when his death occurred.

WESLEY - Born 1887. Lived only to age 19 when he died of appendicitis.

THE NEXT GENERATION

ROBERT EARLBY PINKHAM - Born March 4, 1904 on the farm 3 ½ miles north of Sunderland, Ontario. When I was aged ten, we left the farm when my father bought the Furniture and Funeral Business and we moved to town. That was the customary set-up for those businesses in small towns in those days.

After graduating from high school, Dad thought it would be a good idea for me to become a school teacher so off I went to Peterborough Normal School (Teachers College). The idea didn't work out too well - the kids in the schools were as big or bigger than I was, and I flunked my year. That was enough of that, so back I went to Lindsay Collegiate to complete my senior matriculation (first year at U.).

For the next several years, I helped my father in the business at home. But, it was hard to keep a ambitious young lad "down on the farm" and in the spring of 1929 I got a job with the country's largest oil company - Imperial Oil Limited - in Toronto. Two years later, I was transferred to Hamilton where I met my wife Margaret, the eldest daughter of James and Christina Milne, Hamilton Scottish direct from Aberdeen, Scotland. In 1939, we moved back to Toronto and began the serious business of raising and educating our three daughters, Barbara, Bette and Louise.

Twenty-eight years later, I retired from the company and moved to Cannington to help my brother Ralph with his business there. This was a happy transition from full employment to complete retirement. In the meantime, Margaret and I were preparing our summer home on Balsam Lake for year-round occupancy. Ralph sold the business in 1972 when Marg and I moved to the lake. We haven't spent a full winter there. The months of February and March we have been spending in Florida then with Barbara and her family in California.

GORDON GERALD - Born May 17, 1905. Gordon was the teacher of the family. He made a career as principal of Sunderland elementary schools, Milford Bay in Muskoka Lakes district of Ontario and, lastly, at Oakwood. Gordon was the most like our mother, Annie. The Scottish ancestry reflected in a somewhat serious approach to life, but with a dry sense of humor always at the ready. He was very active in Masonic work as an avocation. He served as Master of his mother lodge at Sunderland, and, later, Deputy Grand Master of Victoria District. Following about a year of illness, he died of cancer on November 15, 1975. His widow, Jessie, lives in their home in Bracebridge, Ontario.

JOHN WESLEY - Born September 7, 1907. After completing high school, he joined the Bank of Commerce in Sunderland. He served in numerous branches of the bank in various accounting capacities. From accountant in Belleville, he progressed to chief accountant at Napanee and Madoc, then was appointed manager at Tamworth. The next move was to Fort Perry. About 1963 he moved to the head office in Toronto and served in the Properties Department, prior to taking early retirement in 1967. He continued to work for some time on a month to month basis.

In 1971, Wes became ill with the flu, and later hospitalized with pneumonia where he died with attendant complications. He left his lovely wife, Dorothy, who now lives in her hometown of Lindsay, and two charming daughters.

RALPH LORNE - Born July 22, 1909. Ralph, the youngest of Lorne's boys, took considerable flack and buffeting from his three older brothers. He was equal to it and came on strong when he assumed management of the business while Dad bowled and played with his horses at the local fall fairs.

In the partnership, Ralph and father got along. Following Lorne's death, he expanded by buying the furniture and funeral business in the neighboring town of Beaverton (*text following faded*). In 1966, he also bought the business in Cannington. In 1970, he sold out completely.

Late in March of 1974, while vacationing in Florida, he suffered heart failure and a stroke which left his right side permanently crippled. He has made some improvement and is bright and alert. Having learned to live with his physical disability, Ralph and his wife, Iva, lived in their longtime home in Sunderland.

~~~~~~~~

This ends the Pinkham story so far as I know it. As mentioned earlier, this branch of the Pinkham name is passing into oblivion with this exception - Neil had at least one son and daughter. I have not heard of them in many years. They are undoubtedly in Western Canada - Alberta or Saskatchewan.

Family lines and genealogical history has always been of interest to me and have felt a bit of sadness that our earlier generations did not pass down written records to those of us who came later. It is a fact that family trees can become very involved and complicated with the addition of each additional generation.

This chronicle is addressed principally to our children, our grandchildren and their children. When you grow up you may have at least some interest in your family background. Remember, there are two distinct passages back into your genealogical history - your father's and your mother's. This will give you a glimpse into your mother's part. As my father often said, "You are English, Irish, Scottish, Yankee-Dutch and Canadian - and be proud of it."

(Signed) R. Earl Pinkham

March 25, 1976
Robert Earlby Pinkham
Long Point on Balsam Lake
RR #3, Kirkfield, Ontario

THE PINKHAM FAMILY TREE

JOHN PINKHAM (b. 1845, d. 1924) married Sarah Anne Irwin (b. 1852, d. 1914) on 20 November 1872.

The Children of JOHN PINKHAM and Sarah Anne Irwin were: Mary Estelle (b. 1873, d. 1917), Lorne M. (b. 1875, d. 1948), Hattie (b. 1877, d. 1936), Lillian (b. 1879-1948), Annie (b. 1882, d. 1911), Milton (b. 1885, d. ?), Wesley (b. 1887, d. 1906).

The children of LORNE PINKHAM (b. 1875, d. 1948) and Annie Gordon (b. 1878, d. 1960) were:

 Robert Earlby (b. 1904, d. -)
  Married Margaret Milne (b. 1908, d. -)
   The children of Robert and Margaret Pinkham:
    Barbara Anne b. January 19, 1937
     m. J. Manrique
     Children: two daughters -
      Anne Louise Manrique b. 31 Oct. 1965
      Daughter b. 9 March 1967
    Bette Margaret b. 7 June 1938
     m. J. Robinson
     Children: three sons -
      James Robert b. 19 Jan 1964
      Jeffery Wade b. 7 Jan. 1967
      Scott Alfred b. 6 May 1969
    Louise Christine b. 7 June 1945
     m. F. C. Allen
     Children (m1): two sons -
      Lee Frederick b. 27 Sept. 1970
      Jeremy Earl b. 26 Feb. 1972
 Gordon Gerald (b. 1905, d. 1975)
  Married Jessie Harris (b. 1914, d. 1972)
 John Wesley (b. 1907, d. 1969)
  Married Dorothy Babcock (b. 1910, d. 1973)
   The children of John and Dorothy Pinkham:
    Lorna Grace b. 22 June 1939
     m. C. Wannamaker
     Children: 3 sons/2 daughters
      Steven Carl b. 31 Jan. 1960
      Patti Anne b. 24 Nov. 1961
      Juli Carol b. 2 Dec. 1963
      David John b. 5 July 1965
    Carolyn Janet b. 5 March 1952
 Ralph Lorne (b.1910, d. -)
  Married Iva Brethour (b. 1911, d. -)

THE IRWIN -PINKHAM FAMILY TREE
1
DAVID IRWIN
circa 1761
m. Janet Graham
1
WILLIAM IRWIN
m. Mary Nelson
1
ROBERT IRWIN
b. 1813, d. 1876
m. Mary Jane Taylor

The children of ROBERT IRWIN and Mary Jane Taylor were:

William Irwin b. 1850, d. 1926, m. Martha Wannamaker
Sarah Ann Irwin b. 1852, d. 1914, m. John Pinkham
Eliza Jane Irwin b. 1845, d. 1921, m. Donald McIntyre
John James Irwin, b. 1857, d. 1938, m. Margaret Hicks
Amelia Irwin, b. 1859, d. 1867
Mary Louisa Irwin, b. 1864, d. 1933, m. John Alton

The children of SARAH ANN IRWIN and John Pinkham:

Mary Estelle Pinkham (b. 1873, d. 1917)

Lorne Mowbray Pinkham (b 1875, d. 1948)
    m. Annie Gordon (b. 1878, d. 1960)
    The children of Lorne and Annie Pinkham:
        Robert Earlby Pinkham b. 1904
           m. Margaret Milne b. 1912
           Children of Robert and Margaret Pinkham:
               Barbara Anne b. 1937
               Bette Margaret b. 1938,
               Louise Christine b. 1945
        Gordon Gerald Pinkham (b. 1905, d 1975)
           m. Jessie Harris b. 1914
        John Weslely Pinkham (b. 1907, d. 1969),
           m. Dorothy Babcock b. 1910
           Children of Wesley and Dorothy Pinkham:
               Lorna Grace b. 1939
               Carolyn Janet b. 1952
        Ralph Lorne Pinkham (b. 1910)
           m. Iva Brethour (b. 1911)

Hattie Pinkham (b. 1877, d. 1936)
> m. James Munsie
> The children of Hattie and James Munsie:
> > Lillian Munsie
> > > m. Len Greer
> > Mary Munsie
> > > m. Bower
> > James Munsie
> > Roberta Munsie
> > Wesley Munsie
> > Robert Munsie
> > Lexie Munsie

Lillian Pinkham (b.1879, d. 1948)
> m. Dr. Charles Piper
> The child of Lillian and Dr. Charles Piper:
> > Mary Alice Piper
> > > m. T. L. Davis, Jr.
> > > The children of Mary Alice:
> > > > Mary Lou Davis b. Jan. 7, 1949
> > > > Kathy Jo Ann Pauts b. Aug. 24, 1952

Annie Pinkham (b. 1882, d. 1911)
> m. Robert Rumney
> The children of Annie and Robert Rumney:
> > Robert Rumney
> > Isabel Rumney
> > Anne Rumney

Frank Milton Pinkham (b. 1885)
> > The children of Frank Milton:
> > Neil Pinkham
> > Son Pinkham
> > Daughter Pinkham

Wesley Pinkham, (b. 1887, d. 1906)

ROBERT IRWIN   Born April 26, 1813 County Monaghan, Ireland. Married
1813-1876   Mary Jane Taylor on October 20, 1849 in Mariposa, Ontario.
                     Died April 19, 1876. Buried Balsover Cemetery.

MARY JANE TAYLOR: Born October 26, 1830 County of Caven, Ireland. Died
                     January 17, 1892. Buried Balsover Cemetery.

The children of Robert and Mary Jane (Taylor) Irwin were:
    WILLIAM JOHN IRWIN b. 1849
         The child of William John Irwin:
         Donald Irwin
    SARAH ANNE IRWIN (1852 - 1914)
       m. John Pinkham (1845-1924)
         The children of SARAH ANNE IRWIN and John Pinkham:
         Lorne M. Pinkham (1875-1948):
            m. Annie Gordon
                The children of Lorne and Annie Pinkham:
                Robert Earlby Pinkham
                   m. Margaret Milne
                Gordon G. Pinkham
                   m. Jessie Harris
                J. Wesley Pinkham
                   m. Dorothy Babcock
                Ralph Lorne Pinkham
                   m. Iva Brethour
         Hattie Pinkham:
            m. James Munsie
                The children of Hattie Pinkham & James Munsie:
                Lillian Munsie
                   m. Len Greer
                Mary Munsie
                James Munsie
                Robert Munsie
                John Wesley Munsie
                Robert Munsie
                Lexie Munsie
       Lily Pinkham:
          m. Dr. Charles Piper
              The child of Lily Pinkham and Chares Piper:
              Mary Alice Piper
                m. T. R. Davis Jr.
       Annie Pinkham:
          m. Robert Rumney
              The child of Annie Pinkham and Robert Rumney:
              Lillian Rumney
                m. Charles Bowins

Frank Milton Pinkham
Wesley Pinkham
<u>ELIZA JANE IRWIN</u> (1854-1921)
m. Donald McIntyre
<u>The children of ELIZA JANE IRWIN and Donald McIntyre:</u>
Archie McIntyre
Ruby McIntyre
<u>JOHN JAMES IRWIN</u> (1857-1938)
m. Margaret Hickes
<u>The children of JOHN JAMES IRWIN and Margaret Hicks:</u>
Lloyd Irwin
m. Grace Day
Ethel Irwin
Pearl Irwin
m. R. J. Sibbery
John Irwin
m. Lillian Baker
<u>The child of John Irwin and Lillian Baker:</u>
Linda Irwin
William Irwin
Lillian Irwin
Irene Irwin
m. Mel Storie
<u>The children of Irene Irwin and Mel Storie:</u>
John Storie
Verla Storie
<u>AMELIA IRWIN</u> (1859 - 1867)
<u>MARY LOUISE IRWIN</u> (1864-1933)
m. John Alton
<u>The children of MARY LOUISE IRWIN and John Alton:</u>
Alice Alton
m. Jack Sinclair
<u>The children of Alice Alton & Jack Sinclair:</u>
Joan Sinclair
m. Thomas Humphries
Donald Sinclair
Alex Sinclair
Mary Alton
John A. Alton
m. Gertrude Davidson
<u>The children of John & Gertrude Davidson:</u>
John Alton
Mary Alton
Ruby Alton
Marion Alton

DAVID IRWIN
m. Janet Graham
i
WILLIAM IRWIN
m. Mary Nelson
i
The children of WILLIAM IRWIN and Mary Nelson:

SUSAN IRWIN
    m. Sampson Hazelton
    The Children of SUSAN IRWIN and Sampson Hazelton:
        WILLIAM HAZELTON
            m. Maggie O'Brien
        THOMAS HAZELTON
            m. Margaret Robinson
        MARY JANE HAZELTON
        SUSANNAH HAZELTON
            m. Frank Belch
ROBERT IRWIN
    m. Mary Jane Taylor
    The Children of ROBERT IRWIN and Mary Jane Taylor:
        WILLIAM IRWIN
            m. Martha Wannamaker
        SARAH ANNE IRWIIN
            m. John Pinkham
        ELIZA JANE IRWIN
            m. Donald McIntyre
        JOHN JAMES IRWIN
            m. Margaret Hicks
        AMELIA IRWIN
        MARY LOUISA IRWIN
            m. John Alton
MARY IRWIN
    m. William Eakins
    The Children of MARY IRWIN and William Eakins:
        WILLIAM EAKINS
            m. Annie Forest
        ROBERT EAKINS
            m. Mary Jackson
        JOHN EAKINS
        ROSANNA EAKINS
            m. William Jewel
        MARY EAKINS
            m. Kenneth Ferguson
        CARRIE EAKINS
            m. William Galbraith

WILLIAM IRWIN
    m. Sarah Purvis
    The Children of WILLIAM IRWIN and Sarah Purvis:
        ELIZABETH IRWIN
            m. Tomilson
        RICHARD A. IRWIN
        ADELIZA IRWIN
        NELSON IRWIIN
            m. Agnes Loucks
        MARY IRWIN
            m. Keith
        JANE IRWIN
            m. Louden
        CAROLINE IRWIN
            m. McKinnon

1776 *1890*

THE NATIONAL SOCIETY OF THE

Daughters of the American Revolution

This certifies that

ANNE LOUISE MANRIQUE

is a regularly approved member of the National Society of the Daughters of the American Revolution, having been admitted by the National Board of Management by virtue of her descent from a patriot who with unfailing loyalty served as a sailor, soldier, civil officer, or rendered material aid to the cause of American Independence during the Revolutionary War

this fifth day of January 2020

National No.	1002805
Ancestor	ABIJAH PINKHAM
State	New Hampshire
Admitted	January 5, 2020

President General

Recording Secretary General

Registrar General

Sources of Reference:

Barry, Bill. People Places: Saskatchewan and Its Names. Canadian Plains Research Center. 1997.

Brewster, Emma Jones. Brewster Genealogy 1566-1907. A Record of the Descendants of William Brewster of the Mayflower/Ruling Elder of the Pilgrim Church which founded Plymouth Colony in 1620. Andesite Publishing. 2017.

Carpenter, Amos Bugbee. A Genealogical History of the Rehoboth Branch of the Carpenter Family in America. Carpenter & Morehouse. Amherst, MA. 1898.

Carter, Ethelmae Eylar. Our Family History. Burgess Publishing Co. 1958.

Curtis, Gates. History of Brasher, New York. The Boston History Company Publishers. 1894.

Dover Historical Society. Vital Records of Dover, NH 1685-1850. Heritage Books, Bowie, MD. 1990.

Harden, Henry Winthrop. New England Historical & Genealogical Registrar. Private Printing by Henry Winthrop Harden. 1916.

Hoyt, David Webster, 1833-1921. The Old Families of Salisbury and Amesbury, Massachusetts. Originally published in 14pts: Providence, R.I.: Snow & Farnham, Co. 1897-1919. Reprinted 1981.

Hubbard, B. F. Forest and Clearings, the History of Stanstead County, Province of Quebec with Sketches of more than Five Hundred Families. Lovell Printing and Publishing Co., Montreal. 1874.

Huntington Family Association. The Huntington Family in America: A Genealogical Memoir. Publisher, Hartford Printing Co., Elihu Geer Sons, Hartford, CT. 1915.

Hughes, Edan Milton. Artists in California: 1786-1940. Hughes Publishing Co. SF, CA. 1986.

Hurd, D. Hamilton. History of Merrimack and Belknap Counties, New Hampshire. Philadelphia. J. W. Lewis & Company. 1885.

Lee, Sarah March. Lee, John, Of Farmington, Hartford County, Connecticut, And His Descendants (1878). Reprint Kessinger Publishing LLC. 2010.

Leighton, Perley M. A Leighton Genealogy: Descendants of Thomas Leighton of Dover, NH. (2 Volumes). NEHGS, Boston. 1989.

Noyes, Sybil, Libby & Charles, Thornton & Davis, Walter Goodwin. Genealogical Dictionary of ME & NH. Portland, 1939. Reprinted Baltimore, 1988.

Phelps, Oliver Seymour. Phelps Family and their English Ancestors. H. P. Smith & W. S. Rann (Editors).

Rollins, Alden M. Vermont Religious Certificates. Picton Press. 2003.

Rubin, Holly & Schneider, Jim. The Ancestry of J. G. Williams and Ursula Miller. Lulu. 2013.

Scales, John. Colonial Era History of Dover, New Hampshire. Heritage Books. 1977.

Sinnett, Charles Nelson. Richard Pinkham of Old Dover, New Hampshire and His Descendants East and West. Higgenson Book Company, Concord, NH. 1908.

Stackpole, Everett S. & Thompson, Lucian. History of the Town of Durham, New Hampshire (Oyster River Plantation) with Genealogical Notes. (2 vols.) Rumford Press, Concord, NH, 1913 (Reprint, Somersworth, NH 1973).

Records:

Data sources (birth, baptism, marriage, death, census) found at Ancestry.com, Family Search, Geni and Wiki genealogical records; NARA; United States & Canadian census records including Canadian National Defense 1855 Militia Act. *FindAGrave/Wikipedia*

Actes de Notarie, 1789-1845 by Leon Lelanne. Source of Notarial Records: Missisquoi, Quebec, Canada. Translation (French-English) rolls 14-17; 17-20.

Biblioteque et Archives, National, Canada

Congregational Church, Canton, Stanstead, Quebec, Canada

Connecticut Births & Christenings, 1649-1906

Curson's Funeral Book. Maquoketa, IA. Volume II, page 279.

Dover Public Library, Dover, New Hampshire. (*Permissions for "Dover Combination"*)

Drouin, Quebec, Canada

Grafton, MA Marriages, Births and Deaths

History of Rutland County, Vermont. Syracuse, NY. 1886.

New Hampshire County Register of Deeds

Massachusetts Vital, Marriage and Death Records

Owen's Jackson County Iowa Gazetteer and Directory, Davenport, IA. 1878.

Portrait & Biographical Album, Clinton County, IA. Chapman Brothers. 1886.

1812 Seward's Book (of Baptisms) for Dunham Circuit, Quebec, Canada

St. Francis Church Records, Stanstead, Quebec, Canada

Vital Records of Massachusetts: Town Records to 1850 (Tan Books, 182 Volume Set)

Wesleyan University Records, Middletown, Connecticut

300 Colonial Ancestors and their War Service by Elizabeth M. Leach Rixford

Genealogical Societies:
Cannington Historical Society, Ontario, Canada
Cape Sable Historical Society, Nova Scotia, Canada
Durham County, Ontario Genealogical Society, Canada
Iowa Historical Society, Des Moines, Iowa USA
Maquoketa Historical Society, Iowa, USA
Mower County Historical Society, Minnesota, USA
Musee Missisquoi, Quebec, Canada
New England Historical Genealogical Society
Rehoboth Antiquarian Society, Rehoboth, MA, USA
Saskachewan Genealogical Society, Canada
Stanstead Historical Society, Stanstead, Quebec, Canada
Uxbridge Ontario Genealogical Group, Canada

Newspapers/Periodicals:
Boston Herald, Boston, MA. (Article dated 15 June 1852)
Canadian Statesman, Bowman, Ontario, Canada. (Obituary dated 17 October 1883)
Congregationalist, Boston, MA. (Article dated 18 June 1852)
Eagle Grove Eagle, Eagle Grove, Iowa. (Article dated 1854)
Edmonton Journal, Edmonton, Alberta, Canada.

Flag of Our Union, Boston, MA. (Article dated 3 July 1852)
Goldfield Chronicle, Wright County, Iowa. (Article dated 3 June 1854)
Jackson Sentinel, Jackson County, IA. (Article dated 19 March 1891)
Log Cabin Chronicles, Eastern Townships, Quebec
Mather's Magnolia, Belknap History, NH, Volume 1, page 205.
Maquoketa Excelsior, Maquoketa, IA. (Article dated 21 March 1891)
Newcastle News, Durham County, Ontario, Canada. (Article dated 4 May 1905)
Misskoui Standard, Eastern Townships, Quebec, Canada.
New Hampshire Gazette, Portsmouth, NH. (Article dated 4 March 1851)
Orono News, Orono, Ontario, Canada. 1883.
Phelps Family Newsletter. February 1985.
"Phelps Family Papers" 1851-1864; Item 33. University of Michigan. Ann Arbor, MI
Sherbrooke Gazette, Quebec, Canada.
Stanstead Journal. Weekly newspaper founded in 1845 by LeRoy Robinson in
          Stanstead, Quebec.
Star-Phoenix, Saskatoon, Saskatchewan, Canada.
Victoria News. Clarke County, Ontario, Canada. 1872.
Winnipeg Free Press, Winnipeg, Manitoba, Canada.

With thanks to:

American Ancestors, Eastern Townships (consultation), Boston, USA

American Antiquarian Society, Massachusetts, USA

Jan Gordon, DAR Los Angeles (California, USA) Eschscholzia Chapter

Cindy Grauer Munsie, Pinkham Ancestry, Vancouver, British Columbia, Canada
          (Harriet Pinkham Munsie Descendant)

Daniel Lepitre, Log Cabin Chronicles, Eastern Townships, Quebec, Canada

Jane Knowles Lindsay, California Genealogical Society

And Mention of:

Canadian Cape Sable Historical Society, Shelburne County, Nova Scotia, Canada:
Pinkham files.

 John Wesley Pinkham married Sarah Ann Irwin:

Robert Irwin from County Caven, Ireland to Fenelon Township, by Ross Weston Irwin
(1921), Guelph, Ontario, 110 pages printed by the Ontario Genealogical Society.

The Bachelder Families of Stanstead, Quebec by B. F. Hubbard (Forests & Clearings):
by Jacqueline Russell compiled and posted online 31 August 2002.

www.ingramcontent.com/pod-product-compliance
Lightning Source LLC
Chambersburg PA
CBHW081430270326
41932CB00019B/3149

* 9 7 8 0 7 8 8 4 2 1 0 8 2 *